NB DCPL000011

D0431500

THE TRUTH ABOUT SYRIA

Also by Barry Rubin

The Long War for Freedom:
The Arab Struggle for Democracy in the Middle East

Hating America: A History

Yasir Arafat: A Political Biography

The Tragedy of the Middle East

Cauldron of Turmoil:
America in the Middle East

Paved with Good Intentions:
The American Experience in Iran

The Arab States and the Palestine Conflict

The Great Powers in the Middle East, 1941–1947

THE TRUTH ABOUT

SYRIA

BARRY RUBIN

palgrave
macmillan

First published in hardcover in 2007 by
PALGRAVE MACMILLAN™
175 Fifth Avenue, New York, N.Y. 10010 and
Houndmills, Basingstoke, Hampshire, England RG21 6XS.
Companies and representatives throughout the world.

PALGRAVE MACMILLAN is the global academic imprint of the Palgrave Macmillan
division of St. Martin's Press, LLC and of Palgrave Macmillan Ltd. Macmillan® is a
registered trademark in the United States, United Kingdom and other countries. Palgrave
is a registered trademark in the European Union and other countries.

ISBN-13: 978-0-230-60407-0 paperback
ISBN-10: 0-230-60407-2 paperback

Library of Congress Cataloging-in-Publication Data

Rubin, Barry M.
    The truth about Syria / Barry Rubin.
      p.   cm.
    ISBN-13: 978-1-4039-8273-5
    ISBN-10: 1-4039-8273-2
    ISBN-13: 978-0-230-60407-0 paperback
    ISBN-10: 0-230-60407-2 paperback
    1. Syria—Politics and government—20th century.   2. Syria—Politics and
government—2000–   I. Title.
DS98.2.R83   2007
956.9104'2—dc22

                                                                    2006039076

A catalogue record of the book is available from the British Library.

Design by Letra Libre.

First PALGRAVE MACMILLAN paperback edition: June 2008

10   9   8   7   6   5   4   3   2   1

Printed in the United States of America.

The great man is the one who surprises his enemies.
*   —Bashar al-Assad, Speech of*
*   August 15, 2006*

I well might lodge a fear
To be again displaced; which to avoid . . .
Be it thy course to busy giddy minds
With foreign quarrels.
*   —William Shakespeare, Henry IV, Part Two*

To my best friends,
Judy, Gabriella, and Daniel

CONTENTS

PREFACE

Modern political life has a number of stock figures. One is the Latin American dictator, a beribboned, corrupt generalissimo whose regime ensures that rich landlords live in luxury on the backs of impoverished peasants, using anticommunist rhetoric to justify crushing any possibility of reform. Clearly, such rulers are seen as villains.

Then there is the Communist regime, gray and bureaucratic, using humanitarian language to cloak a land of gulags, dressing up inefficiency with beautiful slogans, an oligarchy masquerading as the representatives of the downtrodden, promising glorious tomorrows and blaming all its shortcomings on capitalism and imperialism.

Most obvious of all are the fascist dictatorships, not deigning to conceal the iron fist inside a velvet glove, openly broadcasting hate, stridently anti-Semitic, proudly militaristic, boastingly aggressive. This is the easiest of all dictatorial regimes to spot for its villainy.

But now it is the twenty-first century, and all three of these characters are close to being extinct. Their spirit, however, lives on in a new form, consciously camouflaged, obscured by a lack of familiarity with its identifiable features. Today's innovative regime of this type is ruled by a corrupt dictator who ensures that a government-connected and enriched elite lives in luxury on the backs of the people, using left-wing rhetoric and the excuse of Third World sufferings to win over its own people through demagoguery and the West by manipulating its feelings of guilt.

These are the Middle Eastern dictatorships of Iran, Syria, Libya, Sudan, and of Iraq under Saddam Hussein; as well as the aspiring tyrants among a wide range of terrorist groups that include al-Qaida, Hamas, Hizballah, and the Kurdish Workers' Party. Like the Communists, all portray themselves as helping the downtrodden and speak in the language of anti-imperialism. Like the fascists, they are anti-Semitic and aggressive. Like the tinpot dictators, they are corrupt and arrogant.

As has always existed with the other three categories of dictatorship, the Middle East dictators have no shortage of apologists and appeasers in the West, and in the Middle East itself—sometimes purchased; sometimes passionately sincere; often blissfully ignorant. A very limited understanding of such regimes, their past behavior, and the interests that motivate them leads to a series of misunderstandings about them that are easily answered but far more often misunderstood:

Certainly, these regimes and movements have grievances. But that was also true of all the others as well.

Of course, it is possible to negotiate with them. But talking will not change their ideology, methods, or goals.

Without doubt, we, too, have faults. But the ultimate judgment must be based on which side is better.

It might be thought that concessions and proof of good will would dilute their extremism. But they gobble up the concessions, give nothing in return, and are ready to digest still more.

The problem here is not one of misunderstanding but rather of a genuine clash in world views and interests.

The Syrian regime stands as an exemplar of this new breed of dictatorships that—while perhaps an anticlimax after the Communist Soviet Union, Nazi Germany, and Imperial Japan—is the biggest threat to the peace, stability, and democracy of the world at present. These present-day regimes jeopardize the hope for a better future not only for the West but also for those unfortunate enough to live under their rule.

That is why it is so very important to understand how these contemporary systems work, the ways in which they dominate their own people and make fools or victims out of others.

Beyond the political category it embodies, Syria also provides the best case study of what has happened in the Arab world, and thus in the Middle East, during the last half century. When it gained independence after World War Two, Syria was a democratic country with a seemingly bright future. Blessed with fertile land and ample resources, Syria boasted good relations with the West as well as an energetic, entrepreneurial middle class. Yet a combination of radical intellectuals, militant ideologies, and ambitiously politicized military officers pushed Syria down a different path—a path that has led to turmoil and disaster.

How this ideologically bankrupt, economically backward, geographically circumscribed, and militarily feeble nation has nonetheless played a powerful and negative role in shaping the modern Middle East is the story of this book.

For one thing, Syria practically invented the art of state-sponsored terrorism. For generations, its leaders have believed that the only way to navigate around the country's limitations has been to export unrest to the rest of the region, whether through terrorism, military action, occupation, or the spread of radical ideologies. The fact that terrorism is such a terrible problem in the Middle East and the world today has much to do with how Syria has used this tool strategically.

Today, remarkably, Syria is the source of two wars, yet it has paid no price for the destruction wrought across its borders. In Iraq, Syria is the main foreign sponsor of a terrorist insurgency targeting U.S. soldiers and Iraqi civilians. For all practical purposes, Damascus is at war with the United States. It has recruited, armed, trained, equipped, financed, and sent across the border into Iraq hundreds of radical Islamists in the most successful military campaign against American forces since the Vietnam war. Yet tied down in Iraq and needing to avoid a wider conflict, the United States can do little to retaliate.

Meanwhile, Syria has also played a central role inciting and inflaming the Arab-Israeli conflict. It helped create a war between Lebanese Hizballah and Israel in 2006. It provides a headquarters and safe haven, training, equipment, and encouragement to many Palestinian terrorist groups, including those who block any hope of achieving peace. For years it backed two major terrorist insurgencies against Turkey, as well, first by Armenian and then by Kurdish organizations.

As if all that were not enough, Syria has dominated Lebanon for thirty years, sometimes controlling but more often fomenting unrest there. Syria's agents have murdered several dozen Lebanese politicians and journalists. Lebanon is the great prize for Syria, its economic worth exceeding even its strategic value. The Syrian regime will not let go and seeks to create conditions in which the world acquiesces to its hegemony there, no matter how much violence and chaos this inflicts on Lebanon.

The story of what has gone on inside Syria is as fascinating as that country's international role. A professed republic, it has been long ruled by one family, passed down like a hereditary sinecure. A self-described progressive state, it is largely controlled by a small group that enriches itself at the expense of the great majority of its people. A supposed secular regime, it avidly courts radical Islamists abroad and has become increasingly Islamized at home.

No other country in the Middle East is as much of a cauldron of religious and ethnic groups—Muslims, Alawites, Druze, Christians, and Kurds—competing for power. No place in the region has seen such a collision of contending ideologies—Arab nationalism, Syrian nationalism, Islamism, communism, reformist liberalism, and more—battle it out for decades.

Where Syria succeeded has been in the establishment of a stable dictatorship that has kept the country together for so long despite a profusion of failures.

Once the archetypal leftist, Arab nationalist regime, Syria is now the test case for the battle—whose outcome has the most serious implications for the world—among Arab nationalist dictators, radical Islamist revolutionaries, and liberal reformers over the fate of the Arab and Muslim worlds. In our era, this contest will prove the most important in determining the direction of the entire world.

I would like to thank the staff of the Global Research in International Affairs (GLORIA) Center for research assistance. Many friends and colleagues were most helpful, and to them I am grateful. I would also like to thank my agent, Andrew Stuart, who has gone far beyond duty in his kindness and assistance, and the staff of Palgrave Macmillan, especially Airié Stuart and Alan Bradshaw, for their dedication to making this the best possible book.

In terms of transliteration systems, I have employed one that is simple and easily understood by a wide audience. I have generally avoided diacritical marks. For easy recognition, however, I made exceptions, using the spellings of a few words—Assad, Ba'th, Hassan, Hussein, and Nasser—in their most familiar forms.

CHAPTER ONE

WHY SYRIA MATTERS

"It is my pleasure to meet with you in the new Middle East," said Syrian president Bashar al-Assad in a speech to the Syrian Journalists' Union on August 15, 2006.[1] But Bashar's new Middle East was neither the one hoped for by many since Iraqi president Saddam Hussein's 1991 defeat in Kuwait nor expected when Bashar himself ascended the throne in 2000. Actually, it was not even new at all but rather a reversion, often in remarkable detail, to the Middle East of the 1950s through the 1980s. The Arab world, now accompanied by Iran, was reembracing an era that had been an unmitigated disaster for itself and extolling ideas and strategies that had repeatedly led to catastrophes ranging from military defeats to massive waste of resources.

No Arab state has had more to do with this important and tragic turnabout than does Syria, which indeed could be called the main architect and beneficiary of this march backward. Egypt, Saudi Arabia, Jordan, and other Arab states wanted quiet; Iraq needed peace to rebuild itself. Even Libyan dictator Muammar Qadhafi, pressed by sanctions and frightened by the fate of Iraq's Saddam, was on his good behavior. Only Syria remained as a source of instability and radicalism.

Thus, a small state with a modest economy became the fulcrum on which the Middle East shifted and which, in turn, shook the globe. Indeed, Bashar's version of the new Middle East may well persist for an entire generation. Does this make Bashar a fool or a genius? That cannot be determined directly. What can be said is that his policy is good for the regime, simultaneously brilliant and disastrous for Syria, and just plain disastrous for many others.

To understand Syria's special role in the region, it is wise to heed the important insight of a Lebanese American scholar, Fouad Ajami: "Syria's main asset, in contrast to Egypt's preeminence and Saudi wealth, is its capacity for mischief."[2] In the final analysis, Bashar's mischief is in the service of regime maintenance, the all-encompassing cause and goal behind the behavior of the Syrian government. Demagoguery, not the delivery of material benefits, is the basis of its power.

Why have those who govern Syria followed such a pattern for more than six decades under almost a dozen different regimes? The answer: Precisely because the country is a weak one in many respects. Aside from lacking Egypt's power and Saudi Arabia's money, it also falls short on internal coherence due to its diverse population and minority-dominated regime. In Iraq, Saddam Hussein used repression, ideology, and foreign adventures to hold together a system dominated by Sunni Arab Muslims, who made up only one-fifth of the population. In Syria, even more intense measures were needed to sustain a regime that is dominated by the small, non-Muslim Alawite community, only half as large proportionately as the group that formed the basis of its Iraqi counterpart.

To survive, then, the regime needs transcendent slogans and passionate external conflicts that help make its problems disappear. Arabism and, in more recent years, Islamism are its solution. In this light, Syria's rulers can claim to be not a rather inept, corrupt dictatorship but the rightful leaders of all Arabs and the champions of all Muslims. Their battle cries are used very effectively to justify oppression at home and aggression abroad. No other country in the world throws around the word "imperialism" more in describing foreign adversaries, and yet no other state on the globe follows a more classical imperialist policy.

In broad terms, this approach of blaming faults on foreigners to protect dictatorships at home is followed by most, if not all, Arab governments, but Syria offers the purest example of the system. As for the consequences, two basic principles are useful to keep in mind:

1. It often seems as if the worse Syria behaves, the better its regime does. Syrian leaders do not accept the Western view that moderation, compromise, an open economy, and peace are always better. When Syria acts radical, up to a point of course, it maximizes its main asset—causing trouble—which cancels out all its other weaknesses. As a dictatorship, militancy provides an excuse for tight controls and domestic popularity through its demagoguery.

2. Success for the regime and state means disaster for the people, society, and economy. The regime prospers by keeping Syrians believing that their top priority should be the battle against America and Israel, not freedom and prosperity. External threats are used to justify internal repression. The state's control over the economy means lower living standards for most while simultaneously preserving a rich ruling elite with plenty of money to give to its supporters. Imprisoning or intimidating liberal critics means domestic stability but without human rights.

Nevertheless, the regime has survived, its foreign maneuvers have worked well much of the time, and Syrian control over Lebanon has been a money-maker as well as a source of regional influence. But what does all of this avail Syria compared to what an emphasis on peace and development might have achieved? Syria's pattern might be called one of brilliantly successful disasters. The policy works in the sense that the regime survives and the public perceives it as successful. But objectively the society and economy are damaged, freedom is restricted, and resources are wasted. Unfortunately, this pattern is thoroughly typical of Arab politics.

Syria, then, is both a most revealing test case for the failure of change in Middle East politics and a key actor—though there is plenty of blame to go around—in making things go so wrong for the Arab world. If Damascus had moved from the radical to the moderate camp during the 1990s or under Bashar's guidance, it would have decisively shifted the balance to making possible a breakthrough toward a more peaceful and progressive Middle East. Syria's participation in the Gulf War coalition of 1991, its willingness to negotiate with Israel, its severe economic and social stagnation, and its strategic vulnerability, all topped off by the coming to power of a new generation of leaders, provoked expectations that it would undergo dramatic change.

It is a Western, not an Arab, idea that the populace's desperation at their countries' difficult plight would make Hafiz al-Assad, Syria's president between 1971 and his death in 2000—and Saddam, Palestine Liberation Organization (PLO) head Yasir Arafat, or other Arab and Iranian leaders—move toward compromise and moderation. But the rulers themselves reasoned in the exact opposite way: Faced with pressure to change, they became more demanding.

Often, at least up to a point, this strategy works. The West has offered Syria, for example, more concessions in an attempt to encourage reforms, ensure profitable trade, buy peace, and buy off terrorism. Of course, the West is acting in its own interests, but what is most important is that these interests include solving the issues that have caused conflict, building understanding and confidence, and proving their good intentions toward the peoples of the Middle East.

Yet to the dictatorial regimes, this behavior seems not the result of generosity or proffered friendship but rather Western fear of their power and an imperialist desire to control the Arabs and Muslims. Frequently, too, it is seen as a tribute to their superior tactics, which fool or outmaneuver their adversaries. This perception encourages continued intransigence in hope of reaping still more benefits. Eventually, this process has destroyed any possibility of moderation, though not always Western illusions.

Here are two examples of such thinking. In 1986, at a moment of great weakness for Syria and the Arabs, Hafiz told the British ambassador to Syria, "If I were prime minister of Israel with its present military superiority and the support of the world's number-one power, I would not make a single concession."[3]

Yet at that time and thereafter, the United States was working hard to bring the PLO into a negotiated agreement that would make it head of a state. And a few years later, when in even a stronger position, Israel negotiated with the PLO and made massive concessions because it wanted peace. The intention was to solve the conflict by finding some mutually acceptable compromise solution. The other side, however, interpreted such actions as simultaneously a trick of Israel and America that should be rejected as well as a sign of weakness that should be exploited.

Precisely twenty years after his father Hafiz's remark, Bashar made his most important speech to date at the journalists' conference on August 15, 2006. Only power and violence, he argued, forces the other side to make concessions, negotiate, or even pay attention to the issue. Speaking about the international reaction just after the Israel-Hizballah war, he said, "The world does not care about our interests, feelings and rights except when we are powerful. Otherwise, they would not do anything."[4]

The remarks by Hafiz and Bashar tell a great deal. In the absence of pressure, their regime becomes bolder in seeking its goals. When fearful, it retreats to consolidate and survive. Consequently, the only way to get Syria to be moderate in behavior is by applying credible pressure to convince it—at least temporarily—that troublemaking does not pay. This model was most clearly applied when Syria was weak in the 1990s, by Turkey in forcing Syria to stop sponsoring terrorism against itself in 1998, and immediately after the September 11, 2001, attacks when it appeared as if a U.S. war against terrorists and their sponsors might embroil Syria, too.

Yet even on each of these and other such occasions—except for the narrowly focused Turkish intervention—Damascus was allowed to get away with the kind of things that would have toppled rulers in most states. Thus, frequent Western attempts to negotiate, bargain with, or appease Syria only worsen the situation by giving the regime the impression that it has nothing to fear. This is what happened when Syria came to understand at the end of the 1990s and after the September 11, 2001, crisis that the United States was not going to target it. Syria then turned the tables and became even more subversively aggressive.

This brings us to Bashar's task when he succeeded to power on the death of his father in 2000. Since the 1980s, Syria has faced big problems. Its Soviet ally and arms supplier collapsed, the economy has not done well, domestic unrest has increased, Israel has widened the conventional military gap to its own advantage, and Saddam was overthrown by the Americans.

Bashar's father and predecessor, Hafiz, maneuvered very well. He participated in the 1991 battle against Iraq's invasion of Kuwait enough to win help from the rich Gulf Arabs and the United States. His involvement in negotiations with Israel also helped, though in the end he refused to make an agreement. Then Hafiz died and passed on the presidency to his inexperienced son.

Clearly, Bashar is no Hafiz. His father was a far better strategist. Unlike Bashar, Hafiz probably would never have withdrawn all his soldiers from Lebanon in 2005 and would have been more careful to avoid friction with the Gulf Arabs and America. He would never have let Iran turn Syria into something like a client state. And Hafiz treated Syria's client, Hizballah leader Hassan Nasrallah, like one of the hired help rather than an equal, as Bashar did.

Yet the Assad genes are still working by producing an heir who knows how to maneuver and manipulate. Bashar withdrew from Lebanon but kept Syria's security and economic assets in place. Almost twenty major bombings and assassinations in the first two years after Syrian troops left have shown the Lebanese that Syrian interests must be attended to. By killing Rafiq Hariri, the former Lebanese prime minister, in February 2005, Bashar got into some trouble, but he also eliminated the only man with the stature to unite Lebanon, mobilize Western support, attract massive Saudi financial backing, stand up to Hizballah, and defy Syria. By helping drag Lebanon into war with Israel in 2006, he strengthened Hizballah's chances for seizing power in the country.

Bashar's risk-taking seems to be paying off. On the Iraqi front, he waged war on America at almost no cost to himself. Syria equipped, trained, and sent into battle terrorists who killed thousands of Iraqis and hundreds of Americans without any threat of international action or even condemnation.

Then, on the Lebanese front in 2006, he mounted from behind the scenes what was basically a conventional war against Israel using his Hizballah proxies, again with no cost to himself, though the Lebanese have paid a great deal. The war began when Hizballah finally succeeded after several attempts in kidnapping Israeli soldiers in a cross-border raid. Israel responded by bombing Hizballah forces and their arms smuggling routes, which resulted in significant damage to neighboring Lebanese buildings, and attacking into southern Lebanon while Hizballah fired thousands of rockets into Israel. Much of Hizballah's arms and money came from Tehran, with Syria getting a free ride as co-patron. In Damascus, Bashar became a hero for confronting Israel at Lebanese expense. He has also piled up considerable credit with radical Islamists by being their friend and ally in Iraq, Lebanon, and—by backing Hamas and Islamic Jihad—among the Palestinians.

International pressure or domestic upheaval may cause Bashar's effort's to blow up against him some day, but for the moment, he is riding high. And perhaps that answers the question about Bashar: someone who seems to be acting like a fool in Western terms may well be a genius as a Middle East leader.

So how did this young, new leader and his relatively small, weak country help turn the Middle East—and indeed the world—in such a different, bloody, and dangerous direction?

After 1991, there had been hopes in the West, Israel, and among many people in the Arabic-speaking world that dramatic changes around the globe and in the region would produce a new Middle East of pragmatism, reform, democracy, and peace. Given the Soviet Union's collapse, Saddam's defeat, trends toward democracy elsewhere, America's emergence as the sole superpower, and other factors, a better world seemed to be in birth. A generation of Arabs had experienced defeat, tragedy, and stagnation. Surely they would recognize what had gone wrong and choose another path.

Bashar has taken credit for killing this dream of a more peaceful and democratic Middle East while perhaps overstating that achievement's difficulty. "It was not easy . . . to convince many people about our vision of the future," he explained. His goal was to destroy the "cherished Middle East" of the West, Israel, and moderate Arabs, which he viewed as being "built on submission and humiliation and deprivation of peoples of their rights." In its place he would put "a sweeping popular upsurge . . . characterized by honor and Arabism . . . struggle and resistance."[5]

It is all very familiar. After the 2006 Hizballah-Israel war, the Middle East has clearly and probably irreversibly entered a new era with a decidedly old twist. The possibility of a negotiated Arab-Israeli peace and Arab progress toward democracy is close to dead. Whether they achieved political power or not, radical Islamist groups are setting the agenda. For a half-dozen years, things had been certainly heading in this direction, heralded by the Palestinian and Syrian rejection of peace with Israel in 2000; the turn to a terrorist-based intifada; the fall-out from the September 11, 2001, attacks on America; the post-Saddam violence in Iraq; the Arab regimes' defeat of reform movements; and electoral advances by Hamas, Hizballah, and the Egyptian Muslim Brotherhood, along with many other developments.

One of the most visible features of this new, decidedly unimproved, Middle East is an Iran-Syria-Hizballah-Hamas alliance seeking regional hegemony, the destruction of Israel, and the expulsion of Western influence—all the old goals—under the slogan of resistance. Once again the political line is the traditional one of extolling violent struggle in pursuit of total victory rather than viewing moderation as pragmatic, compromise as beneficial, or social progress and economic construction as the highest priority.

Only on two points does the new era of resistance represent a sharp break with the past: unprecedented high levels of Iranian involvement in Arab politics and the creation of an Arab nationalist–Islamist synthesis for which Bashar has been the main promoter and advocate. When one takes into account the fact that Bashar is not really a Muslim—he is an Alawite, a religious community which has never been Muslim whatever outward pretense is made—the accomplishment is stupendous in its audacity.[6]

All of these facts make it no less strange to see the revival of policies so spectacularly unsuccessful the first time around, whose disastrous repercussions are still being felt by Arab societies, the Middle East, and the entire globe. Elements of this worldview have all been tested by time, but they failed by a wide margin.

Consequently, we are left with an intriguing question: Why do Bashar and his allies, colleagues, and clients have an interest in revitalizing a worldview and program that failed so miserably and disastrously, leading the Arab world into years of defeat, wasted resources, dictatorships, and a steady falling behind the rest of the world in most socioeconomic categories?

A large part of the answer is that this state of affairs serves the two groups that matter most in Arab politics: the Arab nationalist dictators and the revolutionary Islamist challengers seeking to displace them. The Arab regimes rejected reforms because change threatened to unseat them. Using demagoguery enabled them to continue as both dictatorships and failed leaderships while still enjoying popular support. On the other side, radical Islamist forces, far more able to compete for mass support than the small though courageous bands of liberals, sought a new strategy to expand their influence and gain power.

In addition to the utilitarian aspects of this worldview, the analytical emphasis on "resistance" to foreigners rather than reform at home builds on a very strong foundation: a half-century-long indoctrination that overwhelmingly dominates Arab discourse in claiming that all the Arab world's problems are caused by Israel, America, and the West. The idea that their problems are not of their own making and that they can be heroic by fighting back makes people feel good. It is an opium for the masses, especially those who can vicariously experience battle by watching others—Iraqis, Israelis, Lebanese, and Palestinians—dying as a result.

Another attractive point is the belief that victory will be relatively easy because Israel, America, and the West are really weak. An Egyptian Islamist wrote that Americans are cowards while Muslims are brave: "The believers do not fear the enemy.... Yet their enemies protect [their] lives like a miser protects his money. They...do not enter into battles seeking martyrdom.... This is the secret of the believers' victory over their enemies." Indeed, the infidels' cowardice leads them to "bolster their status by means of science and inventions."[7] It is almost as if technical advances and social progress are for wimps. The fact that this statement was published in a state-controlled Egyptian newspaper, *al-Gumhuriya,* as an immediate reaction to September 11 shows how Arab nationalist institutions collude to promote "Islamist" ideas that feed the resistance mentality.

If Arabs and Muslims are willing to sacrifice themselves or even their whole societies as martyrs, runs the argument, they can achieve victory. In this respect, Hizballah leader Nasrallah, Palestinian Hamas leader Khalid Mashal, Bashar, and Iranian president Mahmoud Ahmadinejad sound eerily like Palestinian leader Arafat, Egyptian president Gamal Abdel Nasser, Iraqi president Saddam, and Syrian presidents Salah Jadid and Hafiz al-Assad in the 1960s and 1970s. It was this kind of thinking that led to the Arab defeat in the 1967 war and in a number of conflicts thereafter.

Recognizing what had happened, many Arabs in the 1990s concluded that this strategy of radical demands and confrontation with others did not work. "We had given up on the military option. We believed this belonged to history," stated Hani Hourani, head of the New Jordan Research Center. Yet by 2006, most notably in regard to the Israel-Hizballah war of that year, that critique was either forgotten or deemed to be wrong. In Hourani's words, "Hizballah created a new way of thinking about the whole conflict in the region: Israel is not that invincible. It could be beaten. It could be harmed.... Hizballah, even if we don't agree with its ideology, was suggesting a different option to the Arab people."[8]

Evidence was provided to validate this claim, but on examination the data did not support the conclusion. The Palestinian intifada that began in 2000, like its predecessor two decades earlier, did not gain a Palestinian state, much less destroy Israel. Its main effect was to wreck the infrastructure on the Gaza Strip and West Bank, causing massive Palestinian casualties, a loss of international support, and a long postponement of actually obtaining a Palestinian state. For Fatah, the group mainly responsible for these events, that strategy brought its downfall. Unless the goal was to "hurt" Israel regardless of the cost, the Palestinian situation should not have been an attractive example.

Another example cited was that of Iraq. Again, while Americans have been killed there, the great majority of the victims are Arab Muslims, with Iraq's society and economy being driven into the ground. As if that is not enough, communal hatreds have been heightened to the point of civil war causing massive casualties and destruction. Again, as with the September 11 attacks, if the goal was to hurt Americans, then some success was achieved. Yet the cost to the people of Iraq—and of Afghanistan, too, whose government was also overthrown by the United States and which also faced bloody civil strife—has been far higher.

The 2006 Israel-Hizballah war was supposed to be the ultimate example of this strategy's success. Yet it is easy to see that Israel won in the terms by which wars are usually judged. It did not feel the need for a quick cease-fire, inflicted much higher costs on the enemy army, and captured the battlefield. On the negative side, Israel suffered harm from rocket attacks—though the damage was in no way disabling—and military casualties, which have occurred in all wars, including those that saw Israel's biggest victories. Yet the common Arab perception is that the war proved the viability of a military option against Israel.

Certainly, a strategy that functions mainly by making one feel good about supposedly making one's enemies feel bad should not be the basis for a serious or successful political program. It certainly is no substitute for social progress or economic development. In the absence of material victory, such a strategy leaves one hoping for miracles—the intervention of God or of a demigod in human form.

This factor requires the revival of still another element of belief that has consistently failed in the past: faith in a political superhero who will lead Arabs and Muslims to victory. In the 1950s and 1960s, there was Nasser; in the 1970s, Arafat and Hafiz; in the 1980s and 1990s, it was Saddam; and then Usama bin Ladin. All failed, all were defeated. The result should have been the rejection of such a spurious hope. Instead, each new candidate for the job has been acclaimed in turn as if nothing was learned from the previous experience. Yet of the last three self-proclaimed great heroes, Saddam has been executed, bin Ladin is hiding out perhaps in a cave, and Abu Musab al-Zarqawi, leader of the Iraqi insurgency, is dead. Yet the enthusiasm for the next contender lives on.

In 2006, Iran's president Ahmadinejad was a resurrected Nasser from 1966, threatening the West, confidently predicting that Israel would be wiped off the map, and toying with war as a way of achieving a quick, easy victory. Bashar reinvented himself as an Arab Clark Kent, a superhero of the resistance disguised as a mild-mannered young man of gangly frame and failed moustache. He promises to achieve the impossible and has persuaded millions of people that he will succeed.

Finally, the new "resistance" axis promises to solve all problems quickly and simply, albeit through large-scale bloodshed. Why compromise if one believes it possible to achieve total victory, revolution, and wipe Israel off the map with armed struggle and the intimidation of the West? Why engage in the long, hard work of economic development when merely showing courage in battle and killing a few enemies fulfills one's dreams? Victory, said Bashar in his August 2006 speech, requires recklessness. If nobody remembers where this kind of mistaken thinking led before, they are all the more ready to embrace it anew.

In many ways, then, what is happening now is like the revival of a play that bankrupted its backers and ruined the reputations of all the actors. But in the sequel, Arab Victory over Imperialism II, all the parts are cast with a new generation of political actors. Iran plays the role of revolutionary patron that Egypt purported to do in 1966. Syria takes the part of patron of Arab nationalism and revolutionary terrorism that Syria did in 1966. Hizballah and Hamas are the new PLO, promising to destroy Israel through violence.

This experience of past tragedy has not, to paraphrase Karl Marx's remark on repetition in history, discouraged the farce of this second go-round. Indeed, the sad history of such endeavors seems to have no impact on the majority of Arab thinkers, writers, journalists, and others celebrating the revival of intransigence in search of total victory.

True, a small liberal Arab minority is horrified by the turn toward radicalism and increased confrontation with the West and Israel in the name of heroic resistance. It is both hard and dangerous for them to make the case against this worldview and strategy. Emperors do not like it when some of their subjects announce their nakedness. Societies, especially undemocratic ones, are not pleased to see their most cherished beliefs questioned.

The same principle applies to more moderate, but still dictatorial regimes that eschew open or at least loud opposition to the resistance doctrine. They want to use the radical ideas in their own interest—rationalizing their regimes, mobilizing their people for resisting foreigners rather than reforming their own society—while also preventing those ideas being used against themselves. At the same time, the rulers of Egypt, Jordan, and Saudi Arabia also remember a lot more about how this ideology failed in the past than they pretend.

Just as Nasser and Saddam posed threats to the relatively more moderate Arab states in the previous era, the new tyranny of Tehran and sword of Damascus are direct challenges to their survival today. Those rulers who are less extreme often use and reinforce the new ideas while also hoping to water them down somewhat, at least when their own interests are concerned. Yet in seeking to avoid being victims of the revolutionary tidal wave, they are loath to confront this ideology directly and often even play along with it to promote their own interests.

The more moderate regimes can even turn the direct radical threat to overthrow them to their own advantage. For example, they use their at least verbal hostility or refusal to make peace with Israel to justify the continuing conflict, which they then use as an excuse for their dismal domestic systems. The same point applies to using the United States as a scapegoat for their own failings even while maintaining normal relations with it. Equally, they repress liberal challengers and reject reforms by arguing that fair elections or open debate would strengthen radical Islamists.

What, then, are the main characteristics of this new era that sweeps all before it, at least in terms of rhetoric?

- A rise in radical Islamist movements, although the Arab nationalist regimes are still holding onto power and might well not lose it.
- Growing hatred of the United States and Israel, at least compared to the levels in some places during the 1990s.
- The belief that total victory can be achieved through terrorism and other violent tactics.
- A euphoric expectation of imminent revolution, glorious victories, and unprecedented Arab or Muslim unity.
- A disinterest in diplomatic compromise solutions, as unnecessary and even treasonous. To concede nothing is to lose nothing because it is still possible to claim everything one wants and leave open the possibility of getting it some day without any concessions.

- The death of hopes for democracy due to both regime manipulation and radical Islamist exploitation of the opportunities offered by some openings in the system, especially relatively free elections.

While the Islamist and Arab nationalist movements are often at odds over power, their basic perceptions and goals are quite parallel. Bashar argues that there is no contradiction at all, and in his resistance doctrine he highlights the common themes:

- The Arab/Muslim world faces a U.S.-Israel, or Western-Israel, or Zionist-Crusader conspiracy to destroy it.
- A secondary enemy is the majority of Arab rulers whose relative moderation shows them to be traitors. Only those who preach intransigence and struggle are upholders of proper Arab and Muslim values. In the 1950s and 1960s, this distinction pitted Egypt, Syria, and Iraq as the "progressives" against "reactionary" Jordan, Saudi Arabia, and other monarchies. Today it is Iran and Syria against Egypt, Jordan, and Saudi Arabia.
- Since the main enemy is purely evil, there can be no compromise with it.
- By the same token, pretty much all types of violence are justified. Such attacks are said not to be terrorism because they are merely defensive, responsive, necessary, and against a satanic foe.
- Total victory is achievable, and therefore accepting anything less is treasonous.
- Consequently, the people must unite under governments with the proper ideologies and the ability to mobilize the entire society (i.e., dictatorships). The priorities for these regimes should be to destroy Israel, defeat America, and reject Western cultural and intellectual influences.
- And because this plan is so necessary and workable, anything other than struggle and resistance—such as more citizen rights, reform, modernized economic structures, and the like—is a distraction. Only after total victory is achieved can these luxuries be arranged. (Actually, while Islamists continue to promise material benefits, Arab nationalist rulers hardly even make a pretense about providing better lives anymore.)
- In contrast, the idea of liberalism and reform is a Western idea, at odds with Islam and the Arab nations' interests, essentially an enemy trick.

In general, though, while Islamists and Arab nationalists compete for power, sometimes even violently, at the same time they mutually reinforce the intellectual system and worldview that locks the Arab world into the very problems they purport to remedy.

One feature of the new era very similar to that of the period from the 1950s to the 1980s is the expectation of imminent transfiguration, a millenarian sense that dramatic change is about to happen. The idea is that the future will defy the past, that such things as balance of forces or politics as the "art of the possible" will be overcome by the hand of God, the proper ideology, or the right military strategy.

This idea was very much in evidence during the period beginning with the 1952 coup in Egypt and particularly after the 1956 Suez war, which catapulted Nasser into being the closest thing there has ever been to a leader of the Arab world, the hero able to unite all the Arabs. Soon he had followers in every country. Nasser asserted Egypt's pride and strength, ridiculed Western powers, smashed Islamist rivals and the Marxist left at home, intrigued the intellectuals, and intimidated Arab regimes that opposed him. "We would clap in proud surprise," recalled Tawfiq al-Hakim, the great Egyptian liberal intellectual, "when he delivered a powerful speech and said about [the United States] which had the atomic bomb that 'if they don't like our conduct, let them drink from the sea,' he filled us with pride."[9]

Hakim made a devastating critique of this original resistance mentality:

> Are the people made happy because they hear socialist songs although they are submerged in misery which everyone sees? . . . Masses of people wait for long hours in front of consumer co-operatives for a piece of meat to be thrown to them. . . . Or take Arab unity. . . . Did the revolution succeed in bringing it about by political means? Did it bring it closer and strengthen it, or rather did it scatter and weaken it by policies which included intervention, pretension to leadership, domination, influence-spreading, showering money in the planning of plots, fomenting coups d'état, and in the Yemen war inducing Arab to kill Arab, and Arab to use burning napalm and poison gas against Arab?[10]

At the time, though, few paid attention to this kind of critique. And this particular emperor's nakedness was revealed only in Egypt's 1967 defeat and more particularly after his death in 1970. Hakim's book was entitled *The Return of Consciousness*. But today it seems as if the age of the coma has returned; many have forgotten the earlier outcome. It is also instructive to recall that Nasser's victorious reputation rested mainly on the 1956 Suez war, which was actually a military humiliation for Egypt. Only U.S. and Soviet diplomatic intervention saved Nasser from total defeat. The situation at that time parallels Nasrallah's "victory" in the Lebanon war; he was rescued by international pressure for a cease-fire that left Hizballah armed and in place.

Ignoring all this history, Nasrallah's fans now praise him as a new Nasser, playing on the similarity of their names to the Arabic word for "victory." In Cairo, their pictures are carried in demonstrations together, even though their views on Islam in politics are opposite. It is also noted that Lebanon's "victory" took place on the fiftieth anniversary of the Suez one. No one mentions that fifty years after Nasser first took power, Egypt has not progressed much. The return of the Sinai Peninsula, which Israel captured in 1967, was achieved not by struggle but rather through friendship with the United States and a peace treaty with Israel.

Another revived concept is that spirit overcomes everything; the balance of forces or technology—military, industrial, or electronic—is not really important. As early as 1947, Fawzi al-Qawuqji, commander of the Syrian-backed People's Army fighting to prevent Israel's creation, explained that the Arabs would win by saying: "More than the arms I value the people who will be conducting this holy war."[11] In the rhetoric of a 1960s radical slogan, "The power of the people is greater than the technology of the man." This is the idea behind the celebration of Hizballah and Hamas, the Iraqi insurgency, the suicide bomber and the rock thrower as capable of achieving victory against apparently overwhelming odds.

Thus, both Arab nationalists and Islamists cite the Koranic verse "If Allah grants you victory, no one will be able to defeat you" as evidence of their certain victory. "He who has faith, awareness, willpower and readiness to become a martyr can never be defeated," claims the Syrian newspaper *Tishrin*. Foreign Minister Walid al-Muallim exults, "Where there is a people with the will to resist, they will triumph."[12]

Aside from claiming their own past exploits as proof of how this strategy works, Arab nationalists also cite the Cuban and Chinese revolutions as well as Vietnam and South Africa for proof that the weaker side can win through determined resistance and steadfastness.[13] It is all very 1960s retro. "Long live the victory of people's war," said the Chinese back then; the Cubans had their "Year of the Heroic Guerrilla." These ideas live on in the Arab world as if in a time capsule.

For Nasrallah, Vietnam is his model:

> I cannot forget the sight of the American forces leaving Vietnam in helicopters.... Some Vietnamese, who had fought alongside the Americans, tried to

climb into these helicopters, but the [Americans] threw them to the ground, abandoned them, and left. This is the sight I anticipate in our region, but . . . it will take years. The Americans will gather their belongings and leave . . . the Middle East, and the Arab and Islamic worlds, like they left Vietnam. I advise all those who place their trust in the Americans to learn the lesson of Vietnam. . . . They will abandon them to their fate, just like they did to all those who placed their trust in them throughout history.[14]

Nasrallah is now, as Arafat once was, also compared to Che Guevara, the romantic but failed Cuban revolutionary leader, who like Nasrallah did not overthrow any governments but appears on many T-shirts. Islamists point to such examples as their victory over the Soviet superpower in Afghanistan (forgetting the U.S. role in helping that campaign) and such "successes" as September 11 and the Iraqi insurgency. They also claim Israel's withdrawal from south Lebanon and the Gaza Strip as triumphs. The Iranians can add their own revolution, the U.S. embassy hostage crisis, and their standing up to Saddam Hussein in the Iran-Iraq war, a war that they nonetheless really lost.

These alleged victories are illusory and the resistance doctrine merely prompts continuing the strategy of aggressive violence and rejection of peace that have produced the casualties among the Lebanese, Iraqis, and Palestinians—whose suffering allegedly creates the need for resistance in the first place. There is a very good reason why weaker states usually avoid provoking or going to war against stronger ones: They lose. History is full of examples of high-spirited, ideologically motivated states that simply could not overcome the odds of reality. In World War II, the relatively mighty Japanese were defeated. Despite having suicide kamikaze pilots and soldiers, they ended up with their own cities in ruins.

The Arab memory of defeats in so many past wars and conflicts is not a sign of cowardice to be expunged by more fighting or to be transformed into a litany of victories inspiring more bloodshed but a valuable political experience that should be heeded. The years of suffering, dictatorship, and squandered resources in the second half of the twentieth century should have been used to teach the lesson that intransigence and violence do not work, that extreme goals bring about far-reaching disaster.

When in the 1990s many Arabs viewed this history more honestly and directly, they were inclined to rethink their future. Knowing what does not work tells one what needs to be done. If Israel could not be destroyed and the conflict was so costly, perhaps it was better to make peace. If America was so powerful, then it would be better to get along with that country than to fight it. If the Arabs were falling behind in every economic, scientific, and social category, comprehensive reform seems necessary. If exporting terrorism turns against the perpetrators and poisons their own society, reject this path. The idea of change was on the agenda, challenging all the assumptions that had been made, tried, and found wanting.

Now, however, this possibility has been lost. A new generation—a generation that does not remember history and has no one to remind it—combined with a hybrid ideology, which discounts Arab nationalism's dreadful experiences as not applying to itself, repeats all these mistakes. In Bashar's version of history, three generations of Arabs fought Israel and lost but—though Westerners might expect that the desire to fight would decrease due to repeated failure and high cost—now Bashar proudly proclaims that a fourth generation is eager for more battle, and the desire for struggle is in fact increasing over time.[15]

The Arabs did not make mistakes, the radicals explain; they simply did not struggle enough or follow the proper ideology. It is as if someone who has been hitting his head against a brick wall, briefly considers the possibility that this is detrimental behavior, and then concluds that he simply has not been knocking it hard enough and that the wall is actually merely made of straw.

As a result, the greater destruction one inflicted on one's own people, the higher the praise seemingly merited. "Oh, Master of Resistance," the Syrian state-run newspaper *Tishrin* intoned on August 3, 2006, in an ode to Nasrallah, the man who launched a war with Israel that set Lebanon back many years in political and economic terms, "you have cloaked yourself in honor merely by writing the first page in the book of deterring and defeating the Zionist-American invaders, along with all those who are hiding behind them. No one thinks that the [war] will be won today, tomorrow, or [even] next year—but it is the beginning of the end, and the road toward victory has begun."[16]

And so the Arab-speaking world in general, with Syria leading the march, steels itself for still another phase in a long, long road of conflict. Perhaps in a few decades another generation will learn for itself what it should have been taught by its predecessors, and there will be another chance for change. Possibly the need for many more years of suffering is inescapable as the resistance mentality has already shredded much of the memory of what really happened in the twentieth century's second half. Perhaps another generation-long ordeal is required to re-create that history in order to rebuild that awareness. Another opportunity for real progress can be built only on the basis of new defeats and failures.

All of this travail should be unnecessary. A serious assessment of the balance of forces would show that conflict with the West is a big mistake since it is so much more powerful in military and technological terms. But this power is only an illusion, say the prophets of resistance. Muslim spiritual power or Arab courage can triumph because America is a paper tiger; the West is beatable. Perhaps, it is claimed, this contest does not necessarily require war since if the United States and West are so weak, they will back down if merely faced with threats. As Winston Churchill said of Soviet methods in his 1946 speech noting the beginning of the Cold War: "I do not believe that Soviet Russia desires war. What they desire is the fruits of war and the indefinite expansion of their power and doctrines."[17]

As Syria perceives the West in general and America in particular not only as too craven to fight but so stupid as to be easily outmaneuvered, Bashar expects that victory can be attained through threat, maneuver, and indirect violence. While experience gives some reasons for thinking this way, it is still the same mistaken argument that Saddam Hussein made from the late 1980s, through the 1991 Kuwait crisis, and up to the moment he was overthrown in 2003, and the one that Usama bin Ladin said was proven by the success of the September 11, 2001, attacks before being driven into hiding. Doesn't the story's outcome disprove the assumption? Not if it is ignored, it doesn't. The fate of Iraq's dictator did not prevent Ahmadinejad from calling America a "superpower made of straw"[18] or the head of Iran's powerful Council of Guardians, Ayatollah Ahmad Jannati, from saying that America "is weaker than a spider web. . . . If the Islamic countries act like Hizballah, and stand up to America like men, America will be humiliated."[19]

Viewing the West and the United States as weak and easy to defeat did not originate with September 11, 2001, or Hizballah's 2006 war in Lebanon. Like the ideas of destroying Israel without breaking into a sweat or violence redeeming Arab honor, it has been around since the 1950s. The internationally renowned, and sometimes dissident, Syrian poet Ali Ahmad Said (best known by his pen name, Adonis) wrote, for example, a poem in praise of Iran's revolution in 1978:

> I shall sing for Qom [Khomeini's city and a center of radical Islamism], that
>   it may transform itself in my ecstasy
> Into a raging conflagration which surrounds the Gulf
> The people of Iran write to the West:
> Your visage, O West, is crumbling
> Your face, O West, has died.[20]

Thirty years later, however, the West is still around and is stronger than ever. Yet the idea of a Western collapse seems to persist eternally in the mentality that dominates discourse in the Arabic-speaking world.

Saddam thought the same way. Speaking at the Royal Cultural Center in Amman, Jordan, on February 24, 1990, he explained that the Americans had run away from Vietnam and Lebanon (in 1983) and abandoned the Shah of Iran. He argued that they would not fight or at least would not long endure in a battle. Khomeini agreed with him on this point, if on nothing else; on November 7, 1979, Khomeini noted that America "could not do a damn thing" to stop the Islamist revolution.[21]

Bin Ladin himself explained, "[Those who] God guides will never lose.... America [is] filled with fear from the north to south and east to west.... [Now there will be] two camps: the camp of belief and of disbelief.... Every Muslim shall ... support his religion."[22] And, after all, the entire September 11 attack was designed to puncture the myth of American power, to show how vulnerable the country was. To Muslim perceptions on this point, the September 11 attack and the other acts of "resistance" did achieve a great success.

Indeed, the basic approach of Bashar's new Middle East permeates the Arab world, from Yemen's president advocating immediate war with Israel to Sudanese president Umar al-Bashir boasting that he would rather fight the United Nations than let its forces into the province of Darfur, where his troops have been murdering ethnic minorities. "We've done the math.... We've found out that a confrontation is a million times better for us."[23]

Bashir's "math" regarding Sudan taking on the entire world does not add up, but his intention was not to battle UN forces any more than he wanted to fight a war on his own soil with his own army. Bashir's calculation was simply that the world did not care about Sudan's massacre of civilians in Darfur and/or would soon grow tired of having peacekeeping forces there, a fatigue that would be heightened by his threatening to inflict casualties on them.

Bashar holds parallel views about Iraq and Lebanon. He hoped the West would give Syria control over Lebanon in exchange for his restoring order there. After all, that is what happened for most of the preceding quarter century. And both Bashir and Bashar also know that demagogically daring to take on America and the world will win them support at home as well as cheers (and perhaps aid) from other Arab publics and groups.

But beyond plaudits and passions, is fighting a panacea? Isn't developing ultimately better than dying, building better than battling, industry preferable to infanticide? Western history is full of those who made this mistake, but the West has succeeded largely to the extent that it has transcended such thinking.

Indeed, does war even really restore Arab honor? Arabs claimed that it did in the late 1960s with the PLO, during and after the 1973 war, two Palestinian intifadas, and on other occasions. In addition, the argument is made that

Hizballah forced Israel out of south Lebanon and Hamas did so from the Gaza Strip, thus redeeming Arab honor.

The historical problem is that after each highly publicized restoration of Arab honor, it soon seems to be tarnished again, or perhaps it is insatiable, requiring another round of repairs. Reformers often try to persuade their fellows that the true way to raise Arab honor and dignity is not through fighting Israel or the West but by putting the priority on building a productive economy, higher living standards, equality for women, a free society, independent courts, an honest media, and good educational and health systems. Yet once again these things have been pushed off the agenda. Indeed, the philosophy of resistance itself breeds the most resistance to the changes that the Arab world really needs.

A superb example of this kind of thinking is provided by Youssef al-Rashid, a columnist for the Kuwaiti daily *al-Anba,* who wrote that "the Lebanese people may have lost a lot of economic and human resources [in the 2006 war] . . . but [aside] from figures and calculations, they have achieved a lot of gains" because Lebanon's "heroic resistance fighters have proven to the world that Lebanese borders are not open to Israeli tanks without a price. Lebanon was victorious in the battle of dignity and honor."[24]

Upon examination, however, what this really says is that billions of dollars in damage, death, suffering, the return of Syrian influence to Lebanon, the rise of intercommunal tensions to the brink of civil war, and the setting back of the country's economy are all worthwhile because it made people feel better about themselves. And even then, Rashid could not say that Lebanese borders are closed to Israeli tanks; it's just that the tanks cannot enter at no cost whatsoever.

This kind of statement has been common in modern Arab political history. To choose only one example, a 1966 internal Syrian Ba'th party document stated that the struggle against imperialism and Zionism was so important that it was worth sacrificing everything the party and the Syrian people had achieved: "We have to risk destruction of all we have built up in order to eliminate Israel!" It was all very well, the Ba'th party explained, to have summit conferences and make military preparations, but there had to come a moment when this plan for war would be implemented.[25] The next year, 1967, these leaders got their wish and fell from power as a result.

Part of this calculation, a dangerous underestimate of their enemy, has never been corrected. When Nasrallah and other extremist Islamists speak about Israel, they echo word for word what Arafat and Arab nationalists said in the 1960s. Basically, it boils down to this: If enough Arabs or Muslims are only ready to become martyrs, wiping Israel off the map would be easy. In this world view, Israel continues to exist only because Arab rulers are too cowardly and traitorous.

This mistake resulted in four decades of disaster for the Arab world. In 1948 and again in 1967, Arab leaders announced that they would defeat Israel and throw the Jews into the sea. But it was the Arabs who suffered a humiliating loss. Next, Arafat and others bragged that guerrilla warfare would do the trick, an idea that brought Arafat one defeat after another: not Israel's defeat but civil wars in Jordan and Lebanon, more defeats on the battlefield, years of suffering, and the waste of billions of dollars in resources. This idea has wrecked the Gaza Strip, site of three unnecessary uprisings in fifteen years. The Arab states remain virtually the sole place in the world exclusively ruled by dictatorships, since only authoritarian governments, it is argued, can defeat Israel and expel Western influence. And so it goes, down through Saddam Hussein's three costly wars and Usama bin Ladin, to present-day Hizballah and Hamas.

When intellectuals and leaders are irresponsible, there are consequences. Zaghloul al-Najjar, a columnist in *al-Ahram*—not an Iranian publication or some crackpot al-Qaida site but the flagship newspaper of the moderate Egyptian government that had a peace treaty with Israel for more than a quarter century—wrote on August 14, 2006:

> Imagine what would [happen] to this oppressive entity [Israel] if an oil embargo was imposed on it, if its air force was destroyed in a surprise attack, and if all the Arab countries around it fired rockets on it simultaneously and decided to put an end to its crimes and its filth. [If this happens], this criminal entity which threatens the entire region with mass destruction will not continue to exist on its stolen land even one more day.[26]

To show that the publication of that article was no fluke, the same newspaper carried a similar article by Anwar Abd al-Malik, an Arab nationalist, on August 29, 2006, about the miracle of Hizballah proving Israel could be easily defeated.[27] Does Egypt want war with Israel? No. But engaging in this kind of demagoguery gives Egypt a degree of immunity from radical criticism at home and abroad while having the dangerous consequence of further reinforcing the disruptive resistance ideology.

During all these flights of fantasy and failure, the idea that the inability to destroy Israel should make real peace an attractive alternative never took hold. In part this was because conflict was the superior option from the point of view of protecting the regimes. At the same time, Arab nationalists and Islamists let their desire for Israel not to exist persuade them that it was weak, divided, cowardly, and would soon crumble.

Here is Arafat in 1968: "The Israelis have one great fear, the fear of casualties." This principle guided PLO strategy: Kill enough Israelis by war or terrorism, and the country would collapse or surrender. A PLO official in 1970 said the Jews could not long remain under so much tension and threat—"Zionist efforts to transform them into a homogeneous, cohesive nation have failed"—and so they would leave.[28] On September 12, 1973, just before his country and Egypt attacked Israel, the Syrian ambassador confided to a Soviet official that Arab states would need ten to fifteen years to destroy Israel but would soon launch an attack to destroy the myth of Israeli invincibility and undermine foreign investment and Jewish immigration.[29]

Yet while the Arabs did well at the war's start and claimed afterward that they had restored their honor, more than thirty years later, all the same issues of Israeli invincibility, a belief that Israeli society could be undermined, and victory would be certain if Arab self-confidence restored remained. Here is Nasrallah on July 29, 2006: "When the people of this tyrannical state lose faith in its mythical army, it is the beginning of the end of this entity."[30] But Israel suffered far heavier losses fighting PLO terrorists in the 1960s—when the country's population was much smaller—than in the 2006 Lebanon war, and the latter conflict actually produced more national unity and higher morale.

Nevertheless, Bashar and Nasrallah still insist, as Arafat did periodically for over almost forty years, that the fighting has shown, in the latter's words, Israel's army to be "helpless, weak, defeated, humiliated, and a failure."[31] Of course, this is propaganda aimed to win the masses' cheers and the cadres' steadfastness, but the leaders, too, believe it. After all, this is the assessment on which they base their policy.

The strategy for achieving victory of Arafat then and of Bashar, Nasrallah, or Hamas now was to terrorize Israeli civilians. This is why they use terrorism, not because they are intrinsically evil but rather because they think it will be effective. By attacking civilian targets, Arafat said in 1968, the PLO would "weaken the Israeli economy" and "create and maintain an atmosphere of strain and anxiety that will force the Zionists to realize that it is impossible for them to live in Israel."[32] Or, as an article in a PLO magazine explained in 1970, if all Israelis would be made to feel "isolated and defenseless," they would want to leave, and Israel would cease to exist.[33]

What Bashar, Nasrallah, and Iran say today sounds like PLO documents from a quarter-century ago. One entitled "Guidelines for Attacking Civilian Targets in Israel," called for "using weapons in terrifying ways against them where they live," including, for example, attacking tourist facilities "during the height of the tourist season"[34]—which is precisely what happened in the 2006 war. And in calling for Israel's destruction, Ahmadinejad echoed what Arab leaders were saying when he was a child, with no real success.

Similarly, the other main strategic idea of today's Iran-led, Syrian-prompted alliance is the same one developed in the 1960s, in which terror-sponsoring states assaulted Israel through other countries and client groups. Syria used Jordan and Lebanon for this purpose in 1947, even before Israel's creation, when Damascus wanted to hide its involvement in the fighting.[35] The whole history of the PLO and more than a dozen Palestinian terrorist groups is largely based on the principle of state sponsorship and safe havens. Again, it didn't work.

The Arab reaction to the 2006 war in Lebanon follows an old tradition in which military defeats are turned by verbal gymnastics into victories, partly based on the fact that Arab forces did win some battles and fought bravely. In effect, fighting and dying simply become substitutes for the lack of success elsewhere; blood purges failures in politics, society, and economy. An example is the common case of a student who flunks exams, or gets into trouble with the family, finding redemption by becoming a suicide bomber. The Lebanese poet Abbas Baydoun, who writes on cultural matters, cheered Hizballah by saying it "has erased a guilt, and corrected the world's memory, in order to compensate for Arab frustration and expunge a sense of shame."[36]

The 1956, 1973, 1982, and other wars have been transformed to fit this narrative. A superb example of this pattern is what happened at Karama, Jordan, in March 1968. Israel's army crossed the river, drove through Jordanian army units, then attacked and destroyed the main Fatah camp there. Arafat fled, leaving his men to fend for themselves. Israel lost 21 men; Fatah, 150. The battle was an Israeli victory, and the main credit for what Arab military resistance there was belonged to the Jordanian army.

But Arafat persuaded Palestinians and the Arab world that Karama was a great victory for Fatah, making the organization appear heroic in comparison with the Arab armies' apparent cowardice and incompetence in the 1967 war. Thousands begged to join Fatah; Nasser invited Arafat to come to Cairo and be his protégé. Arafat's career, and the tragedy of the next thirty-five years of bloodshed, was set in motion.

Egypt itself used the 1973 war in this manner. While the Egyptian offensive at the start of the war was indeed brilliant and its use of new antitank weapons (another parallel with Lebanon in 2006) was successful, Egypt lost the war. By the end of the fighting, the international community had to rush in and save Egypt when Israeli forces crossed the Suez Canal and surrounded its Third Army. Yet ever since Egypt has claimed this war as a victory. At least, Egyptian president Anwar Sadat used the war as a basis for his peace bid, turning the victory to some productive use. But few in the Arabic-speaking world today view the war in that context.

A more typical case of how things work was the PLO's handling of its disastrous defeat in Lebanon in 1982, which ended with that group being driven from the country. Arafat called it a victory and his colleague, Khalid al-Hassan, modestly proclaimed, "We should not become arrogant in the future as a result of this victory."[37]

There was some dissent on this point. Isam Sartawi, the PLO's leading moderate, presented a different perspective, demanding an investigation of the PLO's poor performance in the fighting. He urged the PLO to "wake up" and leave the "path of defeat" that had led to the 1982 debacle. Sartawi ridiculed the wishful thinking that claimed that war to be a PLO victory. "Another victory such as this," he joked, "and the PLO will find itself in the Fiji Islands."[38]

Yet what happened between Arafat's fantasy and Sartawi's realism? Twenty years later, Arafat was still leading the PLO. Two months after voicing his complaints, Sartawi was murdered by Palestinian terrorists from a group headquartered in Damascus that often served as an instrument of the Syrian regime. Repression, then, is one way to discourage anyone from pointing out the huge holes in the resistance mentality.

Here can be seen a brilliantly designed mechanism that safeguards the radicals and regimes, and a weapon wielded brilliantly by Bashar. If anyone dissents or ridicules these ideas, it is said that this proves him to be a traitorous lackey of the West and Zionism. This is an inescapable fact of life in the Arabic-speaking world. A Lebanese Shia asked in this regard, "How should I react to . . . people . . . that tell me that they are ready to kill themselves, their kids, see their houses destroyed and their jobs nonexistent, while looking at me [and implying], if 'you are not willing to do the same, thus you are an American-Israeli agent?'"[39]

The same treatment is given governments or groups if they seek outside support to protect themselves from the radicals, since that means turning to the West. Sometimes, of course, the threat is so grave that the taboo is broken—as when the Saudis and Kuwaitis got Western help to save them from Saddam in 1990.

Yet there is a terrible reckoning afterward, since this decision was a major factor in the rise of bin Ladin's international jihadism. Anwar Sadat made peace with Israel in 1979 and was assassinated in 1981. The same fate befell

Jordan's king Abdallah in 1951, for merely attempting to make peace, and to Lebanese president Bashir al-Jumayyil in 1982.

This same trick of defining dissent as treason is used by Bashar against other countries which have interests diverging from Syria's and as a way to show his own people that he is the noblest Arab of them all. In his August 15, 2006, speech, Bashar called the leaders of Egypt, Jordan, Lebanon, and Saudi Arabia mere "half-men," midgets who lacked his courage, and even outright traitors. Just as this policy plays with fire by inciting war against Israel, it also foments conflicts among the Arabs themselves. By advocating unity only on his terms, Bashar ensured that there would be none.

As significant, and perhaps even more important, Bashar's resistance strategy is meant to kill off the possibility of the democratization of politics and liberalization of society. After all, if the priority is on resistance, reform is at best a distraction; at worst it is treason. Thus, struggle excuses stagnation. What matters is the glory of resistance rather than the banality of economic reform, improving the school system, and developing an honest media or independent judiciary. "In a state of war," wrote the dissident Egyptian playwright Ali Salem, whose works are banned in his own country, "no one argues . . . or asks questions." They are told that this is not the right time to talk about free speech, democracy, or corruption, and then ordered, "Get back to the trench immediately!"[40]

And when in March 2001 Ba'th party members asked Syrian vice-president Abd al-Halim Khaddam at a public meeting why the regime did not do more to solve the problems of corruption, incompetence, and the slow pace of reform, his answer was that the Arab-Israeli conflict permitted no changes at home: "This country is in a state of war as long as the occupation continues."[41] The irony of this argument—or, more accurately the proof that it was bogus— was that the regime had turned down Israel's offer to return the entire Golan Heights a year earlier.

The regime needed the continuation of the conflict with Israel to rationalize its own dictatorship, corruption, and even continued rule. And this situation also allowed endless chances for posturing bravely. Bashar roared in a 2001 speech, "An inch of land is like a kilometer and that in turn is like a thousand kilometers. A country that concedes even a tiny part of its territory is bound to concede a much bigger part in the future. . . . Land is an issue of honor not meters." And he added that this belief was his inheritance: "President Hafiz al-Assad did not give in," boasted Bashar, "and neither shall we; neither today nor in the future."[42]

Today, radical Islamism—with an assist from the nationalists—is recapitulating the history of Arab nationalism in remarkable detail, including the wildly exaggerated promises of victory, the intoxication with supposed triumphs, the putting of resources into struggle instead of constructive pursuits, and so on. The old con game of offering battle against foreigners to discourage struggle against one's own dictator—as a substitute for democracy, reform, and material progress—is presented afresh as if it had not been used over and over in the past.

In some ways, this worldview does not correspond with reality and is very damaging. But there is much method in the "madness" of those who promulgate it. The resistance mentality is an excellent tool for regime preservation. Ultimately, the main victims are the Arabs themselves. The main beneficiary among governments is Bashar al-Assad and the Syrian regime.

Bashar was ecstatic after the 2006 war. Seeing "millions of youngsters waving" the flag of resistance proved "that this nation is on the brink of a new phase in its history."[43] Perhaps it is true, but it is the same as the old phase, and ultimately so will be its results. In the meantime, the Syrian regime has remained stable and become even more popular. Unless he made a major miscalculation, it was springtime for Bashar.

CHAPTER TWO

THE WORLD'S MOST UNSTABLE COUNTRY, 1946–1970

Between 1949 and 1970, Syria was the world's most unstable country. It simply could not find a coherent identity, worldview, or system. So consistent was this problem that one American diplomat called Syria's condition in 1968 the "stability of instability" because of the many coups that took place there.[1] Yet after Hafiz al-Assad took power in November 1970, the government he established seemed to go on forever. Indeed, since that time not a single Arab regime—outside of two marginal states, Yemen and Sudan—has been overthrown by internal forces.

No one faced more trouble but then learned the secrets of political success better than did those who have ruled Syria. And it wasn't because the job was easy.

An indication of the task's difficulty was conveyed in what Syrian president Shukri al-Quwatli supposedly told Nasser when the two countries temporarily united under the latter's rule in 1958: "You have no idea, Mr. President, of the immensity of the task entrusted to you. . . . You have just become a leader of a people all of whom think they are politicians, half of whom think they are national leaders, one-quarter that they are prophets, and one-tenth that they are gods. Indeed, you will be dealing with a people who worship God, Fire and the Devil."[2]

What this pointed joke hints at is the vacuum of identity in Syria that arose from three factors: the diversity of religions, variety of communities, and discord about borders. The questions to be decided were not only What is Syria? but also Where is Syria? and What is a Syrian? Was Syria to be defined as Arab, Muslim, or multicultural? Was it an entity in itself or the core of a bigger area or of the entire Arab world? Should Syria merge with Jordan, Iraq, Egypt, or other countries, and who would run such a combination? Who was the rightful ruler of Syria itself: the Sunni Arab elite, as tradition dictated; a delicately balanced coalition of communities, as in Lebanon; or one of the minority groups? Which road should Syria follow to development, capitalist or Communist-style socialist? Given the complexity of this decision, no wonder the country underwent such instability for so long a time.

One of the key problems promoting this situation was Syria's ethnic-religious complexity. Sixty percent of the population is Sunni Arab Muslim. Of the remainder, 13 percent is Christian, 12 percent Alawite, 9 percent Kurdish, 5 percent Druze, with a scattering of other groups. All of these communities have areas of geographic concentration, which makes them more potentially politically potent. Nearly 90 percent of the Alawites live, for example, in al-Ladhiqiya province, where they constitute more than 80 percent of the rural population.

This diversity factor has tremendous implications. About one-third of Syrians are not Muslim; about 10 percent—the Kurds—are not even Arab. About one-fifth—the Alawites and Druze—are arguably heretics whose apostasy could be punished by death under Islamic law. In Muslim doctrine and historic practice, living under non-Muslim rulers presents a big theological and psychological problem. That is why, at the beginning of the republic, while minority groups prevented the inclusion in the new constitution of a provision making Islam Syria's official religion, they could not stop a clause insisting that the president must be Muslim. Nevertheless, Syria has had a non-Muslim president for more than four decades, an incredibly explosive point for those who think of the situation in those terms.

The treatment of the non-Arab Kurdish minority shows how "Arab" became the fundamental definition of being Syrian while the even more dangerous issue of Islamic identity was put in second place. Most of Syria's Kurds came from Turkey in the 1920s and 1930s, fleeing the modernizing reforms of that country's secular republic against which they had revolted. They remain concentrated in rural areas of Aleppo, poor neighborhoods outside Damascus, and in the northeast. In 1962 many were reclassified from citizens to foreigners in the drive to make Syria completely Arab. Ethnic Arabs were settled in land confiscated from the Kurds along the Turkish border. The Kurdish language is banned. There is literally no place for Kurds as such in a Syrian state whose foundation rests on a profoundly passionate insistence on an Arab identity.

Despite Syria's problems, things could have been even worse. An Islamic identity would have left out more than three times as many Syrians: the Alawites, Druze, and Christians. Post-Saddam Iraq and the Lebanon civil war are vivid reminders of what can happen when such societies dissolve into communal power struggles.

But this mixture of communities could have been better managed politically in a number of ways. For example, Syria might have accepted an identity as an all-inclusive multiethnic state, as had Lebanon. When the French ruled Syria from the 1920s until just after World War Two, they had built a system in which each group was guaranteed a quota of seats in parliament. The problem in Syria is that this approach raised the constant threat of intercommunal conflict, as has happened in Lebanon.

A second possibility was continued domination by Sunni Muslim Arabs in a democratic or dictatorial system, since after all they were the majority and the traditional ruling group. Their degree of urbanization, level of education, and business experience gave the Sunni elite a definite edge. Of course, most of the Sunnis were poor peasants paying high rents to Sunni landlords. Yet as the subsequent history of Syria has demonstrated, elites have ways of mobilizing support from other members of their communities in what remains even today a society characterized by group rather than individual identity.

Sunni domination might also have easily remained in a militantly pan-Arab nationalist Syria. After all, since most Arabs are Sunni, the nationalist doctrine appeals most to the interests of Syrian Sunnis, whose majority would be augmented further by uniting with other Arab states. The ruling class and main religion of an Arab state stretching from the Atlantic Ocean to the Persian Gulf—and incorporating what are now up to twenty different countries—would be Sunni. Indeed, an Alawite-dominated regime puts so much emphasis on Arab nationalism precisely because it is a quite successful way to appeal to the Sunni majority.

What happened in Syria, however, was a third alternative. After a long period of strife, there came to power a despised minority group with a radical program, the antithesis of what might be expected was needed to create a stable state. That group needed a doctrine that would justify not only its hold on power in Syria but also the state's expansion to dominate its neighbors. On top of that, with its claim to Islam questionable, such a regime would have to find some powerful ways to win support and control such a turbulent country.

History has shown that the easiest way to unite a people is by inspiring a common fear and hatred of others. In Iraq, for example, a Sunni Muslim Arab minority of around 20 percent used the Ba'thist formula as its road to power. By employing constant appeals to national chauvinism, directing hatreds and paranoia outward, and creating a tight system of controls, the Saddam Hussein regime ruled Iraq for almost thirty years. If not for a U.S.-led invasion in 2003, it would still be in power.

You are not a Shia or a Kurd, the Iraqi regime told its people. You are a member of the glorious Arab nation. And your problems, the reason that life is not better, are not due to your government's incompetence, greed, and oppression. Rather, your enemy is the imperialists and Zionists who are holding you back and want to destroy everything you have and enslave you. Therefore, to fight for your rights you must unite behind—not against—your dictator.

The Syrian approach has been much the same. Iraq, however, had to depend more—or perhaps this was simply Saddam's personal style—on repression. Syria banked to a larger extent on demagoguery. Thus, while the Iraqi exile writer Kanan Makiya famously called Iraq the "republic of fear," Syria might be better termed the republic of hate, and the vast quantity of hate generated by personal frustrations, material deprivation, lack of freedom, ideological scapegoating, and ethnic quarrels has been successfully deflected outward to prevent a meltdown of the society.

As if conflict among Syrians was not enough, there was also the issue of Syria's borders. Syria still claimed the area of Alexandretta, ceded under the French mandate to Turkey, which called it Hatay. There was also a tendency to view as Syrian any place that had been governed in the same jurisdiction as Damascus during the pre-1918 Ottoman Empire. Thus, Jordan, Israel, Lebanon, the West Bank, and the Gaza Strip were all seen as part of this Greater Syria. Syria never established relations with Lebanon since it did not accept that neighbor's existence as an independent country. And its territorial ambition both fed off and reinforced the pan-Arab nationalist view that all Arab states should be merged into a single country stretching from the Atlantic Ocean to the Persian Gulf. Rather than settle down to make the most of what it had, Syria has spent decades trying to obtain all these "lost" territories of Greater Syria or, even better, leadership of the proposed new Arab empire.

Nor were these the only huge problems Syria faced. In common with other Third World countries, it had to confront all the normal issues of relative backwardness and poverty. The economy, school and health systems, roads and transport, communications and buildings, and everything else needed to be upgraded.

One approach to the process of solving such problems is to see what institutions, ideas, and methods have to be improved or changed, modernized in line with what has worked elsewhere in the world. Another is to rail against the injustice of the situation, blaming others for one's troubles and believing that removal of this heavy external hand will allow quick and easy progress. Syria has tended very much toward the latter approach, which is far easier and faster to achieve as well as more certain of success.

By the time Assad came to power in 1970, earlier Arab nationalist and Ba'thist regimes had been trying out the idea that a mobilization state would develop the country quickly. Their role models were European dictatorial regimes, Communist and fascist. The Ba'th party founders, when they were students in France during the 1930s, had studied how Communist movements worked, while the Nazi German system had tremendous appeal for Arab nationalists in that same decade. Sami al-Jundi, one of the party's early leaders and its prime minister in 1963, later wrote: "We were racists, admirers of Fascism, eagerly reading Nazi books and books about the source of the Nazi spirit. . . . We were the first to translate *Mein Kampf*."[3]

What especially fascinated the Ba'thists was the ability of the European extremist movements to combine far-reaching goals, use of ideology and propaganda, and comprehensive organizational structures. The Ba'thists believed that a utopia could be built in their own countries by imposing a system of one ideology, one people, top-down rule, a planned economy, a single party, and many other trappings from an original idea by Nazi Germany or the Communist Soviet Union.

It soon became apparent, however, that such a regime, in the Arab world as in Europe, was more effective at keeping control than at turning its subjects' lives into ones of luxury and happiness. Staying alive and in power was an impressive enough achievement in itself given Syria's extraordinarily bumpy history. And so when Hafiz took power in 1970, he focused on keeping it. The regime quickly ran out of ideas for domestic development, either social or economic. It simply had no reform program at home to gain support or make Syrians expect the state's policies would bring them a better life. All that Hafiz could promise was stability at home and glorious triumphs abroad.

The stability at home that Hafiz provided was extremely attractive to Syrians. Their country's history between 1946, when it became independent, and 1970, when Hafiz seized power, made Syria the world's most chaotic country. The reasons were partly due to Syria's uncertain identity and communal complexity, partly to its search for a path to development, partly to the heady new ideas that promised to solve all problems, partly to its location in a turbulent region, and partly because of its unique psychological problems.

For, in a real sense, Syria did not believe in itself as a country but rather came to think that it was a fragment of past Arab greatness and the core for its future revival. Thus, the present, the place where real progress takes place, became a low priority.

Certainly it can be argued that Syria's borders were arbitrary; yet that can be said of many countries. Equally, it is possible to think that Syria would be more important as part—even better as capital—of an Arab superstate. Still, one has to consider whether this goal is achievable and at what cost. Is it worthwhile to postpone such mundane concerns as democracy, peace with neighbors, citizen rights, higher living standards, and general economic progress for this imagined future?

In the seventh and eighth centuries, Damascus had been capital of the Muslim empire of the Umayyads. During later centuries, it was the government center of a province, Bilad al-Sham. If the first experience gave rise to a bid for leading all Arabs, the second created the sense of being the rightful ruler of "Greater Syria," which had now become Lebanon, Israel, Jordan, the West Bank, and Gaza Strip.

The third pillar of Syria's claim to a larger mission was the founding of the Arab Kingdom of Syria in 1920 by the Hashemite family. The Hashemites, rulers of Mecca and Medina under Ottoman Turkish sovereignty, had revolted during World War I and allied themselves with the British against the Turks. In exchange, they hoped to become the rulers of a great Arab state. But the British and French had made a deal between themselves to divide up the area. The French got Syria and Lebanon in the arrangement. But the Hashemites also claimed Syria. In 1920 a French army marched into Syria, easily defeated King Faysal's Hashemite troops, and took over the country, which was then bestowed on France as a League of Nations' mandate. The Hashemites ended up with their old Hijaz lands in western Arabia, which they soon lost to the Saudis, as well as Iraq and Jordan, but not Syria.

Within Syria, the French organized a local military. Since the Sunni elite was too patriotic and aristocratic to participate, half of the soldiers were Alawites. They broke up the largely Sunni Arab nationalist demonstrations and stopped labor strikes on behalf of the colonial rulers. These actions laid the basis for later Alawite domination of the military and hence, through coups, of the government.

Alawite leaders made no secret of the fact that they did not regard themselves as Muslims, knew that the Sunni Arabs agreed on that point, and had no interest in Arab nationalism. They preferred either that their lands be joined with multiethnic Lebanon or that at least the French stay in Syria. In 1936 Sulayman Assad, Hafiz's grandfather, and five other Alawite notables sent a letter to France's prime minister asking that the French continue to rule Syria since otherwise their people would be oppressed and even massacred by the Sunni Muslims. It stated:

> The spirit of hatred and fanaticism embedded in the hearts of the Arab Muslims against everything that is non-Muslim has been perpetually nurtured by the Islamic religion. There is no hope that the situation will ever change. Therefore, the abolition of the [French] Mandate will expose the minorities in Syria to the dangers of death and annihilation, not to mention that it will annihilate the freedom of thought and belief.[4]

Despite these pleas, and under pressure from Syrian nationalists supported by the British and Americans, France finally granted Syria an independence that took full effect in 1946. One can well imagine that the Alawite minority did not rejoice at an outcome it had tried to avoid.[5] Competing Arab Sunni Muslim factions, the National and People's parties, dominated the new country, though in 1950 the minority groups prevented Islam from being declared the state's official religion. Syria had a democratic political system and a free enterprise economic one. Given this promising start, the future might have developed relatively smoothly.

But the system was shaken by severe tremors taking place along several fault lines. One of these was the minority problem; a second was the lack of a distinctive Syrian identity. Other overlapping problems included the challenge of Arab nationalism, the rise of new radical ideas, and the Arab-Israeli conflict. The Arab world's emergence from European rule sparked debates over how Arab unity might be achieved, a struggle over power in each state, competition for leadership of the Arab world, controversies about the best path toward economic development, and strife over eliminating the remaining Western influence. Subordinated classes and communities raised demands; factions clashed over which economic system could bring rapid development.

Syria took Arab nationalism more seriously than did any other Arab state. Egypt, Iraq, and others each mouthed an Arab nationalist line but never ceased to have their own separate state consciousness, a healthy cynicism viewing Arab unity as perfectly fine as long as it developed under their own leadership. Syria was more naively idealistic, eager to dissolve itself into the nirvana of Arab unity, rejecting its own legitimacy as a state. Later the Assads had to provide Syria with a right to exist by selling the idea that it would one day become the core of something larger. Its existence and interests were legitimized by taking the role of Arabism's beating heart. What was good for Syria was good for the Arab world because Syria was the very personification of the Arab world.

Radical ideas—pan-Arabism, Ba'thism, Nasserism, Communism, Greater Syrian nationalism—further undermined Syria during the 1950s. These movements agreed that:

- Socialism was better than capitalism.
- Aligning with the Soviet bloc was superior to working with the West.
- Imperialism was the threat.
- An enlightened dictatorship was more to be desired than a bourgeois republic.
- A planned centralized economy would bring faster progress than private enterprise.
- Secularism and modernization must sweep away traditional society.

These movements found many of their supporters among dissatisfied, marginalized minorities—including those among them who had joined the army—and poor Sunni Arab peasants oppressed by rapacious landlords. As for the Sunni elite, it was content to take the top posts in the military, certain that this was a sufficient strategy to keep control over the Alawite and Druze mid-level officers.

The Sunni elite also embraced the idea of liberal democracy as a way of ensuring stability—so it thought—preserving the status quo. The system of multiparty electoral pluralism maintained a balance among families and between the two competing cities of Damascus and Aleppo. By providing representation for each minority community, this structure also let the leaders of each make deals with each other, as in Lebanon.

But even after Syria became independent, the idea of its being a country in its own right with permanent borders and a capitalist system was never secure. It was further discredited by competing factions and ideologies, each of which wanted a total victory for itself. The enemies of Syria's existing system were confident that once they were in charge, they could create a utopian society far superior to what existed.

The Arab defeat in the 1948 war to destroy Israel was still another nail in the Syrian system's coffin. The Arab side had been totally confident of an easy victory over the Jews. Instead, they had been defeated. Syria's military commanders had not performed well, while the government had proven ineffective and corrupt in fighting the war. Junior and mid-level officers seethed with resentment.

Syria's 1948 intervention in Palestine was by no means entirely altruistic. Some of the money raised for that cause disappeared, with the ensuing scandal even touching the prime minister. Syria's leaders openly spoke of annexing Palestine—as part of "southern Syria"—and Jordan as well. The rulers also attacked their Lebanese Christian neighbors as being as much of a "bone in the Arabs' throat" as were the Jews.[6]

The greatest living Syrian soldier at the time was Yousuf al-Atrash, leader of the Druze and of their 1925 anti-French revolt. While his rebellion would later be claimed by Syrian Arab nationalists as their own, Atrash recalled that the Arabs had not given him much help and suggested the Druze remain neutral in this new war. Explaining why his people would not volunteer to fight in Palestine, Atrash accurately prophesized: "The Jews are well prepared. Should they come to a clash with the Syrian army, they would be more than a match for this miserable force. . . . That would be the end of this regime in Damascus."[7]

Most Syrians, however, had no doubts that the outcome would be in the opposite direction. The Zionists would easily be defeated and Palestine would be Arab, perhaps even Syrian. The Jews in Palestine were not a very worthy foe and were merely, Syrian newspapers explained, only "following orders from New York, the Jewish world capital." The media accused Syria's Jews of espionage, treason, collaboration with Zionism, and spreading cholera. Although Syrian Jews were rarely attacked physically, they were fired from government jobs.[8]

As the first of many Syrian nominees to be their leading political agents in Palestine, the government chose Fawzi al-Qawuqji, who was a Syrian citizen. Born in Aleppo, he fought in the Ottoman army during World War I and with the French against Faysal's short-lived Syrian kingdom. Such a record did not seem likely to produce a dedicated Arab nationalist. In 1925, though, he changed sides and joined the anti-French revolt. After the French crushed the uprising, Qawuqji became military advisor to Saudi king Ibn Saud and later joined the Iraqi army. In 1936 he resigned to lead Palestinian Arab forces against the British and Jews during a rebellion. Under British pressure, he retreated first to pro-fascist Iraq and next to Nazi Germany, where he sat out World War II.

His People's Army, nominally Palestinian and fielding 5,000 soldiers, was really a surrogate force for Damascus in the war. The Syrian government gave him a house, an office, and a budget. According to him, the Arab was a natural-born soldier who could not be defeated. Prime Minister Jamil Mardam promised that Qawuqji's force would soon "teach the treacherous Jews an unforgettable lesson."[9]

On December 17, 1947, the League of Ulama, the association of Muslim clerics in Syria, proclaimed a jihad to conquer all of Palestine. Two days later the People's Army crossed the border on Syrian army trucks. They were quickly defeated. And six months later, in May 1948, the regular Syrian army followed them into Israel along with the Jordanian, Egyptian, and Iraqi armies. Abd al-Rahman Azzam, head of the Arab League, predicted: "This will be a war of extermination and a momentous massacre." But these forces, too, would be defeated.

As Hafiz's foreign minister, Farouq al-Sharaa, explained decades later, "The Arab national plan did not know how to deal with this [issue]. It neither accepted partition [of Palestine into Jewish and Arab states], nor did it reject it [effectively]. . . . What happened was completely the opposite. The rejection increased the share of the territory that was allocated to the Jewish state."[10] Even fifty years later, Sharaa could not admit what had happened. He lied by saying the Arabs were defeated only because their armies were commanded by British officers. In fact, only the Jordanian army had British officers, and it fought better than any of its allies.

There is no argument, however, about the fact that the Syrian government's humiliating defeat and incompetence destabilized that country after the war. Between 1946 and 1956, Syria had twenty different cabinets and four different constitutions. From 1949 to 1970, there were ten successful coups and a lot of failed ones. The first coup, in 1949, was led by Colonel Husni al-Zaim, who had, fortunately for himself, been in political exile during the 1948 war and thus bore no direct responsibility for the disaster. A few months later he was overthrown by Colonel Sami al-Hinnawi, who was himself replaced soon thereafter by Colonel Adib al-Shishakli.

These officers worked with various radical parties and traditional centrist politicians, conspiring for or against various schemes to combine Syria with Jordan or seek a pan-Syrian empire. Trying to extend his hold on power, Shishakli banned newspapers and political parties, including the Ba'th, Communists, the Muslim Brotherhood, and the National and People's parties. Despite pioneering various techniques, such as creating a single ruling party, he was himself overthrown in 1954 by a broad coalition ranging from traditional liberals to the Ba'th.

This was only the beginning of a protracted crisis. For the next four years, Syria was buffeted through endless maneuvers, quarrels, plots, and counterplots. A key factor was the rising role of the Soviet Union, which made itself the sponsor of Arab nationalism beginning with its 1955 arms deal supplying Egypt with modern weapons. In November 1956 Syria made a similar arrangement with Moscow. When Egyptian president Gamal Abdel Nasser became the closest thing to an Arab nationalist leader, Syria gravitated in his direction. The growing Ba'th party, doubting it could defeat all its foes and hold onto power alone, apparently thought it could use Nasser to maneuver itself into overall Arab leadership.

In fact, what happened was the exact opposite. Nasser manipulated the Ba'th into submitting to Egypt. The resulting 1958 merger of Egypt and Syria into the United Arab Republic was a disaster for Syria and the Ba'th party. Nasser set the terms for the union, demanded that all political parties but his own be dissolved, and had a cabinet that was two-thirds Egyptian. He treated Syria like a colony and exiled Ba'thist military officers Hafiz al-Assad and his friend Mustafa Tlas to Egypt, where Nasser's men could keep an eye on them. By any measure of usual political logic, this experiment should have proven that Arab nationalism was a serious mistake. Yet this never happened, for those who dedicated their lives to implementing the myth would not learn from experience in order to change their course. Thus, the group of patriotic—in local Syrian terms—officers who revolted in 1961 and threw out the Egyptians were considered to be traitors by later Ba'thist regimes.

Once again Syria was plunged into disorder. Finally, on March 8, 1963, the Ba'th party seized power, It was a moment that seemed to be the high water mark for Ba'thist ambitions since the party's local branch also took over Iraq. Talks were held with Nasser once again to see if Egypt, Iraq, and Syria might be combined into one Arab superstate. But Nasser, chastened by his earlier experience of failed union with Syria and suspicious of the Ba'th, did not want to try again. At any rate, the Iraqi Ba'th party was soon overthrown. The great moment, if it existed at all, had passed. Still, the Syrian Ba'th party remained in power, putting down an attempted Nasserist coup and as a result being labeled fascist by Nasser.

Within Syria, a Sunni military officer named Amin al-Hafiz was in control along with Ba'th civilian politicians. But they were too tame for the party's impatient radicals. In March 1966 the party's Military Committee, headed by Salah Jadid and including Hafiz al-Assad, grabbed power and established a truly left-wing revolutionary government, committed to social revolution at home, the overthrow of all Arab monarchies, alliance with the Soviets, and immediate battle with Israel and America abroad.[11]

The Jadid regime took very seriously the Ba'th program as an adaptation of Communism in the framework of Arab nationalism, with secularism and socialism as leading principles. Writing in 1956, Michel Aflaq, the Ba'th theoretician, associated religion with the old corrupt social order, oppression, and exploitation of the weak, seemingly influenced by Marx's view of religion as the opiate of the masses, distracting from the proper business of social revolution. Religion was something that was exploited "to numb the people in order to keep them from rebelling against those who would oppress and enslave them." In its declaration of principles, the Ba'th party said it would build, "A new generation of Arabs . . . committed to scientific thought freed from the shackles of superstition and backward customs." In discussing nationalism, this statement deliberately used Arabic words traditionally applied to religion in order to claim that nationalism must replace Islam as the proper belief system of the Arab people.[12]

Not surprisingly, this stance would lead to significant problems with Syria's Sunni Muslim majority. In April 1967 a young Ba'thist officer named Ibrahim al-Khallas, who was an Alawite, wrote an article in the Syrian army journal *Jaysh al-Shaab* [People's Army], entitled "The Means of Creating a New Arab Socialist Person." He explained, "The way to fashion Arab culture and Arab society is by creating an Arab socialist who believes that God, imperialism and all other values that had controlled society in the past are no more than mummies in the Museum of History." Religion, the product of feudalism and imperialism, had made Arabs a submissive, fatalistic people. The new Arab man would rebel as a socialist revolutionary who believed only in humanity.[13]

This was the kind of thing leftists in the West had been writing for more than a century and was a staple in Communist states. But Syria was not a Western country with a strong tradition of secularism. Urban Sunnis protested the article; strikes and anti-Ba'th demonstrations broke out. The regime denounced the article as a CIA-Zionist plot and threw the author and magazine editor into prison. Despite these actions, the Jadid regime was in fact antireligious. It forbade preaching, and restricted the conduct of any religious education, outside mosques; appointed clerics; managed religious institutions; and arrested or executed clerics who opposed it.[14] Yet it also realized the dangers of an open confrontation with Islam.

As in the Khallas case, the Arab-Israeli conflict was the main safety valve for deflecting all internal problems and mobilizing support. But the Jadid government genuinely pinned its hopes, and even survival, on spreading the revolution and destroying Israel in the near future.

An important internal party document in 1965 mandated that the Palestinian struggle had to be supported even if it led to Syria's destruction. Syria's goal was "the annihilation of the state of Israel and the return of the Palestinian Arab people to their fatherland." The party warned that putting reform at home before destroying Israel was "dangerous and illogical if it implies the postponement of the liberation struggle to the indefinite future." Moreover, Syria, the regime's leaders wrote, could not depend on Egypt or the PLO to destroy Israel since Nasser tightly restrained the Palestinians and the PLO was just his front group.[15] In other words, total victory had to be won soon, and Syria was the instrument for securing this triumph.

From the very start, Syria sought to dominate the Palestinian movement and turn it into an instrument. Almost a half-century of effort has not blunted that determination. Arafat and his friends founded Fatah in 1959 as an independent revolutionary Palestinian group. The Palestine Liberation Organization (PLO) was created soon thereafter as an Egyptian client. Syria mistrusted both groups and banned Fatah's magazine.

But Fatah soon became a client of Syria's new Ba'thist regime.[16] If Nasser had the PLO, Damascus would counter with its own Palestinian group. While the PLO issued threats, Syria would prove its revolutionary credentials by actually carrying out attacks against Israel. Fatah leaders called Syria their land of sanctuary; and Arafat's number-two man, Abu Iyad, said that from the beginning, Syria was the movement's heart and lungs.[17]

The first training camps for Fatah fighters were opened in Syria with a hundred soldiers in 1964. Recruits were paid eighteen British pounds a month, a good salary in those days. Most of Fatah's money came from wealthy Palestinians living in Kuwait or Saudi Arabia, though Syria probably also subsidized the organization.[18] By 1965 Arafat had his headquarters in Damascus.[19]

Syria's role as sponsor was shown by Fatah's first choice of a target on January 1, 1965—Israel's water system, the building of which Syria had tried so hard and so unsuccessfully to stop. To avoid trouble with the West or Israel, Syria's regime routed the attacks through Lebanon or Jordan so it could not be held responsible. This set a pattern that would persist for decades. The Syrian government also denied that it had anything to do with Fatah or terrorism, and Western governments, in particular the British Foreign Office[20] and the U.S. State Department,[21] believed its denials, their credulity toward Syria becoming another enduring pattern. Under Arafat's leadership, Fatah staged sixty-one attacks into Israel during its first two years of armed struggle.[22] These forays were so badly organized and ineffective, however, that when Syrian officials told British diplomats they had "concrete evidence" that Fatah was an Israeli front, a British diplomat responded, "Indeed the incompetence and ineptitude of many of the attacks could be held to lend weight to these suspicions." But the British did not believe this claim for several reasons, one being precisely the fact that the attacks were so incompetent: "The Israelis would surely put up a better show," the diplomat wrote.[23]

From the start, too, the targets of attacks were primarily civilian, a strategy that became the movement's trademark. On January 4, 1965, Fatah commandos infiltrated into Israel from Jordan and again tried to dynamite the water

system. Similar efforts in the following weeks and months were also largely unsuccessful.[24] Israel captured its first Fatah prisoner when his rifle misfired. The
first casualty was a Fatah man killed by Jordanian soldiers while returning
across the border after an attack on Israel.[25]

In May 1966 a raid on the Israeli city of Afula and a kibbutz killed nine Israelis, including two children. Two days later Israel counterattacked the two
main terrorist camps on the Jordanian-ruled West Bank, at Qalqilya and Jenin.
In November, after an Israeli reprisal raid at Samu, Jordan, civilians demonstrated demanding that King Hussein arm them. Instead, as Israel had hoped,
he restricted attacks. Syria was reaping the political benefits, while Jordan faced
the consequent internal unrest and Israeli reprisals.

Fatah's rapid growth was due to Syrian sponsorship. But this relationship
also made problems for Arafat in dealing with Egypt, Jordan, and Iraq. After
all, Fatah was a Syrian client whose purpose was to counter Egypt's strategy of
backing the PLO. Why should other Arab regimes help it?

Even within Syria, opinions over Fatah were divided. Jadid viewed Arafat
as a protégé; Hafiz considered Arafat to be an instrument of his rivals. Arafat
said that he was once arrested and held for a day by one Syrian intelligence
agency while transporting dynamite from Lebanon in the trunk of his car just
after the head of another service assured him of its support. Syria's rulers were
especially angered by a Fatah plot to blow up the Tapline oil pipeline that carried Saudi oil through Lebanon to the Mediterranean. The Saudis would not
be happy if Syria sabotaged their main source of revenue.[26]

Syria's rival factions became patrons of competing leaders within Fatah.
After all, while Arafat had assumed the leadership of Fatah and made decisions
without consulting colleagues, it was not inevitable that he would hold the
post forever or outrank all the other co-founders. There were still tactical differences and complex debates over both ideology and relations with Arab
states. Some already saw Arafat as an autocratic leader. In May 1966 the Fatah
Central Committee briefly suspended him for allegedly mishandling funds, ignoring collective decisions, taking unauthorized trips, and making false military reports.[27]

The battle escalated in 1966 as the Assad faction in Syria's regime backed
Major Yousuf al-Urabi, a Palestinian officer in Syria's army and close friend of
Hafiz, to be the new Fatah leader. Arafat later claimed the Syrians planned to
assassinate him, but it appears that he or some of his friends had Urabi killed in
order to eliminate the threat to themselves. As a result, Arafat and some of his
supporters were thrown into the notorious Mezza prison for about six weeks.[28]
Hafiz personally interrogated one of Arafat's top lieutenants, Abu Jihad, about

Fatah activities. Whether Salah Jadid saved Arafat by promising to act more to Hafiz's liking or Hafiz felt that Arafat had been sufficiently intimidated, the Palestinians were finally released.[29]

This incident was to set a pattern of enmity between Hafiz and Arafat that would persist until the former's death more than three decades later. Indeed, in Hafiz's semiofficial biography, the regime claims that Arafat was thrown into jail because he had betrayed a Fatah operation and was really an Israeli agent.

But Jadid was about to provide Hafiz with a much bigger problem. In May 1967 the Syrian and Soviet governments created a major confrontation by claiming, without apparent justification, that Israel was about to attack Syria. Egypt was dragged into a competition among Arab states to see who could make the most extreme threats against Israel. Egypt, Jordan, and Syria forged an alliance. Nasser loudly threatened war, demanded that UN peacekeeping forces be withdrawn from its border with Israel and closed the Straits of Tiran to Israeli shipping. Fatah's raids and the PLO leadership's heated rhetoric intensified the crisis. Returning from Gaza in May 1967, the PLO chief told Nasser that the Palestinian people were "straining for the fight.... The army of Egypt . . . now stands face to face with the gangs of Israel" and the Arab nation was intent "on the liberation of the usurped homeland." War was inevitable, said the PLO leader Shuqayri, and would lead to total victory, after which the Jews would "go back the way they came . . . by sea," to their original countries. If he was not threatening to throw the Jews into the sea, he was certainly promising to put them onto boats.[30]

What happened, however, was quite different from the expectations of Nasser, Jadid, Shuqayri, and Arafat. Israel attacked first, smashing the armies of Egypt, Syria, and Jordan in six days. Israel captured the remnants of pre-1948 Palestine—the West Bank and Gaza—along with Egypt's Sinai Peninsula and Syria's Golan Heights. The resulting humiliation and hopelessness inflamed the Arabs' worst fears that Israel would take over the region.

The outcome did not, however, inspire Syria or other Arab states with a desire to end the conflict quickly through negotiation. The very extent of the disaster meant that no regime would accept it. The "progressive" Arab military regimes in Egypt, Syria, and Iraq—shown to be no more effective than their predecessors—would scarcely allow themselves to be more politically yielding. At the 1967 Arab summit, Syria and other Arab states agreed not to negotiate, recognize, or make peace with Israel.

"There are only two well-defined goals on the Arab scene," wrote the influential Egyptian journalist Muhammad Hasanayn Haykal, "erasing the traces of the 1967 aggression by Israel's withdrawal from all the areas occupied by it in that year and erasing the aggression of 1948 by Israel's total and absolute annihilation. . . . The mistake of some of us is starting off with the last step before beginning the first."[31] For more than a quarter century after 1967, however, Syria would insist that the only satisfactory Arab strategy was to openly seek Israel's destruction.

Another outcome of the war was that Arafat transferred from Syrian patronage to that of a more powerful Egypt. Nasser knew that the old PLO leadership had failed completely and he wanted a way to hit Israel that did not require the direct involvement of Arab armies. The Egyptian leader got the Soviet Union to join him in backing Arafat and helped Fatah set up its new main base in Jordan. The Syrians had been cut out completely.[32]

But Arafat fumbled the opportunity to turn the tide. His cross-border attacks on Israel caused civilian casualties but did not jeopardize his enemy's survival. Meanwhile, Fatah and the PLO acted like a state within a state, antagonizing Jordan's King Hussein and his supporters. In September 1970 Hussein made his move, and the Jordanian army attacked and defeated Fatah. Jadid, who wanted to save his old protégé, sent Syrian tanks into Jordan on September 20, but the United States and Israel made it clear that they would not allow King Hussein to be overthrown, and the Jordanians showed themselves ready and able to fight the Syrian invasion. Hafiz, the air force commander, refused to provide air support for Jadid, and the Syrian forces backed down and withdrew.

The Sunni elite that traditionally ruled Syria into the 1940s had declined; the Communists and Pan-Syrian nationalists had fallen by the wayside in the 1950s, followed by the civilian founders of the Ba'th party in the early 1960s. Only the military was left. But within the army Sunni officers had worn themselves down in a rivalry of attrition. Then came the turn of the most radical Ba'th officers, of Salah Jadid, but his extremism had crashed with the 1967 war and the humiliation over Jordan. And so, in the end, Hafiz was really the only one who could rule, a radical but a relatively pragmatic man who would replace rivalry and revolution with building a solid regime. In effect, he was the Stalin of Syria, as Saddam Hussein would be in a different way for Iraq.

On November 13, 1970, Hafiz easily seized power. Jadid was thrown into prison, where he remained for twenty-five years, dying of a heart attack in August 1993 at the age of sixty-three.[33] The Assad era had arrived; the time of instability, but not of tyranny, was over.

CHAPTER THREE

ASSAD'S SYSTEM, THEN AND NOW

Syria's Ba'thist revolution was born from an idealist ambition to create something grand but ended by imposing the terribly heavy burden of preserving a stagnant system. Surely it has some achievements to its credit—land reform, stability, and the elevation of some people from the previously lowly strata of society—yet it did far more harm by smothering a vibrant society under a gray authoritarianism that has held Syria back, plunged it into a permanent state of war, and wasted its resources. It is not an exaggeration to say that since the 1980s Syria's main purpose has become keeping the regime in power.

There was nothing modest about the goals of the Ba'thist revolution. Like its Bolshevik counterpart in Russia, the Ba'thist's role model, the plan was to seize power, totally transform the country from above, and use that state as a base to take over as much territory as possible. The politicians and military officers who gained control in 1963, in 1966, and in 1970 believed they would unite the Arab world and quickly develop Syria into a modern industrial secular society with a Western level of living standards. These far-reaching objectives were not attained, and the revolution's main achievement—as in the USSR—became their use in keeping hold on power. In short, the goal became not to rule well, but merely to rule.

Building this system was no easy job for Hafiz and his colleagues but, once created, it had a kind of ugly elegance in its ingenious and systematic architecture. Every detail had to be effectively covered, each possible threat to the regime completely blocked. Yet the Assads' creation was much more than just a set of institutions for retaining power, it was also a set of ideas that safeguarded the regime, shaped its own thinking, and maximized its popularity among the citizenry. As a result, while Syria had ten successful coup attempts and more failed ones during the two decades between 1949 and 1970, it has not faced one serious threat from the Syrian political or military elite since then.

To make the regime really strong and stable, Syria's leaders used educators, journalists, intellectuals, and cultural figures to ensure that people did not just obey the dictator, they would love him. Although far from attaining the kind of society portrayed in George Orwell's *1984* or Aldous Huxley's *Brave New World*—cynicism and quiet antagonism has always existed—Syria was about as close as any nation could come in practice. Iraq under Saddam was far more dependent on fear and repression; Islamist Iran, more riddled with sullen resentment and openly expressed opposition. It has its troubles, but Syria's system is a success story from the standpoint of power imposed on a willing populace.

The government did not just sit in its offices and issue decrees. It has had command of the country's wealth, information, ideology, and every conceivable institution. Syrians can conduct business only by making government officials their partners or succeed in most careers only by echoing the regime's ideology, whether they believe it in their hearts or not. It is a society where all the media are under regime control and adhere to the official line; sustained public criticism can lead to torture and imprisonment; cell phones and Internet use are tightly controlled; private conversations may well be reported to the secret police; and any contact with a foreigner is suspect. Yet it is also a society in which the people generally accept the regime's stories and the permanent war footing this worldview demands.

How was this impressive edifice created? "I am a man of institutions," Hafiz accurately explained.[1] To start with, there was the Soviet model, which the Ba'th party sought to copy with adjustments for Arab circumstances. The key is to control all the commanding heights of the society—army, economy, media, education, religion, and so on—both to use them for promoting the regime and to keep them out of anyone else's hands. The army furnishes the guns and the economy provides the money needed to preserve the system. Promotions, jobs, and income tie people to the government. The schools, media, and mosques manufacture popular loyalty and enthusiasm. From top to bottom it is a total system of control and indoctrination.

Next, the party pervades all levels of society and is organized like a disciplined civilian army to justify, support, and inform the leadership. Its branches and cells are located throughout the country, in schools and even in the armed forces. Umar Amiralay, a film director critical of the system who was arrested in 2006, explained, "The only civil society practicing politics, culture, social activities, is the Ba'th Party. You have to join the party to have any opportunities."[2]

Membership in the party has become quite large, comprising as much as 10 percent of the country's population, meaning a high proportion of families have at least one member linked to the regime. In 1970 when Hafiz took power— but by which time the Ba'th party had been ruling Syria for eight years—membership was still only 65,000, rising to 374,000 in 1981, and 1 million in 1992. In 2000 the official figure was 1.4 million. By 2005 it hit 1.8 million. One key point in preserving top-down control, however, is that only about 30 percent of these people are full party members. According to the Ba'th party's 2000 report, two-thirds were below age thirty and about 36 percent were students. Women made up just under 30 percent. The peasantry was significantly underrepresented. The party's focus is to ensure the elite's loyalty—the reason for the importance of students, who are the future elite—while the greatest attraction of party membership is as a ticket to higher status. Thus, 998 of the 1,307 judges were members, as were the majority of Syria's university teachers.[3]

The party's secretary-general is also the country's president. He is selected by the party's regional command, which is elected by the party congress, which itself is elected every four years by the organization's branches. The congress elects a ninety-member central committee and a twenty-one-member regional committee, the country's highest political body.[4] None of this, however, means that the party is democratic since, after all, this system is modeled on that of the Soviet Communist party.

The fist of dictatorship is thinly concealed by the glove of representative government. As mandated by the 1973 constitution, a veneer of parliamentary democracy parallels the real lines of power. Hafiz was five times elected president for seven-year terms from 1970 to his death in 2000. In 1972 the National Progressive Front was established, with the ruling party heading a pretend-coalition government made up of a half-dozen Communist and Arab nationalist parties in what was really a one-party state. Among the many lessons Hafiz learned from his predecessors' failures was to co-opt and tame non-Ba'thist groups that might otherwise challenge the regime.

In practice, though, the president dominates the Ba'th party, which dominates the National Progressive Front, which dominates the parliament, a body with power merely to endorse laws and the executive's policies, not to initiate or challenge them. About one-third of the seats in parliament are held by independent members and some others go to satellite parties, but most are held by Ba'thist stalwarts.

Party members or sympathizers head all significant organizations, so that trade unions and writers', women's, peasants', and professional organizations become arms of the regime.[5] Party membership is a useful, sometimes indispensable, tool to advance one's career. Students who join the party have points added to their grades and more easily enter prestigious universities and degree programs.

In a dictatorship, it is absolutely vital to control those groups most likely to challenge the regime: military officers, who might make a coup; journalists and intellectuals, who could subvert through criticism; businesspeople and unions, who might raise economic demands. In this context, Hafiz al-Assad learned a great deal from the chronic instability of the 1949 to 1970 era. Aside from repression and the regime's ability to dole out rewards, the key to willing consent is organization, ideology, and demagoguery. The traditional techniques of patronage politics also work quite well. Giving people jobs, favors, and money is a very reliable way to win their loyalty.

A good summary of how this persuasive power works is the Ba'th party's slogan: Unity, freedom, and socialism. This slogan poses as the way to defend and further the interests of all Syrians and indeed of all Arabs. Compare this to the American doctrine of life, liberty, and the pursuit of happiness or the French motto of liberty, equality, and brotherhood. The vital difference is that these latter two credos emphasize the rights and well-being of individuals; the Syrian credo champions the power of the state and the subordination of citizens to it.

Western democratic revolutions have been about limiting the powers of the state. But the focus of the Ba'thist doctrine is on the regime's interests, not those of the citizens. Individuals' rights must be limited because the struggle for Arab nationalism and against imperialism and Zionism requires the tight discipline and systematic mobilization that only a dictatorial system can provide while democracy waits forever in the wings. In this universe, "Unity" means the union of all the Arabs, which justifies the state's liberty to subvert its neighbors.

"Freedom" refers to the Arab state's independence from Western influence, not to an individual's rights against state coercion. Protecting Arab freedom means to fight America, Israel, and the West, a battle that is said to be of the greatest personal importance for every individual Arab. Paradoxically, though, in order to achieve this version of freedom, citizens have to obey and support the dictatorial regime that denies them personal liberty.

"Socialism" here is the doctrine of state control, a highly centralized economy ensuring the regime's ability to dole out patronage as suits its interests. The idea is to ensure that too many resources do not fall into private hands, which would set up sectors independent of the state. The alternative to state socialism is the empowering of a Sunni bourgeoisie that could finance liberal reform groups, Islamist movements, or both.

Never has authoritarian rule been justified in more attractive popular terms than in the Ba'thist doctrine.

To make this system work and be freely accepted by its subjects, the regime defined the job of intellectuals, teachers, and journalists as being to support the government's program rather than pursue truth, professional integrity, or democracy. Antoun al-Maqdasi, a Syrian political philosopher, complained that the government's apparent goal was to make citizens as identical as possible in their ideas and views, "as if they were cast in the same mold."[6]

That is, of course, precisely the point: They are supposed to echo government views. As Bashar put it, "The role of the Arab intellectual is not to weep or to cry over the ruins, but rather his role is to present people with the culture and the ideology of the resistance."[7] The Syrian minister of expatriate affairs, Buthayna Shaban, explained that "culture should be mobilized: literature, art, poetry, for the resistance. We must all work to inculcate these [values] in future generations, so that they will not know the taste of defeat and shame."[8]

There is no sense that culture is about teaching and making choices or that citizens might be instructed to search for truth in the most honest way possible rather than having only one version presented to them. Indeed, inculcating the need for battle becomes more important than providing skills or knowledge. Thus, the dean of education at Damascus University explained that the culture of resistance must permeate every aspect of Syrian life. "We can teach the child the following mathematical problem: 25 tanks entered South Lebanon. The brave men of the resistance confronted them. They [destroyed] five tanks and damaged seven. How many of these tanks returned defeated back to where they came from?"[9] Clearly, this is more to be prized than teaching mathematical equations about how many votes did each party get in a democratic election.

Every citizen is to be a soldier mobilized against the foreign enemy and his local lackeys. It is everyone's duty to love the regime and above all the president. As for the intellectuals and the cultural elite, they are richly rewarded for selling their integrity but can also pose as heroes of the resistance for doing so. There are few things better than winning the right to live in luxury and have one's career advanced while at the very same time being smug in one's virtue as a champion of the underdogs. The regime's "left-wing" and secularist veneer, both qualities jettisoned decades ago in practice, also make Western intellectuals more willing to praise or repeat the claims of what is in fact a repressive, greedy dictatorship.

It is also quite true, of course, that many Syrians have benefited personally from the regime's policies, and this is a genuine incentive for loyalty. First, those from poorer backgrounds—many but by no means all of them Alawites—have risen through the opportunity to study. Second, a huge proportion of the population is directly or indirectly in the government's employ and thus receives its livelihood from the regime. Finally, many urban Sunni elite families did do well from the 1980s onward as the political elite encouraged their prosperity both to ensure their support and to get its own cut of the profits.

This reality enabled a regime official, Secretary of the Office of Youth and Students of the Ba'th Party Regional Command Faiz Izz al-Din, to tell liberal critics in 2000, "You cannot come to me and say that as one who is a member of the Ba'th Party for over forty years, I am worthless, and expect me to take this quietly and with a smile." Husayn al-Zu'bi, a University of Damascus lecturer, no doubt spoke for many when he said that if it were not for the Ba'th party, "I could not have studied and become a university lecturer. My father was a simple peasant exploited by feudal lords and the bourgeoisie. Therefore one cannot claim that the regime in power in Syria has done nothing positive."[10] To some extent, though, such a story could be told under any regime, since the expansion of the educated and skilled personnel required inevitably causes the elite's need to recruit from the poorer classes.

In short, the regime has used a classic carrot-and-stick approach. Those who cooperate completely are given good jobs, money, and honor; those who do not are scorned and punished. Most people have no trouble choosing the former option if it is available to them. Although co-optation does not work on everyone, it succeeds often enough to keep the active opposition small, isolated, and intimidated. The regime's flexible approach also reduces the overall level of conflict. If you behave, it is not too hard to get along with the authorities. In contrast to the unforgiving approach of Saddam Hussein in Iraq, the Assads have always been willing to welcome sinners ready to repent.

An interesting example of this technique is the Syrian treatment of the Communist party. The pro-Soviet wing was simultaneously controlled and coddled, partly to please Hafiz's Soviet ally, partly because it accepted the regime and caused no trouble. In contrast, those in the opposition Communist faction who continued to advocate a revolution against the "petit-bourgeois" Ba'th received very long prison sentences.

While many of the regime's structural and bureaucratic aspects were imported from Moscow and its satellites, Hafiz also made an important original contribution to the art of being a successful dictator. He had to solve the puzzle of how to be simultaneously an authoritarian ruler, govern badly, and both stay in office and remain popular. The power structure is built on a foundation of familial and communal relations. All those who benefit have their fates linked to the regime's survival, not only because it is the source of their rank and privileges but also since it ensures the lives and livelihoods of themselves and their loved ones.

First and foremost, then, the regime is a family dynasty, the property of the Assads, their brothers and their sisters and their cousins—and they have them by the dozens—and their aunts. Then comes the extended family, the Kalbiyya tribe, and next the Alawites as an ethnic-religious community. Finally, there is an even larger community, comprised of party members, the elite, and their families—what the Soviets called the "nomenclature"—who feel that they have benefited from the system.

The regime has brought the Alawites, who comprise only about 12 percent of the Syrian population, everything; its fall could cost them everything. Many have become important officials or top officers who, in turn, donate money generously to their home villages and extended families. The limited and acceptable collective price has been a loss of some of their own unique identity as the Assads pressed them to behave like "regular Muslims," shedding or at least concealing their distinctive aspects. The power elite has become more integrated into non-Alawite ways but do not seem to forget their unique aspects, as one sees for example in the choice of names for children. Still, while the regime is dominated by Alawites, they do not use their power, aside from favoring their co-religionists in jobs and their extended families generally, for communal purposes. After all, the regime's rulers are Arab, not Alawite, nationalists.

Historically, Sunni Arab Muslims viewed Alawites as pariahs, not only as backward hillbillies but also as infidels. Even the word "Alawite" itself is a piece of political propaganda. This community was historically called Nusayyris. "Alawite" refers to Ali, the hero of the Shia Muslims, whose name means literally "the faction of Ali." Anyone who is a follower of Ali sounds like a Muslim. In contrast, though, the name Nusayyri derives from Ibn Nusayyr, a ninth-century—and hence post-Muhammad—prophet who founded their religion. Since apostasy by Muslims is punishable by death under Islamic law and Islam recognizes no prophets after Muhammad, every Alawite is technically guilty of a capital offense.

There were Sunni massacres of Nusayyris in medieval times, and the Ottoman authorities launched an unsuccessful campaign to force them to convert to Sunni Islam in the nineteenth century. For example, they built mosques in Alawite villages which the inhabitants ignored. Discrimination, and even violent oppression, therefore, is a historical fact of which Alawites are well aware.

When the French came to rule Syria in 1920, they gave the Alawites a chance precisely because they were alienated from the majority and in search of a protector. Bringing them into the army meant using a group that had little reason to be loyal to the independence-minded Sunni elite and every reason to be grateful to France. As happened elsewhere in the Arab world, the local elite looked down on joining the army, but this career of last resort proved to be a road to power for marginal groups. As a young man even Hafiz reportedly would have preferred to study medicine. Since his family could not afford the tuition costs, he had to go to a military academy instead.

Outnumbered five to one by a group that views itself as Syria's proper and natural ruler, the Alawites had to stick together. Even today, it is very rare to find an Alawite in the liberal opposition and never at all in the Islamist camp.

Outcasts from the status quo, they turned to radicalism and secularism. Instead of the traditional society, where they fared badly, and Islam, where they fared not at all, the Alawites turned to militant pan-Arab nationalism. As long as religion was the chief source of identity for Syria, or for Arabs in general, the Alawites would always be an out group. But if being an Arab was sufficient, they could be equal. This was the attractiveness of the Ba'thist worldview: Religion was to be subsumed in a broad national identity as the glue holding society together; traditional society was to be liquidated; Syria was to be dissolved into the Arab world.

It must be understood that Alawites are not just a religious group but have implicitly seen themselves as a coherent ethnic community with a long collective history. Indeed, since their religious beliefs are kept largely secret from all but the initiated, theology is not an important element in their identity. At the same time, though, the Alawites have always refused to make public their holy books precisely because these would show how widely they diverge from Islam. These works reportedly include such concepts as a mystical trinity comprised of Ali, son-in-law of Muhammad, Islam's founder; Muhammad himself; and a freed slave who became an important follower of Muhammad. The Alawites do not seek or accept converts.[11]

The fact that the Assads managed to overcome all these problems is a stupendous achievement. The Sunni elite saw itself as urban and cosmopolitan, the bearers of civilization, and the Alawites as a backward rural people of suspect beliefs. During Hafiz's reign, intoxication with the notion of Arab nationalism overcame this bias; with Bashar, after 2000, the regime has claimed to own the local franchise on Islam as well.

Hafiz understood that the Alawites could not go it alone, and so the regime cultivated Sunni allies. Against the old urban mercantile and rural landowning Sunni elite, the Ba'th party's land reform benefited Sunni peasants and turned them into supporters. As a result of Hafiz's reversal of the Jadid regime's secular policies and a clever courting of the Sunnis, the regime became more stable. When the Muslim Brotherhood revolted in the late 1970s and early 1980s, most Sunnis did not support it. Those in rural areas were less religious than their urban counterparts, and many of them had benefited from the Ba'th revolution. Most of the urban middle classes liked the stability provided by the regime. Many were relatively secular and modernist, finding the Ba'th more to their taste than the Muslim Brotherhood.

All this counted nothing for the Brotherhood itself, of course. But the issue was how many people would think its way. The Brotherhood's war on the regime—which it openly labeled as being an Alawite one—was a jihad against those seen as infidels or heretics. Having an Alawite government was bad enough; the idea that it was secularist on top of that was too much for the Brotherhood to bear. Still, most Sunnis sided, for whatever reason, with the regime. Much of the Brotherhood's base was regional, coming from the north, which resented the economic domination of Damascus. Thus, Hafiz was able to put down the Brotherhood's rebellion of the late 1970s and early 1980s not only through bloody repression but also by political maneuvering. And the revolt did not recur.

Hafiz was not an Alawite communalist who consciously sought to put his people into power. His Arab nationalism was no doubt sincere. But having an entire community identified with the regime on a life-and-death basis was a tremendous advantage. Still, while the regime used the Alawite community as its base and bulwark, Hafiz was willing to have individual Sunnis in the highest positions.

Many of these men had been Hafiz's personal friends in the military from the early days before he gained power. Mustafa Tlas, for example, met Hafiz when they were students together at Homs Military College. Tlas worked with Hafiz on the Ba'th party military committee and was exiled with him to Egypt in 1959. So much did Hafiz trust Tlas that when they were going home after Syria broke up the union with Egypt, and he was delayed in Cairo, Hafiz asked Tlas to escort his wife and daughter back home. A decade later, as soon as Hafiz staged his coup, he made Tlas minister of defense, a job he kept for three decades. Although Tlas was a loose cannon who probably did the Syrian military more harm than good, for Hafiz, loyalty outranked every other virtue.

Other Sunnis in high positions were Hikmat Shihabi, perennial army chief of staff; Vice-President Zuhayr al-Masharqa; and Prime Minister Mahmoud al-Zu'bi. When he came to power, Hafiz made Abd al-Halim Khaddam foreign minister. In 1984 he was promoted to vice-president and put in charge of Lebanon. His successor at the Foreign Ministry was another Sunni, Farouq al-Sharaa. Having Sunni foreign ministers made sense; they had more worldly experience than the Alawites and could also get along more easily with their Sunni counterparts in other Arab countries.

But when Bashar consolidated power after taking over in 2000, all these men—and most Sunnis in general—were retired and not replaced by others from that community. It was as if they were no longer needed to provide cover for the Alawite-dominated regime. About the only Sunni left in the real top tier was Tlas's son, a close friend of Bashar. Under both Hafiz and Bashar there were always Sunnis in important-sounding jobs—cabinet ministers and members of parliament—but that was not where the real power lay.

Although Hafiz did not run a military regime, the armed forces and security services were the regime's backbone and protector. Hafiz was not only president and head of the Ba'th party but also a lieutenant general commanding the army, all posts Bashar inherited. Hafiz controlled but also respected and consulted the officer corps. And almost 90 percent of the generals at the time of Hafiz's death were Alawites.[12]

Communal screening applied especially to choosing the members for elite units, often commanded by Hafiz's relatives. The Republican Guard, an armored division and the only force the Assads trusted enough to let enter Damascus, was commanded for a long time by one of his nephews. Three of his sons—Basil, Bashar, and Mahir—served in that unit. When Bashar became president, he made his personal secretary a commander in the Guard. Another special force, Unit 549, which defends the capital, is headed by one of Bashar's cousins. An additional elite unit, the Special Forces, is, along with the Third and Fourth Armored divisions, commanded by Alawites.[13]

Equally important are the intelligence forces, also largely run by Alawites. These include the military, air force, general, and political security intelligence units. Military Intelligence has the main responsibility for Lebanon while General Intelligence watches Syria's own people, though it also has agent networks in Lebanon. Both groups provide help to terrorist organizations. These agencies are all coordinated by the Ba'th Party Regional Command National Security Bureau, which also advises whichever Assad happens to be ruling at the time. There are in all fifteen security agencies with 50,000 employees. Thus, one of every 240 Syrians is part of the repressive apparatus, even without counting soldiers and party members.

All the security agencies report directly to the Assad who is president. The Ba'th party also permeates the armed forces as an additional watchdog. As of 2000, there were 27 party branches, 212 subbranches, and 1,656 clubs, with a total of 25,066 Ba'th party members in the military.[14]

Adding together all those working for the government or institutions it controls, those in the armed forces, and party members—despite allowing for overlap—means that about half of all Syrians owe part of their daily bread directly to the regime. This in itself is a powerful control mechanism.

Thus, the Assads have used a multilevel strategy to control the military:

- Hafiz, and later Bashar, commanded the armed forces. Their relatives were in critical intelligence positions and led key units. Officers were selected first from their family, second from their tribe, and third from the Alawites in general. Hafiz also used old personal friends in sensitive command positions. Trusted men were kept in high-level posts for long periods of time.

- Officers received many special privileges ranging from legal ones, such as housing and allowances, to illegal benefits, such as the right to smuggle across the border with Lebanon; shares in business enterprises; and commissions for allowing drug production or processing, counterfeiting U.S. dollars, and other criminal activities. Since salaries remained low even by Syrian standards—a senior officer in the 1990s might earn only $7,000 a year—corrupt practices were inevitable.

- The government kept tight controls over the military to ensure that officers did not gain the primary loyalty of their soldiers; tight restrictions were kept on the distribution of weapons and ammunition; units were forbidden to enter Damascus; and so on. Many of these controls interfered with the quality of the army as a fighting force. Recognizing this problem in regard to Syrian defeats in the 1967, 1973, and 1982 wars with Israel, Hafiz tried to put qualified men into high positions. But he accepted reduced competence rather than take any risks with the armed forces' loyalty.

- Special military units and intelligence agencies kept an eye on each other and carefully monitored the regular army. These groups, made up almost exclusively of Alawites, had the best personnel, equipment, and privileges.

- The armed forces were steadily and dramatically expanded from 50,000 soldiers just before the 1967 war to 170,000 in 1973, 300,000 in 1983, and 500,000 in 1985. But Syria could not afford the weapons and equipment to gain parity with Israel. Consequently, its strategy shifted more to using terrorist groups, especially Hizballah, as extensions of its military force and building up a large arsenal of rockets and missiles that was meant to intimidate Israel at a relatively low cost.

- In theory, governments should seek peace to reduce their military budget and devote the money to economic development. But this is not true for Syria. Aside from needing international tension to justify its rule, the regime spends a lot of money to keep the generals happy, absorb young men who might otherwise be discontented and unemployed, and defend itself from potential domestic threats. One of the main ways of controlling the armed forces is to enrich its personnel and give them what they want.

About the only major failure of the system regarding regime maintenance came in 1983, when Hafiz had a heart attack. One of the special units created in the 1970s was the Defense Companies, commanded by Hafiz's younger brother, Rifaat. With Hafiz disabled, Rifaat sent his men to seize key positions in Damascus to ensure his own succession. The regular army generals were opposed to this action. When Hafiz recovered, he ousted his brother and the Defense Companies were demoted to a regular army division.

Reportedly, one of the causes of Rifaat's coup attempt was that the committee established by Hafiz to oversee the country during his illness had a Sunni majority. Some of the Alawite barons worried they might be cut out in a post-Hafiz regime. Hafiz returned to work quickly and reassured them, and they caused him no trouble thereafter.

The Republican Guard division, created to replace the discredited Defense Companies, was commanded by Adnan Makhlouf, a cousin of Hafiz's wife, Anisa. When Bashar came to power, he dismissed Makhlouf, replacing him with Ali Hassan, a friend and also an Alawite officer. Bashar and his cronies are almost all Alawites he grew up with; as sons of the elite, their loyalty is unquestionable but their military competence is doubtful.

Even though competence was a real concern for Hafiz, it simply could not come first. As a result, the armed forces would not be effective against well-organized foreign foes, especially Israel. The dictatorship also bred other structural flaws in its military forces. For example, intelligence focused on keeping the ruler happy more than on being accurate. A centralized, rigid hierarchy prevented the military from fully using the kind of quick-response tactical flexibility without which victory in modern warfare is difficult.

But such concerns have always been secondary for the regime. The most important priorities were to ensure that the military did not play politics but could suppress domestic threats from highly motivated but poorly equipped Islamist revolutionaries and ride herd on Lebanese militias.

The bottom line of the situation was this: In any actual war, Israel would be able to defeat Syria, and Hafiz either knew this fact outright or strongly suspected it. Therefore, after 1973, the Syrian regime tried to avoid direct war with Israel. Instead it sponsored terrorism, built up a missile capacity to hold Israeli civilians hostage, and issued constant threats. Only once in thirty years was Hafiz pulled over the brink: in 1982, when Israeli forces went into Lebanon. The Syrian army lost badly and the air force did even worse. In this respect, at least, Hafiz almost never made the mistake of believing his own propaganda.

Another factor weakening the Syrian army's international role is its lack of modern equipment. By the 1970s, the United States and the Soviet Union were the only two powers able to supply all the import needs of a Middle Eastern military. American weapons were always superior to Soviet ones, and, after 1991, the United States was the only superpower. The fact that the Cold War ended with a U.S. victory penalized Iraq, Libya, and Syria, all of which depended on Soviet weaponry.[15]

During the second half of the twentieth century, the alliance with the Soviet Union was more important for Syria than for any other Third World country, with the exception of Cuba. During his first three years of rule, Hafiz visited Moscow six times. In 1977 alone, Soviet arms exports to Syria were worth $825 million; that figure rose to $1 billion in 1978. The following year Moscow wrote off one-quarter of Syria's $2 billion debt, so valuable was the strategic relationship with Syria for Moscow's interests.[16] When the Soviet Union finally died in 1991, a senior Syrian official commented, "We regret the Soviet collapse more than the Russians do."[17] There were good reasons for this response. Under Hafiz, the Soviets supplied about $25 billion in military equipment, including 4,600 tanks, 600 fighter planes, 170 helicopters, and at least 2 submarines. About 10,000 Syrian officers received training in the Soviet Union and Russia.[18]

But this golden age came to an end. The military technology gap widened when a weaker, less ambitious Russia replaced the Union of Soviet Socialist Republics. Also, unlike the Soviet Union, Russia would not give cheap credit to buy arms in exchange for political influence, and it even demanded repayment of old debts, shifts that further weakened the Syrian army.

As Russia made something of a comeback, however, it did reestablish military relations with Syria in 2005 and forgave about $10 billion in Syrian debt for past arms' purchases. Moscow was once again ready to sell advanced weapons to Syria, but on a cash-only basis. These weapons included about 1,000 Kornet antitank missiles, a number of which were given to Hizballah and were used against Israel in the 2006 war in Lebanon. Syria's port of Latakia was once again used as a naval base by Moscow, and about 2,000 Russian military advisors travelled to Syria to train that country's soldiers.[19]

Still, these ups and downs in the military's status had virtually no effect on its role in ensuring the Syrian regime's survival at home. That feature was little changed as leadership passed from Hafiz to Bashar. Much the same can be said for the system of repression. To think that Syria's government rests mainly or solely on intimidating its population is a mistake, yet fear is indeed a very potent weapon. There is fear not only of punishment but of having one's career sabotaged or being unable to support one's family. Equally powerful is the terror of being branded a traitor, foreign agent, disloyal Arab, unpatriotic Syrian, or apostate Muslim.

The security forces are expert at playing on the emotions of those it would silence or recruit, making dissidents feel their efforts will be fruitless and reprisals for crossing the regime a certainty. Since Syria has been in a state of emergency since 1963, the regime's minions can do whatever they want. Courts will convict and employers will fire at the government's orders. There is no appeal.

Westerners may believe that the state's heavy hand would create resentment and rebellion, but Westerners have never lived in such a society. In Syria, manipulation and repression breeds obedience. Most people do not want to risk losing their job, going to jail, or being beaten up. Open dissenters are a small minority. To make matters worse, unlike in, say, Eastern Europe under Communism, dissidents cannot easily use nationalism or religion to win supporters against the regime since it nearly monopolizes both of these powerful forces. Instead of praising a dissident, colleagues and neighbors are likely to join in the denunciations, outraged that someone would be disloyal to the Arab nation and Islam while simultaneously worried about being denounced themselves.

Two Syrian jokes illustrate how the repressive system works more effectively than any detailed narrative. At the secret police Olympics, goes one anecdote, the world's best compete in the top event. Two agents must enter the forest and catch a rabbit using only their hands. The other countries' teams go in and capture the rabbit in more or less time. But the Syrians do not come back at all. After a long time, the referee searches for them. Finally, he spots the Syrian team in a clearing, beating a donkey and shouting "Confess you're a rabbit! Confess you're a rabbit." The anecdote points to the stupidity of the Syrian security services but also shows their ability to reinterpret reality as they wish and do whatever they please.

In the second joke, a Syrian dies and goes to heaven. An angel asks him to recount his life story, but instead he just goes on endlessly praising Assad and the Ba'th party. At a loss as to what to do, the angel calls for God, who appears in great majesty. But even God cannot get the Syrian to deviate from regurgitating the regime's propaganda. Finally, God persuades the man that he is indeed the deity, and the man then tells the truth about himself. "But why," asks God, "didn't you do this before when we asked you?" The man replies: "I thought you were the mukhabarat [the secret police]!"

What more can one say about the absolute power the regime's agents enjoy in Syria?

Again, it should be stressed that repression has usually been a weapon of last resort in Syria, or merely one item in the regime's repertoire. Manipulation is a far more flexible tool. For example, when oppositionists from different groups formed a united front in 2006, the security forces worked hard to split them. Everyone was offered something he wanted. For the Kurds, this has meant language rights; for intellectuals, there was the possibility of having their works published and being allowed to travel abroad.

One of Syria's most promising young intellectuals had written critical articles about the regime in a Western publication under a pen name. A few months later at a party, an intelligence officer greeted the man using his pseudonym. The message was clear: We know everything; you will get away with nothing. Next, he was called in for a meeting at the security group's headquarters and given a choice: Support the regime and be published, paid, and honored, or continue being a bad boy and be unemployed, attacked, isolated, and barred from leaving the country. He chose to cooperate. Today one of Bashar's most articulate apologists, he can write whatever he desires—as long as every word is precisely what the regime wants.[20]

When the people are no longer afraid, runs the regime's philosophy, that is when the rulers must start to tremble. Consequently, sometimes the regime must resort to torture and murder. This is not punishment for the sake of revenge but rather, in Voltaire's famous phrase of two centuries earlier, to encourage the others to stay in line.

Ruthless repression comes in most handy when the regime faces a real challenge. In a 1979 attack on an army artillery school graduation ceremony in Aleppo, the Muslim Brotherhood killed eighty-three Alawite cadets. On June 25, 1980, it almost assassinated Hafiz himself. The dictator was saved only because a bodyguard—a U.S. official described him to me at the time as a "poor, deluded man"—threw himself on the hand grenade.

The regime, determined that it would live and its enemies would die, took a terrible revenge. In 1980 the doctors', dentists', engineers', pharmacists', and lawyers' unions held a one-day strike to protest the lack of freedom in Syria. These groups were disbanded and their leaders were jailed. "Between March and May 1980," wrote an exiled Syrian writer, "the regime perpetrated a series of massacres including at Jisr al-Shaghrour (200 killed), Souq al-Ahad (42 killed), the Hananu neighborhood (83 killed), and Aleppo and Tudmor (700 killed) and Hama's al-Bustan neighborhood (200 killed)." Law Number 49 of July 7, 1980, imposed the death penalty for any current or former member of the Muslim Brotherhood.[21]

Two years later, after the Brotherhood tried to organize an uprising in the large city of Hama, the Syrian army besieged the town for twenty-seven days, bombarded it with artillery and tank fire, and then attacked. At least 10,000 civilians were killed, and possibly twice that number. The army expelled 100,000 residents. Whole neighborhoods, including mosques and churches, were leveled.[22]

Rather than hiding these facts, the regime is proud of them. It believes something quite opposite from the Western concept that repression does not work and that brutality stirs dissent rather than submission. Moreover, its behavior received little serious foreign criticism, much less any punishment. Syria has repeatedly proven that no other nations care about the fates of its citizens; thus potential dissidents feel it is hopeless to speak out. In 2006 Bashar recounted that he had told European leaders that if they tried to interfere to help any dissidents, these people would be considered "unpatriotic" and presumably punished more harshly. "You must stop interfering and sending messages," Bashar warned Western leaders. "This matter is closed, as far as we are concerned."[23]

Assassinations are also a tool the regime uses in silencing critics abroad, beyond the reach of its jailers. Among those so disposed of was Lebanese journalist Salim al-Lawzi (after horrible torture); Lebanese leaders Kamal Jumblatt, Bashir Jumayyill, and Rafiq Hariri; Palestinian military commander Saad Sayil; Ba'th party founder Salah al-Din al-Bitar; and Banan al-Tantawi, wife of Muslim Brotherhood leader Issam al-Attar.[24]

Man does not, of course, live by bread alone, but a steady diet is certainly helpful.

The regime learned from its Marxist-Leninist role models that control over the commanding heights of the economy, the means of production, is a load-bearing wall in the temple of dictatorship. This strategy fulfills many functions. The regime has huge assets to carry out its programs rather than having to beg or tax a private sector for its sustenance. The governing elite own the keys to the treasure chamber, gratifying its own desires to the fullest measure. Just as the government holds a monopoly on force, it also has a near monopoly on wealth. Thus, the regime can hand out gifts as it chooses and deny them to whomever it wishes.

Alongside control of the economy, corruption becomes an integral part of the system. Regime supporters receive what is in effect a license to commit corruption. But if they step out of line or fail to cooperate, the security services know how to blackmail or imprison them. At times, the government occasionally takes action against particularly greedy people or those who are no longer useful for public relations' purposes. But corruption is not so much a disease as it is one of the many antibodies the system uses to survive.

The Assad family itself has been deeply involved in the graft. Perhaps the most famous single case was that of a mobile phone contract for Syriatel, a company presided over by Assad cousin and economic manager Rami Makhlouf, which apparently resulted in big profits for the Assad circle. Even this example is known about only because liberal dissident Riyad Sayf issued a report on it in 2001. He was arrested shortly thereafter, an event many think to be the result of having made this particular revelation.

Next to the assets controlled by the government, the two biggest sources of income for Syria have been foreign aid, which comes largely from Iran, and the ownership of Lebanon. These facts explain why the alliance with Tehran and the domination of Syria's next-door neighbor are indispensable for the regime. The greatest gift Syria's own government gave Syrians collectively was the loot of Lebanon. A quarter-million Syrians worked there providing direct economic support for their families, perhaps totaling 1 million people. Saddam gave Iraqis Kuwait's oil wells and bank vaults but held them for only a few months and incurred a devastating defeat as a result. Syria has milked Lebanon for three decades and has paid no price.

Again, though, the key factor in the economy's structure is that the regime always has its hand on the tap at home. The nationalization of factories and agricultural land reform largely destroyed the independent bourgeoisie as a political force that might challenge the regime. There is no class that can feel it is not dependent on the regime or consider itself to be above retribution, that cannot have the rug pulled out from under it whenever the rulers so choose.

Of course, the regime's mastery of the economy is not so simple. Wealthy Sunni Muslim businessmen, with a lot of enterprises and much financial capital under their control, have three political choices: collaborating with the regime, advocating democracy in the hope they will one day win elections, or joining the Islamists in a powerful Sunni revolutionary movement. In the first case, they accept the existing government; in the latter two scenarios they can try to gain state power by joining an opposition but risking everything they have in the process.

Consequently, at least as long as the economy remains unreformed, few businessmen will take on the regime. To make such an outcome even more unlikely, the regime began courting this sector in the 1980s, increasing the presence in parliament of the Sunni middle class and making some small changes to ease their business problems. There was some intermarriage between the political and economic elites, while many individuals entered into partnerships, trading insider influence for cash.

Not all of the Sunni middle class, however, has pledged allegiance to the Assads. Among the most successful business families in Syria has been the Sayf clan. And it was member of parliament Riyad Sayf who was the most outspoken leader of democratic reform during the brief Damascus spring just after Bashar took power. When he became too troublesome, the regime threw him out of parliament and into jail. Other potential dissidents took heed, learning to shut their mouths and focus on making money.

One of the Syrian economy's main problems, however, is that the regime's tight controls, managerial incompetence, and strategy of foreign confrontations keep it harder to make money. Sayf frequently complained about this situation. In January 2000 he described the private sector as "afraid, confused, shackled and unable to perform its proper role in the development process because of inadequacies in the legal system and the absence of a good investment framework." The banking system, he said, had been reduced to "a channel for providing loans to those who don't deserve them" but got them due to political influence.[25] What benefited the regime and its key supporters always trumped the needs of the business sector and hence of prosperity.

The regime responded, in effect, by saying "So what?" Without ever formulating it in so many words, the Assad government has lived by Mao Zedong's dictum of politics in command as surely as it did his doctrine that political power ultimately grows out of the barrel of a gun. The economy did not work well or produce development yet it provided everything that the government needed. Just as peace endangered the system, so did the changes that would have to be made to achieve an efficient economy, meaning that economic reform was neither a necessity nor a luxury but an outright threat. Westerners might think Syria needed or its government wanted such a change, but those in the Damascus palaces thought otherwise.

And what shaped the views of those not living in the palaces? Opinions expressed in the schools, media, mosques, and culture were all in line with the regime's needs and ideology. Such arguments were all the more credible since they pretty much accorded with what Syrians had thought and been taught since the 1940s. Moreover, the regime pretty much kept out any alternative ideas.

In 1963 all the independent newspapers were closed down. The only remaining ones were published by the government or party. The weekly intellectual magazine, *al-Usbu al-Adabi,* produced by the Syrian Arab Writers' Union, presented more of the same. Indeed, rather than protect its members' rights, the union was a tool for policing and censoring them. The same applied to the television and radio stations. Think of the Soviet media under Communism and the parallel is exact. Article 4b of the State of Emergency law gives the state the right to control newspapers, books, radio and television broadcasting, advertising, and visual arts. It can confiscate and destroy any work that is believed to threaten the security of the state.[26]

Taboo subjects include: the president and his family, the Ba'th Party, the military, the regime's legitimacy, and communal issues. Subjects usually censored are the government's human rights' record, Islamist opposition, allegations of official involvement in drug trafficking, the actions of Syrian troops in Lebanon, or material unfavorable to the Arab cause in the Arab-Israeli conflict.[27]

Hakam al-Baba, a Syrian journalist publishing in a foreign Arabic newspaper, came up with the brilliant satirical notion: The Syrian media merely replays the same news report every day. Its daily broadcast begins by describing how the leadership spent the first twelve hours of that day receiving messages of gratitude from citizens and the second twelve hours meeting with foreign dignitaries with whom they agreed about "the importance of strengthening Arab solidarity and the [need] to harness all energies in the struggle against the Zionist enemy." The pictures showed a leader and his guest looking very serious as boring music played.[28]

But then it was decided at the top, Baba continues, that reform was needed. So a big change was introduced: The leader and his guest could be seen actually moving their hands. Another step toward media transparency was the press conference, in which the leader and his guest answer journalists' questions. Baba writes that Syrian viewers were filled with joy at this major step forward. In practice, though, only the same trusted reporters got to ask the same question—he claims they had it written down on a piece of paper that they put back in their wallets for the next press conference—on whether Syria's policies were correct. The leader answered that, yes, indeed, the government's positions were in fact just terrific.[29] Baba's humorous account is actually quite close to the truth.

For many years it was easy for the regime to keep down and keep out any media competition to its monopoly. The government jammed Jordanian television channels and blocked foreign Arabic newspapers from entering Syria. But how could it stop the Internet or satellite television?[30] The first step was to accuse such media, even the radical al-Jazira station, of being controlled by Israel. In addition, Syria pressured them into saying nothing that might offend the regime. The regime blocks troublesome Internet sites to users at home, while Syrian officials demand that Arab counterparts gag the media they fund abroad or that they control on their soil.[31]

In Syria, the media has been given the task of mobilizing the people to support government policies. Most Syrian journalists are employees of the ministry of information; the higher-ranking ones are required to be Ba'th party members. Such journalists seem literally unaware that there could be any other way to function. Fouad Mardoud, editor of the *Syria Times,* explained, "I cannot imagine that there's anyone in Syria who wants to attack our policy."[32] The use of the word "our" underlined his identification with the regime, which after all had put and kept him in his job. Criticizing a specific aspect of how policy had been implemented or how well a particular institution worked was sometimes acceptable—but only after being cleared by the regime. For example, the government decided when there would be an anticorruption campaign, who would be the target of complaint, and what misdeeds were acceptable to mention.

When a *New York Times* correspondent in 2003 asked Bashar about the notorious deal in which his cousin and business manager allegedly took a big bribe for giving a mobile phone contract to a foreign company, the regime omitted the question and answer in its Arabic translation. Of course, no Syrian newspaper dared mention either the deal or the omission.[33]

While Syria cannot control the media in other Arabic-speaking countries, it was able to do so in Lebanon after taking control there in the 1970s. Journalists who were not sufficiently tame were kidnapped, tortured, or killed. Salim al-Lawzi, editor of *al-Hawadith,* suffered all three of these treatments. His right hand was badly mutilated to warn others not to use that appendage to write ill of Syria. And when Damascus started its terrorist offensive in Lebanon after its withdrawal in 2005, many of its targets were journalists.

The regime's campaign to control journalists, intellectuals, and writers is a very deliberate one. Muhammad Kamal Khatib, a Syrian journalist, recalled a prophecy of Ahmad Iskandar, information minister from 1974 until his death in 1983: "If the Syrian intellectuals and writers are not willing to go with us, we will build a new generation of intellectuals that will support us." According to Khatib, this is precisely what the regime achieved.[34] Indeed, a disproportionately large number of today's dissident intellectuals are older; perhaps because only those whose ideas were formed prior to the entrenchment of the Assad system can see through its pretenses.

The government also has had great success in controlling that other great institution for attitude formation, religion. The Muslim Brotherhood called the regime an infidel one; the regime branded the Muslim Brothers (al-Ikhwan) the Muslim Traitors (al-Khuwan). It was bad enough that the Islamists hated the Syrian rulers as secularist and leftist; to make matters worse for the regime, they kept shouting out one of its most dangerous secrets: that it was ruled by non-Muslims.

Any critical clerics had to be silenced. The religious establishment had to be made to accept the Alawites as perfectly good Shia Muslims. According to the constitution, Syria's president had to be Muslim; thus, Hafiz and Bashar had to be Muslims. Hafiz was photographed and later Bashar was filmed praying in mosques. A regime that had begun by sending out patrols in Damascus to tear the veils off women had became a government proclaiming its piety at every opportunity.

As part of his campaign to win over Sunni Muslims, Hafiz also made a religious pilgrimage in 1974, raised clerics' salaries, and convinced the respected—but totally politicized and relatively junior—Lebanese Shia cleric Musa al-Sadr to certify that Alawites were really Shia Muslims. The regime also arranged for Muslim clerics to give sermons to glorify Hafiz, as well as for newspapers to affirm his piety and publish big, front-page pictures of him praying on holidays. Over time, this strategy led to permitting women to go veiled, building mosques and religious schools, and having the media promote Islam. The government placed accommodating clerics as independents in parliament. For a time in 1990, the regime even tried to set up its own pro-government Islamic party.[35]

Muhammad Said al-Bouti, a teacher, author, and host of a popular religious program on state television, was typical of the new breed of pro-regime clerics. "Under the leadership of President Assad," he intoned, "Syria became the focal point of support for the entire Muslim world. The mosques of Damascus are flourishing; the number of worshippers present in them is on the increase." He attacked the Muslim Brotherhood as violating Islam's principles. Ahmad Kaftaru, Syria's state-appointed mufti, the country's chief Muslim official—and incidentally a Kurd—explained, "Islam is the base and the regime's power of rule is the protector." Thus, religion and the state were totally interdependent. Kaftaru quoted Assad as telling him, in words that would have astonished the Ba'th party's secular-oriented founders, "Islam is the revolution in the name of progress."[36]

The government had thus taken control of the religious establishment, the education and ordination of clerics, the building of mosques, and so on. Its goal was to use Islam for four purposes: to combat liberalism by upholding tradition; to discredit the radical Islamists as misinterpreting their own religion; to curse its own foreign enemies as anti-Muslim; and to legitimize the regime as the embodiment of piety.

Under Bashar's reign, the government has taken on an even more active role as promoter of Islam. It recognizes that religion offers a rare outlet for Syrians otherwise frustrated by their lives and society, but it is determined not to allow these feelings to be channeled into support for its Islamist enemies.

As president, Bashar repealed his father's decree forbidding girls from wearing headscarves in school. In June 2003 a decree permitted soldiers to pray in military camps, even though regulations mandated that career soldiers suspected of being religious were to be dismissed. Bashar has even gone on his own minor pilgrimages.[37] Big mosques were built by the state, and schools became more religious in their instruction. The regime portrays itself as the friend of religion, a government any good Sunni Muslim would be proud to support.

Internationally, Bashar also has become a champion of Islamism. He is allied with Islamist Iran, is the Arab patron of Islamist Hizballah and Hamas, and the sponsor of the Sunni Islamist insurgency in Iraq. At least in the short to medium run, domestic Islamic forces have been tamed, even transformed into regime supporters. In effect, Bashar has invented a new ideology, which can be called the Islamist-Arab nationalist synthesis or national Islamism. Islamist and nationalist can work in perfect harmony if they can be focused on fighting the evil external enemies of Arabs and Muslims: America, the West, and Israel. And, of course, this effort requires that both sides enthusiastically support the Syrian regime, which champions their common causes.

Yet this new strategy has even one more advantage for the regime. As Islamic forces become stronger, the regime has told liberals that they must support it, too, lest radical Islamists take over.[38] This ploy has also worked.

Bashar, who before acceding to the presidency was personally quite secular—for example, he liked to drink wine—thus embarked on a brilliant three-pronged offensive:

1. Encourage nonpolitical Islam at home so that Syrian Sunni Muslims will be grateful to the regime.
2. Sponsor radical Islamism abroad so that Islamist groups in other countries will ally with the Syrian government and not support counterparts who want to overthrow it. Syria did more to sponsor Islamist revolution abroad than all the other Arab governments put together. Aside from the Lebanese Hizballah and the Palestinian Hamas and Islamic Jihad, Bashar has hosted leaders of militant Islamist opposition groups from Algeria, Jordan, Sudan, and Tunisia.
3. Persuade liberal-minded Syrians that if they challenge the regime, the ultimate winners will be the Islamists. For reformist intellectuals and women who want more rights, as well as for Christians and Druze, a continuation of the Assad dictatorship would be by far the lesser of the two evils.

This strategy worked to push the Syrian Muslim Brotherhood opposition to the margins on both the domestic and international fronts. For example, at a 1998 conference in Amman called by the Syrian Brotherhood to mobilize support, a Jordanian participant reportedly scolded, "Syria is the only Arab state standing up to Israel, granting support to every opposition to the Zionist occupation. Therefore, it is impossible for an Arab or a Muslim to attack it and try to harm it and its leadership."[39]

Historically, Syria's "anti-imperialist" rhetoric had been couched in Marxist terms. Today Deputy Minister of Waqf, in effect the ministry of religious affairs, Muhammad Abd al-Sattar thunders, somewhat incongruously, on state television: "Jihad is now incumbent upon each and every Muslim, Arab, and Christian. The time has come for the duty of jihad." The enemy are the Jews, who had "killed the prophets," had allegedly been depicted in the Koran "in a very sinister and dark way," and had been cursed by Allah.[40]

It was strange for a Muslim cleric to call on Christians to fulfill the duty of jihad since, after all, jihad is only an Islamic tenet. Yet this was very much in line with the new Syrian approach. On one hand, the idea is to show this as a "nationalist" rather than "religious" holy war, the perfect example of blending the two doctrines. On the other hand, the regime upholds Syria's multi-ethnic character. Making distinctions between religious communities would heighten not only Muslim-Christian tensions but also Muslim-Alawite ones. At any rate, the Syrian regime has, among other achievements, now invented the non-Muslim jihad.

Meanwhile, the ambiguous Islamic tradition toward the Jews is being reinterpreted exclusively in a one-dimensional way to become a virtual manual of anti-Semitism. Sattar has said that the Jews are closer to animals than to humans: "This is why the people who were given the Torah were likened to a donkey carrying books. They were also likened to apes and pigs, and they are, indeed, the descendants of apes and pigs, as the Koran teaches us."[41]

Hatred is not a new part of the Syrian regime's ideology. Stirring up a transcendent, passionate loathing has always been a key part of the system and a vital tool for the regime. This kind of rhetoric, repeated on a daily basis for many years, has inflamed hatred to such a high pitch and with such deep roots that making peace becomes almost impossible. But now every shred of restraint—even if only as a public relations' gesture to avoid foreign criticism—has been thrown out the window.

Like so many of the regime's wagers, this one has worked also, as the world hardly noticed the outpouring of incitement. Meanwhile, the depth of hatred, the pervasiveness of demagoguery, and the dangerous mixing of Arab nationalist and religious ideologies ensures that these attitudes are passed onto the next generation as the proper interpretation of Islam. Mundir Badr Haloum, a Syrian university lecturer, worries that young people are learning as normative

Islam such ideas as considering killing others to be a religious duty and classifying non-Muslims or other types of Muslims as enemies. Even when forced by political interests or diplomatic pressure to condemn terrorism, this is only a pose. "We wear a pained expression on our faces," said Haloum, "but in our hearts we rejoice at the brilliant success—a large number of casualties."[42]

Disinterested foreign observers or potential victims find this situation puzzling; nothing seems to work in defusing the explosive hatreds. It is tempting to assume that there is some way to solve the expressed grievances and that past failures to do so were merely because the efforts were insufficient to secure Syria's trust.

This is precisely the effect the regime is striving for in the first place: to put its enemies on the defensive. The latter are led to believe that something terrible must have been done to make the Syrians so angry. If only Israel or Europe or America offered more, if only Syria would be given the Golan Heights, or Lebanon, or more money, then all the misunderstandings would be cleared up and the problems solved. Thus, the solution is to make conciliatory gestures and present political concessions or economic gifts to soothe the Syrians' pain.

Yet the foreign boogeyman has not been created as the result of misunderstanding or as a reaction to grievances; it constitutes a key factor in the Assad system and that of other Arab nationalist dictatorships. Having so evil an enemy is used to justify any type of action abroad and to necessitate tight controls at home. Communism had the capitalist-imperialist plot; Nazism, the Jewish-capitalist threat. For the Syrian regime, the widely acknowledged Zionist-Israeli and U.S.-Western conspiracies provide the same type of ideological protection, and they are widely accepted as such throughout Syrian society.

Since this incitement is so structurally generated and motivated by the Syrian system's needs, the targets cannot do anything to make the Syrian regime like them better. Any act will be interpreted—and twisted—through the regime's lens. It needs the conflict and must always find new grievances. Then, too, the Syrian regime judges the very concessions that might improve relations as weakness, which encourages it to be more aggressive and raise its demands.

Of course there are real political issues at stake and heated conflicts at play here, but much of this obsession arises from the distorted worldview and false information being pressed on Syrians from all directions. This antagonism is not just a matter of criticism about specific American, Western, or Israeli actions and policies but rather a systematic belief that these evil forces seek the Arabs' enslavement and Islam's eradication. For all of living memory, Syrian schools, mosques, churches, media, modern culture, government, and Islamist opponents have poured out this message. At the same time, any facts or arguments to the contrary have almost never been heard.

It is important to emphasize that systematic, state-sponsored anti-Americanism and anti-Semitism are not marginal phenomena in Syria but are absolutely central ideas, as important as they were in Germany during the 1930s. Bashar himself and the media regularly produce such materials, including dramatic television series, and nothing happens in these domains without government approval. Such things are also exported by Syria to other Arab countries.

When the first Syrian children's television program aired in 1955, its theme was teaching young people to hate the United States. A U.S. embassy dispatch from Damascus about Syrian domestic politics in the mid-1960s was entitled "When You Have a Problem, Blame the United States." Whether it was Lebanon or Israel, Turkey or the shah's Iran, Syria worked assiduously to try to subvert any country friendly to the United States. And no country has surpassed Syria in preaching war and hatred, or sponsoring terrorism, against Israel and America.

Anti-Americanism might seem self-evident because of Syrian opposition to U.S. policies. Yet even despite the existing antagonisms, the United States nevertheless had good relations with the majority of Arab states from the 1950s onward. For most of this period, at least after the early 1970s when Egyptian policy changed, U.S. relations were almost always bad only with Iraq, Syria, and Libya. With Saddam overthrown and Libyan dictator Muammar Qadhafi frightened into cautious behavior, only Syria has such an unbroken record of anti-Americanism.

To its great advantage, and without even dropping the anti-Americanism in its schools and media, Egypt dispensed with its Soviet ally and turned toward the United States, receiving huge amounts of American aid and military equipment on excellent terms. It also made peace with Israel and received back all of its territory that had been captured in the 1967 war. Syria could have done the same thing. Of course, personalities were a factor to some extent here—Hafiz was different from Egyptian president Anwar al-Sadat. Moreover, if Egypt was better off for its policy shift than Syria, Hafiz benefited personally from intransigence by going on for decades more, while Sadat was assassinated in 1981. Yet equally or more critical were the differences between Egypt and Syria. The Egyptian regime was more entrenched in power and stood on a firmer foundation. Syria needed continuing conflict with Israel and America in order to give its people a sense of identity both collectively and in connection with its regime.

Yet while promoting such hatreds might ultimately be dangerous for Syria itself, this technique has also been its secret weapon. It has enabled the regime to evade responsibility for its own serious shortcomings by placing the blame on perfidious Zionism and evil American imperialism. Indeed, Hafiz's and later Bashar's public analysis of the world has been virtually indistinguishable from that of Usama bin Ladin. Even when fellow party members started demanding reform in 2002, the country's vice-president silenced them by saying that as long as there was no peace with Israel, nothing could be changed within Syria.[43] And the regime very definitely wanted nothing to change in Syria.

In this context, then, the orientation toward Israel must be an eternally hostile one. This conflict could never be reduced to a mere debate over the location of borders; it has to be existential. The regime's basic historical theme is that there was no Holocaust and the Zionists are actually Nazi allies. According to Ali Abu al-Hassan, a lecturer at Damascus and Aleppo universities, the contemporary message is, "The crimes of Zionism exceed those of the Nazis." Israel is innately imperialist and expansionist, seeking to control not only its own territory, or Palestine, but the whole Middle East and indeed the whole world. In Hassan's words, this is what Bashar "meant when he declared that 'Zionism is racism whose racism exceeded Nazism.'" But the good news is that Zionism would be destroyed just like Nazism.[44]

Nasr Shimali, another writer and broadcaster, explains that the American policy in Iraq is one of war crimes verging on ethnic cleansing. The crimes perpetrated by Hitler during World War II "pale in comparison to the level of crimes perpetrated by the Americans and Israelis in Palestine and Iraq." But at the same time, Shimali minimizes Hitler's crimes, stating that there is no evidence that the Nazis engaged in genocide, no proof that they wanted to do so. Auschwitz was merely a work camp where the inmates were given educational lectures.[45]

Or there is Ghazi Hussein, a lecturer on international law at Damascus University and an advisor to the Syrian government, who explains how Zionism has "elevated terrorism to a status of religious holiness." And Syrian foreign minister Farouq al-Sharaa himself added that Israel's targeted killings of leading terrorists, which numbered a few score at most, were worse than the ovens at Nazi concentration camps.[46]

Again, such diatribes are not the mere blowing off of steam from the conflict with Israel or the ravings of a few marginal figures; they are a deliberate government policy that forms an integral part of the effort to stay in power and mobilize the people to do its bidding.

This linking of Zionism and Nazism is especially ironic given the close relationship of contemporary Ba'thists and other Arab nationalists to the Third Reich. Indeed, at the moment that the real Nazis were carrying out genocide, Syrian Arab nationalists were, in the later memoir of a Ba'th leader, "Admiring Nazism, reading its books and the source of its thought."[47]

What makes this situation particularly mind-boggling is that Syria gave refuge to fleeing Nazi war criminals who lived in Damascus and worked for its government. Most notorious of those hiding out in Syria was Alois Brunner, an assistant to Nazi war criminal Adolf Eichmann, the architect of the system that murdered 6 million Jews. Brunner was convicted in France in 1954 for the murders of more than 100,000 Jews. He long lived in Damascus, protected by the regime, at least from the mid-1950s into the 1990s. Others included two more Eichmann aides involved in genocide, SS captain Theodor Dannecker and Karl Rademacher. All were employed for at least a time as advisors to Syrian security services. In 1987 Brunner told an interviewer that he "would do it again" and that Jews "deserved to die because they were the devil's agents and human garbage." Syria rejected all requests for his extradition.[48]

And where else but in Syria in 2005 would American Nazi David Duke be received as a hero at the highest official levels, interviewed worshipfully on television, and invited to address a government-sponsored rally in honor of the country's president? Duke simply told his Syrian audiences what the regime and its media had been saying for decades: The United States was occupied by Zionists who controlled the American media and government, indeed controlled many of the world's countries. When Duke explained that Syria's battle was the same as that of the Nazi cause, none of the Syrian journalists or the officials hosting him even seemed embarrassed.[49]

After all, Tlas, Hafiz's closest political friend and perennial defense minister, wrote a book widely circulated in Syria claiming that Jews murdered children to obtain blood for Passover matzo.[50] In 2006 a dentist in Damascus explained to a visiting American reporter casually that everyone knew Jews drank the blood of children during Passover. When challenged on this claim, she was startled, explaining that this is what she had been taught.[51]

The dispute with Israel is very real, but when Israel is portrayed as a satanic, genocidal state whose crimes exceed those of the Nazis—who themselves are, in a rather contradictory manner, excused their big crimes—it becomes impossible to envision that this country has any right to exist or that any negotiated solution with it is possible.

Whatever Arab complaints are against Israel, the conflict might have ended years ago in compromise. There could have been a Palestinian state in the 1970s or 1980s, and certainly an equitable deal could have been reached in 2000. Syria might have taken back the Golan Heights in exchange for peace, too. Yet the very moment when a negotiated solution was possible became the prelude for the greatest explosion of violence, both actual and rhetorical, in decades.

By sponsoring radical Palestinian groups whose terrorism disrupted the peace process of the 1990s, as well as by rejecting any agreement itself, Syria played a leading role in sabotaging any escape from the seemingly endless conflict. And Bashar's accession to power would revitalize these hatreds and conflicts for a new century.

Especially remarkable about Bashar's strategy is the way he encouraged the infiltration of Islamist rhetoric into a Ba'th party and regime that had always seen itself as socialist and secular. Very little is left from that earlier incarnation. The change that occurred just after 2000 is symbolized by the shift from "revolution" to "jihad" as the method of change that Syria supports. Far from being a bulwark against the spread of radical Islamism, the regime under Bashar has become that doctrine's main Arab sponsor. In August 2006, for example, the Syrian media published a religious ruling (fatwa) saying that it was every Muslim's duty to support Hizballah because it had revived real jihad. Typically fatwas are signed by senior clerics. The fact that this document was not shows that it had come directly from the government. In contrast, when a well-known Saudi shaykh took the opposite view in a fatwa, another Syrian newspaper said he should be killed for producing such "infidel filth."[52]

The strategic, however hypocritical, turn toward an Islamist version of Arab nationalism has not increased the regime's moral rectitude but rather has been channeled into a kamikaze-like culture of destruction, not construction. The Stalinist regime once celebrated workers who overfulfilled their quotas and engineers who implemented great building projects. In a similar but far less constructive manner, Syrian intellectuals now extol martyrdom. In the words of Palestinian Syrian writer Adnan Kanafani, the Arab people have

> managed to shape a new culture from these ideas—the culture of martyrdom. The opponents try to bring us down from this honor, with claims about suicide bombers, terrorists, and so on. But we don't care about that, because we have rights, and we sacrifice our souls in order to attain these rights. Therefore, the martyrs are the vanguard of this nation. Because of the blood they have sacrificed, the very least we owe them is to always remain optimistic that victory will be ours one day.[53]

But if one is certain of achieving what is in reality an unattainable victory, the most likely outcome is the continued sacrifice of blood, which becomes an end in itself. Ibrahim Zarour, a Damascus University history professor and Ba'th party member, calls martyrdom the highest value of all. The homeland, he says, is more precious to the martyr than his parents or children.[54] In Western countries, those who die fighting for their homeland are revered because their act is seen as an expression of love for family and freedom. Unlike in Syria and other Arab countries, the heroic dead in Western democracies would not be so honored for being killed in the deliberate act of murdering civilians.

Zarour's view of martyrdom, like that of the Syrian regime, is different: Both extol death as a core value, not a necessary evil. He explains, "The mother in our Arab and Islamic history has always sacrificed her children and prepared them for martyrdom. This is rooted in our religion, our culture, in our values, and our upbringing. . . . Mothers . . . utter cries of joy when they learn that their sons were martyred in battles in Palestine, in the Golan Heights, or Iraq."[55] Martyrdom is a secret weapon that can overcome the enemy's economic, military, and technological superiority. And whether the martyr dies in the act of blowing up a school or supermarket or on the battlefield is irrelevant and no less honorable.

There is something very self-destructive, aside from immoral, in this type of thinking. Are these champions of—other people's—martyrdom really unaware of the fact that a willingness to be killed is a rather unsatisfactory substitute for economic, military, or technological superiority? The dead man is not going to improve his life or society. Choosing one path requires abandoning the other one.

Yet in Syria, this choice does make sense. With no solutions to Syria's real problems and not even a domestic program for addressing them, the regime has turned completely toward mobilizing support through foreign adventures. It is a strategy that seems to work brilliantly. At times of weakness, when it seemed possible that the United States might do something about it—as in the 1990s and briefly after the September 11 attacks—the Syrian government pulled back. As soon as it concluded that it could act with impunity, however, it returned to its usual behavior.

This obsession with foreign quarrels is only one among a number of clever tactics deployed by the regime. To stall and deflect by changing the subject when problems seem to come too close to home is routine. When Syrian officials dodged his question about why Syria was so enthusiastic about Hizballah fighting Israel but did nothing on its own border with that country, a television host in Dubai joked, "You always change the subject and put words in people's mouths. We ask you about the Golan Heights and you talk about Nicaragua."[56]

Another technique is the old protection racket: Act in a belligerent fashion then demand to be paid off to desist. Syria sets fires, notably by stirring up violence in Lebanon and Iraq, and then demands that other countries pay it for putting them out, as well as letting it keep the property or wealth it so "rescues." The regime also insists on being rewarded for actions that very much suit its own self-interest. For example, for Syria to make peace with Israel, get back the Golan Heights, carry out economic reform, help stabilize Iraq or Lebanon, obtain a cooperation agreement with the European Union, or solve other crises, the regime first insisted on major concessions from others. Only if and when it got what it wanted would Syria agree to discuss what it might offer in return, but by then it did not need to give anything.

If the other party was not ready to give in to Syria's demands, the regime was happy to wait until it got what it wanted no matter how much it cost the Syrians. When a good offer was made, Syria rejected it as insufficient. Only Syria could sponsor a war of terrorism in Iraq, back Hamas, encourage Hizballah to attack Israel, slander America every day, and then announce that the United States was at fault for any tension in the bilateral relationship.

In its internal governance and foreign diplomacy, then, the Syrian regime has built up a very sophisticated system with numerous backup and fail-safe mechanisms. These include having a large community, the Alawites, tied to the government for survival; managing the armed forces; mobilizing people through a revolutionary ideology; buying off whole sectors of society; tightly controlling the economy; establishing a strong party apparatus; inflaming enmity toward foreign devils to mobilize domestic support; and ceaselessly manipulating privileges and punishments.

It is almost as if so much energy and talent has gone into creating this structure not much is left for doing anything productive.

Still, it is hard not to admire the political and public relations' skill, as well as sheer brazenness displayed, by the Assads and their minions in perfecting their craft. They are the Michelangelos of modern authoritarianism; the Leonardo da Vincis of contemporary tyranny. They have built a system that has endured and remained popular for many decades without ever governing very well. If there was a Nobel Prize for dictatorship, the Assads and their regime would win it by a landslide.

CHAPTER FOUR

AGAINST ALL NEIGHBORS

In his play *Richard III,* William Shakespeare describes the title character as a man whose character and temperament make him unsuited for the peacetime pursuit of pleasure. "Cheated of feature by dissembling nature,/Deformed, unfinished, sent before my time/Into this breathing world, scarce half made up," he has no interest in making merry, music, or love. And so he stirs up trouble in the pursuit of power. By plots, dangerous arguments, "prophecies, libels and dreams," he sets others "in deadly hate the one against the other."

The Syrian regime, in a real sense, is in a similar situation. Thus, as its main asset, Syria must use what Fouad Ajami has called the capacity for mischief.[1] The cause is a combination between the country's weakness—its lack of Saudi wealth or Egyptian cohesiveness—and the flawed foundation on which the regime stands. Syria suffers from a lack of a discrete national history, logical boundaries, and homogeneity sufficient to provide a secure identity of its own without the tempting dream of pan-Arab empire. The fact its rulers come mainly from the minority Alawite community whose Arab and Islamic credentials are suspect to the majority Sunni Muslims has forced the regime's frantic efforts to prove its Arab patriotism and Muslim fidelity.

Egypt and Saudi Arabia could afford to turn largely inward, seeking to cope with their problems by focusing on their own society, because despite their Arab nationalism, they are coherent societies. When Egypt walked away from the ambition to lead or rule the Arabic-speaking world in the 1980s, its citizens hardly criticized or even noticed that choice. In contrast, the vision of pan-Arab nationalism and foreign entanglements are the foundations of Syrian identity. The country has been glued together and found its identity as being the center of Arabism, the core of a great state, the most valiant warrior, the revolutionary force doing battle with reactionaries, the center of resistance, and the champion of Islam. Over the years the slogans might change, but the actor remains on stage, issuing calls to arms at the top of his voice.

In this respect, the regime cannot abide regional tranquility; the end of instability abroad would be the beginning of instability at home. The problems of Egypt and Jordan came from insufficient resources; of Saudi Arabia, from the need to manage immense riches. Syria's troubles, on the contrary, are political and largely self-made.

There is a parallel between Syria and Saddam Hussein's Iraq, though there are differences as well. Being stronger, Iraq's dictatorship was more ready to take open risks, a tendency that eventually undid it. Still, Saddam could have lived on oil riches and repression; the Assads lack the former and are too shaky in their minority, outsider status at home to take the latter beyond certain limits. Even a post-Saddam Iraq built on majority rule, whatever its internal problems, can easily survive without being adventurous abroad.

By way of contrast, however, if Syria did not control Lebanon—with or without any direct military presence—it could not continue to live in the style to which it has become accustomed. The Golan Heights is far more valuable in its absence as a cause for mobilizing support than in the possession of such a rocky provincial dead-end that offers neither glory nor wealth.

States generally seek to avoid conflict and to make peace if possible because they desire to live as normal countries. Syria, though, can have a degree of normality only when wrapped in confrontation. After all, if Syria was normal, it would not be ruled by an Alawite-dominated dictatorship built on an outmoded neocommunist model incapable of achieving economic or social progress.

In this context, then, has Syria's foreign policy failed or succeeded? The basic answer is that it has succeeded. After all, Syria has achieved total victory on its most important issue, regime maintenance. Of course, that regime never has won the total victories it hoped to achieve. It has not led the Arabs to national unity or expelled Western influence, nor has it destroyed Israel, annexed Lebanon, or taken over the Palestinian movement. Yet Syria has used a combination of intimidation and pretended cooperation to overbalance its weakness, maintain the regime at home, prevent any significant foreign pressure against it, and spread its influence abroad. Syria also has succeeded in helping to block any solution to the Arab-Israeli conflict. From the standpoint of the Assad government, that record is not bad overall.

Syria's immediate environment, what the Russians call the near abroad, is that area it ambitiously calls Greater Syria. It includes Lebanon, Jordan, Israel, and the Palestinians, each of which Syria wants to include in its sphere of influence and preferably to take over entirely. In Tlas's words, the reason "why Palestine and Jordan were just as important for [Hafiz] as Syria" was because he viewed them as part of Syrian territory, refusing to accept the "artificial borders" given Syria by Anglo-French agreements made during World War I.[2] The same point applies, even more clearly, regarding Lebanon, a country whose independence Syria never has recognized and whose common border it refuses to delineate.

Beyond this is the Arab world as a whole, over which Syria has claimed to be the rightful leader because it is the most faithful embodiment of the Arab nation. This unity is, after all, the most basic point of Ba'thist ideology, though Egypt, Iraq, and Syria have disputed which is destined to reunite the Arab homeland. Again though, for Syria, claiming this role as a key element to justify the regime at home has been equally or even more important than achieving it.

As a way to legitimize the subversion of its neighbors, Syria skillfully exploited the appeal of Arab nationalism. Thus Syria could reinvent its blatant pursuit of self-interest as a noble effort to unite the Arabs in fighting for their rights against Zionism and imperialism. As the Arabs' self-proclaimed most patriotic champion, Syria feels entitled to dictate policy to the Jordanians, Lebanese, Palestinians, and Iraqis.

In this context, the Palestinian issue provided Syria with an excuse for taking over Lebanon, isolating Egypt, intimidating Jordan from making peace with Israel, blackmailing Arab oil producers to pay it subsidies, dominating the PLO, being the Soviet Union's main local ally, and excluding Israel from a normal regional role.

Syria's confidence grew when the Soviets made it their leading Middle East ally after Egypt expelled them in 1972. Despite becoming a client, Damascus did not always listen to Moscow. During the 1970s they disagreed on negotiations with Israel (the Soviet Union wanted them; Syria did not) and Syria's 1976 invasion of Lebanon (Hafiz wanted to invade; Moscow preferred otherwise), but the relationship remained strong. After Syria's defeat in the 1973 war with Israel, the Soviets provided more and very sophisticated weapons. In the early 1980s, the Soviets helped Syria double the size of its army and gave Hafiz their best, newest arms, including advanced tanks and missiles. The Soviets, however, were not always happy with Syria as an advertisement for their military equipment; in 1982, Israel shot down eighty-eight Syrian planes while losing none.[3]

But then the Soviet Union collapsed. Syria spent a rocky interregnum in the 1990s when Damascus had to pretend to be nice to America, the sole superpower, but soon found a new ally-protector whose interests far more accorded with its own: Iran. Unlike Egypt and Saudi Arabia, Syria could not really cozy up to the United States as even relative moderation was not its cup of tea. It required a radical, anti-status quo partner.

Regarding Iraq, Lebanon, Israel, and the Palestinians, the policies of Tehran and Damascus are close to being identical. Iran can also supply Syria with badly needed money and some day, it seems likely, with the protection of nuclear weapons. With Bashar now playing the role of pious Shia, it certainly makes sense to ally with the world's only other entirely Shia-ruled state. Syria's continued isolation in the Arabic-speaking world no longer matters; with Iran on his side, Bashar does not feel he needs those countries. He can maintain that he is the leading Arab nationalist even when he antagonizes every other Arabic-speaking country.

Despite shifting situations, nothing has altered Syria's decades'-long effort to dominate its neighbors, though of course policies varied depending on the specific victim and over time. Toward its two weaker neighbors, Lebanon and Jordan, Syria has used all the tools at its disposal to gain hegemony. Doing its Arab "duty," Syria in effect took over Lebanon by sending in its army and ensuring that many Lebanese groups and politicians will obey its orders. Regarding Jordan, Syria has followed a more modest strategy; it has constrained that country from becoming too stable or moderate through direct threats and attacks of proxy terrorist groups.

With the Palestinians, Syria has tried to take over Fatah and the PLO by creating its own agents, trying to split or at least gain veto power over the groups. By helping to keep the PLO from making or implementing a diplomatic solution, it has kept the politically profitable Arab-Israeli conflict alive, ensuring that the organization would make no separate peace with Israel that might isolate Syria as the sole intransigent player. This strategy maintains Arab antagonism against the United States and makes it easier for Damascus to seek hegemony over the Palestinians.

At the same time, Syria has struck at its two stronger neighbors, Israel and Turkey, again using revolutionary terrorist organizations while generally avoiding direct confrontation. It has employed Palestinian and Lebanese groups against Israel; Kurdish and Armenian ones against Turkey. Syria has used Arab nationalism to deny these targets, both non-Arab states, a normal regional role and the possibility of obtaining Arab allies against its own ambitions. Against Israel, Syria also could play the Islamic card. By maintaining the Arab-Israeli conflict, Syria forced other Arab states to support itself and blackmailed wealthy oil-producing countries into providing financial aid.

As for Egypt and Iraq, Syria's main rivals for Arab leadership, it cooperated or competed with them depending on the needs of the moment. But Syria also did succeed in helping to knock them out of the running, leading an anti-Egypt boycott over Cairo's peace with Israel in the late 1970s and siding with the U.S.-led coalition in 1991 to isolate Iraq after its invasion of Kuwait. Although Syria never has had the financial resources or strategic weight to consolidate these advantages, Damascus has been able to ensure that the Arab system protects its interests and supports its stances.

In the end, Syria was the last man standing as the others dropped out of contention for an honor they no longer wanted. By 2003, with Saddam out of power, at last the age of Syria had come—or, at least, that is what Bashar thought. His new, improved resistance product—Arab nationalism plus Islam—seemed ready to take the market by storm.

Finally, the Syrian regime is quite comfortable with using anti-Americanism as a key element in its bid for Arab leadership. It has always been hostile toward the United States for reasons that have never changed over time. Syrian goals favor instability; U.S. interests favor stability. The friends of America—Egypt after the late 1970s, Israel, Jordan, Turkey, and an independent Lebanon—are Syria's enemies, rivals, or targets for intimidation. Syria's allies—the Soviet Union, revolutionary groups, Egypt under Nasser, Islamist Iran, and at times Iraq—were and are also opposed to the U.S goals and role in the region.

Being relatively weak and usually preferring to avoid direct confrontation, the Syrian regime spread its influence covertly. These channels included bribed politicians (especially in Lebanon), subsidized organizations, and terrorist groups. On the political level, Damascus has made use of the Jordanian, Palestinian, and Lebanese Ba'th parties as well as the Syrian Social National Party and the Lebanese Islamic Action Front, Hizballah, and many others. To Syria, it has always been preferable to let others fight and die, with other peoples' lands, not Syrian territory, as the scenes of carnage and destruction.

The variety of terrorist groups Syria has employed include the fully controlled Palestinian al-Saiqa, Asbat al-Ansar, and Popular Front for the Liberation of Palestine–General Command (PFLP-GC); the mercenary forces of Abu Nidal; and the usually cooperative Hizballah, Kurdish Workers' Party (PKK), Palestinian Islamic Jihad, the Popular Front for the Liberation of Palestine (PFLP), and the Democratic Front for the Liberation of Palestine (DFLP). To avoid retribution, even these groups often use false names to conceal their identities. For example, the Syrian-controlled al-Saiqa bombed Jewish community centers, stores, and restaurants in France as the "Eagles of the Palestinian Revolution."

One of Syria's deadliest surrogates in attacking Israelis, Palestinians, and others was Abu Nidal, the world's most proficient terrorist-for-hire. In 1974 Sabri al-Banna (Abu Nidal's real name) broke off from Fatah to form the Fatah Revolutionary Council. Syria was one of his main clients. For example, teaming up with another Syrian surrogate group, the Syrian Social National Party, it set off a bomb on April 2, 1986, on board a TWA jetliner flying from Rome to Greece, killing four American passengers and injuring nine others.

This strategy of hiding behind shadowy connections or front groups that victims cannot easily deter or punish has offered Syria a low-cost, low-risk way of waging conflict. No matter how much it is implicated, the regime can simply deny responsibility, and many in the West will believe it or at least use the denials as an excuse to do nothing. Meanwhile, Syria can assert to its own people—at least if the terrorists are Arab—that it supports people who are really heroes waging a just struggle using acceptable methods.

Proving responsibility for any given terrorist act can be very difficult. And even when judicial inquiries have proven that the very closest aides of Syria's president had tried to blow up an airliner full of people—as happened in Britain in 1986—or murder a neighboring country's prime minister—as happened in Jordan in 1981 and Lebanon in 2005—few are willing to do anything about it or even remember what happened for very long.

What do you do if the U.S. secretary of state comes into your office and presents evidence that you are supporting terrorists? Simple. In September 1990 Secretary of State James Baker met with Hafiz and gave him a detailed account of Syria's terrorism sponsorship. Hafiz did take action: He had the three Jordanian agents who supplied the information tracked down and killed. Syria kept on fomenting terrorism; and the United States did very little in retaliation.[4]

But it gets even better: Precisely sixteen years later, after his betrayal by Hafiz, the White House asked Baker to recommend what policy the United States should take on Iraq and the Middle East in general. In explaining why he favored dialogue with Syria, Baker recalled the "success" of his 1990 talks with Hafiz in supposedly getting Syria to stop sponsoring terrorism, ignoring the fact that it had continued to do so during that entire period.[5]

By 2006, Hamas's top leaders—and the most hard line of all—Khalid Mashal and Musa Abu Marzouq lived under the regime's protection in Damascus, as did Islamic Jihad leader Ramadan Shallah. When Hamas kidnapped an Israeli soldier from a cross-border raid in 2006—helping to inspire the Hizballah copycat attack that would set off a Lebanon-Israel war—Mashal announced the operation's success to journalists at a Damascus hotel.

Yet even this behavior pales in comparison to Syria's masterful use of terrorism in Lebanon. The pinnacle of Syria's campaign to control its neighbors was certainly this almost thirty-year-long domination of Lebanon which has been so very profitable for the Syrian elite (through counterfeiting, drugs, and smuggling) and the general populace (providing support for more than 1 million Syrians through relatively higher-wage jobs in Lebanon). Syria employed terrorism against a dozen targets, including the assassination of not one but two presidents of Lebanon and many other critics there.

These events showed the incredible effect small groups of terrorists could have on public attention, national policies, and the international agenda. Terrorist attacks and kidnappings set off and extended the Lebanese civil war, led to the Syrian occupation and an Israeli invasion, and drove out the Western forces trying to stabilize the country. The hostage-taking there in the 1980s almost wrecked the Reagan administration, which abandoned its most cherished principles to negotiate with Iran over freeing Americans being held in Lebanon.

Understandably, Syrian foreign minister Farouq al-Sharaa paid tribute to the efficacy of terrorism by saying "When a young man sacrifices his life, what power can oppose him?"[6] Based on this philosophy, Syria has consistently provided groups with money, safe havens, propaganda, logistical help, training, weapons, diplomatic support, and protection against retaliation. Being able to receive genuine passports, lavish financing, well-equipped training bases, and state-of-the-art equipment, Middle East terrorists can operate more frequently and in a more deadly manner than counterparts elsewhere in the world.

Although Syria lost the 1967, 1973, and 1982 wars with Israel, it has been able to carry on indirect terrorism against that country and keep the conflict burning for four decades at little cost. Syria was Arafat's original patron. It always has had its own Palestinian surrogate groups, assassinated moderate Palestinian leaders, and maintained its right to make decisions for the Palestinians. In fact, Syria and its client groups may well have killed more Palestinians than Israel has done. In addition, Syria has supported a guerrilla war against Iraq by supporting Kurdish nationalist groups, including one headed by the post-Saddam president of Iraq, Jalal Talabani. Syria also is the main foreign backer of the war waged by Kurdish nationalists against Turkey.

Yet despite this long list of depredations, the cost to the regime has been remarkably low. For example, in 1986, a Syrian agent who entered England on a government employees' passport and received an explosive device directly from the Syrian embassy in London used it to try to blow up an El Al passenger plane. His confession implicated Syria's ambassador to Britain, two diplomats, and air force intelligence. The bomb was similar to those employed by a Syrian client group in 1983 bomb attempts against El Al and an explosion that killed four Americans on a TWA plane over Greece. The British response? It recalled its ambassador home from Damascus for a few weeks.[7]

Rather than being turned into a pariah for its attempt to murder hundreds of people, Syria suffered no punishment at all. But that was not all. Once again the regime played the West for suckers and won. To assuage Britain after a court there found his regime directly involved in the terrorist attack, Hafiz "demoted" the head of air force intelligence, General Muhammad al-Khouli, to be "only" deputy air force commander as a supposed punishment. After all, the regime maintained that Khouli was acting without authorization from the top. But as soon as the British stopped paying attention, Khouli was promoted to air force commander, a post he kept until his retirement in 1999.

Khouli, one of Hafiz's closest associates, would never have dared organize such a major terrorist attack on British territory without his boss's personal approval. But for the West to have recognized that fact would have posed a massive political problem that it preferred to avoid. After all, if the president of Syria was personally involved in planning massive terrorist attacks, someone would have to take action against him and his country. Better, they thought, to pretend that the problem did not exist or hope it would go away.[8]

This was the response Syria repeatedly hoped for and received. The West was proving that covertly sponsored terrorist violence was a priceless instrument of statecraft for the regime, far better than the dangerous, often losing, proposition of using one's own military in conventional warfare. Syrian leaders learned from experience that repeated false denials, stalling, and the tiniest amount of cover could evade any retaliation.

Syria's success in employing terrorism and subversion also arose from always using it in a focused way to achieve well-defined, limited goals. The main priorities for Syria in applying this tactic were to gain hegemony in Lebanon, minimize U.S. and Israeli leverage there, sabotage the Arab-Israeli peace process, convince Syrians their government deserved support for its heroic struggle, and blackmail wealthy Arab oil-producing states into paying subsidies.[9]

American officials in the 1970s dubbed Yasir Arafat "the Teflon terrorist" for his ability to escape responsibility or punishment for his deeds. In this spirit, Syria could well be called the Teflon country. Whenever Western states considered doing something about Syria's behavior, a combination of loud threats and conciliatory rhetoric discouraged them. A final line of defense was the protection of a greater power: the Soviet Union in the 1970s and 1980s, the United States in the 1990s, and Iran thereafter. The only penalties Syria faced from its decades-long sponsorship of terror were inclusion on the U.S. list of terrorism-sponsoring countries, which restricted some trade and loans; American sanctions, which had little effect; and occasional breaks in diplomatic relations, usually an ambassador's brief withdrawal.

Meanwhile, however, Syria has remained the world's biggest center for terrorism. Within Syria there have been training camps, headquarters, and propaganda centers for a score or more terrorist groups. In Damascus, their leaders live secure from any foreign or international law enforcement organization. Just across the border in Lebanon's Biqa Valley, an area directly controlled by the Syrian army for decades, more training camps exist. Hizballah and criminal gangs operate enterprises there for drug-growing and production as well as counterfeiting, especially American $100 bills. The profits finance part of Hizballah's budget and enrich the Syrian officers who protect these operations.

Syrian intelligence organizations that report directly to the president pass money and logistical support directly to terrorist groups. For example, as head of Syria's General Intelligence Directorate and a senior advisor to Bashar, Major General Hisham Ikhtiyar handled the funding of Hizballah and Islamic Jihad. For this and other activities, he was sanctioned by the U.S. Treasury Department in 2006.[10]

In theory, of course, the United States is very tough on Syria. In practice, however, things look quite different. During the 1990s, U.S. efforts to get Syria into the anti-Iraq coalition over the Kuwait invasion and then the Arab-Israeli peace process blocked any additional actions against Damascus's sponsorship of terrorism. This was at a time when major sanctions were imposed on Iraq, Iran, and Libya for similar behavior. Even when, after the September 11, 2001, attacks, the United States made the war on terrorism its principal foreign policy strategy, Syria's fortunes were little affected. Afghanistan, Iraq, and even Libya paid for their support of terrorism, but not Syria, from whom even the tiniest amount of cooperation bought immunity from prosecution. Syria may have been on the U.S. State Department list of terrorism-sponsoring states but it was treated as if it had turned state's evidence and joined the witness protection program.

As if this all were not enough, within two years of the September 11, 2001, attacks on America, Syria became the only state in the world sponsoring bin Ladin's al-Qaida group, for its main global operation in Iraq no less. Such a flat statement seems shocking. Of course, Syria had nothing to do with September 11 and had no direct contacts with bin Ladin himself. Yet Syria had been sponsoring the Iraqi insurgency, which is increasingly led by al-Qaida. Abu Musab al-Zarqawi and his successors who run the insurgency have openly expressed their affiliation with bin Ladin. Syria has helped pay, train, and arm this war. This history and strategy, however, had not prevented Syria being elected to the UN Security Council for a two-year term starting in 2002, even as it was expanding its export of violence.

And what kind of things did this citizen-in-good-standing with the international community actually say and do?

Here is the chairman of the Syrian Arab Writers Association, Ali Uqlah Ursan, giving his reaction to the September 11 attacks. Ursan is not just a bureaucrat but the regime's intellectual mouthpiece, the man who polices the writers, having made himself the association's leader for life who expels those who disagree with him. While ceremoniously expressing pain at the "deaths of the innocent," his tone suggests that those who died were not innocent. His main theme is one of exultation for "the fall of the symbol of American power." According to Ursan, the Americans were responsible for the deaths of many innocents in the Arab world, and in Korea, Vietnam, "occupied Palestine," and Libya "on the day of the American-British aggression" (i.e., when the U.S Air Force bombed Qadhafi's palace and his adopted daughter was killed).

But while, of course, the United States has made many mistakes and committed a few crimes over the years, it should be noted that the United States also tried for decades to resolve the Arab-Israeli conflict while the Syrians kept it going; defended South Korea in a UN-sponsored conflict against North Korean aggression in 1950; and bombed Libya only once—in response to a direct attack on U.S. servicemen—in the course of that country's long terrorist campaigns which had resulted in hundreds of deaths. As for the Palestinians, if they had been willing to make peace in exchange for an independent state on several occasions—a possibility their own leadership rejected and Syria helped sabotage—those deaths would not have happened either.

Moreover, despite all the provocations and even terrorism directed by it, the United States has never gone after Syria. If the United States is so imperialistic, why has Syria been able to get away with so much without facing an attack from this supposedly ravening beast? The Syrian government's brinkmanship was born from the understanding that Washington is far from the bloodthirsty stereotype it portrays daily.

But for Ursan, the apparatchik of a dictatorship that had not hesitated, with his approval, to engage in systematic torture and to level one of its own cities, Hama in 1982, and kill more than 10,000 of its own people at one go, his sorrow at more innocent lives lost did not last long. Seeing the masses fleeing in horror in the streets of New York, he intoned:

> Let them drink of the cup that their government has given all the peoples [of the world] to drink from, first and foremost our people. . . . I [felt] that I was being carried in the air above the corpse of the mythological symbol of arrogant American imperialist power, whose administration had prevented the [American] people from knowing the crimes it was committing. . . . My lungs filled with air and I breathed in relief, as I had never breathed before.[11]

For him, as he said on another occasion, the United States is "the center of evil."[12]

If, however, what bothers Ursan is targeting civilians and misinforming one's people about such murders, he might well listen to his own employer's official radio station. On October 26, 2005, an Islamic Jihad suicide bomber—an organization whose leadership resides under Syrian government protection a few blocks from Ursan's office—blew himself up next to a falafel stand at a shopping center in Hadera, Israel, killing five shoppers and injuring more than thirty others. Radio Damascus called this operation a "crushing blow to the Israeli terrorists and war criminals" by a "hero of the Palestinian people."[13]

Six weeks later, on the morning of December 5, 2005, after Israel had withdrawn completely from the Gaza Strip and the government was discussing a pull-out from the West Bank, another Islamic Jihad suicide bomber blew himself up in a Netanya shopping mall, killing five passersby and wounding more than fifty. Radio Damascus could not hide its glee at this response to Israel's "war crimes" and part of the Palestinian effort to liberate their land.[14] Of course, such operations actually only postponed Israel's departure from the West Bank and the creation of a Palestinian state as part of a negotiated peace settlement.

A look at Syria's role in some of these kinds of operations shows what sponsoring terrorism actually means. Palestinian students at universities in Arab countries have been recruited into Hamas and sent to Syria for training. In camps located in Syria or Syrian-occupied Lebanon, they were trained in firing weapons, preparing bombs for suicide bombers, and kidnapping people, as well as in gathering intelligence to prepare for such actions. Among the "heroic" acts of those trained and armed by Syria were two suicide attacks in Netanya in the spring of 2001, with eight Israeli civilians killed and more than a hundred injured.[15]

At the same moment that bin Ladin's men were plotting the September 11 attacks, the Syrian-owned PFLP-GC was planning to destroy the high-rise Azrieli Towers in Tel Aviv. Two Palestinian men were recruited on the West Bank and sent to Syria through Jordan. At the Syrian border, a policeman gave them a brown envelope with the address of the PFLP-GC office in Damascus. They were trained for two weeks at a camp to use weapons and prepare explosive devices. Upon returning to the PFLP-GC office, they were given plans for various types of attacks including using a suicide car bomber to destroy Israel's tallest building. Weapons and explosives were to be supplied by the top PFLP-GC person in Nablus; ways of communicating with Damascus headquarters were set up. The two men were stopped from killing hundreds of people because they were arrested at the Jordan–West Bank frontier, en route to launching attacks on August 7, 2001.[16]

Syria's sponsorship of Palestinian terrorism goes back to the 1960s, albeit usually through Lebanon or Jordan, in order to reduce the danger of Syria being dragged into a war with Israel. Only on one occasion, November 20, 1974, did PLO terrorists cross from Syria into Israel, attacking a village to kill three students and wound two. The threat of Israeli retaliation has been a strong deterrent to sending terrorists directly from Syria but not from dispatching them by an indirect route so Damascus can deny involvement, at least persuasively enough to undercut Western support for an Israeli attack on Syria.

Although Israel has been Syria's most explicit target, other Arabs have also been in its gunsights. Indeed, the regime has acted as Israel's number-one enemy so often precisely in order to gain leverage over neighboring Arab states and the Palestinians. Syria views itself as the rightful leader and legitimate ruler of Palestine. And since Syria claims Palestine, it holds that Palestinian leaders cannot do as they please.

For Damascus, the Palestine problem is too important to be left to the Palestinians. Just as the Soviet Union claimed to represent the international proletariat's interests, whether the workers liked it or not, Syria has styled itself guardian of every Arab issue or cause.

Therefore, the Syrian regime was never merely—despite its statements to the contrary—fighting for the Palestinians' rights; rather it has waged a struggle to destroy Israel in order to enlarge its own territory. Its policy is not one of altruistic or fraternal aid but of imperialism.

In this spirit, Hafiz once told Arafat, "There is no Palestinian people or Palestinian entity, there is only Syria, and Palestine is an integral . . . part of Syria."[17] The editor of the Syrian newspaper *Tishrin* complained that Arafat's talk of a PLO right to make its own decisions independently was an excuse for making "treasonous decisions. . . . We will not tolerate freedom to commit treason or to sell out the cause. Palestine is southern Syria."[18] As a result of its interests and policies, then, Syria's goal has been not to resolve the Arab-Israel issue or regain the Golan Heights but to ensure that the conflict continues and that Palestine neither becomes independent nor falls into the hands of any other Arab state.

There are very good reasons for this policy. A peace settlement would deny Syria its major—even sole—advantage in the inter-Arab struggle and would increase U.S. influence, inevitably favoring Egypt, Israel, and Jordan over Syria. Even if Israel became accepted as a normal regional power, its interests would still clash with those of Syria. Jerusalem would be far more likely to cooperate with Jordan and Egypt, Syria's rivals. In short, Syria's obstructionism and hawkishness are quite logical. Peace would make it a second-rate power.

The history of Syrian-Palestinian relations shows how this strategy was implemented following the 1967 war. Ironically, the war represented exactly what Syria had been seeking: an Arab military confrontation with Israel. For twenty years, Arab leaders and orators had daily proclaimed such a war as necessary, inevitable, and certain to end in total Arab victory. Instead, the crisis provoked by Syria and Egypt led to an Israeli preemptive attack that brought about a total Arab debacle. In a half-dozen days, Israel first destroyed the Egyptian and Syrian air forces, then captured all the Sinai Peninsula, Gaza Strip, the West Bank, east Jerusalem, and the Golan Heights.

Disappointed with the PLO's inability to achieve anything and seeking an indirect way to attack Israel given the failure of regular military methods, Egyptian dictator Gamal Abdel Nasser took on Arafat as a client, helping install him as the new PLO leader.[19] But if Arafat had Egypt, he did not need Syria; in that case, Syria had to find someone else as its candidate for Palestinian leadership. Simultaneously, Syria tried to split Fatah, replace Arafat, create its own client groups, and direct the PLO's Hittin Brigade stationed in its own territory.

When Arafat briefly tried to impose his own control over the brigade in 1969, the Syrians arrested his choice to be its chief of staff during a visit to Damascus and forced him to resign.[20] Syria did not strike directly against Israel through the Golan Heights and instead routed the operations of its terrorist clients through Lebanon, Jordan, even Europe. While demanding that Jordan and Lebanon give the PLO a free hand in their territory, Syria kept the organization under tight control at home. PLO members there could not wear uniforms, carry guns, or hold rallies except when on missions with Syrian intelligence's permission. Most important of all, they could not cross into Israel or Jordan without written authorization from the defense minister, Hafiz himself.

In the late 1960s, Arafat's greatest asset, obtained with Nasser's support, was turning Jordan into a virtual PLO base, where the Palestinians could operate freely in attacking Israel and creating a state within a state while ignoring Jordan's own government. By 1970 the PLO and Jordan were coming to a collision. In

August, Arafat called for a mobilization of all Palestinian forces against Jordan's army and asked Arab states for help against the regime of Jordan's king Hussein. Clearly, Arafat expected assistance from Syria.[21]

King Hussein, too, sought foreign allies against Arafat. He was so desperate that he asked Britain, his family's patron since the early 1920s, to pass on a request to Israel that it stop any Syrian military intervention against him. The British government refused, favoring Arafat over its old friend and assuming he would take over Jordan. Next, the king turned to the United States, which accepted his appeal, seeing Hussein as an ally against pro-Soviet forces in the Arab world and a force for stability. The United States transmitted Hussein's request, and Israel agreed to help.[22]

On September 20, Syria ordered a force made up of the Palestine Liberation Army's Hittin Brigade and elements of the Syrian Fifth Mechanized Division disguised with Palestinian insignias to cross the border. But these forces soon withdrew for three reasons: Syria feared Israel's threat to attack, the Jordanians fought back, and the Syrian air force, then led by Hafiz, refused to support the operation. For Assad, Arafat was an enemy who had sided with his rival, Salah Jadid, and the assault on Jordan was a dangerous adventure.[23]

Nasser's death from a heart attack just after negotiating a PLO-Jordan cease-fire robbed Arafat of his patron and eliminated Syria's most powerful Arab rival.[24] Egypt's new president, Anwar al-Sadat, wanted to focus on Egypt's internal problems and supported the PLO far less enthusiastically than his predecessor.[25] To make matters even worse for Arafat, his old enemy Assad deposed Jadid and seized power in Syria.

By April 1971 Arafat was hiding in a cave in northern Jordan. While telling his men to fight to the end, he begged the top Palestinian in Jordan's government, Minister of Public Works Munib al-Masri, to rescue him. Masri traveled to the north with the Saudi ambassador and asked Arafat to return to Amman and meet the king. He agreed. But when the car reached the town of Jerash, Arafat asked to be driven across the border to Syria, from where he made his way to Lebanon.[26]

A desperate Arafat threw himself on the mercy of Hafiz, the man who had helped ensure his defeat in Jordan. Syria gave Arafat personal refuge but was not going to let him drag the country into war with Jordan or Israel. The Syrians prevented PLO forces from crossing their border with Jordan to continue the conflict against King Hussein, but they were willing to let Arafat run a covert war of terrorism. At a meeting in Daraa, Syria, Arafat founded the Black September group as a secret part of Fatah to attack the West and moderate Arab states.

Syria must have known a lot about Black September's subsequent terror attacks, which also suited its interests. Still, this did not mean Hafiz was content to accept Arafat as the Palestinian leader. In 1972 he tried once more to over-throw Arafat by backing Hamdan Ashour, a leftist Palestinian who had built his own army in Lebanon's Bakaa Valley and who ridiculed Arafat as insufficiently revolutionary. But again Arafat emerged victorious.[27]

Nevertheless, Hafiz did not give up. Syria's strongest counter to Arafat in the 1970s and into the 1980s was al-Saiqa, headed by Ahmad Jibril, a Palestinian who had assimilated into the Syrian elite. Born in a village near Jaffa in 1936, he went to Syria as a refugee at age twelve. After graduating from a military academy, Jibril became an engineering officer in Syria's army and a Ba'th supporter.

Meanwhile, Syria was also making one more attempt to fight Israel directly. In October 1973 Egypt and Syria launched a surprise attack, stunning Israel and challenging its assumed military superiority. Israeli forces were able to counterattack and advance back to the prewar lines by the time a cease-fire ended the fighting after three weeks. Many Arabs thought the war regained them honor lost in their 1967 military defeat but after losing twice to Israel, Sadat and Hafiz both concluded that a conventional war with Israel was a bad idea. Sadat chose to make peace; Hafiz continued the conflict but switched to surrogate, guerrilla warfare because, in Vice-President Khaddam's words, "maintaining the climate of war in the country would hide domestic mistakes."[28]

Egypt benefited from the war in material terms because Sadat, by showing diplomatic creativity and flexibility, used the crisis to forge an alliance with the United States and to begin a process that resulted in the return of the Sinai. Syria ended up with no such gain because of its intransigence on both the U.S. and Israeli fronts. But Syria won in strategic terms because its militant, uncompromising posture won it support at home and in inter-Arab politics, as well as offering opportunities to dominate Lebanon and the Palestinian movement.

True, Syria did make a disengagement agreement with Israel in May 1974, following strenuous shuttle diplomacy by Secretary of State Henry Kissinger, in which Israel returned to the post-1967 lines. Syria also accepted UN Security Council Resolution 338 ending the 1973 war, but it showed no interest in using diplomacy to achieve a peace agreement. Damascus remained a Soviet client. When Sadat made peace with Israel, Syria organized a rejection front that called him a traitor and launched a boycott of Egypt. Concluding that Syrian policy was not going to change for a very long time, Israel's parliament extended Israeli law to the Golan Heights and built Jewish settlements there.

A decade later, in 1982, alarmed by a buildup of conventional PLO units in southern Lebanon—a parallel to what would happen with Hizballah a quarter century later—Israel's army advanced into that country, defeating both Syrian and Palestinian forces. On the covert side, Israel made a deal with Lebanese

Christian forces dissatisfied with Syrian control of Lebanon and seeking to create a new government.

Hafiz had to take note of two critical elements in the 1982 war. One was Syria's isolation and the growing disinterest in fighting Israel through conventional means, since no Arab state came to its aid during the fighting. The other was the PLO's poor military performance. Arafat's failure offered Hafiz still another occasion to launch a hostile takeover of the PLO. Many Fatah men in Lebanon were outraged by the defeat, blaming Arafat for having promoted commanders known to be corrupt, inept, and cowardly. In January 1983 Said Musa Muragha (Abu Musa), a senior PLO military officer respected for his courage and military ability—though also known for being politically naïve—castigated Arafat at a high-level Fatah meeting.[29]

The rebels, fed up with incompetence and wary of moderation, joined with Syria. Assad saw the PLO's defeat in Lebanon as his long-awaited chance to take over the organization. Assad refused to meet Arafat; the Syrian media attacked him. A Syrian leader explained that Arafat thought the Arab states had to support him completely but since Palestine was a cause for all Arabs, "We have the right—especially after the heavy sacrifices we have made for the cause—to discuss, contest, and even to oppose this or that action of the PLO."[30]

When Arafat fired Abu Musa on May 7, 1983, the rebels responded with the biggest anti-Arafat revolt that had ever taken place in Fatah.[31] Abu Musa announced, "We are the conscience of Fatah."[32] The rebels declared that armed struggle is the only and inevitable way to revolution.[33]

In this battle, Arafat's main card was an appeal to Palestinian patriotism against Syrian meddling. Many other Fatah leaders were unhappy with some of Arafat's policies, but they supported him on this basis. Abu Iyad, whose support the rebellion needed to succeed, explained, "By raising arms against their brothers and shedding Palestinian blood, the dissidents made a big mistake." It was, wrote a Palestinian intellectual, "a Catch–22 situation." The PLO and Fatah leadership had many shortcomings, but letting Syrian agents take over threatened to destroy the movement altogether.[34]

The Palestinian masses agreed with that view. While many of the fighters still in Lebanon joined Abu Musa, Palestinians in Jordan, the West Bank, the Gulf, and elsewhere remained loyal to Arafat. As one Palestinian observer put it, "Arafat is king. If Abu Musa walked through a Palestinian refugee camp [in Jordan], the only people who would follow him would be his own bodyguards."[35]

But Abu Musa had a great deal of support among the Fatah troops in Lebanon, the front most important for Assad, as well as the backing of pro-Syrian PLO groups. As the revolt appeared to gain strength, the Syrians became more active. In Damascus, they helped the rebels seize Fatah's offices and military equipment while arresting Palestinians who supported Arafat. The Syrian media accused Arafat of being "irresponsible" and "arrogant."[36] The rebels went on the offensive in Lebanon, defeating pro-Arafat forces there. As his men in Lebanon retreated, Arafat offered concessions to the rebels, promising to do just about anything but resign, all to no avail. He also begged for help from other Arab states and the Soviet Union, portraying Syria as an American pawn.[37]

Arafat himself sneaked back to Lebanon to deal with the mutiny in September 1983, using an alias and shaving his beard.[38] Shortly after arriving in Tripoli, he called a press conference under a tree in an olive grove. Asked about the revolt, Arafat took out a gold pen from his pocket and said, "Assad wants my pen. He wants [control over every] Palestinian decision and I won't give it to him." Arafat spoke about making Tripoli, as he had previously done in Amman, Jordan, and Beirut, Lebanon, a city he would see destroyed rather than surrender. An American reporter from Texas asked Arafat if this was like the situation at the Alamo, a battle in Texas's war of independence against Mexico. Yes, said Arafat, it was the same thing because the Palestinians were so brave. The reporter then asked if Arafat knew that all the defenders of the Alamo died. Arafat paused a moment, then said that the Alamo "isn't all that similar" after all.[39]

Nevertheless, the Syrians were determined to give Arafat his own Alamo experience in Lebanon or chase him and his remaining supporters from the country. On November 3 Fatah rebels backed by Syrian forces launched a major offensive against Arafat, capturing more Palestinian refugee camps. Arafat's last remaining stronghold was Tripoli, besieged by Lebanese militia groups and bombarded by Syrian artillery. Over a lunch of chicken stew, a smiling Arafat told visitors he was certain that Assad intended to finish him off but hoped the Saudis would save him.[40] For the second time in a little over a year, however, Lebanese politicians demanded that Arafat leave their country.[41] Once again Arafat decided he really did not want to become a martyr for his cause. In December Arafat and 4,000 of his men were evacuated from Lebanon, saved once again, as they had been the previous year, by U.S. and Israeli guarantees of safe passage.

Hafiz now controlled virtually all Palestinian assets in Lebanon and Syria. In Lebanon, the Syrians had their surrogates launch mopping-up operations with heavy Palestinian losses. In what came to be known as the war of the camps, Syrian clients among the Druze, Shia, and Christian militias attacked Palestinian refugee camps, killing perhaps 2,000 people.

The price Syria paid for all these operations, however, was a decline in its influence among the Palestinians. Syria's client and the PLO's second-largest group, al-Saiqa, collapsed due to its involvement in killing so many fellow Palestinians. The PLO expelled those officers who fought on Syria's side. Although badly shaken, the PLO nonetheless survived under Arafat's control.

Hafiz, though, was unrelenting in his anti-Arafat campaign. Under Syrian pressure, Algeria and Kuwait refused to let the PLO hold meetings on their territory. Arafat had to beg his old enemy King Hussein to do so in November 1984. Pro-Syrian Fatah rebels denounced this deal with the Jordanian ruler as proving Arafat was a traitor. The Syrian-influenced PFLP and DFLP both refused to attend.[42]

The Syrians were even tougher in going after the few PLO officials who dared express relatively moderate views. In April 1983 PLO moderate Isam Sartawi was murdered in Portugal by the Syrian-backed Abu Nidal group, which, as a reward, was allowed to move its headquarters to Damascus. In 1984 PLO Executive Committee member Fahd Qawasma, who favored cooperation with Jordan, was killed in Amman. PFLP forces operating from Damascus carried out the 1986 murders of Palestinian moderates Aziz Shahada and Nablus mayor Zafir al-Masri. These and other Syrian efforts helped kill any chance for diplomatic progress and intimidated Jordan from making peace with Israel.[43]

This situation only began to change seven years later. But when Arafat made the Oslo agreement in 1993 to start a peace process with Israel, Syria launched a terrorism offensive to subvert that effort and to challenge Arafat's leadership of the Palestinians. It encouraged an anti-Arafat revolt in Lebanon led by a Fatah commander, Colonel Munir Maqda.[44] Syrian defense minister Mustafa Tlas called Arafat "the son of 60,000 whores" for allegedly making too many concessions.[45] Other Syrian leaders used less rude words but also showed their disdain. Throughout the 1990s, Damascus backed Palestinian groups including Hamas that launched many attacks and helped wreck the peace process. It finally collapsed in 2000 after Arafat rejected U.S. and Israeli proposals for a negotiated solution and instead launched an armed uprising.

Finally, in January 2006, after Arafat's death removed his powerful presence, the Islamist group Hamas won the Palestinian parliamentary elections. For the first time, the movement's leading group was a Syrian client. Meanwhile, the pro-Syrian veteran Farouq Qaddumi became the new leader of Fatah. Qaddumi explained, "I do not differentiate between Syrian land or Palestinian land irrespective of whether it belonged to this state or that. I am a pan-Arab man."[46]

With the rise of its Palestinian clients within the movement, Syria had more influence than at any time since the mid-1960s. At long last the leadership of the Palestinians was held by an organization headquartered in Damascus and sponsored by Syria. This effort to control the Palestinian cause had been a consistent theme in Syria's policy, a campaign starting with Fawzi al-Qawuqji and the People's Army in the 1940s, through Arafat and Fatah in the 1960s, to Jibril with the PFLP-GC in the 1970s, Abu Musa in the 1980s, and then to Hamas.

It might seem ironic that after so many decades of backing Arab nationalist groups, Syria would finally reach its goal of maximum influence with an Islamist one. Yet, after all, Syria's long quest for a powerful but pliant client in Lebanon followed a similar trajectory, ending with Hizballah. The importance and success of this Islamist strategy would have a major effect in turning Bashar toward creating a nationalist-Islamist strategy.

As noted, the Syrian effort to dominate Lebanon had been as consistent, intense, and even more successful than its attempts to take over the Palestinian movement. Here, too, terrorism was a vital tactic. Damascus used both its own agents and surrogate groups whose violence intimidated opponents and eliminated rivals. These allies included the Syrian Social National Party, al-Saiqa, and the PFLP-GC. From the 1970s on, dozens of those opposing Syria were killed in Lebanon; not a single pro-Syrian figure was ever murdered by the other side.

The Lebanese civil war gave Syria a chance to send in its army and take over that country. In 1976, just as an alliance of leftists, including PLO and Druze forces, seemed about to triumph in Lebanon, Syria became the Christians' unexpected savior. Worried that a leftist-PLO takeover would produce a stronger radical rival next door and seeing a great opportunity, Hafiz sent in pro-Syrian units of the PLA and his own troops. The PLO, he proclaimed, "does not have any right to interfere in the internal affairs of the host country." Of course, Syria accepted no such limits for itself. Assad obtained Arab League support to allow his troops to enter Lebanon as a "peacekeeping force."[47] By the end of 1976, the Syrian army occupied two-thirds of Lebanon.

Assad then proceeded to consolidate his control over Lebanon. One of the most effective measures was to eliminate the most determined, charismatic Lebanese politicians who dared oppose Syrian hegemony. Damascus ordered the murder of Druze leader Kamal Jumblatt in 1977, shot in his car, because he was too independent-minded, and President Bashir Jumayyil was murdered in 1982 with a bomb just three weeks after his election, because of his dynamism and peace agreement with Israel, which the assassination foiled.

No one was safe. After denouncing Syrian occupation of Lebanon, the country's mufti, its highest-ranking Sunni cleric, Hassan Khalid, was killed on May 9, 1989. On November 22 of that year, the newly elected president, René Moawad, became the second Lebanese president to be killed, along with twenty-three others nearby, by a car bomb.

By terrorizing Arab and Western journalists, Syria also ensured there would be no critical coverage of its policies, at home or in Lebanon. In 1980, for example, one of the most outspoken editors, Salim al-Lawzi, editor of *al-Hawadith,* made a visit home from the exile into which he had fled after earlier threats on his life. He was kidnapped, tortured, and murdered.

The principal use of Syrian-sponsored terrorism within Lebanon occurred between 1982 and 1984, when Israeli, U.S., British, and French troops were forced to withdraw. Although the actual work was largely performed by Iranian-backed Islamist groups, Syria gave them freedom to train, operate, and transport bombs through Syrian-held territory as well as other logistical support.

Following the Israeli invasion of Lebanon in 1982, a multinational force of mostly U.S. and French troops was sent into the country to try to reestablish peace there. If they had remained in the country, the Western states would have become the key power in Lebanon, ending both Syria's control and its ability to use Lebanon to heat up the conflict with Israel whenever it wished to do so. Thus Syria and Iran helped their clients unleash a wave of terrorism that killed many Western and Israeli soldiers. Terrorist groups in Lebanon also took Western residents hostage.

These attacks included some of the biggest terrorist operations in history. On April 18, 1982, for example, carrying out a plan organized by members of the incipient Hizballah group, a terrorist drove a van loaded with 400 pounds of explosives into the U.S. embassy in Beirut, killing 63 people and wounding 120. Seventeen of the victims were Americans, including a number of CIA analysts.

Then, on October 23, 1982, two simultaneous bomb attacks on military headquarters in Beirut killed 242 American Marines and 58 French servicemen. Suicide terrorists from radical Islamist groups supported by Iran and Syria drove two trucks, each carrying 400 pounds of dynamite wrapped around glass cylinders, through the security perimeter of the U.S. Battalion Landing Team headquarters and the French paratroopers' base four miles apart. The subsequent withdrawal of the multinational force and lack of any international challenge to Syrian domination of Lebanon owed a great deal to this campaign of violence.

Sometimes the suicide bombers did not conceal their links to Syria. In July 1985, for example, a twenty-three-year-old Lebanese named Haytham Abbas blew up himself and his car at a checkpoint of the Israel-backed South Lebanese army. The previous day, Abbas, a member of the Lebanese branch of Syria's ruling Ba'th party, had given a television interview praising Hafiz (whose picture was visible on his desk and wall in the videotape), calling him "the symbol of resistance in the Arab homeland and the first struggler."[48] Other suicide terrorists were members of the Syrian-controlled Syrian Social National Party. Also during this period, Hizballah was being built up as a force to organize the Lebanese Shia population and to fight the continuing Israeli presence in the south.

As disorder proliferated and the Lebanese civil war continued, the international community, the United States, and Israel—as well as many in Lebanon itself—literally begged Syria to take control and restrain the violence. The Western forces quickly withdrew from Lebanon. As a favor, Syria later helped free the hostages—those who hadn't been already murdered—being held by pro-Syrian groups and was warmly praised for this good deed. To defeat your adversaries is one thing; to get them to thank you for it and beg you to accept the prize of contention is deserving of a gold medal at the international affairs' Olympic games.

Using terrorists to chase Western forces out of Lebanon and get them to back Syrian control of the country as a way to keep things calm was, however, only phase one of the regime's plan. Once Syrian control was reestablished and reinforced, then Vice-President Khaddam later recalled, Hafiz decided "to start a war of attrition against Israel [from] Lebanon...based on a conviction that a traditional war was not possible." The Syrians would carefully avoid operations into Israel from the Golan Heights, lest this lead to an Israeli attack on Syria itself, and instead channel all operations through Lebanon using Hizballah.[49]

Thus, a Syrian-directed Hizballah replaced the independent-minded Fatah as the dominant group confronting Israel from Lebanon. For the first time, Syria really controlled the south Lebanon front against Israel. The man at the center of this spider web was Syria's intelligence chief there from 1982 to 2003, General Ghazi Kanaan. He was nothing less than an imperial viceroy whose word was law in Lebanon, sufficient to kill or arrest anyone, veto any decision made even by the highest Lebanese politician, and make or break any of them. An Alawite from a village near Hafiz's hometown and belonging to a family allied to the Assads, he came from the heart of the regime's establishment.

Kanaan's great achievement was to build links to prominent Lebanese political and militia leaders, including many who had long opposed Syrian influence. His most impressive conquest in this respect was the Christian nationalist Lebanese Forces, whose leaders had been responsible for the 1982 massacres in the Palestinian refugee camps of Sabra and Shatila. Kanaan used this wide variety of surrogate forces to destroy the May 17, 1983, U.S.-mediated Lebanon-Israel peace agreement and drive out the international force that had arrived in an attempt to end the civil war. Those Lebanese who resisted were killed, kid-napped, or learned how to behave properly toward Damascus by seeing what happened to those who do not.

One of Lebanon's leading intellectuals living abroad tells of an experience that shows Kanaan's omnipotence. He was invited back for a visit to Lebanon by the current president's son, who even offered to send a private plane to bring him. The man called his elderly aunt in Beirut to ask her opinion. "Don't come!" she insisted. "It doesn't matter who is your host. If a Syrian sergeant wants to arrest you, even the president of Lebanon can't do anything about it."[50]

Not only did Syria control Lebanon, it managed the situation so well that everyone in the world pretty much accepted the situation. The Syrian position, which is only partly true, was that it had been invited in by the Lebanese gov-ernment. Of course, with Syria largely controlling the Lebanese government, no one was going to ask it to leave. Bashar's view of this bilateral relationship is of scarce comfort to other Arab states: "We consider our relationship with Lebanon an example of the relationship that should exist between two broth-erly countries."[51]

Even Israel accepted the Syrian military presence in Lebanon as long as that army does not cross certain "red lines." These criteria included keeping its army out of the far south near the Lebanon-Israel border, not deploying anti-aircraft missiles to Lebanon, and not interfering with Israel's planes overflying Lebanon or its ships watching the Mediterranean coast. Mostly, Damascus abided by these unofficial agreements, but it periodically broke them to see if Israel would act decisively to force a return to the status quo.

For example, in January 1977 a Syrian army battalion moved into the south but it was withdrawn when Israel threatened to attack. Four years later, Syria put antiaircraft missiles into eastern Lebanon. This move was one factor prompting the 1982 war. While Syria lost militarily, the war ultimately had no effect on Syria's domination of Lebanon. Thereafter, it used terrorism to chase U.S. and European soldiers out of the country and to harass Israeli-backed Lebanese forces which controlled the far south.

In 1985 Syria again installed antiaircraft missiles in Lebanon but Israeli threats backed up by U.S. support got them removed within three months. During 1993 and 1996, Israeli air strikes hit Hizballah bases and on one occa-sion a Syrian position in Lebanon. War raged between Hizballah and Israel's clients, the South Lebanese Army, but Damascus was careful to avoid a direct war with Israel, using its Lebanese surrogates to insulate it from direct reprisals.

Control over Lebanon has also been valuable for Syria in a defensive sense. Its presence there has made it harder for Israel's army to advance north into

Lebanon and then swing eastward across the border into Syria. More immediately, the strategy made it easy for Syria to keep up pressure on Israel by indirect attacks. Most important of all, Lebanon has produced the loot needed to keep the Syrian regime afloat at home and to enrich its elite in the face of Syria's own mismanaged economy.

Syria has had much less success projecting influence on Jordan, after its direct attempt at military conquest in 1970 was foiled, or on Turkey. Officially, the Syrian regime recognizes Jordan as an independent state but still hopes to absorb it some day into its intended empire. Assad declared in 1981: "The reactionary regime of Jordan was established on a part of the Syrian lands, on part of the Syrian body. We and Jordan are one state, one people, one thing."[52] For its part, Jordan successfully sought protection from the United States, Egypt, Iraq, and even covertly from Israel at various times. Moreover, since the country had a strong central government and a charismatic ruler in King Hussein, it was far harder to subvert than Lebanon.

Nevertheless, during the 1980s, Damascus was quite successful in using intimidation to prevent Jordan from moving toward peace with Israel. From 1981 to 1983 and in 1985–1986, Syria organized numerous attacks on Jordanian diplomats and airline offices abroad to deter any progress. The most daring operation was the sending of a hit squad in 1981 to kill Jordanian prime minister Mudar Badran in Amman. The group was captured and forced to make a three-hour public confession on Jordanian television, but again Syria paid no price for such behavior. The next year it sent a half-dozen terrorist teams to Europe to hit Jordanian targets and critics of Syria. One of them was caught in Germany; another blew up an Arab newspaper in Paris, killing a passerby. Again, Syria suffered no punishment despite clear evidence of direct government involvement in this operation.[53]

In 1983 a wave of attacks by Syrian-sponsored groups killed Jordanian diplomats in Spain and Greece and wounded Jordanian ambassadors to India and Italy. In 1985 a rocket was fired at a Jordanian airliner taking off from Athens, the Jordanian airline's office in Madrid was attacked, a diplomat was killed in Ankara, and a Jordanian publisher was murdered in Athens. As soon as Jordan's king Hussein gave up the idea of serious negotiations with Israel, the assaults ceased. A decade later, however, Syria could not prevent the signing of a Jordan-Israel peace treaty in 1994.

In general and despite economic incentives for good relations, Syria and Jordan rarely get along well. In fact, only in the late 1970s (when both were quarreling with Egypt and Iraq) and for a short period around 2000 did the two have good relations. The problems between them were widened by the different political styles and international alliances of Syria, a radical republic allied with the Soviet Union, and Jordan, a conservative monarchy linked to the United States. The states also backed different sides in Persian Gulf conflicts. During the 1980 to 1988 Iran-Iraq war, Syria supported the former and Jordan the latter. At the time of the 1990–1991 crisis over Iraq's seizure of Kuwait, Jordan (intimidated by Saddam Hussein) feared angering Baghdad; Damascus was on the side of Kuwait and Saudi Arabia.[54]

After both Hafiz and King Hussein died, however, in 2000 and 1999 respectively, the latter's successor, King Abdallah II, thought he could get along with his fellow young ruler, Bashar, whom he mistakenly saw as a Western-oriented, high-tech-loving reformer. It did not take Abdallah long to realize that Bashar was nothing of the sort but rather a wolf in internet surfer's clothing.

Jordan thus fared quite differently from Lebanon. But with a few twists of fate things might have turned out quite differently.

Syria's neighbor Turkey was a tough country in its own right and rather too large (not to mention non-Arab) for Damascus to ever consider swallowing. Still, Syria has sought to keep it off balance and too preoccupied to intervene in the Middle East. As a result, Syria backed Armenian and later Kurdish terrorists of the Kurdish Workers' Party (PKK) against Turkey. The PKK, headquartered in Damascus, received ample help from Syria in waging a war that cost tens of thousands of casualties in southeastern Turkey. Finally, in 1998, the Turks went to the verge of war with Syria to get Damascus to desist. The Turks won the confrontation, and Syria expelled the PKK's leader. This example provided a rare case of a neighbor so credibly threatening Syria as to force it to back down.

Over a period of decades, and with a wide outcome ranging from full success (Lebanon), through ability to constrain (Israel, Jordan, Iraq, and the Palestinians), to ultimate failure (Turkey), Syria has tried to destabilize all its neighbors and conducted what amounts to a permanent covert war against them. Although only in Lebanon did Syria gain control of its intended prey, its efforts have severely disrupted the region and caused a huge amount of bloodshed, as well as triggering wars with Israel and several major crises.

Syria's destabilization strategy did not emerge from heartfelt grievances or misunderstandings but rather due to the needs of the Syrian regime at home and its ambitions abroad. Nothing can bring an end to this general hostility as long as the Assad regime and an Arab nationalist ideology, especially now that it has been melded with Islamism, rule in Damascus.

CHAPTER FIVE

SURVIVING THE 1990s

Everything seemed to go wrong for Syria in the 1990s, but Hafiz maneuvered brilliantly—and his supposed enemies let him get away with a lot. At the end of the decade he was able to deliver to his heir an intact Syria that had not suffered during this era despite its great weakness, numerous enemies, and determination not to make substantive concessions. The way Hafiz achieved this triumph tells a great deal about how Middle East politics works and why the West has been so ineffective in dealing with the region.

Certainly, surviving the 1990s so successfully was no easy task. Tremendous problems were coming at Syria from every direction.

First, every Communist state had collapsed. This included not only Syria's traditional patron, the Soviet Union, and its satellites, but also Romania and Yugoslavia. Indeed, the Soviet Union and Yugoslavia, states whose multiethnic composition paralleled that of Syria, ceased to exist altogether. So devastating for Syria's interests was this crash that Hafiz, in March 1998, called Israel the main beneficiary of this development.[1]

Aside from weakening Syria by destroying its main arms' supplier and strategic protector, Communism's fall also gave the regime warnings as to its own possible fate. After all, the Communist system was the Ba'thist regime's role model, now so thoroughly discredited. Also notable for Syria's leaders was the apparent immediate reason for the downfall of the European Communist dictators. By easing their repressive controls and opening up their societies, Syrian leaders concluded, those governments brought about their own fall and the disintegration of multiethnic countries. The Assads and their colleagues were determined not to make the same mistake.

The parallels between their own country and events in Eastern Europe also did not escape the notice of Hafiz's subjects. In 1990 graffiti appeared on Damascus walls proclaiming "Every Ceausescu's day will come" or "Assadescu," a combination of the names Assad and Ceausescu.[2] Nicholae Ceausescu, Romania's all-powerful dictator, had just been overthrown. Then he and his wife were put up against a wall and shot.

Understandably, the Assads and their supporters saw preserving the Syrian regime as, literally, a life-and-death matter, not just a question of preserving power but of saving one's own family from a terrible fate. They also were quite aware that Syria might fall apart into ethnic strife, as did Yugoslavia, a conflict in which the Alawites would be vastly outnumbered by those who might like to wipe them out for many mutually reinforcing reasons including religious hatred, political rivalry, and revenge for past sufferings at the hands of the dictatorship.[3] The terrible ethnic strife that broke out in Iraq a decade later shows that this nightmare was no fantastic dream. Indeed, a communal civil war in Syria might well be far bloodier than the terrible acts of terrorism and murder Iraq witnessed after the overthrow of Saddam Hussein.

The apparent lessons for Hafiz here were the need to struggle in order to preserve the regime, find a new patron, and unite the country behind himself in a way that pushed religious and communal passions aside, all the while avoiding real reform. In other words, he had to, at least temporarily, conciliate potential foreign threats while keeping Syrians loyal but without giving them anything in material terms. This was a Herculean task.

This problem was mirrored and reinforced by a second huge disaster for Syrian interests in the 1990s: America's new role as the world's sole superpower. The United States had won the Cold War; Syria had been on the losing side. For decades, Syrian leaders had been insisting that the United States was an imperialist ogre bent on destroying Syria. They had defied America and opposed virtually all of its policies and interests in the region. Now the reviled Americans were in a position to take their revenge. How could Syria, isolated and relatively weak, possibly survive?

After all, Hafiz had long predicted the catastrophe the United States allegedly wanted to inflict on the Arabs in general and Syria in particular. As he put it in a 1981 speech: "The United States wants us to be puppets so it can manipulate us the way it wants. It wants us to be slaves so it can exploit us the way it wants. It wants to occupy our territory and exploit our masses."[4] If he was right, his own regime would certainly be doomed.

The only hope was for Hafiz to play the Americans just right. In Iraq, Saddam Hussein continued his defiance, going on the offensive and trying, with minimal results, to mobilize all Arabs and Muslims behind him. Hafiz was far foxier, pulling back and pretending moderation without taking any irreversible steps. The Assad regime survived and Hafiz's son Bashar would mount the throne after him. The Saddam Hussein regime fell and Saddam's two sons would be killed in a shoot-out with U.S. forces in Baghdad.

Ironically, of course, Hafiz triumphed precisely because he knew something that Saddam did not seem to understand. The Syrian dictator, unlike the Iraqi one, did not want to call America's bluff. As long as Syria did not become too threatening, the United States would basically leave it alone. Ironically, Syria did so well because its propaganda was indeed false. Contrary to what the regime was telling its people, the United States did not want to overthrow the regime and brutalize Syria's people but instead to avoid conflict and prove it preferred friendship to hostility.

As it had already done with Egypt and would later do with the PLO and even Libya, America was prepared to get along with those who could persuade it that they wanted to behave moderately. U.S. policymakers were eager to resolve the Arab-Israeli conflict by trading land captured by Israel in 1967 for real peace. Such a changed relationship would even open the way to the provision of massive U.S. aid. Hafiz was not ready to become moderate in real terms—his regime's interests prohibited such a step—but he was quite ready to play along as long as was needed.

So while Saddam Hussein decided to fight America, Hafiz came up with the better strategy of fooling America. He manipulated the United States quite effectively. The Americans' good intentions, eagerness to make friends, and wishful thinking were all weapons in his arsenal. Americans tended to assume that the Syrian regime wanted peace with Israel, since this would get Syria back the Golan Heights, and domestic reform, to achieve prosperity. And all these wishes and illusions went double for Europe.

It was in Syria's interest to cooperate with the United States in the 1991 Kuwait crisis; although it was very difficult in psychological terms, it cost little to talk with Israel or to let 4,000 Jews leave Syria as a sign of respect for human rights.[5] In the end, though, Hafiz would yield nothing and the Americans would do nothing to him. As soon as the balance of forces seemed to change, Syria could return to business as usual.

Aside from these two wider problems with the global scene, Syria faced difficulties with all of its neighbors: Iraq, Turkey, Israel, Lebanon, Jordan, and the Palestinians. Since Syria had been sponsoring terrorism against all of them, the Assad regime had plenty of reasons to worry that they might take revenge.

By the end of the 1990s, however, the balance sheet was not at all bad from Syria's viewpoint. True, Turkey forced Syria to stop backing Kurdish terrorists, Jordan signed a peace treaty with Israel, and the PLO entered a peace process with Israel. But no one launched an all-out offensive to punish Syria or defeat it decisively. Moreover, in the end the PLO-Israel peace process produced no separate peace. The decade ended with Syria not making any concessions to Israel or having to abandon its historic goals of destroying Israel and controlling Lebanon.

Syria's biggest apparent concession—its participation in the 1991 war against Iraq, simultaneously its near duplicate and chief rival—was actually very much in line with its interests and reaped the regime rich rewards. Hafiz and Saddam had similar worldviews, policies, and ambitions. Due to these ambitions, however, they were enemies. A strong Iraq endangered Syria as much as it did Kuwait or Saudi Arabia, and in 1990 Iraq looked very strong indeed.

After defeating Iran in their 1980 to 1988 war, Saddam was portraying himself as the rightful Arab leader. Indeed, his bid for power employed precisely the same rhetoric about the need for a tough Arab response to American "hegemony" that Syria's leaders always used.[6] Nevertheless, the long quarrel between Hafiz and Saddam arose precisely from their conflicting claim to be the proper leader for the Arabs and Ba'th party in fighting America, Israel, and more moderate Arab states. When Saddam's aggression next turned against Kuwait, in August 1990, Syria had the chance to oppose Baghdad, let others do the fighting, and collect financial aid as well as Western support for its hegemony over Lebanon.

Meanwhile, Turkey, Syria's neighbor to the north, was getting increasingly angry about Damascus's support for the Kurdish Workers' Party (PKK) terrorist group that was killing thousands of people in its revolt there. Syria and Turkey also had a dispute over territory—Turkey's Hatay province, which Syria claimed—and the use of the Euphrates River, as new Turkish dams reduced the flow of water to Syrian farms. Turkey's growing alliance with Israel during the 1990s was largely a response to the resulting tension, a conflict that would turn into a confrontation in 1998 (from which Hafiz wisely backed down).

Control of Lebanon was Syria's main foreign policy asset, not only a geostrategic but also an economic one, since that country offered ample employment opportunities for Syria's surplus workers, a bumper opium crop, and a smugglers' paradise. But how could Syria secure its hegemony over its neighbor at a time when the United States and other forces might take advantage of its weakness to wrest away the prize?

Hafiz had the answers. First, since Syria helped out in the Kuwait war, and in order to encourage Syria's peace process with Israel, the United States accepted Damascus's colonial rule over Lebanon.

Second, Syria built up the power of its Lebanese client groups, especially Hizballah, which attacked the remaining pro-Israel forces in south Lebanon without dragging Syria into a direct military conflict. When Lebanon's government, perhaps inspired by the heady atmosphere after Saddam's overthrow, decided to send its army to the south in 1991, the Syrians stopped this small show of independence. After all, as Vice-President Khaddam later recalled, being able to launch attacks from the area was "part of a Syrian strategy to pressure Israel and prevent a possible Lebanese government tendency to reach a peace agreement with it."[7]

Third, to provide a safety valve for the Lebanese themselves, Assad let the independent-minded Rafiq Hariri become prime minister in 1992, forcing him out when Syria felt more secure regarding its hold on that country. Already in 1989, Syria had used U.S. help to consolidate its position in Lebanon through the Taif Accord, a diplomatic agreement ending that country's civil war that left Syria the arbiter of Lebanon's politics and security. These maneuvers were brilliantly successful in enabling Syria to keep its most important asset despite its own weakness.

Syria got a lot less in Jordan but was no worse off either. It had long tried to subvert that kingdom, with the Jordanians responding by helping Syrian Islamists or at least letting its own Muslim Brotherhood support them. Jordan and Syria were continually at odds. Still, Damascus kept Amman too frightened to cause any real problems.

Israel was hardest of all. If Syrian leaders really believed that Israel was the ultimate, evil enemy, what would happen if that nemesis was so strong—and enjoyed full support from the world's sole superpower as well—while the Arabs were so weak? Was Syria so caught in a corner as to consider doing the unthinkable and make peace, or would it be a better tactic merely to pretend to do so to satisfy the United States? Hafiz certainly did not rush toward such a deal. In fact, he did not seem that eager for it at all. In the end he would escape from the peace process without any damage or cost, but of course during the 1990s this result could not be assured.

Even all of this did not exhaust the list of problems Hafiz faced. Although he had defeated radical Islamism within Syria by crushing the Muslim Brotherhood in 1982, it was a rising force in the region. Syria was not in the best position to deal with this threat. After all, the regime was controlled by a non-Muslim sect and boasted of its secularism, as well as having the blood of many Islamists on its hands. Again, though, Hafiz dealt with the problem effectively.

One tactic was to build up Syria's alliance with Iran, Hizballah, and Hamas, a process that first began in the 1980s and accelerated in the 1990s. Having such friends was not just a gambit on Hafiz's part but an essential requirement for the regime's survival. By portraying the Alawites as Shia Muslims, he successfully reinvented their image at a time when others were being reviled as infidels or heretics for far less. Syria could torture domestic Islamist revolutionaries all it wanted and still wipe away its sins by backing Islamist causes abroad.

Still another headache for Hafiz was the fact that his natural constituency and basis for rule at home, the forces of radical pan-Arab nationalism, were fracturing and weakened in the Arabic-speaking world. Even the enthusiastically Arab nationalist Bashar later acknowledged this decline: "The state of the Arab nation and the weak ties among Arab countries prevailing... during the 1990s is no secret." This process went so far "that any talk of Arab nationalism or Arab solidarity seemed . . . to some to be romantic or a waste of time."[8] Syria was in danger of being isolated. But Hafiz clung close to Egypt while winning Saudi and Kuwaiti approval—and massive funding—for his role in the anti-Saddam coalition that freed Kuwait.

On one issue—Syria's domestic scene—Hafiz did virtually nothing. This strategy, of course, was totally different from the expectations of many foreign observers. Yet it was the regime's goal to save itself by avoiding any change at home. More than that, Syria's rulers viewed internal reforms as the greatest danger to their power. Foreign policy, as would happen so often before and after, was a substitute for better performance in the actual governance of Syria.

Thus, Hafiz made no real political, social, or economic reforms at home. All the country's problems continued to smolder but not to burn. His response made sense in terms of the regime's interests. Maneuvers on the foreign policy scene were enough to bring sufficient domestic support for the government. Nationalist appeals rallied the people. With the Islamists crushed and liberals virtually nonexistent, Hafiz faced no internal challenges.

His successful use of these strategies to manage—or at least to fend off—gigantic problems rightly earned Hafiz the nickname the "fox of Damascus" from admiring foreign diplomats. Of course, if Hafiz was a fox, Syria and Lebanon were his chicken coop and their people his cuisine. Both at home and abroad, his mighty struggles succeeded in preserving a status quo of stagnation and bloodshed.

As Hafiz played skillfully the game of nations, in 1990 the onus of prime regional troublemaker fell on Iraqi president Saddam Hussein. On August 2, 1990, he invaded Kuwait, quickly seizing and annexing that country. Purporting to bring to life Arab aspirations, Saddam actually acted as an imperialist using these passions as a cover. And when he held the knife to the throat of Kuwait and Saudi Arabia, they begged the much-maligned United States to save them.

Nine days later, at an Arab League meeting, all members except for Iraq, Libya, and the PLO condemned Iraq's behavior and decided to send a peace-keeping force to Saudi Arabia. Syria joined the Saudi- and Egyptian-led coalition not out of moderation or love for the Gulf Arabs but in the service of its own interests. Economically, Syria was in bad shape. It could no longer depend on aid from the quickly expiring Soviet bloc or oil-rich Gulf Arab states that preferred to spend their money on themselves. Politically, it was isolated, involved in quarrels with Iraq, Israel, Jordan, Turkey, and the PLO. Since Syria had supported Iraq's enemy, Iran, in the 1980 to 1988 Gulf war, Damascus knew it was on Saddam's list of future victims.

The Kuwait crisis was a welcome relief to this dismal situation, giving Syria a chance to escape isolation and obtain large amounts of Saudi aid by supporting the coalition, which was in its interest anyway. Syria had to do little to make these gains except send some troops to sit in the desert. Saddam's condition, as part of his price for leaving Kuwait, that Syria also had to pull out from Lebanon, gave Hafiz an even greater incentive to oppose Iraq. Saddam's putting this together with a demand that Israel must leave the West Bank and Gaza Strip thus equating Syria with Israel—added insult to injury for Hafiz. Syria had no choice but to join the anti-Iraq coalition, even if it had not been so richly rewarded for doing so.

The Syrian regime thus got precisely what it wanted at little cost to itself. It was not forced to make peace with Israel, reduce its support for terrorism, or ease its control over Lebanon. On the contrary, for participating in the coalition, the Bush Administration not only forgave Syria's dictatorship for past anti-American terrorism and human rights' abuses but also accepted Syrian hegemony in Lebanon. The Saudis gave Syria at least $2 billion in aid, largely spent to buy new military equipment to pursue its ambitions and repress its people.

As Saddam was defeated in the war and driven out of Kuwait, Syria's image was transformed from radical troublemaker to member in good standing of the alliance of moderates and a client of the world's sole superpower, which it nevertheless continued to revile. It still had to undergo another initiation exercise to be in that exclusive club, however: participation in a peace process with Israel.

That process was the most psychologically difficult issue that Hafiz faced during his thirty-year-long tenure as Syria's dictator. Up to 1991, it was a basic article of faith for Arab nationalists that there could never be any peace and preferably not even any negotiations with Israel. Egypt had broken with that consensus by making the Camp David agreement in 1979, a sin that Syria had used to isolate its rival in the contest for Arab leadership. During the 1990s, however, both the PLO and Jordan signed agreements with Israel. How was Syria to deal with this dramatically changed situation?

The new framework was largely dictated by historical experience. After more than forty years of effort and despite its vast superiority in money, territory, and population, the Arab world had been unable to beat or destroy Israel. The Arabs had been defeated in the 1948, 1956, 1967, 1973, and 1982 wars with accompanying losses of territory, money, prestige, and stability. Every tactic used against Israel failed: conventional war, guerrilla fighting, terrorism, economic boycott, or pressure on the West to stop supporting the Jewish state. For many Arabs, there seemed no good reason to believe that this situation was going to change in their favor.

On the contrary, the resulting instability and discrediting of the Arab nationalist regimes fostered revolutionary Islamist opposition movements, expensive arms races, and catastrophic civil wars. As Syrian foreign minister Farouq al-Sharaa reflected in describing the many failures, "We have faced setback after setback, stab after stab on the Arab body, and a crack after crack in the Arab national plan. On the other hand, the Zionist plan kept advancing, thanks to the mistakes in the Arab plan."[9] Yet the really significant question was, Did the Arab plan merely include tactical errors, or was the whole effort a mistake and a totally new approach needed?

By identifying the Arabs' biggest mistake as failing to unite to fight Israel, Sharaa merely repeated in the 1990s the old Arab nationalist argument from the 1950s. The second largest error, he continued, was becoming involved in any other issue besides the Arab-Israeli conflict. Sadat should never have made peace with Israel; Iraq should never have diverted Arab resources by attacking Iran and then Kuwait. In short, after decades of failed conflict, Sharaa's conclusion was that the only way to win would be to try even harder.

In the 1990s, however, there were thoughts by some Arabs of making some change in strategy, at least temporarily. Israel, Sharaa warned, was more powerful than all the Arab states combined. The United States supplied Israel with advanced weapons ranging from rifles to rockets and planes, plus powerful computers that even the Europeans did not have. Israel was making advanced arms of its own, exporting them even to China.[10] At the same time, Syria's leaders knew they could not afford the kind of weapons and spare parts they had once purchased with Saudi aid and at discounted Soviet prices.

Sharaa and other Syrian leaders never noted that much of Israel's advantage arose from the fact that it was—unlike Syria—a democratic and economically flexible society. Acceptance of this lesson might have suggested that social transformation at home was a prerequisite for victory abroad. That idea, however, would have been too dangerous and lay beyond the limits of the regime's ideology.

An interesting example of how Syrian leaders distorted things even in their own minds was Sharaa's claim that Israel's arms spending was twenty times that of Syria's. In fact, Israel's 2000 defense budget was $9.3 billion while Syria's was $4.8 billion. Even this two-to-one gap, however, is overstated, since a large portion of Israeli spending was for soldiers' wages and benefits that cost Syria far less. Regarding the priority on military budgeting, in 1992, 26.2 percent of Syrian government spending went for military purposes; by 1997, that figure rose to 39 percent. These spending levels were higher than any major state in the region except wealthy Saudi Arabia. By this measure, Syrian spending was double that of Israel and four times more than Egypt. Syria had triple the number of people that Israel did—and oil fields as well—but could not generate anywhere near as much revenue for its national budget. Nevertheless, it spent far more proportionately on its army.[11]

From Israel's standpoint, military spending was a "necessary evil" to defend against foreign attack; for Syria, however, a large army was also needed to absorb otherwise unemployable manpower, keep happy an officer class that might otherwise stage a coup, and have an institution capable of repressing its own people. Thus, high military spending for Syria was an inflexible cost for the regime, neither easily cut nor something the political leadership wanted to reduce.

Still, given Israel's military strength, Syrian leaders in the 1990s concluded that they did not have the option of going to war. The bottom line, as Sharaa explained, was that the Arabs seemed to be "really cornered and faced with one of two choices. Either we have to accept a peace that is akin to capitulation and surrender, which can never be the peace we want, or we have to reject peace without a solid ground on which to base this rejection."[12]

Many foreign observers interpreted this kind of talk as indicating that Syria wanted, or could be easily persuaded, to make peace with Israel. A typical article, published in Britain's *Financial Times,* was aptly titled "Syria's Golden Opportunity: Making Peace with Israel." It explained that Syria's disastrous domestic economic situation could be fixed only through such a deal and presented other reasons why peace should be imminent. Syria was isolated in the

Arab world. Assad was about to lose his bargaining chip because Israel's impending withdrawal from south Lebanon, the author claimed, "would deprive Hizballah and Syria of any legitimacy for resistance." In conclusion, "Damascus has realized that a unique opportunity may be at hand. . . . Syria is no longer resigned to making peace with its Jewish neighbor but genuinely seeking it."[13]

Of course, a few weeks later, Hafiz belied this expectation by turning down peace in exchange for getting back all of the Golan Heights. He did not say no out of a whim or due to his rejected demand for a tiny sliver of territory Syria had seized from Israel in the 1948 war. Rather, he was pursuing Syria's interests, for which peace with Israel had far more minuses than pluses.

A rational analysis showed many more reasons for Syria to avoid rather than to make peace with Israel. Syria had a great deal to lose if diplomacy succeeded. It did not want to see an increase in regional stability, a greater U.S. role, or the normalization of Israel's position in the area. Extremely dissatisfied with the status quo, Syria's rulers saw the Arab world's return to past militancy as a way to escape isolation and seize leadership. Otherwise, their hope of gaining (or keeping) influence over neighbors and becoming the area's dominant power would be lost forever. The existence of a Western-oriented Palestinian state that did not side with Syria's ambitions, but whose existence might even reduce tensions or end the Arab-Israeli conflict, would do nothing for them either.

An Israel-Syria peace treaty would be equally bad for the regime. Such a diplomatic achievement would open the door for most other Arab states to have relations with Israel and to work with it on matters of common interest. But Israel would remain determined—and be far more able—to oppose Syria's ambitions for sway over Jordan, Lebanon, and the Palestinians. In a peacetime Middle East, the United States would also use its stronger influence to block Syrian goals. In addition, an Israel-Lebanon agreement would follow any Israel-Syria accord, reducing Damascus's leverage in that country and bringing international pressure for a Syrian withdrawal.

These strategic costs would not be matched by any economic or political gains for Syria, certainly not on the all-important domestic front. A Syrian agreement with Israel would not bring much Western aid or investment. More open access for foreigners to invest or do business directly in Syria and more open commercial opportunities for Syrian businesspeople would weaken the dictatorship's hold over its own subjects. Freer communications would give Syrians more access to news and information, including ideas and facts the regime did not want them to know.

As a result of such changes, Syria would lose prestige, aid, and deferral to its interests. These were advantages that being a militant confrontational state once brought it in the Arab world. Today these same factors make Syria a superpower in terms of the demagogic appeal used to keep its people in line, marching behind the regime.

In short, the Arab-Israeli conflict is good for Syria. Losing the issue itself was worse than losing a dozen battles against Israel. Syria would be relegated to being a secondary power in the Middle East. At home, the result could be the regime's overthrow and a devastating civil war or revolution. As one pro-regime Syrian writer warned, Israel's proposal to give Syria the Golan Heights in exchange for real peace "is like a minefield; it conceals things that are not apparent on the surface."[14]

Syrian liberals, small in number and denied access to the media, were cynical about how the regime manipulated the Arab-Israeli conflict so well as to find it indispensable. But they were not in a position to do anything about it. "Conflict has been very important for the regime," explained one. "When there were human rights abuses or corruption, the ultimate excuse was the conflict." Another added, "Syria must always have an enemy" to help create political cohesion. "No question, the fig leaf has been Israel," agreed a Lebanese analyst in Beirut. "The [Syrian] regime fabricated its legitimacy under that fig leaf. Assad used the discourse of war to block any discourse rejecting his policy. It worked."[15]

At times, especially in the 1990s, the rationale for using the conflict to justify whatever the regime wanted to do was weaker. As one Syrian pointed out, "People wonder: 'If you were really fighting Israel, then you wouldn't be importing all these Mercedes.' And the record of the regime is not commensurate with the sacrifices we have been asked to make. That's why after 30 years it sounds hollow."[16]

Yet it was easier to revitalize the conflict than to find a substitute that might work as well. The more critics pointed out the regime's vulnerability on the issue, the greater the need to ensure that Syrians—and if possible all Arabs and Muslims—saw the conflict as inescapable and all-important.

Although hollow, the argument still was effective. Sharaa warned that the preferred strategy, rejection of peace with Israel, must rest on "solid ground." This did not mean abandoning the conflict but finding a persuasive reason for why the continuation was the fault of Israel and not of Syria. Hafiz and Sharaa insisted on terms that Israel could not accept while requiring that all of their demands be met before negotiations began. In this way, Syria's leaders could insist that they wanted peace but Israel was refusing to accede.[17]

This new idea was one of the most brilliant insights in Arab nationalist history. For decades, Arab states had publicly insisted that they would never make peace with Israel. After Egypt did so anyway in 1979, this stance was taken up even more stubbornly as the standard for Arab nationalist legitimacy, to prove that a regime, movement, or politician was not a traitor like Sadat. Then Arafat made a deal in 1993 and Jordan signed a peace treaty in 1994. Many of those who remained obdurate, especially those in the nationalist as opposed to the Islamist camp, came to see that the old position was a public relations' disaster.

The shift in Syria's orientation was one of image management rather than substance. The regime finally comprehended that as long as the Arab side explicitly rejected peace, Israel would have the diplomatic and media advantage. What must be done, according to Sharaa, was to say that the Arabs were ready for peace, to repeat their demands and so, "in a convincing way," persuade the international community that Israel was at fault for the conflict since it rejected Arab demands.

If an Arab regime started insisting it wanted peace with Israel—even if it took no actual step in that direction—the world's diplomats beat a path to the regime's door, making offers and concessions to create a political process and show good will. This would happen even if they eventually got nothing in exchange. In addition, the onus for the failure of any peace process was usually put on Israel or the United States, which critics would say could have done more to achieve a solution.

A subtle corollary further extended the value of this gambit. If Israel did offer to return the land or even actually did so, new disputed land could be discovered. Thus, after Israel pulled out of all south Lebanon, Hizballah began demanding the return of the Shabaa Farms and some villages lost in border changes made long before Israel's creation. When Israel made clear its willingness in principle to give back all Syrian territory captured in 1967, the regime insisted it also get pieces of real estate that were supposed to be part of Israel but had been seized by Syria in 1948.[18]

Here is how Sharaa put it prophetically in 2000, a few days before Syria actually rejected getting all its land back through the peace process:

> If we do not get our land through the peace process, we will win the world and Arab public. For Israel has continued to claim that it is always with peace and that the Arabs are against it. True, the media are directed against us and are in favor of the enemy to a large extent, but it is possible to penetrate these mighty, hostile media. . . . Our strong, solid, and persistent position

and the reaffirmation of our constants in a convincing way are bound to have an effect.

A strong argument is important in the media. We only want our land and rights. They are the ones who are exposed now because they want to keep the land. This process of exposure is, in my opinion, very important. We must expose them because they do not want peace.[19]

Conventional wisdom about Syria-Israel negotiations, at least periodically, is that there was a "window of opportunity," a temporary chance to make progress that would disappear soon. But another way to look at the situation is as a "window of weakness" that Syria sought to survive by playing along in a process it never intended to complete.

The "window of opportunity" argument and Syria's stance were usually explained by three points, all of which were seen as promoting Syria's willingness—even eagerness—to make a deal.

1. The desire to regain the Golan Heights before Hafiz died—and thus to leave a more stable situation and ensure a smooth transition for his son to succeed him in office
2. A need to escape international isolation in regard to both the West and the Arab world
3. The desire to end the Arab-Israeli conflict and improve relations with the West to enable Syria to make domestic economic and other reforms.

Generally speaking, the truth was the precise opposite of these assumptions.

For example, making peace with Israel and ending the conflict would in fact create a less stable situation within Syria and make Bashar's succession more difficult. Such a deal would increase Syria's isolation from its closest ally, Iran, from Iraq (then ruled by Saddam Hussein), and from radical Islamist groups. It would also remove Syria's excuse for continuing to control Lebanon, thus greatly weakening its national economy. Domestic reforms also would reduce the regime's power; growing demands for change would in fact ensure the downfall of the regime.

What did serve Syria's interest was to get something for nothing. On one hand, pretending to negotiate would defuse the threat from the United States and give Syria leverage in getting gifts in exchange for cooperation. The most important of these gifts was support for its continued domination of Lebanon. By negotiating even without ever reaching an agreement, it got more backing from the West; by simultaneously posing as a heroic country that would demand its full rights and yield nothing, Syria mobilized more domestic, some Arab, and Iranian support.

Assad well understood that reaching a peace agreement would produce far more domestic stress and difficulties than would stalling and, when time was up, playing Dr. No.

Indeed, there are at least fifteen reasons why Syria needed the conflict to continue and saw real peace as dangerous, even fatal, to its survival.

First, there are five strategic reasons why Syria did not want a deal to end the conflict:

1. Syria's leaders were still debating among themselves on the issue. They found it very difficult to face the most difficult decision in the country's history.

2. Syria's leaders still believed they could get everything they wanted while giving up nothing in a deal. This is another example of a common Arab world tactic of *sumud*, or steadfastness: We would rather suffer many years and take large risks than compromise even if we are in a position of weakness. Of course, this can also be an indication that the status quo is not so terrible and that change might bring significant domestic and other costs. A contributing factor in this particular case was Assad's desire to prove that he got a better deal from Israel than did Egypt, Jordan, or the Palestinians. But Syria simply lacked the leverage for such an outcome.

3. Syria's leaders mistakenly believed that violence—most obviously from Lebanon—would bring more Israeli concessions. Yet Israel preferred to withdraw from southern Lebanon rather than let Syria use attacks there as blackmail. Even then, however, Syria saw its support for radical groups in Lebanon as a card with which to weaken Israel and mobilize support against it. In Sharaa's words, "The entire Lebanese resistance . . . continues fighting to this day. You have heard about the big losses that are inflicted on Israel [by them]."[20] The value of this tactic would be richly demonstrated in the 2006 Lebanon war.

4. Hafiz was still alive, but his ailments and declining energy had reduced his ability to be a strong, active leader, making it harder for him to be agile in negotiations or to push through a deal with Israel at home.

5. Syria's rulers were reasonably happy with a situation in which they had declared themselves willing to negotiate but did not make the

necessary effort to close an agreement. These circumstances let Syria pose as moderate to the West, exercise veto power over the Arab world by positioning itself as the most noble and militant regime, preserve its hold on Lebanon, mobilize domestic support, and seek more western concessions by playing hard to get. Syria tantalized the West by suggesting that more concessions and less pressure would bring about a breakthrough.

Next, there are five good regional reasons for avoiding peace:

6.   Israel as a normal player in the Middle East, the inevitable result of a successful peace process, would be a disaster for Syrian interests because the two countries were opposed on almost every issue: Their attitudes toward strong U.S. influence in the region, the political direction of a Palestinian state, the power balance in the Arab world, and Lebanon, among others, were completely opposite.

7.   A peace agreement would be the beginning of the end for Syrian control over Lebanon, even if Israel implicitly accepted Syria's domination there. If Syria lost control of Lebanon, it would mean the termination of advantages for Syria's poor and its ruling elite.

8.   Syria does not want the United States to be even stronger in the region by having brokered a successful peace process, since it knows that the Americans oppose Syrian ambitions and even the regime's very existence. The regime needs to blame the United States for the continuing conflict and its support for Israel.

9.   A successful Israel-Palestinian deal and the creation of a truly independent Palestinian state would rob Damascus of the valuable Palestinian card, forever ending Syria's chance to take over the Palestinian movement and/or Palestine.

10. Syria's militancy against Israel is practically the only asset it has in the area. If this pillar was removed, Syria would be reduced to a third-rate power with little influence in the Arab world. In Sharaa's words, "Some [Arabs] said, the Syrians are just like all the others"— that is, ready to sell out in order to justify their own concessions. But Syria's tough line proved this was not true. The Arabs had to acknowledge that Syria's policy "was really smart.... It adhered to its national rights and sovereignty and faithfully defended the honor of its homeland and people."[21]

And, finally, there are five domestic reasons why peace with Israel endangered Syria's stability:

11. The Syrian rulers do not want to open the economy or society too much; this step would weaken the regime and take away the profits the rulers enjoy by controlling the statist economy.
12. The rulers do not want to enrich the Sunni Muslim merchants who would benefit from peace and a far-reaching economic reform. Doing so would strengthen a group that might prefer to overthrow the regime.
13. Syria's leaders know they will not get much aid or investment from abroad as a result of a peace deal.
14. They wanted to prevent the domestic opposition from portraying them as traitors who sold out to Zionism, especially at the time of a delicate transition to Bashar. Such a moment was clearly not the best time to undertake a risky, complex foreign policy initiative.
15. Even with a peace agreement, Syria would still have no reliable military supplier—and still lack funds to buy arms—to keep its generals satisfied and to provide weapons to ensure continued domestic control. Without the conflict, maintaining a strong military establishment might also be more difficult.

Consequently, Syria's ideal strategy was to appear to negotiate seriously while demanding so much that Israel would not agree. This was a win/win situation, since Syria could appear to be moderate in the West and steadfast in the Arab world. Either Damascus would get everything it wanted, or it would not have to take the risks involved in making peace and could portray Israel as the villain.

In the negotiations, Syria's unshakable stance was that Israel must first commit itself to a complete withdrawal from the Golan Heights, which belonged to Syria, and the area of the demilitarized zone on Israel's side of the border, which Syria had captured in 1948. The shorthand for this demand was the June 4, 1967, borders, rather than the international or 1948 borders. Then, and only then, when Israel had conceded to all of Syria's demands—and thus given up any leverage it might have—would Syria discuss what it would give and the nature of peace arrangements. Syrian diplomats made clear that holding talks did not in any way constitute recognition. At one point, the chief Syrian negotiator referred to the party he was meeting with as "what you call Israel."[22]

Of course, Syria was hypocritically demanding that Israel give up all the land it had seized in wartime while considering its own conquests sacred parts of the homeland. Both Egypt and Jordan had already accepted the international borders in their agreements with Israel. But that was precisely the point: Syria wanted to show that it was able to get more than other Arab states and would rather fight on for a century than give up an inch of ground. Moreover, the small parcel of land Syria wanted beyond its own border was of vital strategic importance to Israel, but not to Syria. Possession of that area would put Syrian troops on the down slope from the Golan Heights, making it easy to advance through the completely flat land between there and the Mediterranean. Syria would also control key Israeli water sources and be able to claim part of the Sea of Galilee, the most important water source of all.

There was no chance that any Israeli government would agree to such terms. Syria's demand that Israel must concede all the Golan plus areas on its own side of the border before any other issues were even discussed doomed negotiations to failure. Israel was willing to make major concessions but only in exchange for a clear commitment that the conflict would come to an end and normal relations would be established. This understanding on what both sides would give was especially necessary since ceding territory was a material concession while diplomatic arrangements were an abstract, potentially reversible, arrangement.

The purported new era in Syrian policy began with the 1991 Madrid conference. It was the first time that Arab states had sat down with Israel to talk about making peace and, as such, was a defeat for Syria's historic line. Syria could not stay on the sidelines because almost every other Arab state, as well as a Palestinian delegation selected by the PLO, was participating. The United States saw this meeting as a way to make a breakthrough based on the defeat of Saddam and what seemed to be a dramatic reconsideration in the Arab world. Bringing together a number of Arab states and the Palestinians to sit down and talk about peace with Israel was a genuine achievement. And Syria did more than any other country to scuttle it.

Indeed, the Syrians tried to organize an Arab walkout; it failed because no one else would join them. Nobody else was as hard line as Syria, and only the Lebanese could be intimidated to "coordinate" with it. According to Sharaa's own account, he lied to Secretary of State James Baker by pretending everyone else would follow Syria's lead. Baker, however, insisted on actually asking the Palestinians and Jordanians what they wanted to do. Sharaa then supposedly warned Baker that the Syrians would walk out if he did not meet their demands. Baker was said to have responded angrily: "You are threatening the United States." It was, Sharaa concluded, "a long, heated argument."[23]

Sharaa portrayed the conference as a victory, as if Damascus were eager to negotiate while Israel was against it. Israel, he claimed, wanted to keep all the territory it had captured in 1967 plus southern Lebanon. In an ironic twist, Sharaa claimed as proof of this assertion that Israeli prime minister Yitzhak Shamir "wanted the talks to continue for 10 years without making any progress." In fact, almost exactly ten years after the Madrid conference, Israel offered to return the entire Golan Heights, and Syria turned it down.[24]

Following the conference, two sets of separate talks were held. One was bilateral—between Syrian, Palestinian, and Jordanian delegations on one side and Israel on the other—hosted by the United States; the other was multilateral, focusing on different key issues and conducted by various other countries. Syria tried to persuade other Arab states not to attend the latter meetings; again it failed. If the rest of the leaders, including Arafat, had listened to Syria, Sharaa later stated, "I believe that no one would have dared attend the multilateral talks."

Far from cooperating, Syria was determined to sabotage the process if at all possible. Yet Syria, whose line had so long dominated the Arab world, was being left behind by apparently changing circumstances. During this period, Syria continued to participate in the meetings, though not to negotiate. The Syrian delegation made long, polemical speeches regarding all the wrongs Israel had done to their country and to the Arabs in general in the past. It must have been quite frightening for the Assad regime, with Jordan and the Palestinians, supported by the Gulf Arab states and Egypt, going their own way toward, in Syria's view, "capitulation."

But even worse was to come: In 1993, secret Israel-PLO negotiations of which Syria knew nothing came to fruition. Sharaa called the train of events "a plot to turn the Syrians against the Palestinians, and the Palestinians against the Syrians and the Arabs. This is very serious and it must stop. It is as if we do not belong to one nation. This is inconceivable."[25]

Of course, the Syrians did have legitimate concerns about Israel making a full withdrawal. During Israel's 1992 election campaign, for example, both of the leading candidates—Yitzhak Shamir and Yitzhak Rabin—agreed that Israel should keep the Golan Heights. Rabin had said, "To raise the thought that we descend from the Golan Heights would be tantamount to abandoning, I repeat, abandoning the defense of Israel."[26]

Yet once Rabin was elected prime minister, he reversed this position. In September 1992 he stated in a radio interview that Israel "would be ready to implement Security Council resolutions 242 and 338, which means acceptance of some territorial compromise." Two months later he went further by declaring "the depth of withdrawal will reflect the depth of peace"[27]; in other words, full withdrawal for full peace. Israeli leaders were convinced that they must prove to Syria their readiness to do what was needed to make a deal.

Israel proposed in an April 1992 "non-paper"—a speculative, informal, semiofficial memorandum—that the two sides discuss basic confidence-building measures and agree to refrain from military activities against each other during the negotiations. This document raised several questions for Syria: Does it accept the legitimacy and right of existence of Israel? Does it accept the applicability to Israel of Article 2 of the UN Charter, which makes it incumbent on members of the UN to accept each other's sovereign equality, the legitimacy of their statehood, and their basic rights as nation-state members of the United Nations?[28]

The Syrians responded on August 8, 1992, with a "non-paper" of their own, a document that was so vague that it was hard to tell whether it was, in the words of Israeli negotiator Itamar Rabinovitch, even dealing with the subject of Israel-Syria peacemaking. The memorandum did not mention Israel by name.[29]

Rabinovitch tried to put the best face on the meetings, but it was hard to find much of substance in them. He noted, "Through hint and allusion, our interlocutors suggested to us that there were several elements of normalization; some of them remained unacceptable to Syria, while others had to evolve over time. We in turn sensed that there was greater flexibility to the Syrian position in that matter."[30] Rabinovitch concluded that for Assad, "Israel remained a rival, if not an enemy, and the terms of the peace settlement [would] not serve to enhance its advantage over the Arabs . . . but rather to diminish it."[31]

To break the deadlock, the United States came up with the idea of a "hypothetical exercise." Each side would ask the other a question. Israel's would be "Assuming we satisfy your demands regarding withdrawal, what would be your position on peace and normalization?" Syria would ask "Assuming we satisfy your demands with regard to peace, what would be the extent of territorial withdrawal you would undertake?" Rabin agreed on August 3, 1993, authorizing Secretary of State Warren Christopher to explore with Syria what would happen if Israel met its demands regarding withdrawal. Would there be a peace treaty, normalization of relations, or any confidence-building measures before withdrawal was completed?[32]

Christopher clearly mishandled the exercise. Rather than making clear the activity's hypothetical nature and the need for a hypothetical Syrian response, he gave Syria the impression that Israel had agreed to all its demands without any response on its part. The result was to make things even worse. The Syrian delegation insisted that Israel must agree to all its demands before anything else happened at all. And Syria's response was so totally hedged with conditions as to amount to nothing. Assad even told Christopher he could not accept the idea of normalizing relations between the two countries.[33]

Attempts to make progress by discussing the possible economic advantages of peace similarly went nowhere. Pursuing the idea that Syria needed economic reform and would be motivated toward peace by material advantage was if anything counterproductive. Israeli leaders had put forward the concept of a "New Middle East," focusing on cooperation for development. But Syrian ambassador Walid al-Muallim pointed out that Syria rejected bilateral economic ties with Israel because it feared Israel's economic domination. A meeting of Israeli and Syrian generals also produced disagreement on just about everything.[34]

The real problem was not the format of the negotiations or the details of terms but a total misunderstanding of the Syrian position. The regime believed neither that it needed peace nor that ending the conflict would be beneficial to it. This stand had "disadvantages" in terms of keeping the Syrian economy closed, "forcing" the government to keep military spending high, maintaining the conflict, and discouraging any progress toward democracy. Yet the Syrian government welcomed these costs as beneficial to its survival. Syria did not want peace, not because the regime was blind or stubborn but because it understood its own interests very well.

As if this were not enough, however, intransigence in itself yielded benefits. U.S. president Bill Clinton genuinely wanted to resolve the conflict, both for the benefits this would bring to U.S. interests and for the glory it would bring his reputation. Reluctant to accept failure, Syria's hard line did not make him angry at Damascus; it made Clinton all the more eager to persuade it. To some extent, he blamed Israel for not offering even more and asking for less, precisely the effect Assad wanted.

This is a common pattern for Syria in its dealings with the United States and with Europe. The more an Assad, Hafiz or later Bashar, said no, the more he was offered or the more generously he was treated in the hope of convincing him to say yes. Thus, Clinton refrained from pressuring Syria or threatening it at a time when U.S. power was high and Middle East opposition to the United States was at an all-time low. Christopher wore holes in the carpets of Assad's presidential palace so frequent were his visits. Clinton himself met Assad in January 1994 in Europe and in October 1994 in Damascus. Clinton went on the latter visit after being told that Hafiz would make a public statement clearly condemning terrorism. Instead, Hafiz insisted in front of the surprised president that Syria never supported terrorism against Israel and that resistance in Lebanon was never terrorism.[35]

The American president, whose country was reviled in Syria daily, eventually would call Syria "the key to the achievement of enduring and comprehensive peace" in the Middle East.[36] Although Clinton made this statement after leaving office, there is every reason to believe he thought that way when he was in the White House. U.S. policymakers never seem to realize that the more importance they bestow on Syria, the more leverage they give it. The fact that Syria was a charter member of the U.S. State Department's list of terrorism-sponsoring states since its inception in 1979 made all the more bizarre Clinton's efforts to seduce a radical dictator through praise and toleration of his exploitation of Lebanon, extremist rhetoric, support for terrorism, and human rights' violations. After all, if Syria does not have to be afraid of the United States, then it has no incentive to behave more cautiously or moderately.

The Syria-Israel talks continued until 1996, when a wave of Hamas terrorist attacks on Israel and the election of Benjamin Netanyahu as prime minister, largely as the result of this bombing campaign, temporarily ended them. Three years later, in 1999, they began again at a higher level of intensity, with high-level meetings at Shepherdstown, West Virginia. The American hosts were eager, even desperate, to succeed before Clinton's term ended in January 2001. But the talks ended in failure in January 2000, as did Clinton's meeting with Hafiz in March. Nominally, the Syrian dictator's complaint was that Israel was offering him "only" all of the Golan Heights up to the international border; the real reasons ran far deeper.

This pressure of time had made the U.S. policymakers even more eager to persuade Syria to be cooperative, albeit only through friendly methods. There were never any threats of what might happen if Syria rejected the peace process or chose to continue its enmity with the United States. Instead, high-ranking American officials trooped off to Damascus as supplicants. Syria was treated as if it was in the drivers' seat and the United States had to ask for favors. This was exactly how the Syrian leadership saw the situation, and it responded accordingly.

Thus, the existence and course of this supposed peace process greatly benefited Syria as it was given immunity from prosecution, so to speak, for its past or current involvement in pro-Soviet, terrorist, and anti-American activities. Syrian occupation of Lebanon was accepted as a way of trying to get Syria to end Israeli occupation of its own territory. Yet despite all this coddling, nothing happened in these talks either. Syria's position, except for a willingness to meet, remained absolutely unchanged during a nine-year-long process.

As always, by merely saying no, Syria ensured its strategic victory, a victory that it regards as keeping its "principles" and "honor," but not, of course, a victory in terms of any material gain. This is what Sharaa meant when he promised the regime's hard-line supporters "Rest assured we are in a stronger position despite their weapons."[37] It is hardly surprising that Syrian leaders said Syria was strong, had nothing to fear, would make no concessions, and would surely emerge triumphant. They were right. After Assad rejected peace in 2000, there was no retaliation from the United States; indeed, there was not even strong criticism of Syria's actions. If Syria was vulnerable, Washington certainly did not exploit the situation.

In general, Western policymakers do not understand the issues at stake in Arab-Israeli conflict negotiations. The West assumes that since the Arab side is suffering from defeat, occupation, and—in the Palestinian case—the lack of a state, their forces are eager for a negotiated peace. In fact, due to ideology, competition over who is more militant, and dictators' priority on retaining power, the Arab side is eager to avoid a solution.

When Israel did offer almost everything the Arabs sought, the Arabs found other issues to explain why they refused to settle. Such issues include the Palestinian demand that all refugees should return to Israel (where they can sabotage it from within). Then there are always tiny, forgotten pieces of territory, as with the Hizballah claim that Israel is occupying a small piece of Lebanon (the Shabaa farm) which everyone else (including Syria) regards as Syrian territory; or the Syrian demand for Israeli land illegally occupied by Syria in 1948, which would give Damascus a claim on Israel's main water source.

There was always the pretext of prisoners being held by Israel (those who committed the last round of terrorist attacks) or quibbling over language. Has Hamas recognized Israel's right to exist? Well, it has maybe, perhaps, sort of implicitly hinted that it has, if you read between the lines and ignore what Hamas leaders say in Arabic to the contrary.

And so in 2006, six years after Israel offered to give up all the land it captured in 1967, it is possible to persuade the world that . . . Israel has not offered to do so. Immediately after Israel withdrew from the entire Gaza Strip and proposed large withdrawals from the West Bank, much of the Western media and even governments were convinced that the problem is that Israel is still an occupier.

No wonder Sharaa concluded, "So, in either case, we will not lose." The regime, as Sharaa put it, views the liberation of Palestine as coming in phases. The first phase is "regaining the occupied Arab territories and guaranteeing the

Palestinian Arab people's inalienable national rights," and the second is the elimination of Israel.[38]

Meanwhile, Syrian leaders, schools, media, and clerics explain that the goal of Israelis is the destruction of the Arabs and of Islam. Those who believe peace with Israel is attainable, wrote Sabir Falhout in the state-controlled *al-Thawra* newspaper in 1999, "are only fooling the Arab masses" because Zionism views all non-Jews as subhumans it wants to enslave.[39] It is evident that the Syrian regime still believes what the 1965 Ba'th congress concluded: "Not a single one of the aims of the Arab nation could be fully achieved as long as Israel exists.[40]

A parallel problem for dealing in a friendly manner with the United States makes Syria unlikely to be assuaged by any conceivable action America could take. After all, if the United States is so deterministically anti-Syria, anti-Muslim, and imperialist in its intentions, no real conciliation would ever be possible. A lot of these ideas were derived from radical Arab nationalist thought, but such beliefs also entered the regime's worldview through the Soviet Union and Marxism.

Syria's single real confrontation in the 1990s was not with either Israel or the United States, two countries that did not want to escalate conflict, but rather with Turkey. The Turks' determination to put credible pressure on Syria succeeded where the diplomatic methods of the world's sole superpower failed.

The issue was over Syrian support for the Kurdish terrorists wreaking so much havoc in southeastern Turkey. Gunmen from the PKK were seeking a separate, Marxist Kurdish state in the part of Turkey that was predominantly Kurdish. Their methods included stopping buses, inspecting the passengers, and killing those who were ethnic Turks. It was a vicious war that cost 30,000 lives and took place largely because Syria trained and assisted the terrorists, giving them cross-border access, much as Syria did against Israel and would later do against Iraq.

Syria had several grudges against Turkey. One was that the Alexandretta region had been given to Turkey in 1939 by the French who ruled Syria in a border rectification agreement. Syria wanted it back. The Euphrates River flowed through Turkey before reaching Syria. As Turkey began building dams on the river—starting with the massive Ataturk Dam in 1990—Syria complained that Turkey was taking too much water. Turkey rejected these claims.

Like many others, the Turks had frustrating experiences with Syria. For example, after a top-level 1993 meeting, the two countries said they would prevent any activity that would jeopardize their neighbor's security. On returning home from Damascus, Turkish prime minister Suleiman Demirel said the visit had "started a new era" in relations.[41]

But Syria continued to back the PKK. As it had done so often, Syria was sponsoring a terrorist war against a neighbor, killing its citizens and threatening its stability, at no cost to itself whatever. And as others would find, the international community and the West would do nothing about the problem. Europe hotly criticized Turkey for the way it was suppressing the revolt but said and did nothing against Syria for provoking this war.

By 1996 Turkey's patience had begun to run out. In February, a Turkey-Israel military agreement was signed. While both parties stated that the pact was not directed against any third country, it was clearly intended to put Syria on notice. Turkey had asked the Syrian government to expel the PKK headquarters in Damascus and the group's leader, Abdallah Ocalan, and Syria refused. At that point, Turkey suspended all governmental contacts with Damascus. In May 1997 Turkish defense minister Turhan Tayan visited the Israeli-controlled Golan Heights, another warning to Syria.[42]

Turkey continued, however, to try diplomatic methods, holding several bilateral meetings during 1998. When this did not work, Turkey made a serious and credible threat. At the Turkish parliament's opening session on October 1, 1998, Demirel warned: "We reserve the right to retaliate against Syria, which has not abandoned its hostile attitude despite all our warnings and peaceful initiatives, and that our patience is nearing an end." Chief of Staff General Huseyin Kivrikoglu said that Turkey was in a state of undeclared war with Syria, put the army on alert, and massed troops on the Syrian-Turkish border.[43]

Eight days later Syria decided to expel Ocalan and to stop helping the PKK. Damascus had considered Turkey's readiness to go to war. With Israel on its southern border, Syria could not fight a two-front war. Real pressure could force Syria to change its policy after soft words and concessions had failed. In addition, after the crisis, Turkish-Syrian relations improved and Ankara made no further demands on Damascus.[44] Thus if Syria is willing to compromise, even under pressure, its problems with neighbors can also be resolved. They are willing to accommodate reasonable Syrian interests. The problem lies with Damascus, not with Israel, Jordan, Lebanon, Saudi Arabia, Turkey, or post-Saddam Iraq.

Syria has been able to handle most of its other problems without concessions. That included maintaining its most valuable asset, control over Lebanon. Indeed, Syria used the latitude provided by the American courting process to consolidate its power there. On October 22, 1989, Lebanon and Syria—with the United States and Saudi Arabia as co-sponsors—signed the Taif Accord, officially known as the Charter on National Reconciliation. On the positive side, the fourteen-year-long Lebanese civil war was over; on the negative side, Syria was the real victor.

Syria controlled all important aspects of Lebanese political and economic life. As a report by Lebanon's Christian bishops put it, Syria "gives orders, appoints leaders, organizes parliamentary and other elections, elevates and drops whomever it wants . . . interferes in [Lebanon's] administration, judiciary, economy, and particularly politics."[45] It also decided what books or newspapers could be imported and ruled over the media. Damascus maintained a network of informers, wire-tapping, and its own prisons within Lebanon.

When the Christian nationalist Michel Aoun rebelled against the pro-Syrian Lebanese regime in 1990, that government invited Syria's army to help defeat him. As all Lebanese militias except the pro-Syrian Hizballah disarmed in 1991, the chance of anyone fighting Damascus declined further. And in May of that year, Lebanon and Syria signed a treaty of "brotherhood, cooperation, and coordination" that further legitimized Syria's hold on the country.

Syria's confidence along with its desire to stabilize the situation and increase the value of its Lebanese subsidiary led it to accept Rafiq Hariri as Lebanon's prime minister in October 1992. Hariri, a Sunni Muslim who also held Saudi citizenship, was a fabulously wealthy businessman. He used corruption to maintain power, was ready to work with Syria and its Lebanese lackeys, and had little interest in Lebanon's poorer people.

But he also was dedicated to economic reconstruction and wanted to see Lebanon independent. The deal struck between him and the Assad regime was that Hariri would work on rebuilding the country after the debilitating civil war while Damascus and its clients handled political matters. Hariri kept his part of the bargain, mobilizing aid and loans from both the West and Gulf Arab states.

Yet the Syrians wanted to keep a tight grip, constantly manipulating Lebanese politics and playing off the numerous politicians ready to serve Damascus's interests. In 1998 Hafiz decided to extend the term of the compliant President Elias al-Hrawi, which required amending the country's constitution. Hariri opposed the plan. And so one week before the September 3 vote, Hafiz summoned Hariri to Damascus and in a short meeting apparently made him an offer he could not refuse. Hariri and his party suddenly voted as Hafiz desired. Hariri had bowed to Syria but would not kneel; on October 20 he resigned as prime minister.

In Lebanon, Syrian General Ghazi Kanaan was Hafiz's proconsul, the real ruler. When a former member of Lebanon's parliament, Yahya Shamas, refused to sell Kanaan a piece of land he wanted, the man was jailed on drug trafficking charges.[46]

Elections, too, were stage-managed by Syria to produce the desired results. From 1990 on, no one openly critical of Syria's presence or demanding its withdrawal was elected to parliament. The techniques used to ensure this result included the manipulation of electoral district lines, the granting of citizenship to 300,000 Syrians (equal to 10 percent of Lebanon's entire population), bribery, having voters put prepared ballots in boxes in front of Syrian agents, and so on. During the 1996 parliamentary campaign, Hizballah secretary-general Hassan Nasrallah told a rally that his group had irreversibly decided to run its own lists. A week later, after being summoned to Damascus, he announced that he had changed his mind. When an independent-minded member of parliament tried to lease billboards for his campaign, the company was pressured into turning down his business and replacing his posters with those of the rival Syrian-backed candidates.[47]

What made this strategy even more remarkable was that the United States was enlisted to support it. To encourage Syrian participation in the peace process, the State Department kept its criticisms of Syria's methods very mild. After Syria had sabotaged the peace process, the United States merely encouraged Syria to make sure the Lebanese election results did not put too many Hizballah candidates in office. Syria was being paid off for merely distributing power to its own clients somewhat differently.

During the 1990s, then, Syria survived intact despite tremendous problems and pressures. In general, it had done so through intransigence coupled with stalling and minimal accommodation where necessary. Only the Turks, by going to the brink of war, had forced Syria to change its behavior on one secondary issue.

Speaking of the prospects of Syria-Israel peace, a senior Western diplomat remarked, "It would be a terrible tragedy if both sides cannot find a way to make it happen. This is the best opportunity to solve the problem for a long time."[48] This was truly the best chance ever to solve the conflict, but Syria preferred the "tragedy" of failure over the "opportunity" for a breakthrough. And as discussed, this was not an irrational choice from the regime's standpoint.

There existed a basic contradiction between peace with Israel and Syria's ruling worldview, ideology, geostrategic interests, and regime. This is one of the most important truths so often not understood about Syria and the Palestinians and the Iranians, Hamas and Hizballah, and Saddam Hussein.

True, peace would have permitted an end of conflict. But the Syrian regime needed the conflict to continue in order to mobilize its own people. Peace would have enabled a thoroughgoing reform of the Syrian economy. But such a reform would be a disaster for the regime, removing control of wealth from its hands and creating an independent middle class that would be the foundation of an opposition movement. Peace would have enabled a reduction of military budget, but keeping the army happy and providing privileges for elite officers was vital for the rulers. In every case, this logic of regime maintenance applied. With peace, Syria would no longer have leverage in the Arab world; rather it would face domestic critics (especially Islamists) and foreign ones trying to outradical Damascus. Without peace, Syria could outradical them.

The Syrian regime had always seen its caution in the 1990s as only temporary. Having won then while being on the defensive, Syria would return to the offensive in the new century under its first new leader in thirty years.

CHAPTER SIX

DICTATOR AND SON, INC.

It is not an easy thing to divine the character of Hafiz or Bashar al-Assad. In comparison, men like Yasir Arafat and Saddam Hussein were open books, colorful public performers who loved the crowd's attention and gloried in being dictators. But Hafiz was one of the most anticharismatic figures ever to boss an entire country, while Bashar seems a strange hybrid of eccentric bungler and crafty strategist who has far from grown into his role.

Hafiz rose from the huts of his ancestors' remote village to the marble palaces of power. Not only did he rule Syria for thirty years, but he elevated his Alawite people from the despised, impoverished infidels of an exotic non-Muslim creed to become masters of the country. Unlike Saddam Hussein or Arafat, he was not a flamboyant risk-taker but a shrewd calculator whose dealing with such diplomatic grandmasters as Henry Kissinger made him admired by them.

One key to this tale is that Hafiz, unlike Yasir and Saddam, two civilians who liked to put on uniforms and play soldier, was a professional military man who had followed the career of officer, not politician. Like his fellow former air force general Egyptian president Husni Mubarak, Hafiz came from a world where discipline was supposed to be the highest virtue and having too much personality could be dangerous. His military background taught him to listen to staff advice and to make sure there was a clear chain of command. This was not a man who could sway masses, but he didn't need to because he had come to power by ordering soldiers, not making speeches at mass rallies. Hafiz might have worn only business suits thereafter, but he was never quite out of uniform.

Fortunately for Hafiz, he did not have to act like a politician. Because he did not like going out very much, he worked mostly from home in the palace.

He did not tour gladly or rejoice in making speeches. There was nothing attractive or zestful in his mien; he was a sort of Arab equivalent of the gray Soviet leaders such as Leonid Brezhnev. His daily life was secluded; his manner, stiff. In meetings or interviews, Hafiz sat straight and still and rarely gestured. Such a man could never have risen in the world of politicians or staged a real revolution, as opposed to a palace military coup against other officers.

If Hafiz was indeed the fox of Damascus, perhaps his greatest skill in being so—at least after his initial period in power—was an ability to be changeless, to say no in the service of the status quo. He knew how to maneuver, but he used this ability to stay in the same place, swimming strenuously and skillfully to tread water.

Born in 1930 in a village near Latakia in the Alawite heartland of Syria, Hafiz belonged to the Matawira tribe. He was educated locally and went to the air academy in 1952. That was a fateful year for Arab nationalist military officers since their colleagues in Egypt set an example by seizing power and establishing the first Arab nationalist regime. By then Hafiz had already been a Ba'th party member for five years, being simultaneously a pilot and a revolutionary conspirator in uniform.

After a three-year-long exile in Egypt where Ba'th officers were sent by Nasser to be kept out of the way during the 1958–1961 Egypt-Syria union, Hafiz returned home when a coup broke it up. After Salah Jadid's 1966 coup Hafiz became minister of defense and air force commander. By the time he took power in his own right, then, Hafiz had almost twenty-five years of political intrigue and twenty years of military experience behind him, far more than Nasser or Saddam Hussein possessed when they became dictators.

Aside from his character and training, Hafiz's approach was to prove one part realism, one part ideology, and one part family-based mafia. While his seizure of power in 1970 was on behalf of the Ba'th party's military committee and he pushed the Ba'th politicians into irrelevance, the regime did retain a strong element of being run by a top-down, institutionalized party with a clear ideological line. In this sense, Hafiz was not an individualistic dictator lusting for power and accumulating wealth so much as he was the chief bureaucrat. The Ba'th party was designed by its founders as the Arab nationalist version of a Communist party, and it modeled itself on the Soviet Union's approach. The regime sought to control every aspect of life—the economy, military, literary, media, schools, and mosques—both from imitation and from an understanding that this was the best way to stay in power.

At the same time, though, Hafiz was also the head of a family, clan, and ethnic community, chief guardian of their power to use the state as a personal or collective source of wealth and security. His Alawite heritage was, literally, written on his forehead, artificially made higher in the old Alawite custom of laying a baby on a wooden cradle without a pillow. He was responsible for the community's welfare, prosperity, and even its survival among a hostile majority. In this aspect of his leadership, the parallels between the Assad saga and "The Godfather" were strong. He was in effect Don Hafiz who, like Don Vito Corleone, survived by placing relatives and kinsman in key positions, doing people favors they would have to repay some day, and recruiting among his own ethnic community. In Hafiz's case, this meant Alawites instead of Sicilians.

In keeping with the regime's tribal aspect, Hafiz intended to pass power to his oldest son, Basil, in the role of Sonny Corleone. But like that character in "The Godfather," he was killed on a highway, albeit in an accident that was his own fault. Another son, Majd, was completely bypassed in the power arrangements since he, like Fredo Corleone, had psychological infirmities. Hafiz thus turned to Bashar, in the role of Michael Corleone, plucking him from his "legitimate" career and quickly grooming him as successor.

Continuing to parallel "The Godfather," there was a tempestuous love affair between the don's daughter, Connie Corleone, played by Bushra al-Assad, and a minor soldier in the mob, Carlo Rizzi played by Asif Shawkat. As in the film, brother Basil hated Asif and opposed the marriage. But, unlike the fictional version, after Basil died Bushra and Asif married and lived happily ever after. Asif became Bashar's right-hand man, his consigliore. As head of military intelligence, Shawkat was one of the three—along with Mahir al-Assad, Bashar's other brother—most powerful figures in Syria.

Like Don Corleone, Hafiz also did a good job of moving aside his own generation to clear the way for Bashar, though Ghazi Kanaan, long-time Syrian strongman in Lebanon and later interior minister—like Corleone lieutenant Salvatore Tessio—had to be killed because he would not accept the new order. As with the Corleones, the Assads owned numerous politicians and judges while skimming off profits from a number of criminal enterprises, smuggling, drugs, counterfeiting, and the protection racket. And certainly, the Assads like their fictional doubles did not hesitate to remove permanently those they viewed as dangerous rivals on their own turf or in Lebanon, making sure that they slept with the fishes. Many a Lebanese politician was also made an offer he couldn't refuse though, at least so far, none is known to have woken up to find a horse's head in his bed.

Probably Hafiz, like Vito Corleone, hoped that his college-educated son would represent a combination of continuity and added sophistication for the regime. If these two patriarchs had any concern about the succession it was whether their heir had the needed ruthlessness to be the dictator of their respective empires. In both cases, they need not have worried.

Born on September 11, 1965, Bashar was educated in Syria. He spent six years at Damascus University and graduated from its medical school, worked at the Tishrin Military Hospital there between 1988 and 1992, then went to London only to complete his medical residency in ophthalmology. He was there for just two years—there is no reason to believe that experience had much effect on him—being recalled home in January 1994, when Basil died in the car crash.[1] Thus Bashar was a child of the regime, brought up in the narrow confines of its elite, his playmates being from this group. In contrast, his father had a much wider circle of acquaintances and broader experience of life.

Once Bashar took power in 2000, the regime became even more of an Alawite and family affair. One brother, Mahir, heads the Presidential Guard; a cousin on his mother's side, Adnan Makhlouf, commands the Republican Guard; and two other cousins, Adnan and Muhammad al-Assad, are leaders of the Struggle Companies. Thus, all these elite forces are in the hands of dependable men. Indeed, almost the only non-Alawite among them merely confirms the rule of hereditary power since that person was Manaf Tlas, son of perennial defense minister and one of Hafiz's oldest friends, Mustafa Tlas.

But, to return to Hafiz, it is impossible to determine just how much he acted or felt himself a dictator who made decisions as he personally pleased.[2] Writing of his negotiations with Hafiz after the 1973 war, Kissinger recalled that before receiving the U.S. proposal for a disengagement agreement with Israel, Assad called in Chief of Staff General Hikmat Shihabi and Tlas; interestingly, both men were Sunni Muslims. "Clearly, he did not wish to take sole responsibility for major steps. And he wanted to be sure that his colleagues (and potential rivals) could not claim later that he had been taken in."

Perhaps this was an example of Assad's basic style, or possibly it was more typical of the earlier period of his rule. Yet Hafiz was also aware of his country's tumultuous history, his society's tendency toward factionalism, his regime's lack of a majority communal base, the potential appeal of the Islamists, and the need of Syria to compete in militancy with other Arab states.[3]

Twenty years later, Kissinger's successor, James Baker, conducted similar negotiations with Hafiz, who also then cited public opinion as a factor to be taken into account in decision making. "If," remarked Assad, "you were in my place . . . you wouldn't be more flexible than I am now." At another point, he remarked that if he went too far in Arab-Israeli peacemaking, "We will lose Arab domestic public opinion. . . . They will know what is going on. This would not only be adventurism, it would be a form of suicide. It is one thing to adopt a suicidal policy if it brings benefits to the people, but it is truly fool-hardy if there is no positive result."[4]

In contrast to Kissinger, Baker thought such statements were actually mere negotiating tactics to gain concessions, concealing the fact that Assad exercised sole power. At one point, Assad told Baker, "I can't give you an answer without consulting with the institutions of the party and the Progressive National Front." Baker wrote, "It was, I knew, the ultimate brush-off; there was no one in the Syrian Arab Republic with whom Assad needed to consult, except him-self. 'Okay let's leave it,' I abruptly concluded, slamming my portfolio shut to make sure Assad absorbed my irritation."[5]

Yet both Kissinger and Baker were looking at the issue in a Western con-text. Even if Assad could do whatever he wanted, it was certainly playing it safer to bring in others—especially non-Alawites—to take responsibility, to make sure they agreed and would not use any hint of relative moderation against him. The rulers knew that the majority of their people might easily hate them if they stopped enhancing their popularity by demagoguery and gave up their use of the United States and Israel as external enemies. Assad might have sole power within his own regime but he also knew, based on his life experience, that another regime would come along if he made a mistake. To him and his son, real moderation seemed the ultimate error.

Moreover, the public opinion aspect of Syrian politics could be seen in a different light. Having the issue of anti-Westernism and the Arab-Israeli con-flict were major pillars of the regime's survival. To abandon them would under-mine the whole structure of the Syrian system. The problem was not just how the public would react to the decision itself but how public opinion would be generated after the decision was implemented. Public opinion was something to be feared but only if it were not managed and manipulated properly.

If Syria faced domestic opposition to making peace with Israel, after all, this was largely an artifact of its own policies. All Syrian institutions—schools, mosques, media, organizations, government—vilified Israel and the United States without the slightest effort at even the tiniest balance. First-grade stu-dents were taught in their textbooks that "the Jews are criminal villains." In math, multiplication problems included such problems as how many "Jewish soldiers" had been killed. As for scholarship, Syrian defense minister Tlas had written a doctoral dissertation, published as a book by a state company, claim-ing that Jews murdered children in order to use their blood for making Passover matzos.[6]

These activities were not the product of popular demand but of systematic government-organized incitement. Such a strategy was useful for a regime that needed to keep attention and hatred focused on foreign enemies to excuse its own domestic shortcomings and justify its rule. Yet given Syria's political culture as well as the cumulative effect of such activities, there was a very strong reservoir of wildly passionate hatred against Israel and the same applied to the United States.

In this regard, Assad made a very revealing remark to Baker: "We don't want anyone to say we have given up what we have been talking about for twenty years."[7] That statement applied to both kinds of domestic critics: those hard-liners who would claim the regime had sold out and those liberals who would say that once the conflict was settled, there was no more need for a dictatorship.

The same problem applied to foreign rivals who would love a chance to portray themselves as more militant than Syria. Radicals, such as Iraq or the PLO, would try to subvert Syria as a traitorous hypocrite while Syria would no longer have its militancy to use as a stick to beat moderates. And once Islamism became a major force on the regional scene, both aspects of this issue—the offensive and defensive uses of radicalism—would become more important than ever.

Assad told Kissinger, "People here who have been nurtured for twenty-six years on hatred [of Israel] can't be swayed overnight by our changing our courses." But his regime continued to nurture that hate for the next twenty-six years in its own interests, ensuring that any such change would continue to be both unattractive to the people and unprofitable for the regime. Chief of Staff Shihabi told Kissinger that any disengagement agreement with Israel had to be one that they "could defend domestically against bitter radical opposition."[8] Yet by the same token, fomenting militancy against Israel at home and abroad would raise radical opposition against Syria's regional rivals, a weapon it used to dominate Lebanon, fend off U.S. influence, and for many other purposes as well.

The bottom line was that Assad knew how Syria worked far better than those foreigners who constantly wanted to teach him to think as a "pragmatist" and lecture him about where Syria's "true" interests lay. Militancy and survival were intertwined, and the regime was always ready to pay a high cost for maintaining them. This was its own brand of pragmatism, and it made very good sense for anyone sitting in a Damascus palace who wanted to continue that lifestyle.

This same set of criteria applied to Hafiz's policies in the 1990s. In each case, he made the minimum possible nod toward moderation and flexibility but only to maintain the status quo. Like the air force pilot he had been, Hafiz nursed his stricken plane back to base. His task was made easier by the fact that no one attacked him when he was in distress, mistakenly thinking their mercy would convince him that they were not enemies after all. Unfortunately, confidence-building measures do not work with someone who needs your enmity.

And so for many reasons, when Hafiz died in June 2000 and turned over Syria to Bashar, he left a legacy both rich and troubled. On one hand, the regime was secure at home; on the other hand, it faced a dreadful economic situation, its society was stagnant, and it was isolated both in the region and internationally. Given both sides of this equation—at least viewed superficially, ignorantly, and from a Western perspective—the thirty-four-year-old Bashar was expected to make major reforms.

These major reforms did not happen. But his father's work in clearing the way for Bashar, one of Hafiz's most brilliant accomplishments, did guarantee the son's hold on power. He first began with Basil, born in March 1962, who was groomed for the succession. Basil went to officers' school and was moved steadily up in the army until he became commander of a Republican Guard brigade. And along the way he was also head of the Syrian Olympic riding team and both founder and head of the country's computer society.

But Hafiz had to start from scratch in 1994 when Basil rammed his car at high speed into a bridge abutment on the Damascus airport road. Hafiz knew he would have to risk his regime's future by accepting second best, but was determined to make it work. The process to prepare Bashar for the presidency and ensure that the elite accepted him took six years. Bashar was sent to officers' courses and then made a Republican Guard brigade commander. He rose quickly from captain (1994) to major (1995), lieutenant colonel (1997), colonel (1999), and finally—on taking over as president—to lieutenant general (2000).

Meanwhile, Hafiz pushed senior officials into retirement to eliminate any alternative candidates, potential challengers, or even carping critics who thought they could do a better job: Chief of Staff General Hikmat Shihabi went in 1998, after fourteen years at that post, as did intelligence chief Ali Douba. Vice-President Abd al-Halim Khaddam was clearly on the way out as Bashar took over the task of being Syrian imperial satrap over Lebanon. Among the others retired were Chief of Staff Ali Aslan; his deputies Abd al-Rahman al-Sayyad, Farouq Ibrahim Issa, Ibrahim al-Safi, Shafiq Fayyad, and Ahmad Abd al-Nabi; the head of the Political Security branch of intelligence, Adnan Badr Hassan; and the head of Military Intelligence, Hassan al-Khalil.

Almost none of them made any fuss. Why should they? They were in their later years, had been in power for a long time, were wealthy, and had no ambition to seize power. The regime would continue to look after them and their families. There was no great incentive to rock the boat. Indeed, in many cases their sons would hold high positions under Bashar and their daughters intermarried with the rest of the elite. Hafiz did not need to tell them, "Don't go against the family," because they were reasonably satisfied members of the family.

The timing of this bloodless purge went hand in hand with Hafiz's physical decline. He was unable to open the December 1998 parliamentary session in person, allegedly due to a cold. Visitors noted his difficulty in focusing. When in March 1999 he was sworn in for his fifth term as president, his inaugural address was distributed in writing rather than read by him. Aside from everything else, the pressure of his fading health and the impending transition doomed any prospect for a Syria-Israel peace deal at this stage.

Domestically, however, things went very smoothly. Everyone seemed eager to facilitate Bashar's coronation. There was only one big exception during Hafiz's lifetime: Rifaat al-Assad, Hafiz's younger brother, who thought he should be heir to the throne. Instead, in 1998, his title as vice-president was taken away from him.[9] Rifaat had long been a source of trouble for the family; but once the succession neared, any threat, however minor, could no longer be tolerated.

Born in 1937, Rifaat may have held an honorary PhD in politics from the Soviet Academy of Sciences, but he was a thug through and through. His career in the Syrian army, which he joined in 1963, was entirely due to family and party connections. Within two years he became commander of a special security force and helped in his brother's takeover of power. He then became head of the elite Defense Companies unit, Syria's equivalent of Iraq's Republican Guard.[10]

Rifaat's corrupt enterprises were so sizable that in the 1970s a weekly market was held in Damascus just to sell his smuggled goods. He gained the title "King of the Oriental Carpets" because his men in Lebanon took from anyone whatever woven floor coverings took their fancy. Such criminal activities and growing power did not endear him to the real career officers who commanded the army. They waited for him to make a mistake and they were not disappointed. When Hafiz had a heart attack in November 1983, Rifaat sent his units to grab key parts of Damascus in a bid to ensure he would be the successor. But Hafiz did not die. As soon as he recovered, Hafiz began whittling down his wild brother's power. He took the Defense Companies away from him and relegated Rifaat to a prestigious but meaningless post as one of Syria's three vice-presidents.

Unwisely, Rifaat again tried to seize power. According to the Assad court biographer, Hafiz sent his mother from their home village to stay at Rifaat's house. Then Hafiz went all by himself to confront his brother in front of the matriarch. Cornered and unwilling to upset their mother, Rifaat backed down in exchange for a promise that his interests would be left intact.[11]

Hafiz was willing to let Rifaat keep his wealth but not his influence. First, he sent Rifaat to the Soviet Union on a mission in May 1984 and then purged any officials thought to sympathize with him. Unwelcome in Damascus, Rifaat went on to Switzerland, France, and Spain. Only after his mother's death in 1992 did he return to Damascus, being forced to leave once again in 1998, when he lost the vice-presidential post.

Rifaat's second exile was to ensure he would not get in Bashar's way. Rifaat tried to cause trouble and enjoyed ample media support, since his son was head of the London-based Arab News Network satellite television station, established in 1997 to back Rifaat's interests. He tried rather ineptly to stir up trouble. Finally, in September 1999, regime security forces invaded his Latakia estate, much of which was on public land he had grabbed (11,410 square meters, according to the official complaint). A few shots were fired but his guards were easily overcome, after which the regime closed his offices in Damascus and arrested his remaining supporters.[12] The government warned that if he ever came back to Syria, he might be put on trial. Rifaat was finished and the family's unity ensured.

And so there was no alternative to Bashar, who was portrayed to the Syrian public as a bright, young, caring, modern leader. He was promoted rapidly upward in the army. Off he went to Arab capitals and to Paris to familiarize himself—and his hosts—with his future leadership role. He hung out with Jordan's prince and soon-to-be king Abdallah, who was temporarily persuaded that they were soul mates, a new set of moderate, pragmatic, forward-looking leaders. "Bashar," he explained, "is like me; we are the Internet generation."[13]

Paid-off Arab reporters wrote paeans of praise to the young paragon of virtue, not only in the Syrian state-controlled media but in foreign Arabic newspapers as well. According to the London-based *al-Sharq al-Awsat,* quoting a "Syrian source," Bashar "reflects the spirit of youth aspiring for its nation's resurgence and catching up with the age and its technical developments, particularly computers, the Internet, information technology, and modernization of the state's work processes." Everybody is happy to see Bashar as their leader because "he has the high qualifications . . . that will consolidate stability, continue the economic and social modernization and development, and deal with the challenges facing Syria with a high spirit of national and pan-Arab responsibility."[14]

Those reading *al-Majalla* on Sunday, June 6, 1999, for example, would have learned that Bashar was an intellectual, fluent in French and English; modest, tall and slim; and an avid reader of science books. He was disciplined, loved justice, and surrounded himself with other intellectuals. According to this article, "He believes that man is the essence and sole purpose of all aspects of activities and development. He believes that modern technology in general and information technology (IT) in particular provides a real opportunity and the means for raising the Syrian people's living standards." The author, however, also expected no one would notice that most of the article was plagiarized from a Syrian Computer Society press release, in other words from a piece of Syrian government propaganda.[15]

Bashar's involvement with that society was one of the highlights of his resume. He was elected chairman after the death of his brother Basil in 1989. Basil had been a thug and playboy whose only interest in surfing would have been of the beach variety. Bashar's being president of the society no more proved his interest in high technology than did his inheriting the presidency prove his political perspicacity.[16]

When Hafiz died and Bashar stepped up to the plate, some Arab intellectuals felt as if it were the final insult, the ultimate humiliation of how a "progressive" republic had turned into the Assad family's property. A radical regime that had always rejected hereditary monarchy as disgusting now behaved as if Syria were a family fiefdom. Syria had always been a dictatorship, but now it seemed to be a feudal one, openly mocking the values it supposedly espoused.

The Palestinian writer Hassan Khadir mourned that nothing had changed "after thirty years of autocratic and totalitarian rule" in Syria. There seemed to be no hope for democracy, he concluded. What made it even more depressing for Arab democrats was how typical Syria was of Arab polities. Another Palestinian, Hani Habib, wrote, "The 'Syrian constitution' is in fact the constitution of all the Arabs from the [Atlantic] ocean to the [Persian] Gulf."[17]

In contrast to the disgust of so many Arab intellectuals, Western observers thought Bashar was a jolly good fellow. Before taking power he had built a good impression in the West, which was of course a deliberate strategy to ease the transition. Officials and journalists who met him concluded that Bashar was intelligent—which was true—but also that he was forward-looking and knowledgeable about Western ideas, which was false. In short, they were taken in completely. Thus, he was given a clean slate and a fresh start. Without doing anything, he was regarded with expectation and hope, another edition of the endless exercise in wishful thinking with which many in the West view the

Middle East. For example, Bashar had spent two years in London; Hafiz's visit to Paris in 1998 was his first official visit to the non-Communist West in twenty-two years.[18] Bashar was thus relatively more exposed to Western influence, but the contact was still quite limited and had no real effect on his worldview, as his later statements would show.

The way the regime machine steamrollered him into power after his father's death at the age of sixty-nine on June 10, 2000,[19] should have left no doubt as to his future course. First came the funeral on June 14, an event quite dramatic for the old, uncharismatic dictator. Women wept; young men slashed their chests and bled in mourning; people collapsed from grief and heat exhaustion. Hundreds of thousands turned out to chant his name as the coffin was carried, appropriately, on a gun carriage. A hundred foreign delegations from fifty countries and including a dozen heads of state came to pay their respects, with condolence calls made to Bashar. The coffin lay in state at a hilltop palace, then made the trip—the precise reversal of Hafiz's life journey—back the 200 miles north to his home village of Qardaha.[20]

Then, Khaddam, as acting president, managed the actual succession process quite smoothly. Bashar was unanimously elected Ba'th party secretary-general on June 18, nominated as president two days later, approved by parliament one week thereafter, and elected president on July 11 with 97.29 percent of the votes.[21] Since his father was elected in 1999 by 99.9 percent of the votes,[22] the 2.6 percent reduction in unanimity must represent the degree of democratic opening the new era brought about.

There was, however, a small impediment. Syria's constitution mandated that the president be more than forty years old; Bashar was six years too young. It was amended with the speed of summer lightning to fit Bashar's age of 34 years old precisely. Only one parliament member, Munzir al-Mousili, merely dared note that the legislature was legally required to say why it was reducing the minimum age for president. The speaker cut him off and Syrian television turned off its cameras, resuming coverage only to show the speaker attacking Mousili and concluding, "The respected member's sinful part of his soul led him into error, and he just realized his mistake and repented."[23]

In his inaugural speech of July 17, Bashar made clear his view of democracy:

We cannot apply the democracy of others on ourselves. Western democracy ... is the outcome of a long history that resulted in customs and traditions that distinguish the current culture of Western societies. ... To apply what they have we have to live their history. ... As this is obviously impossible, our democratic experience must be unique to us, stemming from our history, culture, and civilization and as a response to the needs of our society and the requirements of our reality.[24]

This of course makes perfect sense in principle. But the problem is that Bashar defined the status quo as the perfect system for Syrian society. At most, as he expressed it in that speech, all that was needed to make it work a bit better was to reduce inefficient administration, waste, and corruption.[25]

Bashar had an easy time purging or urging into retirement the rest of the old guard; thus, the rejection of reform cannot be blamed on their influence. Indeed, within his first two years in office, three-quarters of the top sixty officials in the regime's government and military whom he had inherited in 2000, men who had been thoroughly screened by Hafiz, had been replaced.[26] The cabinet was fired and deposed Prime Minister Mahmoud Zu'bi "committed suicide" on the verge of being arrested in an "anti-corruption campaign."[27] These actions neatly identified corruption with the previous generation.

The last phase came in June 2005, when the remaining veterans were retired, including Defense Minister Mustafa Tlas; the two-vice presidents, Zuhayr al-Masharqa and Khaddam; and the assistant secretary-general of the Ba'th party, Abdallah al-Ahmar, and others. The party's Regional Command was made smaller and packed with Bashar's men. In October 2005 came the apparent assassination of Ghazi Kanaan, Syria's veteran viceroy in Lebanon who had been pushed aside to become interior minister. Kanaan, who had just been questioned by international investigators looking into Syrian involvement in the murder of Lebanese political leader Rafiq Hariri, was offered up as an old-guard scapegoat for the killing. Khaddam, Kanaan's friend, fled to Paris, presuming he was next on the list.

A typical and visible example of the gap between the pretense of reform and the reality of continuity is the cult of personality for the leader. An old Syrian joke had it that the population of Syria was double what the statistics said and consisted of 50 percent people and 50 percent pictures of Hafiz. Bashar said that he did not want so many pictures of himself displayed publicly, and many Western newspapers reported that this change was being made. In fact, the cult continued. There are posters of Bashar everywhere in endless variety: versions with and without sunglasses, bicycling with his family, shown with his wife, and the three Assad brothers together—Basil, Mahir, and Bashar.

But was Bashar up to the job or simply a poster boy instead of a strong leader? His appearance was not encouraging. He is tall, gangly even, and looks something like a teenager who grew up so fast he is not yet quite comfortable with his body. At the age of forty, his mustache—a sign of virility in the Arab-speaking world—remains sparse. He giggles, gesticulates, and is clearly not completely comfortable as a speaker. During one speech, he lost his balance and crashed into a microphone. Some of his more outrageous remarks are ad-libbed, as he departs from his script and says things that get him into some trouble. Bashar seems to be the world's first nerd dictator.

At the same time, though, he is genuinely popular among at least young, urban, and more educated Syrians because he, too, is young and relatively so-phisticated. The fact that he appears in some pictures with his wife is in itself quite different from the previous generation's practice. Ironically, this would-be champion of anti-Westernism has an appeal precisely because he seems more modern and Western in habit and culture, the image in which his counterparts seek to cast themselves. In private, he is adept at fooling those who want to be-lieve he is a closet moderate, seducing them into giving him a good press or other favors, then slamming the door on his promises.

To get the flavor of Bashar's thinking, one must get the sense of his rheto-ric. He sounds like the radical Ba'th party leader that he is. There is no hint of Western-style thinking or moderation in his public statements. They are full of the extremist phrases and analyses—sounding like knock-offs of Soviet Com-munist-style views—that have been typical of Syrian leaders for decades. Cer-tainly he is a warmer speaker than his very stiff father, but the message is nonetheless chilling.

As a case in point, take Bashar's speech at Damascus University, on No-vember 10, 2005.[28] This is an especially interesting talk since he gave it at his alma mater to an audience among the most technocratic and intellectual in Syria. If Bashar was going to expose his more visionary, reformist side, it would certainly have been at such a forum.

In fact, as shown by both his speeches and his actions, Bashar is virtually indifferent to economic or social issues. He has no serious concern for educa-tion or development or building institutions. Nor does he show any real knowledge about or understanding of other countries. His sole message is the traditional one: The Arabs are under assault by evil forces and must respond with resistance.

No serious analysis comes from Bashar, only a caricatured world of con-spiracies, plots, and enemy agents, of traitors and heroic warriors—the echo of similar speeches given for a half-century, and which with very little change could have been made by any of the last five dictators of Syria. Indeed, with a few twists of rhetoric and specific references, it could have been given by Nasser, Arafat, or Saddam Hussein, among others. It is also revealing that

Bashar's sole mention of Islam is to ridicule the Americans for talking about Islamist terrorists in Iraq. Religion, despite all pretenses at convenient moments, is of no importance for Bashar and does not really stir his feelings.

In the university speech, Bashar complains that developments in the region have tragic consequences for which "Arab citizens pay a high price in terms of their livelihood, security and dignity." Yet these developments never relate to internal economic shortcomings, corruption, or the failure of reform, but only to international political events for which the Arabs are blameless. Indeed, these problems are the deliberate creation of "international circles, and their agents in our Arab establishment," which promote "destructive political schemes under exciting names." In other words, the real threat is the idea of reform and democracy, whose local proponents are nothing more than enemy agents acting against Arab interests.

When Bashar talks about perilous threats, he is never referring to radical Islamism. Indeed, his complaints and analysis are almost identical to theirs. For Bashar, the danger comes from a Western-directed "media, cultural and scientific war which targets our young generations," trying to separate them "from their identity, heritage and history . . . pushing them to surrender to the illusion of certain defeat." The problem, then, is that some say the Arabs have been defeated—that is, they have not destroyed Israel or defeated the West and thus should try something else. Bashar defends the continuation of all the old policies and ideas, ignoring their complete failure for a half-century.

It is ironic that he says the brainwashing war targets young people "because they do not recall, or have not lived the details of the political events in the past two decades and earlier." The problem is the exact opposite. *He* is the one who wants to erase that history of so many lost wars and wasted opportunities. Precisely that memory is the factor that motivates those advocating a change of course.

In Bashar's mind, that tale of woe should rather be regarded as the good old days, the golden age of resistance. "Syria was able then to stand the storms blowing from every direction" and ensured the campaign to destroy the Arabs "failed to achieve their objectives." He wants to revive the worldview and strategies of the years before the 1990s, erasing a time when Syria had to adapt to such changes as the Soviet Union's collapse, Saddam's defeat in Kuwait, and the U.S. status as sole superpower.

What Bashar wants is not change toward reform or peace or democratization but a renewal of the old struggle. He told his young audience, "Your generation will prove to the enemies and the opponents that it is not less capable of standing fast and challenging than those who preceded them." It should accept the glorious inheritance from previous generations. There can be no lessening in the battle since "our age, like any other, is the age of the powerful only; and there is no place in it for the weak. Rather than consider compromise, Syrians must mobilize "all our national energies and capabilities in order to protect and safeguard our . . . independence and sovereignty" from the Zionist-imperialist danger.

Again, Bashar gives no hint that the best way to do so is through economic development and internal social improvement. Rather, Syria is targeted by some foreign powers precisely because it wants independence and they seek to impose their will upon it. In fact, of course, Syria has never been attacked because of its independence but due to the regime's efforts to destroy the independence of others, including Iraq, Israel, Jordan, Lebanon, the Palestinians, and Turkey. The battles Syrian governments fought have been offensive, not defensive in nature.

Bashar then asks: Has Syria made mistakes to justify the criticisms of it? His answer is no. All it did was refuse to bargain over the just resistance in Lebanon, Iraq, and among the Palestinians. It was only because Syria is right that the country is being attacked. The core problem, according to Bashar, is that Syria proudly upholds its "pan-Arab national identity." Enemies want Syria to forget this identity so they can become its masters.

If foreigners criticize Syria over its failure to make reforms, then, this merely shows their desire to dominate the country and proves the reforms are merely a form of sabotage. "We did not know that they cared more for us than we cared for ourselves. We did not know that they were appointed as our guardians." Hardly surprising in a dictatorship, Bashar wants people to believe that the people's interests are totally identical with the dictator's interests. Thus, anyone who attacks the regime attacks the people as well.

But Bashar goes beyond that, and in this he is no doubt sincere: The reforms being pushed are disastrous for the system as it currently exists. He explains, defining freedom as having no "controls so that they could blackmail any regime from the inside." Economic reform really means "they want us to open our markets" in exchange for very little in return. Cultural reform means "to get out of our skin and become a copy of them." So what is it appropriate for external forces to do? Only to "restore our occupied land and to prevent aggression against us" and to support Syria's current economy. If Syria does not get everything it wants or is asked to give anything in return, it is always better to say no.

Take, for example, the problem of Iraq's "political and security chaos." The crisis there, Bashar explains, is a major danger to Syria and the Arab world because it is "in the process of fragmentation and disintegration." He is hardly going to admit that this situation's cause is an ethnic civil war provoked in large part by Syria itself. Bashar says that talk about Syria being behind the insurgency is a lie to destroy the good relations between the Syrian and Iraqi peoples, just one more aspect of imperialist propaganda. Instead, he attributes the conflict to a Western conspiracy aimed at "eliminating [Iraq's] Arab identity."

It is not credible for Bashar to claim that Syria cannot control its borders. A tightly controlled dictatorship with a ubiquitous security apparatus is hardly so helpless. There is no case on record of Syria not being able to control its borders except when the government decided they should be crossed by subversive or terrorist groups attacking its neighbors. However, if the West is so concerned about the problem, Bashar invites them to provide technology to his intelligence forces.

Bashar cannot even engage honestly with the fact that, aside from Syria's own interference, the dispute in Iraq arises from the communal interests of a non-Arab Kurdish and Shia majority that understandably wants to control its own country. Of course, this is certainly what Bashar fears could happen in Syria as well if the Sunni Arab Muslim majority were to rise up. By destabilizing Iraq, however, isn't he also helping to create a precedent that could endanger Syria far more?

The ironies of his worldview abound. Promoting an Arab nationalist ideology make good sense from Bashar's perspective to take the curse off the minority status of his regime and maximize its appeal at home and abroad. Bashar defines Syria, with some real justification, as a multicultural success. The role model for the Arab-speaking world, he says, is "Syria in its diversity." After all, Sunni Arab Muslims, Alawites, Christians, Druze, and Kurds can live together peacefully under an Arab nationalist banner that suppresses communal conflicts. In contrast, a religious or ethnic definition of identity would lead to civil war or at least strife, possibly including the country's disintegration. Yet one might well ask at this point why it is that his regime has based its foreign policy on exacerbating such communal differences in Iraq, Lebanon, and Turkey.

This is especially true in Lebanon where, Bashar asserts, the West objects to Syrian control only because it wants to destroy the "patriotic" forces there and make that country "a base for conspiring against Syria and its pan-Arab stands" as well as an Israeli stooge. Bashar attributes the call for disarming Hizballah to Israel alone, ignoring the real Lebanese "patriotic forces" that believe only this step can make possible a stable, sovereign country. Equally, he omits the fact that the West supported Syrian domination of Lebanon for decades until the Lebanese majority itself rose against it, as well as the fact that Syria itself agreed to the disarming of all militias in the Taif Accord.

When it suited him, Bashar even implied that the international community wanted his troops to stay in Lebanon and thus its pull-out constituted a victory for Syria. Lebanon is now an anti-Syrian country and enemy agent. Syria, of course, Bashar says indignantly, had nothing to do with the killing of former Prime Minister Hariri, as all Lebanese politicians know. Those who seek "to destroy the Syrian-Lebanese relationship" would "destroy the region with it." For what is good for Syria is good for Lebanon and vice versa. But those who pushed Syria out, who "derive their power from the power of their [foreign] masters," will not long survive. Their fall "will not be far off." His policy amounts to a threat to plunge Lebanon into communal civil war unless it succumbs to the rule of Syria, Iran, and Hizballah.

The reasoning used by Bashar and the strategy arising from it, as we will see, reached its full development in 2006. It is driven and shaped by the most propagandistic notions, full of the spirit of belligerence—what he would call "resistance"—and of viewing the world with no shades of color. It endorses the disastrous last half-century of Arab history and brands those who disagree as enemies who must be smashed. Compromise is equated with surrender.

What Bashar represents, in political practice, is the Middle East version of Stalinism, doctrinaire and aggressive. Far from any interest in reform, he wants continuity. Bashar may well be both more dangerous and more extreme than his father. Hafiz arose in opposition to the ideologues of the Ba'th party. He came from a pragmatic background, in which one did whatever was needed to survive. For Hafiz, caution was a byword. His talent lay in political maneuvering rather than risk taking, ideological intoxication, or confusing propaganda with reality. No doubt life had imbued him with a large measure of cynicism.

In contrast, Bashar has a far more limited experience base—notwithstanding his two years in London—and is more prone to being a true believer who confuses slogans with strategy. He is also influenced by a real need to prove his toughness and orthodoxy. Bashar's statements constantly reveal this psychological need—which is also, of course, a political necessity: "It is important to gain respect, rather than sympathy. It is important to go with [firm] opinions and decisions."[29]

His father, of course, did not feel he had to prove anything. He was a career military officer, a pilot and real military commander, a political conspirator who outmaneuvered dangerous rivals to seize total power. For Hafiz, nothing could be more out of character than revolutionary romanticism. Disgusted with the dangerous risk-taking of the one-time colleagues he overthrew,

Hafiz considered Saddam and Arafat to be unreliable adventurers; Hizballah, a subordinate client; Iran, a necessary ally. He retained enough of the old Ba'th leftist secularism and the non-Muslim Alawite skepticism to distrust Islamists. Hafiz also was a realist in safeguarding whenever possible his links to other Arab regimes, especially Egypt, Iraq, and Saudi Arabia.

For Hafiz, Hizballah leader Hassan Nasrallah was a crude and somewhat distasteful instrument; for Bashar, he is a hero and role model. Hafiz refused even to meet with Nasrallah, while Bashar basks in his reflected glory, allowing the Lebanese Islamist to treat him as a boy to be patronized. Certainly Hafiz never would have treated Hizballah as an equal, much less act like head of the Hizballah fan club. Bashar's reverence seems quite sincere. To one visitor shortly after he took power, Bashar described Nasrallah as a man who understood broad social and public forces from whom he could learn a great deal. Bashar even invited Nasrallah to speak at a ceremony in his family's village on the first anniversary of Hafiz's death, a eulogy that must have set his father to spinning in his nearby grave.[30]

In addition, Bashar has let Syria slip more deeply into a junior partnership with Iran. As Khaddam put it, "Bashar Assad is not a strategic ally of Iran, only a strategic tool."[31] Khaddam knew that Hafiz would never have allowed his country to slip in that fashion. Bashar even let scores of billboards appear all over Syria showing Bashar, Nasrallah, and Iranian president Ahmadinejad as the revolutionary trinity. Hafiz, however, was not a man to let anyone forget for a moment who was the sole political figure to be worshiped in Syria.

Finally, Bashar is distant enough from the golden days of pan-Arabism to act like a Syrian nationalist who does not care what other Arab countries think about what he does. It is not just that Bashar is ready to insult them but that he seems to enjoy doing so unnecessarily. He does not just cope with Syrian isolation in the Arabic-speaking world but sees that status as a point of pride. While Hafiz maneuvered, Bashar charges straight ahead.

In a real sense, to continue with the Corleone analogy, what for Hafiz was business—a realistic assessment of what was needed at a given moment—is for Bashar more personal—the need to prove himself and his desire to fulfill the Ba'thist dream. For both men, radicalism made sense in terms of the regime's interests. But Bashar is dazzled by the means and more likely to lose sight of the more mundane purpose of his strategy.

Certainly, Hafiz's anti-Western policy made sense in terms of regime interests. Syria sided with the Soviet Union in exchange for very real material benefits, including thousands of Soviet military advisers and hundreds of advanced

Soviet-made fighter planes, antiaircraft and ground-to-ground missiles, tanks, and other equipment. Since the United States would not have wanted to replace Moscow and sponsor Assad's dictatorship, Damascus had no real alternative. Similarly, Syria refused to abandon its conflict with Israel or ambitions against other neighbors in order to obtain U.S. patronage.

Indeed, that last point contains an important clue. All Arab regimes opposed Israel; but only the radical regimes with designs on their Arab neighbors (Nasser's Egypt, Syria, Libya, and Iraq) had to maintain their general antagonism to the United States. Those states genuinely seeking to preserve their own sovereignty from aggressive Arab neighbors (Sadat's Egypt, Jordan, and Saudi Arabia) were able to follow a different policy. Washington does not inhibit their domestic systems but would oppose the radicals' foreign policy designs. Thus these relatively moderate states learned how to ensure their regimes' survival on their own terms while working with the West.

During the 1990s, Hafiz found his own way of temporarily doing this without actually changing either domestic stagnation or foreign ambitions. To deal with the crisis of Syria's weakness, he avoided confrontation or rifts with other Arab states (except Iraq, and even that for as briefly as possible) while working hard to get close to the United States by cooperating in the 1991 Kuwait crisis and saying he was ready to talk peace with Israel. In the end, this strategy worked quite well. Hafiz gave Washington very little while the United States gave him pretty much everything he hoped to receive.

Bashar, in contrast, puts the priority on confrontation. In Iraq after Saddam's fall, he basically waged a proxy war against the United States while giving safe haven to high-ranking Iraqi officials wanted for crimes, Iraqi unconventional weapons materiel, and a lot of Saddam's money while allowing the recruiting, training, and arming of Iraqi terrorists on Syrian soil. Such adventurism in Iraq, as well as in Lebanon and by baiting Israel, is a big risk, probably more than his father would have taken in the same situation.

In behaving this way, Bashar seems strikingly similar to a previous president of Syria. Not his dad but rather his father's arch-rival, Salah Jadid. Hafiz overthrew Jadid precisely because the latter had led Syria into two messes—the losing 1967 war and the abortive 1970 invasion of Jordan, both foiled. By risking the regime's survival in the name of ideology and assuming victory was inevitable, Jadid had committed an unpardonable crime. As punishment, Hafiz imprisoned him for thirty years until his death. Although there is some exaggeration in the statement, former Vice-President Khaddam was making an important point when he claimed, "Hafiz al-Assad staged a military coup against the slogans that his son is raising now."[32]

Bashar is in this regard a real contrast to his father, in style if not in substance. It was often said in Syria that Hafiz was an archconservative in the sense that he considered change to be bad unless the situation was so dangerous as to require it. By way of comparison, Bashar is a radical student of the 1960s generation that yearned for instant revolution. He is not just trying to prove that he is as tough and ruthless as his father but that he can advance the cause beyond his father's achievements.

Bashar justifies the need to prove himself sufficiently militant as a necessity:

I know that many countries and [political] circles wanted to test me and discover the points of strength and weakness in my personality. I know some in Lebanon have assumed that the departure of Hafiz al-Assad, with his historic personality, his special ability and his influence, would leave a great vacuum.... I felt this in some countries and in some political leaderships, and especially in Lebanon. However, I believe everybody has realized by now that I do not surrender to blackmail and I will not make any decision under pressure. I adhere to the principles I was raised on in the home of Hafiz al-Assad, which reflect the will of the people in Syria. Moreover, I feel committed to these principles.[33]

Thus, Bashar's historic task is not to change Syria or moderate the regime's goals but to fulfill its historic program. For Bashar, reforms are dangerous, as shown by Soviet experience. Bashar also made an interesting remark about Lebanese politics in the 1970s that seems to apply to Syria as well: "[Had] the reform of the political regime demanded the slaughter of half of the citizens, who would have remained [alive] to correct all society?"[34]

Following his father's path, even while trying to go farther down it, Bashar simply does not comprehend that any alternative exists. He genuinely does not seem to understand democracy, although he recognizes that it probably would be fatal for the system he wants. As Bashar himself has said, he is the product of growing up in the household of Hafiz al-Assad, not of having spent two years in England. Regarding the idea of a free, independent media, Bashar has remarked: "I am amazed by the insistence of those who are influenced by what is going on in the Western society, and especially American society, that the press is 'the fourth governing authority.' How can the press be a fourth governing branch in our backward third world, where the leader does not share the rule with others?! This issue can cause, sometimes, damage."[35]

Indeed, though, what can also cause damage are serious miscalculations about the world. By being too aggressive against Israel; too servile toward Iran; too inflexible regarding Egypt, Jordan, and Saudi Arabia; too greedy about

Lebanon; and too antagonistic with the West, Bashar could trigger a crisis that would be both dangerous to him and very costly to the region. He was right when he said, "As much as the analysis is correct, so will the decision be correct."[36] But there is a problem with his analysis of how the world works, augmented by his poor understanding of other countries, Israel and the United States especially.

Bashar often states the most remarkably transparent untruths. He is just too used to getting away with them. The Syrian and most other Arab media would never contradict him for political reasons; Western media either lacks the knowledge to do so or thinks it sufficient simply to report what he says. For example, in 2003, he told the *New York Times* that during the 1980s, "Saddam Hussein would send large railroad cars loaded with explosives in order to kill hundreds and thousands of Syrians. He killed more than 15,000 over the course of four years."[37] This is a total invention. Presumably Bashar was saying this to portray Syria as simply another victim of Saddam Hussein at a time when America was celebrating that tyrant's downfall and the United States seemed powerful. He was also trying to conceal the fact that he was Saddam's closest ally just before the Iraqi dictator was overthrow.

In the same interview, after being challenged by the journalist, Bashar insisted that reformist dissidents were still allowed to function in Syria. He specifically cited a discussion group that had already been shut down and whose leader had already been sentenced to five years in prison.[38] After even more repression had closed down the reform movement entirely, Bashar explained that the United States and Europe were responsible because of "the clear and direct obstacles [they had] placed before the reform process in Syria." Syria had carried out reform "in spite" of this sabotage, he continued, concluding, "Imagine how things would be if the situation was normal and there was regional and international support for reform."[39]

And in a speech to an Arab summit meeting, Bashar linked Islam to Arabism by stating in regard to one Muslim prophet, "We should not forget that Arabic was the language of Jesus Christ."[40] Of course, Jesus spoke Aramaic, a language far more closely related to Hebrew than to Arabic. The brazenness and consistency of the fabrications by Bashar and his colleagues often carry the day, proving the effectiveness of the "big lie" strategy.

None of his behavior implies that Bashar does not understand how to keep control over his own country, something he comprehends far better than do foreign observers. Everyone thought Syria had to make reforms—except the Syrian leadership. Instead, Bashar's slogan might be "Make war, not reform; make hate, not love."

Bashar is good at playing on these illusions, at exploiting such naiveté, good intentions, and wishful thinking. In this vein, former U.S. assistant secretary of state Martin Indyk records his feelings after meeting with Bashar in September 2005: "I came away from the meeting thinking that he had developed what appeared to be a very shrewd strategy; that he would cooperate with us over Iraq, that he would pursue peace with Israel in a serious way, and that he hoped in that way we would leave him alone to have his way with Lebanon."[41]

Leaving aside the proposed cost of such cooperation regarding Iraq and Israel—giving Lebanon the same treatment that Britain did to Czechoslovakia in order to get along with Germany in 1938—Bashar was snowing his visitor. Indyk was soon disillusioned, but it often seemed that he—along with such Bashar skeptics as French president Jacques Chirac—was in the minority.

That widespread, misplaced trust protected the Syrian dictator from his many mistakes: murdering Lebanon's most prominent politician, then showing weakness by withdrawing from that country; playing footsie with Saddam at the worst possible moment; alienating even the French; embracing Lebanese terrorists and Iran at a time when the United States was supposedly in a regime-changing mood; and crushing moderate reformers at home at a time when the world's sole superpower was focused on democratization.

Yet he does seem to be getting away with it, a fact that marks the difference between a fool and a genius in the game of nations. Inherent weaknesses in the Western approach to the Middle East have preserved him, as has the way Arab politics work. Bashar understands all this far better than those who underestimate him know. Respect is more important than sympathy; only power counts; and the weak will be crushed, he explains.[42] To be ruthless, to be crafty, to be feared are the most important requirements for success in his line of work. His father taught him this principle well and entrusted him to use it to preserve the family estate.

CHAPTER SEVEN

THE GREAT CHALLENGE AT HOME

"For Syria," wrote a Western journalist in 2000, as Bashar was taking over, "reform has become a question of when, not if, and the longer the delay the more acute will be the pain of adjustment.... Social and economic pressure is building.... Slowly but surely...the situation is approaching the breaking point." A Western diplomat added, "They say that reform threatens stability: We say that lack of action by them poses a far bigger threat." "It's at the point where something has to give," said another Western observer. But all these remarks, albeit logical, were wrong.[1]

The condition of Syria was so bad in the 1990s that everyone said the country must change; everyone, that is, but the rulers, who decided that the correct medicine required was simply more of the same. Clearly, the system's corruption, repression, incompetence, inflexibility, and many more characteristics seemed to be taking it down. If Syria was an ordinary state or located anywhere else in the world, its rulers could well be accused of courting suicide by their stubborn refusal to change.

This conclusion, however, would be misleading. The leaders of Syria would have been more suicidal if they had listened to the advice to be pragmatic. As they have long recognized, reform is a greater threat to stability than inaction.

Certainly, the most productive sector of what resembled an independent middle class, intellectuals and businessmen, was frustrated with economic stagnation, political incompetence, lies, and social claustrophobia. Consequently, they became supporters of reform. This is a classic pattern elsewhere in the world, where these categories of people have demanded liberalization and democracy, often becoming the new ruling class when such measures were taken. In contrast to some elements in the regime, they also believed that economic and political reform went hand in hand. There could be no prosperity without liberty. Michel Kilo, a Syrian liberal journalist and reform activist, reflected that view when he warned that there "could be no economic reform without political reform."[2]

It seemed as if the country faced a stark choice. One alternative was for Syria to embark on a program of massive reform to reduce government controls, foster trade, increase freedom, unleash the country's able commercial sector, and attract foreign investments by opting for peace and stability. The other course would be to accept continued decline, heading straight toward a massive crisis that could bring the regime's collapse and perhaps the disintegration of Syria itself.

But the former alternative was not so obvious or attractive as it seemed, at least from the standpoint of the nation's rulers. They conceived of the economy's function in a different way from foreign observers or intellectuals. For those running the regime, the priority was not to provide higher living standards or more successful development but rather to enrich the elite and ensure that the maximum possible resources stayed in its own hands and away from potential rivals.

Things already looked bad by the 1980s, when low oil prices hit Syria hard, especially since it had so much less petroleum resources than did the rich Gulf states. The situation was not helped by Hafiz's costly and doomed drive to gain military parity with Israel. The lower oil incomes and new priorities of Gulf Arab monarchies made them uninterested in giving money to Syria. The Soviet Union's collapse meant the end of Soviet bloc aid and cheap weapons. Rapid population growth strained Syria's society further. The combination of stifling bureaucracy, tight currency and price controls, low interest rates, overpriced currency, overregulation of the private sector, suspicion of high technology, low pay, high prices, the absence of a private banking system, and rampant corruption did not help matters.

Between 1998 and 1999, on the eve of Bashar's ascendancy, the economy barely grew. If population growth is factored in, it actually shrank. Foreign trade did not grow. A big drought in 1999 reduced harvests. Unemployment skyrocketed, electricity was periodically shut off, and food was rationed.[3] While things improved somewhat thereafter, largely due to high oil prices, the economy remained weak.

That Syria is lagging badly is clear from the figures for per capita gross national product (GNP). In this category, using 2006 figures, Israel's per capita GNP is at $24,600; Saudi Arabia's and Iran's, helped by massive oil production, are at $12,800 and $8,300 respectively. But even the per capita GNP of Jordan, which lacks any oil resources or Syria's rich agricultural land, stands at $4,700; impoverished, overcrowded Egypt is at $3,900. Syria is at the bottom of the list, along with war-torn Iraq, with a per capita GNP of $3,400, a remarkably poor showing that can only be attributed to mismanagement and bad economic policies.[4] Even compared to other Arab dictatorships, then, Syria is lagging. Egypt's per capita GNP rose from only one-third that of Syria's in the 1980s to surpass it, and Egypt is not exactly a model of rapid economic growth.

Nevertheless, the Assads and their supporters were unenthusiastic about real economic reform, particularly since they thought it might require political change, too. If prosperity required opening up the society to foreign influences and domestic freedom, this road—and not the route of continued militancy and dictatorship—seemed the real highway to disaster. A Syrian merchant, expressing the frustration of his fellows, complained, "The only logic I can see in this system is that someone wants the industry in this country to be killed."[5] But this evaluation was not quite right. The government did not want to kill the goose that lays the golden eggs; it simply was determined to keep most of the eggs for itself, even if that reduced overall egg production.

Regarding economic liberalization, Syria also has a unique problem. Alawites, the government's main supporters, greatly benefited from regime patronage as well as jobs in the bureaucracy and military. The real private businesses and entrepreneurial skills belonged overwhelmingly, however, to the Sunni Muslim majority, whose loyalty was not necessarily as reliable. Thus, privatization and deregulation would weaken the Assads' base of support while giving more power and assets to those who might like to see them fall. Entrepreneurs could use the personal independence they gained to be less reliant on government, and some of their profits might go into financing the opposition.

At most, then, the regime hoped for technocratic improvements that would bring more economic benefits without political or social changes. As Bashar puts it, "We need a strong state. . . . For us reform is to have prosperity."[6] But while he certainly maintained the strong state, he provided neither reform nor prosperity. According to a 2005 study, five years after Bashar took over, "Syria's growth has been lagging, with opportunities diminishing due to its dwindling (known) oil reserves and the dearth of higher skills within the labor market. While stable, Syria's political institutions are stagnant and its regional sphere of influence is diminished by the loss of hitherto powerful foreign policy tools."[7]

Even if the regime could buy domestic support by raising living standards, it has failed to take the steps needed to do so. What, then, is the plan of Bashar and his colleagues? How did they deal with the pressure building up for change that might otherwise destabilize the regime and blow up the country?

The answer to this question is that they are not concerned about fixing Syria's real problems because they have a cheaper, safer, and easier alternative along the lines of traditional Arab nationalism as perfected by the Ba'th: Conduct a demagogic foreign policy to mobilize the people against shadow enemies—"shadow" not because there are no disputes but because they could be resolved peacefully. Compromise solutions might benefit Syria as a country but would probably destroy the regime. So instead the Syrian government would break all the rules of pragmatic Western thought and politics while obeying the curious Bizarro World[8] doctrines of Middle Eastern politics and thought.

Thus, rather than seek peace and regional stability to encourage foreign investments, increase domestic freedom to improve the functioning of a society so necessary for development, follow a friendlier policy toward the West or even Gulf Arab monarchies to obtain more aid, or open up the economic system to bring a greater level of investment and initiative, the regime does the exact opposite. And this strategy is working. Even if the economic situation is a mess, the regime survives and has become wildly popular at home. There is a medical joke that the operation was a success but the patient died. In Syria's case, it might be said that the operation was a success; the patient was crippled by it, but felt wonderful and profusely praised the surgeon.

Unlike traditional dictatorships, the regime has not gained the gratitude of its oppressed citizenry by ignoring but by manipulating public opinion. An Egyptian newspaper pointed out that after what happened to Saddam in Iraq, the Syrian regime "realized that a population that is dissatisfied will not defend its government in times of crisis."[9] There was, however, more than one way to satisfy one's subjects. The Romans had "bread and circuses"; Arab regimes have anti-Americanism, anti-Zionism, nationalism, and Islamism. No one knows better how to use these tools than does the Syrian government.

Its economic strategy uses a combination of factors. This is why one of the main goals of Syrian policy has long been a constant search for ways to legitimize its continued rule in Lebanon. Bashar denied that Syria ever had hegemony over Lebanon and portrayed their relationship as one of Syrian altruism. "Did we in Syria aspire for money?" he asked. "Are there natural resources in

Lebanon for us to seek? Is there oil in Lebanon that we want to appropriate? Did we take Lebanese electricity, Lebanese water? No. We took nothing from Lebanon, but we gave blood."[10]

In fact, however, Syria made billions of dollars a year from Lebanon. Aside from smuggling, counterfeiting, and illegal drug profits, Syrian workers in Lebanon received double their pay at home, Syrian military officers pursue land grabs and protection rackets, and Syrian agricultural products are dumped on the Lebanese market.[11] The profits flow only in the direction of Damascus. When Lebanon's prime minister, Rafiq Hariri, negotiated an agreement with his Syrian counterpart for a free trade zone, Syria's government then sabotaged the agreement. Its finance minister explained, "If we have a free passage of goods and produce, then Lebanese apples will flood the Syrian market at the expense of Syrian apples."[12]

The regime also is moving closer to Iran for economic as well as strategic motives. Iran is subsidizing their joint client, Hizballah, thus saving Syria a lot of money since it would have to provide the funds if Tehran did not pick up the tab. Smuggling with Iraq brought in money before Saddam's fall, as did higher international oil prices after 2000. Syria has been muddling through, albeit with mounting debts. Still, the economic situation remains serious, making the regime's willingness and ability to ignore the situation all the more impressive. A list of the elements of economic disaster Syria faces is shocking, though some of the worst problems actually benefit the regime.[13] The main problems include the following:

- There are too few jobs for a rapidly growing population from which an army of young people enter the workforce annually.
- Workers take unproductive jobs in the state bureaucracy or in regime-subsidized companies that are already overstaffed with unneeded employees. According to the government, half the population lives off wages or pensions from the regime.[14] But this situation strengthens the government since it ties people to the regime's survival and makes them suspicious of reforms that might wipe out their jobs.
- Low wages force workers to take second jobs and force couples to delay marriage or live with their parents.
- High levels of corruption pervade the system. These include: smuggling by government officials and the elite, tax evasion, illegal foreign currency holdings, kickbacks on contracts, and demands by employees for bribes to do their jobs. But corruption also is used by the government to reward its supporters, puts money into the recipients' pockets,

and gives the regime an excellent chance to blackmail or imprison any-one who does something illegal—which means pretty much anybody.

- A growing gap exists between a small group enriched by regime con-nections and a relatively impoverished majority. Among the biggest beneficiaries are the Assads themselves, and everyone knows it. Still, this gives the elite an incentive to stick together. The rulers also have built mutually profitable alliances with key Sunni merchants, who join forces with the largely Alawite political elite.

- Tight regulations and government controls strangle the economy but also keep it under the regime's thumb. They provide many ways for the elite and their relatives to enrich themselves and buy support from those they need.

- Syria's foreign debt has increased, from 18.6 percent of gross domestic product in 2001 to 26 percent in 2005.[15]

- Syria's greatest single asset, oil, is quickly disappearing. Production fell from 540,000 barrels a day in 2000, to 400,000 in 2006. In fifteen or twenty years, unless new reserves are found (and Syrian economic poli-cies do not encourage exploration by international companies), all the oil will be gone.[16]

In this dismal situation, three elements keep Syria afloat. The main factor has been Syria's relatively small and declining oil production, which neverthe-less earns the country 60 to 70 percent of its export income. High petroleum prices (as in much of the 1970s and after 2000) cushioned all the country's other shortcomings; low oil prices (as in the 1980s) deepened the crisis.

The second element has been Syria's very profitable hold on Lebanon. Even after pulling out its troops, Syria still is reaping economic benefits. In fact, about 10 percent of the Syrian workforce continues to hold jobs in Lebanon at twice the pay rate they would receive if employed within Syria, where they would probably be unemployed.

Third is foreign aid. Generally speaking, except for losing small amounts of U.S. aid and trade by so behaving, Syria has found that acting in a radical and destabilizing fashion is profitable. In 1980 and 1981, the United States gave Syria $228 million in the hope that it would follow Egypt's example of making economic reforms and peace with Israel. Instead, Syria sponsored kid-nappings and terrorist attacks on Americans in Lebanon; by doing so, it got al-most ten times as much money from Arab states for leading the group that rejected the Egypt-Israel peace deal. Being a "confrontation state" and "rejec-tion front" leader was easier and far more lucrative.

At the same time, Syria received many billions of dollars of aid or easy credit from the Soviet bloc, much of it in the form of arms, for supporting Moscow's ambitions in the region. So strategically useful was Syria—and so hard were its debts to collect—that the Soviets never tried too hard to get the money they were owed. Once Russia replaced the Soviet Union, however, the successor government refused to give Syria any further easy credit since it had its own economic troubles and far fewer international ambitions that might require Syrian help.

During the 1980s, Damascus had found still another way to make money from foreign aid, this time by betraying its loudly voiced Arab nationalism to support non-Arab Iran against the Arab brothers in Iraq during the Iran-Iraq war. This action totally violated the Arab nationalist rule that Arabs should always support each other against those of other persuasions, yet Syria threw this basic principle overboard without seeming to lose any of its Arab nationalist legitimacy. Tehran bought Damascus's support by selling it oil at discount prices, which Syria could then put on the international market for hard currency. Even after the war ended in 1988, the arrangement continued as Syria became Iran's junior partner in various ways, including in their mutual backing for Hizballah and Hamas.

Then, in 1990, by joining the coalition to drive Iraq out of Kuwait, Syria obtained between $4 and $5 billion from Saudi Arabia and other Arab oil-producing states. After Saddam was defeated and under sanctions, Syria turned around and, between 2000 and 2003, made huge profits by similar oil deals with Iraq that broke the sanctions. In the Iraqi case, defying the whole world cost Damascus absolutely nothing and netted it about $8 billion. Syria received preferential deals to sell goods to Iraq, while Iraq used a pipeline and trucks to smuggle oil through Syria, paying Damascus 60 percent of the oil's value on the international market.[17] When Secretary of State Colin Powell protested, Bashar promised to close the pipeline. Of course, he did not do anything, and neither did Powell.

Despite this trickery, however, these sources of income were running dry. By 2003, Syria's aid income had reached a low point. It still had Iran but there was no more Soviet Union. Gulf Arabs would not pay for a pro-Iraq policy, Saddam's days were numbered, and the United States was not going to subsidize a country on its terrorism-supporting list.

The Syrian regime had one other source of potential help, Europe, the customer for half of its exports and supplier of one-third of its imports. But rather than trying to win European support by meeting its demands, the Syrians followed their usual strategy of treating the stronger party as a suppliant seeking its favors. This strategy is at least partly working. For years, the European Union had been negotiating an agreement similar to one that it has with several other Arab countries that would let Syrian goods into the EU on better terms and encourage European investment in Syria. The agreement is conditioned, however, on Syria promising not to build weapons of mass destruction and to do better on human rights. Despite the benefits of such a deal, Bashar brushed aside these demands and has been in no hurry to complete the agreement.

The agreement was initialed in October 2005 without Syria making any concessions on weapons or repression, but despite additional years of talks it has never been completed. The Europeans did not gain any actual political leverage from their economic power over Syria yet they also pressed Damascus no further. They cannot quite believe it is happening, but Bashar refuses to change any of his policies in order to complete the deal, even though it would benefit Syria, his country, far more than the EU. It is a typical piece of Assad diplomacy, turning the tables on those who ostensibly have the edge, trying to make them beg Syria to let them give it gifts without receiving anything in return.

Even when pressed to the wall, then, Syria was still coupling intransigence with extortion and blackmail as an integral part of its diplomacy. In October 1990, for example, Farouq al-Sharaa hinted that three British hostages in Lebanon would be freed more quickly if the United Kingdom restored full relations with Syria, reduced after high-ranking Syrian officials were caught backing an attack to blow up an Israeli passenger plane in London. When Britain continued to support EU sanctions on arms sales to Syria, Information Minister Muhammad Salman repeated the offer.[18] A deal was finally reached not long thereafter on Syria's terms.

No one can accuse Hafiz or Bashar of surrendering to the West in order to get money, but the costs to Syria's economic situation have been dire. Most Syrians had lower living standards, less housing, worse education, and in general poorer lives in every respect. They were steadily falling further behind other, comparable countries. For example, in Syria, male illiteracy was at 12 percent, among females it was 41 percent. In comparison, the overall figure for adult illiteracy in South Korea was just 2.5 percent, in Thailand, 5 percent, and in impoverished Peru, just over 10 percent.[19] The number of personal computers per 1,000 people—despite Bashar's internet surfer reputation—was only 14 in Syria, compared to Peru at 35, South Korea at 182, and Israel at 246.[20]

As a result, such men as Nabil Sukkar, an economist who headed a Damascus consulting firm, and Rateb Shallah, president of the Federation of Syrian Chambers of Commerce and Industry, warned that rapid reform was a necessity.[21] They posited just two alternatives: Either Syria's rulers would reduce government control, unleash the country's able commercial sector, and attract investments by opting for peace and stability or the country would head straight into a huge crisis that could bring about the regime's collapse.

But the regime had a third alternative: to make its people indifferent to materialistic considerations by filling them with pride in Syria as the font of nationalistic and Islamic resistance. That is how the region's dictatorships had played the game for a half-century. The old tricks were still not worn out, nor the audience too jaded to leap to its feet in a standing ovation.

This is not to say that public opinion was becoming less important or more totally under the regime's control. In fact, the opposite was true in both cases, making the performance the government was about to give all the more impressive. The day was past when the populace was totally the prisoner of Syria's state-controlled media. Now they could tune in international television stations like al-Jazira.

Syria's dinosaur bureaucrats, spoiled by having had a monopoly on truth for so long, could not compete very well. It was not easy for them to go on al-Jazira television, as did one pro-regime analyst, and explain that all the Arab regimes were dictatorships because the masses would need a hundred years before they were ready for democracy. He was ridiculed by the moderator, other guests, and callers. Similarly, although the regime had driven the local Muslim Brotherhood out of business, the exile group could now bring their case directly to the people on al-Jazira. Even the most sensitive internal issues were debated in the studio; the regime's most sacred cows were publicly dissected.[22] At the same time, half of the official Syrian newspapers being printed each day went unsold; Syrians simply did not want to bother when the state's media told them nothing.

This did not mean that Syrians enthusiastically embraced the new ways being offered from outside the country. As a scholar concluded after interviewing people there, "Viewers in Damascus... say that Syrian audiences are alarmed at hearing vehement contradictory views about such basic issues, being used to hearing only one correct version of the 'truth.'"[23]

Prepared by their ideology and worldview plus more than a half-century of conditioning, most Syrians were quite willing to be citizens of the Assad universe. To think that people are just waiting for the chance to embrace a Western-style democracy or worldview despite their own experiences and political culture is simply not accurate. The Syrian regime had some problems with public opinion, but it never really lost control and knew precisely how to ensure popular support.

Aside from economic woes and some restiveness in public opinion, a third issue was shaking things up as Bashar took office. Lebanon, largely occupied by Syria for decades and directed by it in so many respects, had become virtually part of the country's domestic situation. Now, on the very verge of the new era in Syria, a new era in Lebanon was beginning. On May 22, 2000, Israel pulled its troops out of southern Lebanon after an eighteen-year-long presence there. Some Lebanese began to advocate the idea of Syria leaving, too.

Syria claimed the pull-out as a victory, with all the state-controlled newspapers headlining "Israel's Total Defeat in South Lebanon."[24] Syria and Iran filled the vacuum in southern Lebanon to their own liking. Hizballah took over, despite the fact that the United Nations had called on the Beirut government to reestablish its own authority there. These developments also made Hizballah a more reliable and stronger force augmenting Syrian power. The group, whose members had long portrayed themselves as revolutionaries bringing Islamist rule to Lebanon, and thus as enemies of other Lebanese factions and Arab nationalist regimes—now proclaimed itself a patriotic movement defending Lebanon and the Arab world from Israel.

This new situation also increased Syria's leverage over Israel, basically returning to the pre-1982 situation (albeit with Islamist Hizballah in place of the PLO). Syria could heat up the border when it chose or offer to keep things quiet for a price.

And while the UN had declared Israel's withdrawal complete, a new pretext for war was created as Hizballah claimed that Israel was still occupying a tiny, barren area called the Shabaa Farms. It was another example of Middle Eastern comic opera that would have been regarded ludicrous in any other part of the world but was the source of bloodshed and crisis there. Before Israel's withdrawal, there had been no mention of Lebanon's "sacred right" to this piece of land; in fact, it had always been regarded as part of Syria. After all, Israel had captured it during the 1967 war with Syria, a war in which Lebanon was not involved. And now, although Syria officially claimed the land as part of its own territory, it cheered on Hizballah and Lebanon, insisting that Israel must yield the area to Lebanon.

This is not to say, however, that the Israeli withdrawal did not create some problems for Syria within Lebanon. The 1989 Taif Accord, which Syria had agreed to in finally settling the Lebanese civil war, mandated Syria's withdrawal from Lebanon, though this provision had been ignored for a decade. As early as 1999, Gibran Tuayni, owner of *al-Nahar,* had courageously raised the issue, followed by Druze leader Walid Jumblatt. In November 2000, anti-Syrian demonstrations were held in Beirut.[25]

For some reason, this time Syria was responsive, whether due to Saudi pressure, to an effort to end Lebanese complaints, or to Bashar's initial weakness or uncertainty. Between June 2001 and February 2003, about half of Syria's 30,000 soldiers in Lebanon went home, and their bases were transferred from Beirut to the countryside. But Syria was not leaving Lebanon. Its intelligence network and workforce stayed in place. Apparently, power would be exercised indirectly, through bribed or intimidated Lebanese politicians.

This was the situation during the early period of Bashar's rule when he took over after his father died on June 10, 2000. The irony of this succession was stupendous. Syria, a radical republic that had always rejected hereditary monarchy as the height of reactionary backwardness, was openly handed down as a family fiefdom.

What better symbol of the nature of dictatorship could there be? Along with the humiliation, however, was a sense of hope. Bashar had a carefully cultivated image as a moderate and a reformer. And certainly he did have potential alternatives for dealing with all Syria's problems—if he only chose to use them.

The most remarkable discussion of the possibilities of that moment came from the Lebanese leftist Hazim Saghiyya who showed what might have been. Writing in 2000 in the London newspaper *al-Hayat,* Saghiyya wrote what he called "The Speech that Bashar al-Assad Will Never Make," indicating how the new president might provide democracy and freedom in a context which could preserve the regime:

> The arduous times that Syria went through necessitated a regime that is no longer needed. The world has changed and so have we, or at least we should, so as to find the time to [deal with] our real problems and compensate for the long years we were busy handling problems that withheld our progress.
>
> The Cold War has ended and sooner or later so will its Middle Eastern parallel. The [continuation of the conflict] is more harmful to us than it is to Israel, which is building a thriving technological economy while neutralizing its [internal] conflicts by the democratic means it has developed over decades.[26]

If Saghiyya and other Arab liberals had their way, Bashar would tell his people that Syrians must "live as a normal state in a normal region." He would then announce free elections, a multiparty system, the rule of law, the release of political prisoners, the end of emergency laws, a reduction of security controls, an anticorruption campaign, major economic reforms, and a reduced military budget. He would also pledge to make a full withdrawal from Lebanon. Once

Syria took such a stance, Saghiyya explained, the world would support it entirely, Israel would be ready to make an acceptable deal, and a new golden age would dawn for Syrians and the Middle East in general.

But Assad never made such a speech because the reform option was not so attractive for him as the liberals believed. He viewed the economy's function in a different way from foreign observers or local businessmen: The goal was not to provide higher living standards for the people or more successful social development but rather to enrich the elite and ensure that the maximum resources were in its own hands, not those of potential rivals. Similarly, Bashar was determined to preserve, not dismantle, the regime that had raised him overnight from eye doctor to dictator.

In short, the man who was supposedly going to destroy Syria's regime was in fact the one most determined to preserve it. In doing so, he enjoyed a complete mandate from his family, the army, and the political elite.

Ridiculing the idea that Bashar might bring reform, Muhammad al-Hasnawi, a Syrian dissident writer living in London, told of the mother of a political prisoner jailed in Syria who wept when she heard of Bashar's succession. She understood that this event meant that nothing would change in Syria. Why did an illiterate woman have no illusions about the situation, Hasnawi wrote, while Syrian liberals who thought themselves fit to lead the country understood nothing?[27]

Another skeptic was As'ad Naim, an exiled Syrian scholar, who warned that many reformers, being insiders who had benefited from the regime in the past, would go back to supporting the government once they were pressured. He bitterly predicted that his countrymen would discover that Bashar was going to give them the same kind of lives they had suffered for thirty years.[28]

In his inaugural speech, however, Bashar was happy to help people go on fooling themselves about his alleged moderate sentiments while also making clear his real intentions. True, he explained, a ruler needed constructive criticism and should examine different viewpoints. But there were limits to this process and any solution must be done in Syrian style, since "we cannot apply the democracy of others to ourselves."[29] So, for example, in the first interview he gave after becoming president, Bashar explained, "When we discuss granting a permit to a newspaper the primary question is what is the goal of the paper [and] do the ideas of the newspaper serve the national and pan-Arab line?"[30]

He did make some small changes. Although they were remarkably limited, even partly illusory, he got tremendous propaganda mileage out of them. More than 600 political prisoners, mostly Islamists who had been held for twenty years, were released. One prison, notorious for its ill treatment, and military courts for trying civilians were closed. Yet even these things were far tinier alterations of the regime's fabric than they seemed. For example, Hafiz had always pardoned prisoners periodically, and these aged relics of the 1982 revolt were no longer dangerous. Indeed, many of those released, lawyers charged, were near the end of their sentences any way; others on the list to be let go were actually still in prison.

The same kind of trickery applied to Bashar's highly publicized suggestion that fewer pictures of himself or banners praising him appear in public. Nevertheless, the number of Bashar images around the country is still stupendous. Similarly, although newspapers ran a few articles supporting reform, these said that change should come solely at the government's direction. Bashar met with several reformers and told them they could criticize the state on economic matters, but only if the state-run Syrian newspapers were willing to print their complaints. And even then, within a year most of those people were in prison. Small parties allied with the regime were offered the possibility of opening their own newspapers but only under censorship and on condition that they reflect the government line. Such newspapers however, never appeared.[31]

As a sole exception, the regime permitted publication of a satirical magazine, *Addomari* (The Lamplighter), by the cartoonist Ali Farzat, who said he hoped to "chase the police out of the people's minds."[32] So hungry were Syrians for something to read which did not follow the party line that the first issue sold out within hours.[33]

Yet such victories were small, rare, and short-lived. Certain marginal problems far from the leader himself—such as rising prices, pay hikes for officials, or low-level corruption—could be mentioned, but it took only a couple of months for Syrian authorities to decide that even one independent publication was too much. Cartoons in Farzat's magazine that criticized the prime minister were censored. The magazine's print run was cut, its distribution sabotaged, and several issues canceled. Sadiq al-Azm, who seemed to be Syria's sole officially sanctioned dissident (and who paid his dues by supporting the regime at key junctures), explained that the magazine's existence proved the old guard "realized that the country cannot be run in the same way any more."[34] But wasn't Syria still being run in 99.9 percent the same way? As for the remaining one-tenth of one percent, within two years, the regime shut down Farzat's magazine.

Those interested in change wanted far more than Bashar was offering. In September 2000 a manifesto was published abroad signed by ninety-nine Syrian cultural and intellectual figures. It urged the regime to end the state of emergency and martial law in effect since 1963; pardon all political prisoners and exiled dissidents; recognize freedom of assembly, speech, and press; and stop spying on the public.[35] Their goal was to establish a multiparty democracy and strong civil society. Only political reform, they argued, would enable Syria to deal with its problems. The state-run media refused even to mention the declaration, and the regime banned the importation of foreign newspapers that printed it. However, no action was taken against the signatories themselves.

Encouraged by the apparent start of a new government-tolerated reform movement, more than 1,000 Syrians, inside the country and abroad, signed a second manifesto in January 2001 that went even further than the first one. It directly urged the end of single-party rule, and advocated for freedom of speech and of the press, political pluralism, an expanded role for women in public life, and democratic elections under the supervision of an independent judiciary. Even the Muslim Brotherhood supported it.[36] Seventy Syrian lawyers signed still another petition calling for the government to conduct political reforms, revoke emergency laws, and permit independent parties.[37]

Reformers founded the National Dialogue Club, which held meetings at the home of Riyad Sayf, one of the few independent-minded members of parliament, to hear lectures on democracy and civil society. At a January 2001 gathering, the speaker, Shibli al-Shami, an engineer, said words that would have been impossible to voice just a few months earlier: "Since 1958, the Syrian regime has been a dictatorship. The main problem is oppression. The oppression is from the inside," he said, and "The West is not bad." He also stressed, however, that reformers should be patient and give the new leadership a chance to develop its programs.[38]

Sayf came from a powerful Sunni family, among the country's largest private employers. First manufacturing mass-produced shirts, they diversified into all sorts of clothes and shoes. The Sayfs had a reputation for being pious Muslims—thus they had good contacts with both the liberal and more religious sectors among the urban Sunnis—and as good employers who treated their employees well. Thus, Sayf was not some ivory castle intellectual but a man who represented the best elements among the Syrian bourgeoisie.[39]

Bashar's planning minister could not even speak to the Syrian Society for Economic Science without Sayf popping up from the audience, amid cheers from the crowd, to complain "We have no transparency, no exact monetary figures, and no accountability. We don't have any development. We don't have dialogue. We don't have strong institutions. We have no anti-corruption campaign."[40]

Sayf asked for permission to form a new party, to be called the Civil Peace Movement. At an organizational meeting of 350 people, he criticized the one-party state as using pan-Arab rhetoric to carry out failed radical socialist policies that damaged the economy and to censure everyone else's ideas. Five professors who were members of the ruling Ba'th party, no doubt planted in the audience for this purpose, stood up to accuse him of collaborating with foreign elements.[41]

Sayf's call for Syria to become a pluralist democracy that would accommodate the country's different religions and ethnic groups was what most horrified the regime. The government preferred a unitary state in which all such differences were subsumed under an Arab nationalist identity. If the communal issue was unleashed, the Sunni majority might overthrow the Alawite-dominated system or the country might erupt in civil war, as later happened in post-Saddam Iraq. Leading government and Ba'th party officials said that such talk would destroy the country's stability and bring catastrophe.[42]

From the regime's standpoint, the reform movement was not a group of people trying to make Syria better, stronger, and more prosperous, but a malignancy that threatened national survival. At a 2001 meeting of regime loyalists at Damascus University, Vice-President Abd al-Halim Khaddam insisted that no citizen has a right to destroy the very foundations of his own society. He warned that reforms would push Syria toward a breakdown like that occurring in Algeria, which faced a bloody uprising after the regime blocked Islamists from winning an election, or Yugoslavia, which was torn apart by ethnic strife when the heavy hand of dictatorship was removed.[43]

According to Khaddam, himself a Sunni, pluralism was a Western plot to shatter countries by demanding self-determination for ethnic groups, a step that would set off a civil war in Syria. An example of how Syria might erupt occurred in March 2004. During a soccer game, Syrian Kurds in the crowd shouted slogans about Iraq's new constitution, which gave their counterparts autonomy in that country. Syrian Arabs, including police, responded with chants backing Shia hard-liners in Iraq. The security forces fired at the Kurds, killing several. Police again opened fire during the victims' funerals, setting off two days of riots. Many Kurds were arrested, beaten, and tortured. Clearly, the communal situation in Syria is fragile indeed.

Aware of such potentially explosive internal problems, Khaddam granted that reformist critics might not consciously be foreign agents "but, even if their intentions are good, the way to hell is still paved with good intentions." Bashar did not even leave that much of a loophole. "In criminal law," he explained in 2001, "the element of intent is significant in determining the punishment." In politics, though, "only the result determines guilt."[44]

The two sides have clear, conflicting themes: The regime argues that reformers are agents of foreign powers; the liberals respond that oppression

comes from inside the country. The battle between reform and status quo re-
volves around the broader question of whether Syria's problems, like the difficulties in the rest of the Arab world, are caused by internal or external factors.
The government's assets include not only the power of the state to repress or
reward but also the long conditioning Syrians have undergone to accept the
regime's claims, its control over a wide range of consciousness-shaping institutions, a similar worldview everywhere in the Arab world, and the emotional power of nationalism and, to some extent, religion. The contest is
most uneven.

The underlying problem is that the rulers recognize that, despite the liberals' honeyed words, any real change undermines them. Because they are so vulnerable, they are desperate to stop their subjects from criticizing them. The
rulers have too much to hide. A free press means exposing the system's work-
ings. Revealing specific instances of corruption undermines the elite's income
and attacks its mechanism for bribing key social groups to ensure their support. As a Syrian dissident asked, how can one monitor corruption without
seeing that it involves the entire regime and all its officials, no matter what
their rank?[45]

For example, in June 2002, the state-built Zayzoun Dam collapsed just
five years after being completed; the reasons were poor design and probably the
use of substandard materials. Five villages were destroyed by the ensuing flood;
dozens of people were killed. After forty years of total control at home, complained a dissident Web site, the government could not solve the simplest domestic problems. Even the military, on which so much money had been spent,
was effective only in killing its own citizens. The real dam that must fall down,
these critics concluded, was the regime itself, because as long as it stands, the
Syrian people will never obtain either liberty or honor.[46]

As the Syrian writer noted, even in the case of a badly built dam, the struggle against imperialism and Zionism was the great excuse used to justify the
regime's incompetence. Yet xenophobic demagoguery does work to stave off
complaints. The regime and its minions merely have to say "Palestine," "Iraq,"
"Israel," "the United States," or slogans along these lines to kill discussion of
any subject.

Liberals tried to use ingenious—and often ingenuous—counterarguments
to try to turn this handicap into a weapon for themselves. Kilo claimed that
only reform could rescue Syria from American domination. If there was no reform, the United States would invade and take over the country. The danger
was so great, he warned, because there was some truth to accusations that the
regime tortured its own people and kept them in a state of poverty and unem-

ployment, that the health and education systems were declining, and that the economy was in bad shape. Kilo got away with mentioning such problems by quoting foreign media in the guise of pointing out the details of the West's anti-Syria campaign.[47]

As always, manipulating the Arab-Israeli conflict was one of the regime's main ways to stifle dissent. Thus, when even Ba'th party members started complaining to Khaddam at a meeting, demanding that the regime do more to defeat corruption and make reforms, the vice-president could simply respond that the Arab-Israeli conflict permitted no changes at home. "This country is in a state of war as long as the occupation continues," agreed Information Minister Adnan Umran. "You have threats coming against Syria every day, and the capital is only 60 miles from the front line."[48]

Knowing this, the reformers carefully avoided mentioning the Arab-Israeli issue and focused intently on domestic affairs. Actually suggesting that peace with Israel would be beneficial for Syria was too dangerous; they knew that saying so would be an excuse to call them Zionist agents. Of course, the government also used the very fact that they avoided the controversial question to brand them as Zionist agents.[49] Such is the nature of Arab politics. Khaddam, for example, asked, "Was it mere coincidence that the reformers' proposals did not include a single word about the Arab-Israeli conflict? Can any Syrian or Arab citizen's life be separated from what goes on in the conflict between the Arabs and Israel?"[50]

Ali Diyab, head of the Ba'th party's Foreign Affairs Bureau, scolded that no issue in Syria could be discussed without reference to the conflict. Anything that strengthens Syria's ability to fight is good; anything that creates internal divisions or detracts from the primacy of this battle merely serves the enemy.[51]

The irony of this argument, however, is that the regime itself has the power to end the conflict quickly and easily whenever it chooses to do so. In exchange for real peace, Israel had offered to return to Syria every square inch of the Golan Heights. Is the real issue preventing a diplomatic resolution Syria's demand for twelve additional square miles of land on Israel's side of the international border, or is the endless state of war the government's insurance policy against domestic problems?

As if to demonstrate that point, when Saudi crown prince Abdallah proposed in 2002 that the Arab states restart a peace process by agreeing collectively to normalize relations with Israel in exchange for its complete withdrawal from territories it captured in June 1967, Bashar lobbied hard to sabotage the effort. Despite U.S. attempts to have a better version of the plan adopted, Syria pushed until the promise of normalization was dropped and a demand that all

Palestinian refugees could go live in Israel was added. Israel predictably saw the proposal as a trap and immediately rejected it.[52]

Liberals rarely take on this sacred cow of Arab politics, the Arab-Israeli conflict. One such interesting exchange, between Syrian-Palestinian author Hisham Dajani and the famous Syrian poet Ali Ahmad Said (best known by his pen name, Adonis), is most revealing. Dajani argued that most Syrian intellectuals supported peace with Israel and gave three basic reasons for doing so. First, a realistic examination of the situation showed that negotiations and compromise were the only way to get back the Golan Heights: "Due to the balance of power," Dajani explained, Arab states and the Palestinians could only get land back by making "some concessions on the issues of water, security arrangements, and normalization of relations." There could be no illusion of capturing the Golan Heights by force; it could return to Syria only through negotiations.[53]

Second, getting back Syria's territory would be a sufficient gain to warrant making peace. The destruction of Israel was not a necessary objective. Regaining all of Syria's land would restore Arab pride.

Third, Syria need not fear peace with Israel. It was silly to believe that Israel would swallow up the Arabs if there was peace. This has not happened to either Egypt or Jordan after they signed treaties with Israel. Indeed, peace would strengthen Syria by allowing it to devote its resources and energies to solve its domestic problems, such as corruption, lack of democracy, and economic backwardness.[54]

Dajani faced a distinctly uphill battle in breaking old attitudes that were strong even if irrational and destructive of real Arab interests. All Said had to do to win the debate was to reiterate the traditional Arab arguments with all the passion and power they invoked. Moreover, those repeating the usual Arab line could look forward to material benefits for doing so. Although Said had often been critical of Syria's government in the past, he knew the regime would support his viewpoint. Indeed, after his attack on Dajani, the regime lifted its ban on Said writing for the state-owned newspaper, *Tishrin*.

Especially worth noting was Dajani's linkage—common among liberal Arabs—between peace, on one hand, and reform, democracy, modernization, economic change, and the struggle against corruption, on the other hand. If peace was going to lead to such undesirable things, the establishment and its supporters thought, than all the more reason for blocking a negotiated solution to the conflict.

The return of Syria's territory and even the creation of a Palestinian state would not settle the issue because compromise was unjust, Said responded.

Moreover, Israel would never be satisfied with peace and would strive to conquer the Arabs. "These are murderers and nothing more," he insisted. "They—including those among them who now seem sympathetic to peace—are willing to treat us only as second-rate human beings that must be killed, or whose killing is not worth bothering about. They say: 'Let us stop the bloodshed. Let us rest for a while. We have tired of the killing. We have tired of killing you.'"[55] Even if Israel made peace, it would just wait for another time to slaughter the Arabs. No Israelis really favored peace. This showed they were sub-humans who should be killed. Syria places high political value on making Israel an irrational evil entity incapable of normal political behavior. If peace is impossible, the battle must continue. And if that is true, discussing alternatives or promoting change is either foolish or treasonous behavior.

When Israel withdrew from south Lebanon, for example, the Beirut government would not or could not end the conflict. Nasrallah faithfully made the case for his foreign patron's continued domination over his country. The Syrian army's presence in Lebanon, he told a rally, was "a regional and internal necessity for Lebanon" and a "national obligation for Syria."[57] The prime reason why it was an "internal necessity," of course, was that the occupation greatly benefited Hizballah itself.

For the politicians in Beirut, then, Syrian pressure, Hizballah's power, and domestic public opinion seemed more worrisome than the consequences of continued tension on the Israel-Lebanon border even though this risky game could undermine reconstruction by forfeiting Lebanon's chances of attracting investment or gaining stability. As a result, Lebanon refused to take control of its own territory, which heightened the threat of confrontation with Israel. Indeed, Hizballah's attacks set off a war in 2006 that inflicted great damage on Lebanon and gave Syria the chance to reestablish its hegemony there.

Three years earlier, when there was still hope of change for the better, here is how Kilo made the most effective try to expose this con game and turn it against the rulers. "Every day," he wrote, "we hear shrieking corrupt voices that claim that the situation should not be reformed as long as the [Israeli] threat exists, as if corruption is the tool that will deflect" this danger. The people knew the real fault was with Syria's leaders. The implication was that the Israeli threat was used as a cynical excuse to deny reform and accuse its advocates of being traitors. But in fact by refusing to make major changes and by keeping the country weak, Syria's rulers—not the reformers—were the real traitors who were endangering the Arabs.[56]

Instead of dealing with Syria's real issues, the rulers seized every opportunity to parade their own patriotic demagoguery and steadfastness. Bashar roared, "An inch of land is like a kilometer and that in turn is like a thousand kilometers. A country that concedes even a tiny part of its territory is bound to concede a much bigger part in the future. . . . Land is an issue of honor not meters." And he added that this was his inheritance: "President Hafiz al-Assad did not give in," boasted Bashar, "and neither shall we; neither today nor in the future."[58]

Nor would he give in to the demands for reform. The Arab Writers' Association, a Stalinist-style government front group, published an article claiming that Syria's 4,000-year-old [*sic*] Arab culture already had enough civil society.[59] In January 2001 Information Minister Adnan Umran proclaimed that, like ethnic pluralism, civil society was an "American term." Umran explained that "neocolonialism no longer relies on armies." The idea of democracy was merely a form of imperialist subversion. The implication was that Syrian reformers were fifth column traitors who would be punished as such. The very next day, one of the signers of the "1,000" and "99" petitions who was organizing a reform club, novelist Nabil Sulayman, was attacked by two assailants and badly beaten.[60]

Kilo tried to respond to the threats and criticisms by reasoning with the rulers. "I do not dream of toppling the state," he explained. "This is not our goal. I believe that the state's functioning can be improved. We make sure to act within the confines of the law and publicly. . . . The dialogue in itself expresses the good health of Syrian society. The spirit of change is blowing in Syria."[61] But his words did no good. The regime's mind was made up and there was no real dialogue. The sound Kilo heard was actually the government blowing out the candle lit by the reformers.

The regime proceeded to repress the opposition in a skillful way that involved a minimum of violence. Much of the assault was verbal, simply letting people know that they must stop this nonsense about civil society or face serious consequences. Bashar made his view clear: Whatever the reformers' intentions, the fact that their ideas would produce disaster meant they are guilty of the most dangerous crimes against the fatherland.[62] Turki Saqr, editor of the ruling party's newspaper, said the reformers merely represented one more wave in the imperialist assault on Syria, trying to force their anti-Arab ideas on the people.[63]

Bashar ridiculed the idea that there was a need to do anything differently from the way the Ba'th had ruled Syria for the previous four decades. He pronounced himself amazed, for example, that anyone could propose that the media might have any independent role in Syria. That was a Western notion, Assad explained, that did not work in a country where the leader shared power with no one.[64] In a statement full of unintentional irony, Bashar explained that Syria really did have freedom of speech and only the most dangerous dissidents were punished. After all, he told a Western interviewer, if the regime imprisoned all its critics, there would be no room in the jails.[65]

In a sense, Bashar spoke honestly. Compared to Saddam's Iraq, the Syrian regime did not want to imprison and torture everyone who said something opposing it. Instead, the government merely denied its critics any access to wider circles of Syrians, took away their jobs, harassed them, and called them in for interviews with security services. Only if this did not work was a spell in prison used as a lesson.

This kind of treatment had three advantages: It helped convince others to keep their mouths shut, it kept the regime's international image from getting too bad, and it held out the possibility that former dissidents could change sides and once again become state lackeys. Most of the time, the system worked.

But the strongest argument of all was the traditional one. If, as the regime argued, the Arabs' woes came overwhelmingly from imperialism and Zionism subverting and trying to destroy them, only domestic unity and support for the regime could save Syria, the honor of the Arabs, and the religion of the Muslims. Internal debate and criticism, much less democracy, would weaken Syria in its desperate, life-or-death struggle of good against evil. To make matters worse, the reformers wanted to import the enemy's ideas and institutions, actually assisting in the subversion of Arab culture and independence.

This worldview was no mere whim but the existential bedrock of the entire system of governance in Syria. After all, if foreign powers were not the villains, then the domestic rulers were. Without the threat of demonic enemies, the Arab regime would have to offer some more worldly goods to its people: peace, prosperity, and freedom. Rather than patriotic champions, the regime would be responsible for everything wrong. In that case, the correct path would not be to join ranks behind the leadership but rather to resist the regime itself. Instead of being carried on the shoulders of a grateful people, the ruling class would be torn to shreds by the mob, as happened literally to their Iraqi counterparts during Iraq's 1958 revolution.

Bashar, then, did not sit passively and ponder whether his regime should survive. As a substitute for reform, Bashar's strategy was to enhance his credentials as a militant Arab nationalist, a fighter against Israel, defender of Islam, friend of revolutionaries, and sworn foe of America. The motto summing up this strategy is "resistance." It is a fascinating choice of words. "Resistance" is to battle against something, not to have any positive program of one's own. The word gives away the secret; it is a reactionary effort to maintain an undesirable status quo. What exactly is being resisted: imperialism and Zionism, or democracy and reform? Resistance most of all means opposition to change, and that describes the Syrian regime perfectly because it was indeed very happy with a status quo that was, by any other measure, a tragedy and a disaster.

Yet there is still more to be learned by deconstructing the word "resistance" in this context. After all, only one type of resistance is being legitimized. Does Lebanon have a right to resist Syrian control? Do the Iraqis have a right to resist what amounts to Syrian covert aggression? Do the Egyptians, Jordanians, and Saudis have the right to resist an Iranian-Syrian attempt to take over the region? Does the West have the right to resist Syrian-sponsored terrorism and destabilization of the region? Bashar and his colleagues are most skillful in their trade. Certainly within Syria and to a large extent in the Arab-speaking world, the concept of resistance is defined in their way alone.

Regarding every alternative he had, Bashar made his choices in this direction. After Israel's unilateral withdrawal, he could have accepted Lebanon as a sovereign nation. Instead, he helped plague Lebanon with a Hizballah state within a state, ordered terrorist operations against advocates of that country's independence, and continued to manipulate Lebanese politics, interfering with the smallest decisions and lowest-level appointments. This strategy ensured that sooner or later, as happened in 2006, an Israel-Lebanon war would break out.

He could have kept his distance from Iraq, knowing that the Gulf Arabs feared and the United States hated Saddam. Participation in the Gulf war coalition in 1991 against Iraq had been one of the few assets Syria possessed in its dealings with the West. Nevertheless, Bashar moved steadily toward alignment with Baghdad, partly as a profit-making venture. This strategy would lead to his sustaining an anti-American, anti-Shia insurgency that would cost tens of thousands of lives after Saddam was overthrown.

Finally, he could have taken a less extremist stance against Israel. Instead, he tried to prove that he was the most hard line of Arab leaders. In his speech to the March 2001 Arab summit, for example, Bashar called for renewing the economic boycott, said no Israeli leader was interested in peace, and condemned all Israelis as war criminals more racist than the Nazis.[66] When the Pope visited Syria, Bashar made a remarkable anti-Semitic speech claiming that the Jews "tried to kill the principles of all religions with the same mentality in which they betrayed Jesus Christ and . . . tried to betray and kill the Prophet Muhammad."[67]

This strategy also had the advantage of coping with the real threat to the regime, which was not the Jews but rather the Muslims. After all, handling a few hundred liberal intellectuals, journalists, and lawyers was relative child's play for the regime. What it truly had to fear was thousands of Islamists who could mobilize millions of Sunni Muslims against it. But with Bashar blowing the anti-American and anti-Israel trumpet while backing Islamist insurgencies in Iraq and Lebanon, he could claim to be the Islamists' best friend. Overwhelmingly, Islamists inside and outside of Syria accepted him as their patron.

Within Syria, activists demanding a bigger role for Islam in society are favored while the liberals are crushed. The regime has given unprecedented leeway for opening mosques, setting up Islamic-favored social institutions, and preaching fiery sermons as long as they are not directed against Bashar. The Ba'th party militia, militantly secular, had once marched through the streets tearing veils off women. Now bearded men and covered-up women are on the increase with the regime's blessing. It was a real accomplishment for Bashar that a man who is not even a Muslim could reinvent himself as a champion of jihad.

By early 2001, with the Islamist flank covered, the crackdown against the liberals intensified. The government reminded the public that martial law made it illegal for more than five people to gather for a political meeting without a permit. To obtain a permit, security agencies must be given two weeks' advance notice of any gathering, the speaker's name, a copy of the speech, and a complete list of attendees. Bashar explained that "no timetables for the development process can be set because it depends on the 'natural development of the society.'" And he admitted, "The development of civil society institutions is not one of my priorities."[68]

As for political reform, the regime would continue a policy it had always used and perhaps the only one it was capable of doing. Tight controls show who is boss and discourage dissent. Very small reforms provide a safety valve, maintain hope, and fool foreigners. Hinting that Bashar really yearns to be a moderate and a man of peace touches the hearts of a seemingly endless supply of gullible Western politicians, journalists, and "experts." The highest possible military budget keeps the generals happy and loyal. As it had always done, inflaming the Arab-Israeli conflict and promoting anti-Americanism mobilize mass support, silence dissent, and provide an ideal excuse for keeping everything the same.

Bashar would not only make this strategy work; he would go on the offensive to become an Arab hero. And as if that were not enough, the West not only did not attack him, it beat a path to his door offering him favors.

CHAPTER EIGHT

TURNING THE TABLES

In Bashar's first years of rule, Syria and its regime were in terrible shape, isolated within the Arabic-speaking world and under assault internationally due to the regime's support for terrorism, role in fomenting the Iraqi insurgency, and mischief in Lebanon. At home, all the old problems continued unabated: stagnation, corruption, weak economy, and minority rule. A reform movement was getting bolder, demanding change.

Bashar's own former vice-president, Abd al-Halim Khaddam, who had served Hafiz when Bashar was a little boy, had defected to Paris. Demanding Bashar's overthrow, Khaddam denounced him as Rafiq Hariri's murderer and joined forces with the Muslim Brotherhood in a new opposition alliance. Indeed, things looked so bad that one Western expert wrote in October 2005: "Bashar Assad's regime in Syria has reached its end phase.... The regime will find it almost impossible to overcome its international isolation and its loss of domestic legitimacy." Given U.S., French, and Saudi hostility; possible indictment over the Hariri murder; the withdrawal from Lebanon; and the failure to deliver political reform, Bashar was supposedly doomed. The only possible outcomes, according to many, were that either the country would disintegrate or there would be a coup.[1] As so often happened to those who failed to understand the regime's structure and strategy, obituaries for the Assads were greatly exaggerated.

The two-year period from the September 11, 2001, attacks until shortly after the U.S. overthrow of Saddam Hussein might be called a new version of the 1990s. The Americans were mad as hell after the terrorist attacks, and the United States was in a period of relative strength, while Syria was weak. The regime could well worry about whether it was the next target on Washington's hit list.

Reformers in Syria hoped this fear would make Bashar more likely to allow reform or, at least, too intimidated to crack down on the liberals. Anwar al-Bunni, one of the most active and courageous human rights' activists, commented, "The government's fear that it will be next on America's 'regime change' list may make it wary of committing gross violations of human rights.... Some of us say that it is only because of what America did in Iraq, the fright it gave our rulers, that we reformers stand a chance here."[2]

To deflect American wrath and regain freedom of action, Syria cooperated—or perhaps, more accurately, pretended to do so—in 2001 as it had done a decade earlier. The two situations, however, were not exactly parallel. During the 1990s Hafiz generally did try to avoid antagonizing the United States, and his labors were more substantial—namely the peace process with Israel—which could reasonably be expected to require a long-term effort. In contrast, Bashar was far more provocative and gave absolutely minimal assistance in hunting down a tiny number of terrorists. Hafiz showed his intransigence only at the end, while Bashar betrayed any U.S. hopes of moderation almost immediately. Still, both dictators got away with their behavior rather easily.

Bashar's enemies did not consist just of Syrians at home or in exile. After decades of intimidation, the Lebanese majority was finally standing up to Syria. The West was more antagonistic to Syria than at any time in decades. The United States would have liked to see Bashar ousted since he was providing the logistical support and safe haven for terrorists in Iraq who were killing thousands of Iraqis and hundreds of American soldiers. In addition, Syria was attempting to foil the U.S. effort to produce a stable, democratic Iraq. Bashar was also the leading sponsor of terrorism against Lebanon, Israel, and Jordan. He refused to make peace with Israel and worked to ensure that no one else could.

The list of Bashar's enemies does not end there. By ordering Hariri's assassination in February 2005, the Syrian regime had also alienated France, the Arabs' best friend in the West. French president Jacques Chirac, who viewed Lebanon as virtually a protectorate of France, was furious at the murder of his Lebanese friend. The UN began an investigation, Washington recalled its ambassador to Syria, and U.S. and European Union leaders stopped visiting Damascus.[3]

The West finally seemed ready to take on Syria, having learned a lesson at long last. British foreign secretary Jack Straw later summarized this conclusion by saying: "What we...know from the history of dealing with Syria...[is] that where the international community is firm and united, in the end the Syrian government gets the message."[4]

In Lebanon itself, such a wave of anti-Syrian anger erupted in response to the killing of Hariri that Damascus felt it wise to withdraw its army. The Druze leader Walid Jumblatt especially was not afraid to tell off Bashar in the strongest language. One of his later statements gives the flavor of this discourse: "You yourself are an insignificant, criminal, and hostile minority. . . . We want blood vengeance from . . . Bashar. Oh ruler of Damascus, it is you who are the slave, and we are free." Lebanese leaders like Jumblatt demanded that Syria respect their country's independence, that Hizballah be disarmed, and that the Beirut government take over the south. "We reject the pretext of the Shabaa Farms, we reject the Syrian-Iranian axis. We reject the seizing of the homeland at the expense of its aspirations of liberty and independence."[5]

Everywhere one looked, people were sending that message. They insisted that the regime must reform, that change had to happen. On and on they chattered about how the solution was economic reforms, more human rights, democratic openings, and making peace—in short, moderation and pragmatism. If this did not happen, some in the West began to think about a second alternative defined by a new phrase, "Ba'th light": a palace coup that would continue the regime, without Bashar, on a somewhat more moderate course.

Yet Bashar made all of these problems go away with his magic wand, not by doing something new—or the kind of thing that might be expected from an allegedly Western-influenced, jazz-loving, internet-surfing kind of guy—but by returning to the most basic trick in the Arab regime playbook: fomenting violence and hatred. He was his father's son; in fact, he was trying to surpass the old man.

That is not to say Hafiz would have done the same things Bashar did, far from it. Hafiz was an obdurate man, yet his tough experiences in turbulent domestic politics and an unforgiving external world had also taught him to be a cautious one. But Bashar was indeed a prince of the Ba'th realm even if he had not originally been intended to be its crown prince. If he lacked confidence in his own ability, he and those around him—many of them also sons of the original Ba'thist revolutionaries who had seized and run Syria for thirty years—had confidence in a system they had inherited rather than built. With this background supplemented by the impetuosity of youth, they understood that extremism, not moderation, not adventurism, not diplomatic compromise, was the solution.

Bashar did not need decades of experience in power or depths of wisdom to comprehend the overwhelming value of demagoguery. He had seen it in action every day. Besides, it took far less money, effort, and talent to implement this policy than, say, a thoroughgoing reform of the economy and a systematic jihad against corruption. It was less risky, too, as long as he knew when to stop. Such a strategy could make his people happy, cheering the rulers with wild enthusiasm. Arabs on the street would extol his heroism and patriotism. World leaders would flock to his door, trying to find some tempting, tasty gift to buy

his favor. Many Western journalists and editorial writers turned him into a vir-
tuous victim, a feared adversary, or at least a sought-after interlocutor.

His trump card was that of national patriotic appeal. Syria, he argued, is
under threat by Israel, the United States, the traitorous Arab regimes, and the
West in general. The ungrateful Lebanese and other Arab regimes are cowardly,
eager to surrender. Democracy is subversion. The nature of this evil assault requires all Syrians, Arabs, and Muslims to stick together. Syria is the beating
heart of Arab resistance against Zionist aggression and American attempts to
destroy the Arabs and smash Islam. Syria is bold in leading the resistance. Ironically, of course, Bashar embarked on this course only after he determined that
the so-called ravening beasts were not all that likely to bite him.

Was the Syrian regime basically atheistic and neocommunist, dominated
by a non-Muslim minority? With a wave of his hand—though on the basis of
his father's long preparation—Bashar reinvented Syria as part of an Islamist alliance, standing alongside Iran, Hamas, Hizballah, and the Iraqi insurgency.
The insurgents were the real men—along with the occasional female suicide
bomber and legions of mothers applauding martyrdom for their sons—sacrificing themselves for the cause.

And to turn popular opinion to his side, all Bashar had to do was to set off
a war that inflicted $10 billion in damage to Lebanon and Israel without scrap-
ing one brick in his own country. If one wants to look for the perfect case study
of precisely how Arab and Middle East politics work, what Bashar did in 2006
is the model for understanding everything.

Of course, Bashar did not just base his strategy on a war in Lebanon. Indeed, the war was only the indirect result of his strategy, a logical outcome in
broad terms but an accident in terms of its details. He started five years earlier, maneuvering to defuse the American challenge without giving up anything, smashing the domestic reform movement, re-intimidating Lebanon,
and building an alliance with the Islamists. On this basis, Bashar expressed
confidence. Asked in 2006 if Syria was not in a weaker position, given all the
problems and enemies it was facing, he confidently responded that the situation was, in fact, the exact opposite: "The Syrian role has now become much
better than it has been in years."[6] How did Bashar pull off this massive reversal of fortune?

Bashar simply applied two key rules of Syrian politics which often apply to
the rest of the Arab world and Iran as well:

1.   The worse you behave, at least up to a point—Saddam Hussein
     went too far but he could easily have avoided his fate by a bit more

caution—the better you do in terms of public support and Western forbearance.

2. The stronger the regime gets, the worse it is for the society and economy. But the regime survives and is even cheered by those it victimizes. In a sense, Syria is the closest living embodiment to the system foreseen by George Orwell in his novel *1984*. Successfully controlling how people think, rounding up dissidents, as well as creating an external enemy produces a situation in which despite lack of freedoms and shortages of goods, the populace exclaims: "We love you, Big Brother."

And so Bashar:

- Started a covert war against America and his neighbors in Iraq
- Helped Hamas radicalize the Palestinians and engage in a war of terrorism against Israel
- Built up Hizballah's power as Syria's surrogate in Lebanon and to provoke Israel
- Repressed reformers at home
- Reconciled the Sunni Muslim majority at home by giving their religion more freedom of action and taking up Islamist causes abroad
- Developed a new version of the regime ideology to meld Arab nationalism and Islamism under the banner of resistance
- Murdered the most outstanding Lebanese politician and made it clear that without Syrian hegemony, Lebanon would know no peace
- Cooperated with Tehran to build their alliance into a force contending for regional power
- Blamed everything wrong with Syria, Arabs, and Muslims on America, Israel, and the West.

These points may seem simplistic when presented directly. Bashar may not have formulated his program so clearly, and, of course, in action there were contradictions, complications, and setbacks. Still, these were the main themes, and overall they worked quite well.

Much of this approach accorded with traditionally successful Arab political strategy; Bashar proved his audacity in undertaking it at the very moment when a failed example was so close at hand. His course of action can be compared to a man embarking on a crime when his next-door neighbor has just been convicted and hung. By looking out his window, Bashar could see what had happened to neighboring dictator Saddam Hussein. The United States had overthrown him in no small part as an example, in the great phrase of the French philosopher Voltaire two centuries earlier, to "encourage the others" of his ilk to behave better.

If Bashar could articulate why he felt his strategy would end up differently, he might have cited these six points:

1. The United States was tied down in Iraq, with its resources stretched near or to the limit.
2. Israel did not want a war with Syria.
3. The Europeans would work to restrain both of his enemies and generally seek peace at almost any price.
4. Just as Syria had once been protected by the Soviet Union, it was now Iran's client.
5. While Saddam had done things to inflame his domestic majority against himself, Bashar would please his subjects with a strong dose of Arab nationalism and Islamism.
6. When necessary, a few verbal gestures of moderation and an expressed eagerness to talk with the West would persuade politicians and officials there that Bashar was ready to make a deal. Many would complain that their own governments were at fault for not talking to Syria or offering it enough.

Beyond all this, however, was an additional factor that neutralized almost all the dangerous elements in his brew. Foolishly Saddam had acted directly: He attacked Iraq and invaded Kuwait with his army; he defied America and the world through public governmental action against the disarmament and sanctions mandated after his 1991 defeat.

In contrast, Bashar would act indirectly through no less than four sets of deniable surrogates: Syria's agents in Lebanon (both his own and locally purchased politicians), Hizballah, Hamas, and the Iraqi insurgency. Anyone who wanted to could pretend that Syria had nothing to do with all the violence next door. In each case, the victims themselves could be portrayed as the aggressors.

The indirect method also had another advantage. By acting publicly and directly, Saddam had thrice brought war onto Iraqi soil. Bashar would instead fight his wars on other people's territory. Syrians could be persuaded that any damage done in Lebanon or Iraq was part of a glorious struggle while they positively rejoiced in any harm the regime was able to do in Israel.

By such methods was Bashar able to turn the tables. The West did nothing to punish Syria; the regime credibly, if falsely, claimed victory over Israel in Lebanon without a single bomb falling on Syria and using mostly Iranian

money no less. To make the outcome even better for Syria, international op-
probrium has seemed to fall mainly on Israel. In Syria, everyone loves Bashar;
in the Arab-speaking world, the masses sing the praises of the Syria-Iran-
Hizballah-Hamas alliance. And if Syria is still isolated among Arab regimes, it
claims this situation is only the result of its superior virtue as the valiant warrior suffering from the sabotage and jealousy of hypocritical traitors.

Such a strategy has solved all Bashar's problems. Of course, Syria is still a
mess, falling steadily behind the rest of the world and lacking freedom. Yet
these problems are subsumed in the celebration of pride restored and honor ex-
alted. How did Bashar succeed in his goals?

First Bashar needed to ensure his power at home. Hafiz had done his work
well. After a consolidation period once Bashar took power, the Alawite elite,
Ba'th leadership, government officials, and generals had been brought into line
behind the new dictator. It was not the old guard but Bashar's own wishes that
killed off reform.

The next step was to destroy the pressure for reform from below. After the
early disappointed hope that Bashar would be more flexible than his father, the
Syrian reform movement tried to prove its loyalty to the regime. The government largely ignored the two ambitious reform manifestos in September 2000
and January 2001; thereafter, almost 300 Syrian intellectuals, professionals,
lawyers, and political activists tried in a May 2003 letter to Bashar to tie the
regime's ideology and interests up with reform.

They hoped to change Bashar's mind by using traditional arguments and
invoking the regime's own goals. Reform was needed, they stressed, because Israel's occupation of the West Bank and Gaza along with the U.S. occupation of
Iraq threatened the homeland, which was caught between two strong enemies.
Only reform would make Syria strong enough to handle that threat.[7] In this
way, liberals hoped in vain to strengthen their case and reduce the risk of repression. Yet that more cautious, seemingly clever strategy had the drawback of
reinforcing the very ideas that ensured the dictatorship's continuity and the
radical Islamist opposition's strength.

For example, the May 2003 letter argued that the regime's diagnosis was
right, only its proposed solution was wrong. National survival, the reformers
insisted, required reform. Arab governments were impotent or collapsing,
and Syria was surrounded by enemies, especially the "aggressive, racist, ego-
tistical, and evil policies" of the United States and Israel. The only way for
Syria to save itself and stop the United States from taking over the region was
by a sweeping program of reforms that included the release of political prisoners, allowing all democratic freedoms, and reducing the power of the security forces.[8]

Bashar was not persuaded, and his regime never accepted this argument. Even if it wanted economic progress, it would not buy it at the price of reform. In the 1990s, the regime had even proposed the slogan of "development without change."[9] Thus, appeals to Syrian leaders to reform themselves are unlikely to produce results. As the reformist activist Maamoun al-Humsi put it in retrospect, attempts to coax reform by praising the regime were doomed to failure.[10]

By September 2001, the regime felt secure enough to arrest both Sayf and Humsi, the two liberal dissident members of parliament, on charges of trying to change the constitution by illegal means. The "illegal means" in question seem to have been speaking freely in advocating a multiparty system in liberal discussion clubs and writing appeals to the regime to rein in the security services and end high-level corruption. As Sayf was taken off to serve his sentence, he shouted, "This is a badge of honor to me and others like me. Long live the people!"[11] Like Sayf, who owned the Syrian franchise of Adidas sportswear, Humsi was no naive academic but a successful self-made businessman, showing how the regime had alienated the most talented part of the bourgeoisie—those eager and able to build a better economy—by its waste, incompetence, corruption, and mismanagement.[12]

In a similar vein, the former head of Damascus University's economics department, Arif Dahla, was sentenced to ten years in prison. New crimes were invented to keep up with technological advances. Thus, a state security court in Damascus sentenced three people to prison terms ranging from two to four years after they sent material on Syria to a Gulf Internet publication. They were accused of "transmitting to a foreign country information which should have stayed secret," of "writing articles banned by the government and damaging to Syria and its ties with a foreign state," and "publishing false information."[13]

There was still a little reform activity and a great deal of grumbling, expressed in private or in the foreign Arab press. In March 2004, twenty Syrians held a demonstration outside parliament until they were arrested. Others organized an Internet petition drive, with several thousand people signing, calling for the abolition of military law, an end to arbitrary arrest, the release of political prisoners, and the right to establish political parties and civil associations.[14] But basically the reform movement was dismantled.

When one examines how reformist dissidents were treated, it is easy to understand why so few join them. A prime example is Sayf's account of his personal experiences. Shortly after his release from prison in January 2006, having served four years out of a five-year sentence, he was called in by one of the regime's highest-ranking secret policemen, the head of General Intelligence, and warned not to meet with a UN Human Rights' Commission delegation. The next night he was taken blindfolded and handcuffed to an office of military security, an organization headed by Bashar's brother-in-law, where he was beaten in an attempt to make him promise not to talk to journalists, diplomats, or other foreigners. He was given a choice: forget about politics and enjoy the regime's help or spend the rest of his life being harassed and humiliated.[15]

Four days after this incident, Sayf was summoned by the head of still a third agency, the Department of Domestic Security, who expressed anger at Sayf's having given an interview to a Lebanese newspaper. Unless he published a retraction, Sayf was told, he would return to prison. Once Sayf complied, however, the demands escalated. Now he was warned not to make any statement at all to journalists or at meetings. Otherwise, the police suggested, he could be imprisoned or even put to death, with the regime ignoring any foreign protests about his treatment. Again Sayf gave in but tried other means to continue his resistance activities. In March 2006 he participated in a sit-in by Kurdish groups on the second anniversary of a massacre committed by government agents. Sayf was seized and imprisoned for a day. The head of Domestic Security told him that he was now considered an enemy of the state.[16]

His office manager and secretary were called in for questioning by the secret police, whose spies lurked outside his office, home, and his children's houses. Sayf was followed wherever he went; his visitors, relatives, and friends were interrogated. The police tried to persuade them to file some false complaint against Sayf that might damage his business or moral reputation. Starting in July, Domestic Security ordered him to visit its office daily. The second time, as he was leaving, two agents assaulted and severely beat him.[17]

Such treatment would be sufficient to convince most people to stop engaging in political activities that, after all, appeared to be futile. Faced with such conditions, another activist, Maamoun al-Humsi decided to leave the country altogether and continue his campaign for human rights in exile. The regime, he explained, forces a choice between being a rewarded collaborator or facing pressure, slander, and imprisonment. Both choices "lead to the silencing" of dissidents and at worst to their "parroting the views of the regime" and serving its interests.[18]

Everyone in Syria understood that Sayf and Humsi were wealthy and internationally known figures, scions of the most respected, commercially successful Sunni Muslim families in Syria. If they could be so treated, those of lesser repute could fear much worse. The regime was not shy about eliminating those it perceived to be threats. The potential penalty for challenging the regime could be death. For example, the popular Kurdish cleric Muhammad Mashouq al-Khaznawi, who had worked to ally Kurdish groups with the secular opposition and the Muslim Brotherhood, was murdered in 2005, apparently by the government.[19] When his son dared make this accusation, a warrant was issued for his arrest.[20]

In the face of this onslaught, the Syrian liberals might well have quoted lines from folk-singer Tom Lehrer's satirical lyrics about the Spanish Civil War: the regime may have won all the battles but they had all the good songs. The liberal's arguments were impeccable, but no one was persuaded by them. The liberal call to reason could not overcome the overwhelming appeal of such a deeply entrenched, passionately positioned ideology coupled with the power of an omnipresent state.

Despite the wide range of problems it faced, Syria once again outmaneuvered the external threats as well as it did the domestic challenges. During the 1990s, Syria had fended off American pressure at a time of weakness by cooperating in the war against Iraq and participating in a peace process with Israel. In exchange, it received U.S. acceptance of its control over Lebanon as well as relative noninterference regarding its sponsorship of terrorism and its poor human rights' record. A similar process would happen at the start of the next decade as well, with Bashar's strategy echoing that of his father's, albeit less skillfully and less completely.

In 2000, on the eve of his own death and in the Clinton administration's waning days, Hafiz had ended his long dance with the peace process by bowing out of it entirely. But his refusal of a deal premised on his getting back the entire Golan Heights in exchange for full peace with Israel was overshadowed by Arafat's similar rejection. Indeed, the dramatic developments around the failed Camp David conference, the rebuffed Clinton plan, and Arafat's return to terrorist violence, coupled with Clinton's own departure from office, prevented any strong U.S. reaction to Syria's behavior. Damascus continued to enjoy the benefits of relatively soft treatment by America even after it had reneged on reaching a peace agreement, the behavior that had motivated this U.S. policy in the first place. The same point applies to Syria's turnaround to embrace the Iraqi regime in the late 1990s, after receiving billions of Gulf Arab money and American gifts for opposing Saddam.

Then along came September 11, 2001, once again wiping Syria's slate clean, at least in terms of practical matters. The terrorist attacks on New York and Washington by Usama bin Ladin's al-Qaida supposedly changed everything. But, still, some terrorists were more equal than others. Although Syria remained on the list of countries sponsoring terrorism, al-Qaida was an independent group rather than the client of any Arab state. President George W. Bush proclaimed al-Qaida the main target in the war on terrorism, America's top priority. U.S. forces went after it by invading Afghanistan and overthrowing its Taliban regime, then trying to chase down al-Qaida's leaders and assets.

Given this focus, though, the war on terrorism seemed to have become a war on just one terrorist group. The West ignored the fact that Syria sponsored and hosted Hamas, Hizballah, Islamic Jihad, the Popular Front for the Liberation of Palestine, the Popular Front for the Liberation of Palestine-General Command, and a long list of other terrorist organizations. Forgotten was Syria's role in the attack on the U.S. Marines in 1983, which had accounted for the biggest death toll of Americans in a single terror attack before September 11. But Syria was not a sponsor of al-Qaida.

In this respect, the September 11 attacks seemed to be a repeat of the crisis of a decade earlier. Just as Syria had gained U.S. tolerance by siding with it against Iraq's invasion of Kuwait, the same thing seemed to be happening by Damascus's doing so against al-Qaida. The irony of a terrorism-sponsoring state becoming an ally in the war against terrorism mirrored the earlier irony of a radical Ba'th party–ruled dictatorship joining the coalition in the war against another radical Ba'th party–ruled dictatorship.

Once again, too, Syria was prepared to buy virtue and immunity on the cheap, acting in its own interest and doing nothing beyond that. After all, what did Syria owe to al-Qaida, one of the few terrorist groups it did not sponsor? The regime was more than happy to supply the United States with some intelligence about bin Ladin's organization.

Ironies abounded. Syria apparently provided safe passage for al-Qaida men fleeing Afghanistan to pass into Lebanon, where they could do more mischief. In January 2002 Bashar told a visiting delegation of U.S. legislators that America could benefit from Syria's knowledge as a country that "successfully fought terrorism." Senator Richard Durbin concurred. Standing a few blocks away from the headquarters of the leading terrorist groups in the world, Durbin praised Syria's "rich experience in fighting terrorism," which might benefit the United States. "The analysis we heard on Syria's history, experience, and handling of [the terrorism] that struck at it is a useful lesson for us and for many countries in the world."[21]

Leaving aside the fact that Syria's "rich experience" consisted mostly of training, arming, encouraging, and protecting terrorist groups, an exiled Syrian dissident, Subhi Hadidi, was appalled by what was said to constitute the allegedly "positive" aspects of Syria's record regarding terrorism. After all, Bashar was boasting about Syria's destruction of the Muslim Brotherhood in the 1980s, a campaign that included murdering thousands of innocent civilians. For the United States to apply Syria's experience, he explained, meant flattening whole cities, as the Syrian army did in Hama, or sentencing to death retroactively anyone who had ever belonged to the Taliban or al-Qaida. "Should the American military commander," he asked, "have climbed atop a tank, ridden to the heart of Kabul, and announced via megaphone that he was prepared to kill 1,000 people a day, as the Syrian military commander did in Aleppo in 1980?"[22]

Once again the Syrian regime was treated as a privileged dictatorship, a most favored terrorism-sponsoring nation, and a forgiven massive violator of human rights. Every day the Syrian media, schools, mosques, and officials systematically slandered America, training the populace in hatred and steeping them in lies. The regime's smug confidence was exemplified by Imad Fawzi Shuaybi, a professor at Damascus University, who explained, "Relations exist on two levels. Publicly there is conflict, but on the second level the U.S. knows that it needs the Syrians."[23]

The wording of that statement is telling. Shuaybi did not claim that while publicly there was conflict, in private there was cooperation—a concept that might well be applied regarding U.S. relations to, say, Egypt or Saudi Arabia. Instead, he admits that the equation is between Syria maintaining conflict with the United States and at the same time Syria having leverage over the United States, a win-win situation for Damascus. This analysis is an accurate reflection of the Syrian attitude: It can act as it pleases because it has the upper hand in the relationship. And indeed this is what Syria's "rich experience" in dealing with the United States and the West in general have taught it.

And what precisely did Syria do to gain this apparent leverage? Syrian security forces—the same men who had fomented terrorism against Israel, Jordan, Lebanon, and Turkey—spoke to CIA officials about al-Qaida. Intelligence-sharing, according to the *Washington Post,* reached "unprecedented levels,"[24] which probably meant it had gone from zero to one-tenth of 1 percent. "They have said and done some things, and have cooperated with us recently, that suggest that they're looking for a better relationship with the United States," said Secretary of State Colin Powell. Bush called Bashar to say thanks. Yet Syria was not looking for a better relationship but simply to get the heat off itself without changing any of its policies. A half-dozen congressional delegations visited Damascus in January 2002, a period known locally and jokingly as the American month. Bashar suddenly decided to meet all the American counterterrorism tourists personally, even though he had previously ignored such pilgrims.[25]

What had Syria actually done? As far as is known, it provided information that helped disrupt one attack planned against American soldiers in the Persian Gulf (presumably not in Iraq where it did not want such attacks to be stopped) and assisted in the arrest and investigation of Muhammad Haydar Zammar, a Syrian-born German citizen who had recruited three of the September 11 hijackers in

Hamburg. No doubt these actions were useful but raise the question of how much Syrian intelligence knew about hundreds of such operations in Iraq designed to kill American soldiers or about Zammar's activities when the September 11 attacks were still in the planning stage. Syria also reportedly arrested, presumably temporarily, some people the U.S. authorities wanted and turned over files on them with, in the *Post's* words, "a speed and ease surprising for a former Soviet ally that is frequently mistrustful of American intentions." Indeed, American officials pronounced themselves as "surprised" at just how cooperative Syria was being.[26]

But why should anyone have been surprised? After the bloodiest terrorist attack in American history, the United States was, literally, on the warpath. Anyone deemed to have helped stage this operation was going to be seen as a deadly enemy worthy of punishment; anyone who helped capture the terrorists would reap benefits. In exchange for a bit of assistance in rounding up terrorists who were not in its employ, and might conceivably be operating against it, Syria could get on the bandwagon. Damascus could even choose the terrorists on whom it did or did not inform.

If Syria had really wanted good relations with the United States—or truly feared its antiterrorist wrath—it could have closed down terrorist offices in Damascus, as the United States had been demanding for years. Syria then would have gotten off the list of terrorism sponsors and become eligible for increased trade benefits and even U.S. aid. Yet Syria was unwilling to pay that small price. Even worse, it did not feel such a gesture necessary because the regime believed that American forbearance could be bought on the cheap. If Bashar had not already understood this lesson from his father's teachings, here was more proof that this was a good tactic; he no doubt filed this experience away for future use: America should be fooled rather than feared.

Some other very telling aspects of this moment in history should have been added to the "rich experience" of the United States and the West in dealing with Syria. First, one of the actions Syria has been credited with, in an anti-terrorist context, was the fact that Hizballah attacks on Israel temporarily stopped soon after the September 11 attacks. But if Syria actually can be thanked for having so much influence on Hizballah as to make it desist, Damascus can equally be held responsible for when Hizballah did stage attacks and can be seen as the address for punishing them. Indeed, the attacks soon began again, the coast seeming clear and with an apparent green light from Damascus.

Second, the United States forgot history, as happens so often in Washington but never in Damascus. As an example, the *Washington Post* told its readers: "For more than a decade, Syria's policy has favored peace with Israel conditioned on full return of the Golan."[27] Yet this was written just a year after Syria rejected peace with Israel on precisely this basis, despite being offered full return of the Golan Heights.

Third, at the very moment U.S. policymakers were praising Syria and trying to engage it, Bashar's government established a new committee to promote a boycott of American goods. Restaurants in Damascus posted signs saying that no Americans were allowed to dine there. In one case, a U.S. diplomat was thrown out of a restaurant; its owners were lauded as local heroes.[28] In addition, inciting violent anti-Americanism in the Syrian media went on without any diminution.

To Syria, fooling the United States government—and this was the tough second Bush administration, not some allegedly soft-on-bad-guys liberal Democrats—and media seemed as easy as stealing candy from a baby or, perhaps more to the point, from Lebanon. Of course, the United States rationalized that cozying up to Syria yet again was also due to the limited options the Middle East offered it. Still, immediately after September 11, Syria might have been pressed to do more to win such a full pardon, like closing down terrorist offices and helping to arrest those (pro-Syrian) terrorists who had blown up the U.S. embassy and the marine barracks in the 1980s and held, sometimes killing, American hostages. The country might also have been pressed to move away from Iran or toward making peace with Israel.

Most obviously of all, Syria might have been asked to turn over the four Hizballah terrorists listed by the FBI as among the world's twenty-two most wanted. They were known to be operating in Syrian-controlled Lebanon, no doubt frequently visiting Damascus, and probably working closely with Syrian intelligence officials.[29] These men included the notorious Imad Mughniyya, involved in the 1982 Beirut bombing that killed 242 American soldiers in Lebanon in 1982, among other achievements.[30] When Assistant Secretary of State William Burns asked Bashar about these men, he said he had no idea where they might be.[31] The United States then dropped the issue entirely, without criticizing or pressuring Syria.

Born in a poor neighborhood in Beirut's southern suburbs in 1962, Mughniyya had joined Arafat's elite Force 17 security unit as a teenager and rose quickly from rank-and-file gunman to important Fatah intelligence figure. By the 1980s, Mughniyya was head of the terrorist apparatus of Syria's client Hizballah group, which was taking American hostages. Besides the 1982 Beirut bombing, he was probably involved in the April 1983 bombing of the U.S. embassy there that killed 63 Americans.[32]

Indicted in absentia by a U.S. court for the 1985 hijacking of a TWA plane in which an American navy diver was murdered, he also made the FBI's list of the world's twenty-two most wanted terrorists issued after the September 11, 2001, attacks. Three others on that list were also Hizballah men, one of whom was wanted by the Argentine government for the 1992 bombing of the Israeli embassy in Buenos Aires in which twenty-three people were killed.[33]

Rather than the United States pressing its advantage, the Syrian distinction between "good" and "bad" terrorism—the deliberate murders of civilians that served Syrian interests and those that did not—was allowed to stand. "The only problem between Syria and the United States is distinguishing between terrorism and national resistance," explained Haytham Kaylani, a former Syrian general and analyst at the Arab Center for Strategic Studies in Damascus.[34] It was not the nature of the acts that defined them as terrorism, Syria held, but their political intentions. This distinction periodically returned to haunt American policy. It was a case of one man's terrorist being another's asset to subvert neighbors and ensure that no peace ever came to the Middle East.

The arguments of those boosting cooperation with Syria were hardly impressive. "Although the U.S. Embassy in Damascus has been attacked twice in the past four years, including a serious assault in 1998 that U.S. officials contend was partly organized by Syrian security," explained the *Washington Post,* "the embassy also sponsors English lessons, cultural events and other trappings of a normal relationship." Who needs a tough policy when they let you teach English for free to their citizens?

As for the December 1998 Syrian attack on the U.S. embassy, it was among the most severe such assaults in modern history. Demonstrators protesting the American "Desert Fox" air attack on Iraq, which had come in response to an Iraqi plot to assassinate former president George Bush, broke into the American Cultural Center and ambassador's home, damaged them, and tore down the American flag. As if this were not enough, the day after President Clinton met with Hafiz at King Hussein's funeral, Defense Minister Tlas called the assault "an act of heroism." The Syrians merely apologized, paid $500,000 for the damage, and distanced themselves from Tlas's remark.[35]

Then, as happened so frequently, Syria's regime was forgiven. But even the new, post–September 11 honeymoon, and presumably Syrian cooperation against selected terrorists it didn't like or need, was not to last long. The United States had thrown away its massive strategic leverage over Syria without achieving anything except a small amount of intelligence on al-Qaida.

The attack on the embassy was also a signal of Syria's turn toward an alliance with Saddam. Within two years, it would bring a return to open hostility against the United States. By that time, though, the momentum generated by the post–September 11 period had dissipated, and Syria was even more convinced that America was a paper tiger. Then, too, a new U.S. confrontation with Iraq in 2003 undercut any U.S. willingness or ability to confront Syria, just as had happened with the 1991 battle with Baghdad.

Of course, the Syrians had good reason to oppose a U.S. invasion of Iraq. Such a move created an uncomfortable precedent that might be used against themselves some day, either by the Americans or by their own people. Syrian television avoided screening reports from Baghdad's central square, where Iraqis celebrated the toppling of the statue of Saddam Hussein. As one Syrian activist put it, statues can be found in Damascus as well.[36]

Having American troops on Syria's border was also a real strategic worry. Bashar even admitted that he thought Syria would be the next American target if it succeeded in Iraq.[37] In addition, Saddam Hussein, faced with a growing American threat, had been working hard to improve relations with Syria, including a huge increase in trade starting in 1997. When U.S. military operations against Iraq had briefly increased during Operation Desert Fox in 1998, the Syrian regime ordered up violent anti-American demonstrations to warn against targeting the Baghdad regime.

This rapprochement was certainly not due to any friendship between Hafiz and Saddam. The two dictators hated each other, having quarreled going back to the 1960s, when the international Ba'th party split into two factions. Aside from ideological differences, the real dispute was over which country should lead the Arab world, Syria or Iraq. Saddam, more ruthless than his Syrian counterparts, seemed to frighten them a bit. Even Bashar called him "a beast of a man."[38]

Despite these personal dislikes, Syria had some good strategic motives for accommodating Iraq since it feared Israel and was under pressure from Turkey to stop supporting Kurdish terrorists. But there was also a material motive far more potent than Arab nationalist brotherhood. In 1998 Syria and Iraq agreed to reopen their petroleum pipeline, a violation of the international sanctions on Baghdad. U.S. officials warned that Syria should "think carefully" about doing so. Syria thought about it, did it any way, and the Clinton administration did nothing in response.[39] Neither did its successors. By 2002 Syrian minister of information Adnan Umran could state publicly, "Our relations with Iraq are back to normal."[40]

Nothing was very well concealed. In 1999, for example, a *New York Times* correspondent stood beside a Syrian highway watching scores of trucks laden with Iraqi oil pass as Syrian police watched them. When the U.S. and British governments protested, Syria responded that it was unable to control the border. Yet this was not a very difficult task since the trucks were openly crossing the frontier on only two roads.[41] Syria later used the same argument to excuse its alleged inability to stop the flow of weapons into Iraq and Lebanon to arm insurgencies there.

Meanwhile, the Syrian regime made a huge amount of money from the sanctions against Iraq. The big bucks were in oil smuggling, much of which also was conducted quite openly through the pipeline from 2000 until it was shut off by American troops in Iraq almost three years later. The petroleum—about 200,000 barrels a day, one-third of Syria's own production—was sold to Syria at $10 to $15 a barrel and used inside the country, letting Damascus export more of its own oil for $24 a barrel, at a profit estimated to total $3.4 billion.[42] The funds from Syria furnished Saddam's largest source of illegal income.[43]

Saddam used part of the money he received from Syria to buy arms, and Bashar helped here, too. According to captured files that *Los Angeles Times* reporters obtained from the al-Bashair Trading Company in Baghdad, prior to the U.S. attack in 2003, it bought tens of millions of dollars in arms from Syria, holding more than fifty contracts with a Syrian counterpart, SES International Corporation. The general manager of SES was Asif Isa Shalish, a cousin of Bashar; another of the biggest shareholders was Major General Dhu Himma Shalish, a Bashar relative and head of the presidential security corps. When Saddam was overthrown, the director-general of al-Bashair, Munir Awad, fled to Syria, where he lives under government protection.[44] Clearly, Awad is a man whom the Syrian authorities would not like to be captured and questioned about his business activities.

Washington did protest the blatant violations of the sanctions' system but Syria ignored the complaints. Bashar even lied directly to Powell's face during his 2001 trip to Damascus by claiming that the Syria-Iraq oil pipeline was merely being tested and not carrying large amounts of petroleum. When the large-scale oil shipments continued on a daily basis, it was obvious that far more than a mere testing was going on. Yet the United States took no action. At the same time, Syria was also violating the sanctions in other ways: Its business dealings with Iraq included a new air route, railroad line, free trade zone, and joint investment institution. Indeed, at the very moment Bashar was telling Powell that Syria was not helping Iraq evade sanctions, a twenty-two-member Syrian trade mission was arriving in Baghdad to promote economic ties.[45]

One incident in Syria-Iraq relations at this time was far more shocking than the rest and should have raised a danger flag about how reckless Bashar might be. At a meeting between Bashar and Saddam, the Syrian regime reportedly agreed to let Iraq send an army corps to the Golan Heights. Four Iraqi divisions began to move toward Syria. The Saudis were extremely upset and urged the United States to join them in giving Bashar a serious warning against such a provocative move. After all, not only would this escalation lead to a potential crisis with Israel that might result in war, it would give Saddam a chance to drag Syria into a conflict whenever he wanted. If, for example, Saddam wanted to blackmail the West into dropping sanctions or forestall a U.S. attack against himself, the Iraqi dictator might easily unleash a new Arab-Israeli war. The Saudi envoy, Prince Bandar, claimed he told Bashar something along the lines of "You think you are using Saddam but Saddam is using you." Bashar sensibly backed down and canceled the plan.[46] If, however, Saddam had remained in power, it is possible that Bashar would have later chosen his wily neighboring tyrant as role model instead of turning toward Hizballah's leader, Hassan Nasrallah.

When Syria raised its successful candidacy for membership on the UN Security Council in 2002 for a two-year term, the fact that it had broken UN sanctions and helped the international organization's number-one enemy did not become an issue. Openly violating UN sanctions against Iraq and UN resolutions on Lebanon, plus sponsoring terrorism, even proved no barrier to Syria taking its turn at chairing the Security Council in June 2002, despite its domestic and international behavior.

The only gesture Syria made toward helping curb Iraq was its November 2002 vote in favor of UN Security Council Resolution 1441, which demanded that Iraq let international weapons' inspections start again or face consequences. This could be viewed merely as a response to international pressure. At any rate, Syrian officials explained that they considered the proposal a way to save Saddam in spite of himself. Iraqi concessions on inspections would not hurt Syria; an American invasion would. Syria, like most other countries (and unlike the United States), did not interpret this resolution as giving a green light for any attack on Iraq.

Meanwhile, the Syrian regime's promotion of across-the-board anti-Americanism was relentless. Even if the United States is willing to ignore or forget this permanent campaign, it has sunk deep roots in the Syrian people's way of thinking. Certainly and understandably, there are many elements of U.S. policy that Syria does not like. But what is objectionable and dangerous is not the fact of opposition but the passionate hatred, solely negative presentation, slanderous misrepresentation, and demonizing interpretation.

Basically what the Syrian regime is saying and disseminating through every aspect of the country's media, schools, government statements, and mosque sermons precisely parallels the line of Usama bin Ladin, which triggered the September 11 attacks and against which the United States has declared war. The message is that America sought to conquer the Arab world, turn the Middle East over to Israeli control, and destroy Islam. Consequently, it was necessary and proper to fight the United States.

If the Syrian regime believes this—and there is every indication that it does—the conflict could never be resolved by patient explanation or negotiation. Syria's hostility toward the United States is more intense than that of any other Arab state. After all, Egypt—and somewhat later, Algeria and Libya—successfully "changed sides"; other Arab states, such as Saudi Arabia, Jordan, Morocco, and Tunisia, have always gotten along with the United States.

Like these other countries, Bashar had two alternatives to the course he selected. He could have made a deal with minor concessions, trading relative Syrian inaction in sponsoring terrorism and opposing U.S. efforts in Iraq for various benefits, including the acceptance of his regime and its continued domination over Lebanon. Even Iran, at least temporarily, chose to stand by while its most dangerous foe, Saddam, was destroyed despite the strategic threat of an American presence next door. Or, more ambitiously, Bashar could have made a deal with the United States and tried to transform Syria through economic and political reform, peace with Israel in exchange for the Golan Heights, and massive Western aid. Instead, he opted for confrontation.

The key to understanding this choice is the same as the one needed to comprehend how his father had earlier dealt with a parallel situation. It was not merely a matter of ideology or personality but of a fundamentally correct assessment. The Assads concluded, in the 1990s and the next decade as well, that to make friends with America, peace with Israel, economic reform, and democracy at home would be to ensure the destruction of their regime.

The rulers in Damascus believed they must avoid the experience of the Soviet bloc, Romania, and Yugoslavia. A basically minority communal regime built up on a system of privilege and corruption could not make a transition to democracy and a free enterprise system. It has no hope of ever winning any fair election; the Alawites might well be massacred by the Sunni majority; the elite would end up in prison or facing a firing squad. Thus, a radical response was not a mistake or a result of Bashar's incompetence—though there are always better and worse ways of implementing any strategy—but of necessity.

And so at the start of the 2003 war, Bashar stated that the United States was attacking Iraq to seize its oil and help Israel dominate the region. "Being friends with America," he warned, "was worse than being its enemy."[47] Why did he think that? An obvious reading is that being on America's side would require states to give up militancy; thus his comment was a slur on Saudi Arabia, Jordan, and Egypt. But they had not particularly suffered from their relationship with the United States. On the contrary, Jordan and Egypt got back all the land Israel had captured in 1967 and received a lot of aid. Saudi Arabia received real protection from Iraq and Iran. What Bashar was actually saying was that he desperately needed the United States as an enemy. He and the Alawite-dominated Ba'th party could not remain in power unless they could mobilize the masses eternally against the evil Americans.

In addition, there is always the ethnic issue. Any democracy in Iraq would mean a regime headed by the country's majority, Shia Muslim Arabs and Kurds, rather than the Sunni Muslim minority. Wouldn't this put ideas in the heads of the Sunni Muslim Arab majority in Syria, not to mention inspiring complaints by Syrian Kurds, who have been so badly treated by Bashar's regime?

Perhaps Iraq would even break up into separate ethnic states, another Syrian nightmare, highlighted by Bashar's false claim that Israel and the United States want the existing Arabic-speaking countries to be split into smaller ethnically defined states. "There are countries in the Middle East with diverse nationalities," Bashar said, "but they have social and historic cohesiveness."[48] Syria fits that description; he no doubt worries whether its cohesiveness will prove to be merely a matter of wishful thinking. The regime is really worried about interethnic warfare and a collapse of its own system at home. Either way, whether Iraq succeeds as a federal state or fails amid a civil war, these outcomes hold dangerous implications for Syria.

Most revealing is Bashar's claim that Bush would fail because he "does not understand that for the Arabs honor is more important than anything else, even food."[49] Bashar's dinner table is not noticeably bare because of this sense of priorities. Yet he is also correct and comprehends his people far better than do American policymakers. This passionate search for pride and revenge means that material benefits—higher living standards, more rights, security from violence—can be trumped by religious and patriotic appeals. Such was the very mechanism by which the regime controlled its subjects. The Romans called it ruling through giving the masses "bread and circuses." In the Arab world, according to Bashar, circuses alone suffice.

There is also an interesting consistency in the pattern of Syria's policy toward the other Arabic-speaking states. Traditionally, Syria had tried to distinguish itself as the most militant, the true knights of Arab nationalism. From the 1950s to the 1980s, Syrian leaders generally insisted there were two camps—the patriots, led by Syria; and the traitors, led usually by Egypt or Saudi Arabia. At times when Syria needed Egyptian political backing or Saudi money, it temporarily reduced its hostility to either state.

Now Bashar has revived the confrontational approach that his father had discarded while on good behavior in the 1990s, though given his other prob-

lems, Bashar arguably needs the help of Cairo and Riyad to escape his isolation
and cope with Syria's economic problems. Nevertheless, at the March 2003
Arab Summit in Sharm al-Shaykh, Egypt, he eviscerated Egypt and Saudi Arabia, which he said were betraying Iraq. He called Qatar an American colony
and a base for subjugating the Gulf, because it hosted U.S. military headquarters. This reveals a major Syrian weakness. For in its need to be the peerless
leader and to downgrade everyone else, Syria has always found it hard to keep
any Arab ally for very long.

So the Syrian government and media pours abuse on the United States and
any Arabs deemed to be siding with it or even neutral. The Iraq war of March
2003 was portrayed as an assault on Arab honor to enslave them, destroy their
religion, take away their culture, and steal their oil. Syria could not allow there
to be any hint of the fact that—rightly or wrongly—U.S. policy was based on
concern over Saddam's aggressive intentions, brutal behavior, and ambitions to
obtain weapons of mass destruction.

The Syrian line was that, as Radio Damascus put it, "The forces of evil in
the world have conspired to gain control over the wealth and resources of the
Arab nation. The superpower in the world is acting today in a biased way in
order to achieve its aims and its Satanic arms bring harm to peaceful peace-lov-
ing peoples."[50] It is not surprising, then, that Syrian foreign minister Farouq al-
Sharaa compared Bush to Hitler and the United States to the Third Reich and
that he told Syria's parliament, "We want Iraq's victory."[51]

Naturally, the United States was not pleased. The efforts to win Syria's
friendship, which had been ongoing since 1990, came to an end in 2003. Secretary of State Powell said the United States would carefully watch Syria's
weapons of mass destruction program and support for Hizballah. Deputy Secretary of State Richard Armitage warned that the United States might respond
to Syria's backing for terrorism with force. Still, the United States did not want
trouble with Damascus. Powell offered Damascus another chance to avoid
conflict, while Bush even praised Syria—hoping his wish would be fulfilled—
for desiring to be cooperative.[52]

Yet things were about to get worse, much worse. On the military front, the
Syrians were no doubt disappointed at the speed and ease with which the
United States defeated Iraq and captured the country. The Syrian media did
not broadcast the scenes of American forces conquering Baghdad and of rejoic-
ing Iraqis. The pulling down of Saddam's statue would obviously put ideas into
the minds of Syrian citizens regarding idols closer to home that might be similarly treated. Moreover, Syrian leaders were annoyed that Iraq had fallen so easily. They seemed to feel that Syria had risked a lot to protect Saddam's regime;
how dare it surrender without much of a fight?

From the U.S. standpoint, Syria took the enemy side by smuggling military equipment into Iraq (including night-vision goggles) and letting wanted Iraqi officials, millions of dollars of Saddam's money, and possibly some equipment for the production of weapons of mass destruction cross the border to safe haven into Syria. In addition, after the defeat of the Saddam regime, an insurgency began that depended largely on Syria as a rear area. Pro-Saddam officials there used smuggled money to finance and direct a war against the coalition forces as well as the Shia-Kurdish majority. Terrorists from abroad or Syrians themselves were trained, armed, and dispatched into Iraq.[53]

Syria was making a fool out of the U.S. government and the Bush administration was helping it to do so. After discovering that Bashar had lied to him about closing the Iraqi oil pipeline in 2001, during his next visit, in May 2003, Powell insisted in his airplane on the way to Damascus that he remembered the experience and would not be fooled again.[54] Shortly after he landed, however, Bashar again sold him the same old swampland by falsely telling Powell that terrorist offices in Damascus had already been closed down, good news that the secretary of state announced to the American reporters accompanying him. Unfortunately, it quickly became apparent, in the most humiliating way for Powell, that he had been taken in once more. Reporters simply telephoned the offices of Hamas and Islamic Jihad and found that they were still open for business as usual.[55]

This did not prevent Bashar from again falsely announcing in January 2004 that the terrorist offices had been closed.[56] They remained in operation ever after, ordering attacks, issuing propaganda, and arranging for the training and equipping of terrorists. Over and over again Bashar pulled this trick on the Americans. And even when they caught on, they just protested until the scam once more receded from memory, leaving at least some officials and politicians eager for new rounds of negotiations in the hopes that Bashar would really change that time.

The post-Saddam situation in Iraq should have laid such fantasies to rest amidst a new and much hotter conflict between Washington and Damascus. For the first time in history, an Arab country was directly sponsoring a full-scale war against the United States. Statements from Syrian officials, including state-appointed clerics, urged Arabs and Muslims to fight the coalition force's "savage aggression."[57] American officials charged Syria with helping terrorists cross the border into Iraq to attack both American troops and civilians, murdering thousands of people. On March 24, 2003, U.S. helicopters flying inside Iraq were hit by fire coming from Syria, possibly by Syrian border guards.[58] In September, Paul Bremer, the U.S. administrator for Iraq, stated that half the foreign combatants captured fighting as insurgents were Syrian, apparently entering the country from their homeland.[59]

The Syrian government responded to American diplomats' complaints about the flow of terrorists and arms to the Iraqi insurgency by claiming to know nothing. When detailed information was presented to prove that this smuggling was going on, the highest officials in Syria—including Bashar—publicly denied that the United States ever provided any proof of its allegations.[60]

Another source of friction was the U.S. government belief that $2.5 billion from Saddam's regime was in Syrian state banks, apparently being used to finance the insurgency. At times, the regime denied the presence of such funds; at other times, it falsely promised that the funds would soon be returned to Iraq. Damascus refused to cooperate with a visiting American delegation seeking to discover who controlled this money. In addition, even more money for the war in Iraq was reportedly being laundered through Syria by foreign donors.[61]

There is even some evidence of direct Syrian espionage against the United States. Ahmad al-Halabi, a Syrian American airman working as a translator with al-Qaida prisoners at Guantanamo Bay, was arrested in July 2003, charged with spying and aiding the enemy, for giving the Syrian embassy information about those captured and details of base operations.[62]

In contrast to Syrian claims, it should be recalled that the U.S. goal in Iraq was to get a government established there and leave as quickly and to the greatest extent as possible. The insurgency has succeeded in forcing America to keep large numbers of troops in Iraq, which increases the friction between the Arab world and the United States while heightening the violence, destabilizing Iraq, and making it harder to secure a democratic government there. These things, of course, are precisely what the Syrian regime wants.

"Syria has a choice and they need to make the right choice as far as the new future we are trying to create in the Middle East," said a State Department official in June 2003. But how could there be any doubt as to what the Syrians would decide? What, if anything, would be done to persuade them to alter their course if they made the wrong choice?[63] The answer to the latter question was: not much.

One of the most upsetting incidents was only made public much later. In October 2003, as the new insurgency began, U.S. officials discovered that Bashar had urged Iraq's top Shia leader, Ayatollah Ali al-Sistani, who had been cooperating with the United States, to launch a jihad against the Americans instead. The U.S. government was "stunned" at this revelation, according to Paul Bremmer. Already, many Sunni insurgents were coming in through Syria. If

Bashar were to succeed in inciting a Shia rebellion, it would mean "an extremely bloody" situation, "costing additional thousands of lives."[64]

There was, then, plenty of provocation for the United States to take action against Damascus. Syria's government was inciting, training, equipping, and aiding terrorists to enter Iraq to kill Americans. Yet instead of bashing Damascus in any material way, the United States took far more cautious steps. Being bogged down in Iraq (a situation largely due to Syrian actions), the Americans hardly wanted to take on another foe.

Avoiding a military confrontation was, of course, a wise decision, but how should the United States respond when the Defense Department warned that Syrian actions directly threatened the lives of U.S. soldiers? Secretary of Defense Donald Rumsfeld accused Syria in May 2003 of continuing to actively direct terrorist groups and of helping ship arms into Iraq. He drafted for the White House an options' paper proposing various ways to press Syria to stop its covert war on Iraq. Powell and other officials warned many times that the United States was considering steps against Syria because of its behavior regarding terrorism, Lebanon, Iraq, and weapons of mass destruction.[65]

Syria might well have been denounced and pressured, both covertly and overtly, to a far greater extent short of military measures. Yet although the administration was not known for its restraint or softness toward perceived enemies, it kept backing off Syria. At most, it warned that Syrian behavior would prevent any improvement in bilateral relations. The White House discouraged members of Congress from passing anti-Syrian legislation. Bashar certainly was not worried, telling an interviewer in 2003 that the Bush administration opposed such measures.[66]

To understand why Syria's rulers don't usually take U.S. deterrence seriously, examine the April 2003 issue of the State Department's *Patterns of Global Terrorism* report. In earlier years, that document had criticized Syria for giving terrorist groups logistical support, bases, and a safe haven, as well as delivering Iranian weapons to Hizballah.[67] But now with Syria increasingly brazen in backing anti-American terrorism and at a moment when the U.S. government was supposedly angry about its activities, the new edition dropped all mention of these things. Space was even given to Syrian government claims that it had nothing to do with terrorist groups' operations and that Israel was the real terrorist. The report also emphasized that Syria promised to protect U.S. citizens, as if that were proof of Syria's good intentions rather than something that should have been taken for granted. Indeed, the report made it seem as if the United States wanted to placate Damascus, the attitude most likely to embolden the regime.[68]

Despite some leaks and signs that the United States was going to take a tougher line, not much happened. When Israel retaliated for an Islamic Jihad suicide bombing at a Haifa restaurant that killed nineteen civilians on October 3, 2003, by hitting that group's training camp near Damascus two days later, President Bush expressed support for this act of self-defense by saying "We would be doing the same thing." State Department spokesman Richard Boucher remarked, "If Syria wants, eventually, to have peace, and is willing to have peace with Israel, one has to question why they continue to allow the operation and support the operation of groups who are fundamentally opposed to that goal."[69] The administration also dropped previous objections to a proposed law to put minor sanctions on Syria.

But that was about it. Syria did not change its policies. In fact, its verbal defiance escalated. Speaking at an Islamic summit conference on October 16, Bashar called U.S. policymakers "a group of fanatics" waging war against Islam and said America was financing radical Islamist groups like al-Qaida to justify its own aggression.[70]

Contrary to Syrian claims, Israel also was not seeking any confrontation with Damascus. The October 2003 air attack on the Islamic Jihad base was a relatively isolated occurrence, the first time Israel had struck deep inside Syrian territory in thirty years and an attempt to make Syria stop its surrogates from murdering Israeli citizens. In April 2001, after a Hizballah rocket attack from southern Lebanon, Israeli planes had hit a Syrian radar station in southern Lebanon, killing three Syrian soldiers. After a second such operation some months later, Hizballah attacks on Israel declined, presumably because Damascus had its clients desist. In August 2003, after a young Israeli had been killed by a Hizballah artillery shell, Israeli fighters flew over an Assad family home, loudly breaking the sound barrier to send a message. Two months later Israel publicly released a map showing the location in Damascus of terrorist offices and the homes of local representatives of those groups.[71]

Yet in the face of continuing provocation, Israel still wanted to avoid a war with Syria. One major reason for Israel's restraint—as would soon be true of America as well—was that it was already preoccupied by a conflict partly of Syria's making. The Palestinian war on Israel, much of it waged by Syria's clients Hizballah and Islamic Jihad, was its top priority. The bottom line, then, was that Syria was able to continue sponsoring terrorism against Israel at virtually no cost.

Diplomatic factors pointed in the same direction and undercut Syrian claims that it was always the victim. Israel, rather than Syria, was condemned for the October 2003 reprisal attack on a terrorist base, responding to that group's attack on civilians. Germany's leader said the Israeli attack was unacceptable; the French Foreign Ministry called it "an unacceptable violation of international law," as did Spain's UN ambassador.[72] Once again, Syria got the message: As long as it did not openly proclaim its systematic involvement in launching terrorism against its neighbors, Syria was immune from retaliation.

An interesting epilogue to this incident shows the Syrian government's real intentions. Syria introduced a resolution to the UN Security Council criticizing the Israeli raid. France and Germany responded that they would support the proposal if it also included a brief condemnation of the terrorist attack in Haifa that had provoked Israel's reprisal attack. The Syrian government turned down this offer, even though it would have given it a big diplomatic victory.[73] Syria, then, would accept unilateral concessions but would not make any concessions itself, even to get most of what it wanted. Syria's main priority was not avoiding Israeli reprisals but retaining the freedom to encourage terrorist attacks through surrogate groups.

As noted, the U.S. government's response to Syria's many provocations was tepid. In December 2003 Bush did sign into law the Syria Accountability and Lebanese Sovereignty Restoration Act, a bill passed by Congress without enthusiastic administration backing. If Syria did not stop supporting Palestinian terrorists, occupying Lebanon, seeking weapons of mass destruction, and stirring up problems in Iraq, the law let the president impose some added sanctions, though in material terms these did not amount to much. After giving Syria five months to change its ways, in May 2004 Bush did indeed stop exports to Syria of American goods, except for food and medicine, and blocked landing rights for Syrian airlines in the United States. Certain transactions with Syria's state bank, which was holding Saddam's money and financing terrorist groups, were also prohibited.[74] But these efforts were mere pin pricks, hardly enough to inconvenience Damascus much or frighten it at all. What purportedly showed America's teeth really displayed only gums.

In implementing the law, Bush claimed Syria posed an "unusual and extraordinary threat" to U.S. national security. He also warned that Syria would "be held responsible for attacks committed by Hizballah and other terrorist groups with offices or other facilities" in the country, a threat that became relevant when Hizballah attacked Israel two years later. Yet Bush did not even use all the powers the law gave him. He could have frozen Syrian assets in the United States, prohibited American businesses from investing in Syria, reduced diplomatic contacts, and restricted the travel of Syrian diplomats on U.S. territory. Of six options available to him, Bush chose to implement the least important two.[75]

Consequently, all of Bashar's actions produced a handsome political profit. After all, at a paltry cost, Bashar ensured that the United States was too preoccupied to attack or harass him more, weakened U.S. influence in the region, and prevented the consolidation of a pro-American, democratic Iraq. Most important, he turned his potentially greatest domestic threat—radical Sunni Islamists—into an ally. I'm on your side in Iraq, he could tell them, and helping your struggle. What difference did America's impotent anger make in the face of such gains?

The U.S. effort to pressure Syria was also undercut by its supposed ally, the European Union (EU). The EU wanted the United States to condemn Israel's October attack on an Islamic Jihad training camp near Damascus that U.S. intelligence sources had confirmed was in operation. And while Bush was making his speech on sanctions, an EU trade delegation arrived in Damascus. The EU was, its officials stated, following a "policy of engagement" with Syria to encourage political and economic reform there. On December 10 it initialed a deal letting Syria sell goods to the EU on favorable terms. Since 60 percent of all Syrian exports went to Europe—fifteen times its trade level with the United States—the Syrian government could well say that the U.S. sanctions would not have much effect.[76]

Despite optimism in some quarters that Syria would prove more helpful, the Syria-Iraq border remained porous and the insurgency continued to be murderous. Syria took a defiant stance that often displayed a kind of surreal, unintentional sense of humor. After the fall of Iraq's Ba'th party government, Syria organized hard-line Ba'th party forces there into a new pro-Damascus group trying to reestablish an Arab nationalist dictatorship in Baghdad. The sheep-like name in which they chose to clothe this extremist wolf in moderate clothing was the Reform party.

One Syrian member of parliament, Muhammad Habash, expressed his regime's attitude of victory in November 2005 in this way:

> You [America] can send your fleets, your tanks and your frigates, but what will you do with these peoples who defy humiliation and degradation, and refuse to break, kneel, or bow before anyone but Allah? . . . You have committed all these massacres in Iraq, but the flag of Israel will never be raised in Iraq because our people there adhere to their convictions, and reject humiliation. . . . The Syrian army will never defend your occupation in Iraq.[77]

From this quote, one would never know that the overwhelming majority of the Iraqi people—who were Muslim and Arab—wanted the Syrian-backed insurgency to end and had elected a government of their own. Syria could not admit that its real concern was fear of a democratic, stable Iraq that would benefit its people and that the insurgency's end would allow U.S. forces to leave, not to mention that all this had nothing to do with Israel. Bashar's hostility was not due to concern for the well-being of Iraq's people but due to fear that a successful post-Saddam Iraq would mean the end of Ba'thist Syria.

Even many Arabs took this view. For example, Kuwait's minister of commerce, Abdallah Abd al-Rahman al-Tawil, could not contain his enthusiasm about how Iraq's becoming a liberal democracy with a functioning civil society would change the region. The Syrians, he happily claimed in 2003, are "scared witless."[78] That same year the courageous editor of *al-Siyasa* in Kuwait, Ahmad al-Jarallah, expressed his hope that Saddam's fate "will awaken the Arabs and make them see the real truth behind the patriotic slogans raised by this type of leader."[79] Mentioning Syria specifically, he noted that the fall of Iraq's regime was a warning to those who "massacre their people, bury them in mass graves, detain them in dungeons, invade their neighbors, and loot others' properties" that they must change their ways or suffer the same fate.[80] Among these regimes' greatest sins, Jarallah added, was calling their reform-minded critics "traitors, betrayers, supporters of Zionists, imperialists."[81]

But the Syrian regime understood all these points very well and knew how to counteract them. What if Iraq could be kept, through terrorism, from becoming a liberal democracy with a functioning civil society? What if Bashar could raise patriotic slogans that prevented Arabs from awakening and seeing the real truth? What if the Syrian regime could convince its people that the reformers were traitors and that resistance to Zionism and imperialism was more important than freedom, democracy, and material progress?

In short, what if the Syrian regime could prove that all the old techniques worked, reviving them with a strong dose of Islamism as well as Arab nationalism? Then its fate would not be the same as Saddam's. On the contrary, its enemies would be the ones scared witless, and the region would change in a very different way from what Tawil and Jarallah, much less U.S. policymakers, had envisioned. That is precisely what the Syrian government set out to do and largely what it did accomplish over the next three years.

CHAPTER NINE

THE COUNTERATTACK

Michel Kilo, Syria's leading reformist journalist, warned Bashar in 2003 that his policy of rejecting domestic reform while embracing foreign adventurism would bring disaster on Syria's head. If Syria kept supporting attacks on Israel, Kilo wrote, that country would launch a new war and defeat it. Don't let the backing for radical groups, Kilo urged, "bring about the demise of Syria just like it brought about the demise of Palestine!"[1]

Yet Bashar was about to do precisely what Kilo saw as disastrous. Indeed, not only did his strategy include an indirect war on Israel but it also created conflict with America, Lebanon, France, and Iraq! And even more remarkably, he would make this seemingly suicidal strategy work to his advantage.

What set the stage for this bold offensive, marking Syria's high point as an international power during a quarter-century or more? Briefly, the broader historical background might be described in the following way: From the 1950s to the 1990s, the Arab world had pursued an Arab nationalist agenda whose priorities were Arab unity, Israel's destruction, and the defeat of the West (especially the United States). Economic or social development, democracy, and stability were to be sacrificed for that struggle. This approach failed miserably on all fronts.

The 1990s were a period of reconsideration. Liberal thinkers grew more vocal; the Soviet pillar was gone; America was the world's sole superpower; and Israel appeared stronger. The USSR's collapse and Saddam's defeat in 1991 forced radical forces to retreat. Islamists failed to overturn any governments and had to reconsider their strategy. Hafiz steered Syria through these shoals, putting Syria's ambitions on hold while preserving—even reinforcing—its empire in Lebanon.

But the regimes, and Syria's most of all, realized that any real reform would threaten their existence. Democracy and openness might bring Islamists to power. The old levers of power, using demagoguery and xenophobia to stir the masses, still worked just fine. The old tools, hatred of Israel and the West, were still in place. The warnings of Arab liberals, Western appeals to self-interest, and attempts by those demonized to prove they were not so bad were not going to change anything.

What happened next, coinciding neatly with the new millennium, was the rulers' rejection of the alternative road and choice instead of a return to the past. The regimes preferred to revitalize the old system. Despite the constant claims of victimization, the Arab world was responding to the perceived weakness of their adversaries rather than any bullying by them. No one forced Arab states to make peace with Israel, to be pro-Western, or to embrace democracy. Rather, they were offered Israeli concessions and American conciliation. It was precisely the realization that there would be no real pressure—no real limit on what they could do—that made nationalist regimes and Islamist oppositions so bold and intransigent.

The irony is palpable. The relative moderation of America, the West, and Israel—the behavior that proved the dominant Arab assessment wrong—was precisely the factor that let the regimes maintain the status quo. In short, the fact that the foreign "threats" were not a threat, generally speaking, made it clear that portraying them as a threat was the best policy. It was risk free at home and relatively risk free abroad. And the one great exception—Iraq—would be perceived as proving that rule.

First in the series of events leading to the Middle East being turned upside down—or perhaps it is more accurate to say, returning to normal—was the Palestinian and Syrian rejection of peace with Israel in 2000. At the Camp David summit in mid-2000 and through the Clinton plan at year's end, Israel offered an independent Palestinian state with its capital in east Jerusalem. In the latter offer, Palestine would have the same amount of land as the territories Israel captured in 1967: all of the Gaza Strip and almost all of the West Bank, with territorial swaps to replace the small areas Israel wanted to annex for security purposes. In addition, the opening offer of the United States had been to raise $22 billion for compensating Palestinian refugees. Arafat flatly turned this proposal down even as a basis for negotiations.[2]

The same thing happened with Syria. Israel offered to give back the entire Golan Heights, albeit not the small area Syria had seized across the international border, and Assad rejected the plan. This happened despite the fact that Israel had met Syria's extreme demand of agreeing to return the whole Golan

Heights before Syria said what it would give in exchange. This kind of behavior made for a great deal of skepticism regarding Syria's good faith in any future negotiations.

As a result of a decade's experience with the peace process, it seemed that both Palestinians and Syrians would not abandon their hope of a future total victory by which Israel would be wiped off the map. A parallel reason for their refusing to make peace was that the conflict itself, even without such a victory, was too politically useful to these leaderships to give up. They would rather continue the battle forever than concede on these two goals. The regimes did not mind paying the cost because that price was relatively low for the elites and they deemed it far lower than what the alternative would do to hurt their interests.

This strategy worked well starting in 2000. Arafat launched an intifada, using a great deal of terrorism against Israeli civilians. Far from remembering their commitments to support Israel if it followed their advice and took big risks for peace, many Western governments—along with much of their intellectual, academic, and media elites—vilified that country. Clearly, this sent a signal to Syria and others: using violence did not turn the West against them; their intransigence did not increase but actually reduced international support for Israel; no pressure, or even criticism, would be applied against them due to their rejectionism. And aside from all that, there was plenty of support to be mobilized at home by using a strategy of outspoken militancy.

The September 11, 2001, attacks reinforced this trend. Bin Ladin's new strategy of striking directly at America arose from the Islamist failures of the 1990s. Why had they not succeeded in making revolutions in places like Egypt or Algeria? The real reason was two-fold: the regimes managed the conflict cleverly and the people were not with the Islamists. Acknowledging these realities, however, would not strengthen the Islamist cause which had to claim that all honest Muslims supported them. Bin Ladin and his colleagues instead switched to the traditional approach: the spotlight of blame must be focused on the United States and the West.

By attacking America, they hoped to incite passion for jihad (holy war) among their own people and channel it into support for themselves. They also wanted to sell the idea that it was the United States that blocked the Islamist triumph, not the regimes' power or the Muslim masses' preference for tradition-oriented Islam and an Arab nationalist identity. Moreover, by striking directly at America, they wanted to demonstrate that it was weak and could be defeated. After all, if they only showed the United States to be an all-powerful, ruthless, satanic adversary, shouldn't this fact inspire fear, a willingness to make concessions, or even the decision to join its side? "No," came the answer; the United States only appeared frightening, but the brave Arabs and Muslims, steeled by the proper ideology, could cut that superpower down to size. Few people in the Arabic-speaking world notice the contradictions in their beliefs.

Despite the operational success of the September 11, 2001, attacks, bin Ladin failed to make himself leader of the Muslims but did succeed in getting his ideas into the Arab mainstream. This was helped by the fact, of course, that they were by no means new ideas. They had been expressed in various forms by Nasser, Arafat, Hafiz, Saddam, Khomeini, and many others. But now they were revitalized and given an Islamist spin. Western imperialism against the Arabs, long adapted by the Arab nationalists from the Marxist lexicon, now became the Zionist-Crusader offensive against the Muslims. This combination of Arab nationalism and Islamism into "National Islamism" worked something like the atomic bomb, in which bringing together two pieces of radioactive material results in a gigantic explosion.

Granted, there was some fear in Syria when the United States overthrew bin Ladin's Taliban friends in Afghanistan and then invaded Iraq. This was, after all, the kind of massive force that the Syrian regime worried might be used against itself. But that was the beauty of its ideological system. If America did nothing, this showed it was weak and attacks against it should be escalated; if America reacted strongly, this proved it was aggressive and must be resisted. Relatively few Arabs said anything different; those who did were not heard by many, since Arab nationalists and Islamists controlled all the microphones.

It was not long before the counteroffensive began. Within Iraq itself, an insurgency rose up against both the foreign coalition presence and the domination of the country by a regime that was not under Sunni control. Syria sponsored the war of terrorism; groups and individuals in Saudi Arabia and Jordan contributed money and men. Iran, while not siding with the insurgency, added to the disorder by pouring in money and incitement. Syria wanted to ensure that the Iraqi experiment in democracy failed in order to preserve itself from the spread of democracy's appeal and a stronger U.S. position in the region. Most Arab states feared the triumph of Shia Muslims in Iraq and sided with their own Sunni counterparts there. Iran sought to turn Iraq into a sphere of influence for itself.

The overall result was massive bloodshed in Iraq, sabotaging a democratic state that could have been a role model for the Syrians. Rather than being seen as a liberator, America was successfully portrayed as an imperialist aggressor among Arabs. The United States was pinned down in Iraq, devoting most of its military forces and huge amounts of money there. The war's unpopularity in the United States and in Europe guaranteed that such an operation would not soon be repeated against Syria.

The Syrian regime thus insulated itself from both domestic and international pressure. What had first seemed an asset for the United States and a major threat to Syria turned into the exact opposite situation. The message once again was that violent resistance could bring big results at little cost to the sponsors. What could be better than for Syria to fight wars against its enemies in which all of the damage and casualties took place in Iraq and the Palestinian areas, to which Lebanon and Israel would soon be added?

One should pause here for a moment and realize the enormity of what has happened. Otherwise it is too easy—as so often happens in the Middle East—to take a remarkable event for granted. Syria was financing, training, arming, encouraging, transporting, and very possibly giving direct orders to an armed force attacking a neighboring country and the American troops stationed there. Thus, it was engaged in a shooting war against the United States and cooperating closely with al-Qaida, the prime target of the war against terrorism and the leading group in the Iraq insurgency. Yet these two facts had almost no real effect on U.S. or Western policies toward Syria. The old Assad magic was still working.

In other situations, one might imagine the UN condemning a regime that did such things, urgently planning international action and sanctions against it. Iraq would be demanding support against this aggression and punishment of its neighbor. The United States might even engage in some military action against that country. None of this happened because of the restraints of Arab politics on Iraq and of a whole range of factors on America. Once again, Syria had gotten away with it.

Syria's manipulation of the situation was equally impressive on the Arab front. After all, the Syrian regime was simultaneously able to benefit from Arab nationalism even while violating its most cherished principle since it allied itself with Iran against most of the Arabic-speaking world. With the Alawites identifying as Shia Muslims, like those in Iran, Bashar's strategy also put him on the wrong side of that divide from the standpoint of the Arab majority. Yet almost no one, and certainly no Arab government, systematically made the argument that Syria had betrayed Arabism. That kind of criticism was reserved exclusively for countries that were friendly toward the West or made peace with Israel.

By no means was this all that Bashar accomplished. Israel withdrew from southern Lebanon in 2000 and from the Gaza Strip in 2005. Within Israel, these steps were seen as both clever and strategically correct moves. Under normal conditions, the world would have acknowledged Israel's moderation and desire for peace, but this effect—though it did exist to some extent—was much muffled by the peculiarities of how the globe dealt with that country. The withdrawal gave Lebanon a chance to obtain peace, in practice if not formally, with Israel, and to disarm the militias and really end the state of anarchy plaguing the country since about 1968. Expectations that the withdrawal would also undermine the rationale for Syria staying in Lebanon and eventually force Damascus to pull out also proved correct.

Syria, however, found a way to maintain its influence. The Israeli pull-out had the big, unintended effect of strengthening Hizballah's power. The Lebanese government—weak, divided, and manipulated by Syria—let Hizballah take over the south and did not disarm that group, despite its pledge to do so in the 1989 Taif agreement. Hizballah claimed it had won a great patriotic victory by driving Israel out of the south, an area where Israel had no interest in being unless Hizballah built up forces there and periodically launched cross-border attacks. Meanwhile, too, Syria and Iran armed Hizballah to the teeth and financed it lavishly enough that it could buy support and influence within Lebanon. The scene was set for bigger events to come.

Five years later, Israel withdrew from the Gaza Strip. The situation was roughly parallel to that of southern Lebanon. The Palestinians might have used the opportunity to raise living standards, create an orderly government, and attract foreign aid. They could have shown the world how well the Palestinians might manage a state and prove to Israel that they would be a reasonably peaceful neighbor, thus paving the way for an Israeli withdrawal from the West Bank and establishment of a Palestinian state. Again, however, the ideas and groups favoring violence easily held sway since the outcome was attributed as a victory for terrorism rather than an opportunity for moderation. Both the south Lebanon and Gaza pull-outs also fed the notion that Israel was weak, losing its backbone, and vulnerable to blackmail by terrorism.

Syria considered Europe to be the weakest link of all, the most susceptible to intimidation. European hostility to Israel and antagonism to the United States generally signaled a rift in the "enemy" ranks. Europe was eager to accommodate the Arab and Muslim side. At most it might be won over; at least, the rift between the United States and Europe blocked the West from taking decisive action.

There is nothing more tempting than to challenge a foe who seems simultaneously all-threatening and very weak. For in this case, the threat makes resistance necessary and the enemy's weakness makes success appear ensured. This was how the Syrian regime viewed the situation around 2005.

A few additional elements that came later in this period should also be mentioned. After having been soundly defeated in the 1990s, revolutionary Islamists saw two new strategic opportunities which were at the exact opposite end of the behavioral spectrum from each other. One was jihadism; the other was elections. Regarding the use of violence, bin Ladin's operations, the Palestinian intifada, Hizballah, and the Iraqi insurgency showed the utility of irregular warfare.

At the same time, with U.S. policy pushing democracy and the ballot box, the regimes felt threatened and the Islamists saw a chance. For example, Yousuf Qaradawi, the senior Muslim Brotherhood spiritual adviser, urged Islamists to run in elections, predicting that they would easily defeat both the unpopular Arab nationalist regimes and the few supporters of secular liberalism.[3]

Islamists had already done well in the 1991 Algerian elections, though this triggered a military coup and civil war. Now Hizballah scored high in Lebanese elections, followed by a victory for Hamas in the January 2005 Palestinian elections and the Muslim Brotherhood receiving 20 percent of votes in Egyptian parliamentary elections later that year. Islamists were convinced that they were really popular and could mobilize that support by demonstrating their militancy. By jumping on the Islamist bandwagon—allying with Iran and supporting Hamas and Hizballah—the secular, non-Muslim regime in Syria could exploit this trend.

One more element in this mix was Iran's drive to obtain nuclear arms. Not only did this prospect of having the ultimate weapon give Tehran increasing confidence, but Western weakness in confronting the issue was one more proof of how easy it was to out-maneuver and bully the West. Starting in 2004, the United States and Europe tried to persuade or dissuade Iran from its nuclear program. Tehran violated every promise, rejected concessions, and was caught lying repeatedly. Yet no serious action was taken to pressure or punish it.

As the war in Lebanon began in the summer of 2006, it was a critical moment in this process. Iran was violating its pledge to respond to a U.S.-European plan which, if rejected, might lead to UN-mandated sanctions. Like Syria, with the Hariri investigation and other problems, Tehran also badly needed a diversion to shake up the area and push their troublesome issues off the table. More generally, Persian, Shia Iran needed a way to win over Sunni Arabs if it was ever going to become a great regional power.

Finally, there were many Westerners careless, ignorant, or malicious enough to give the Syrian elite even more reasons to see its adversaries as weak and divided. One of many examples occurred in September 2004, when former U.S. Assistant Secretary of State Martin Indyk came to Damascus to meet Bashar. Indyk's criticism of Bush's Iraq policy convinced Bashar that America was faltering, that stronger attacks might drive it out of that country, and that the United States could not credibly threaten Syria. Indyk also told Bashar that the United States was interested in Iraq not Lebanon, making the Syrian dictator feel safer in taking a tough line on Lebanon without fearing U.S. retaliation. In former Syrian Vice President Khaddam's words, "The idea that was planted in President Bashar al-Assad's mind was that the United States would come crawling to him in order to negotiate with him about Iraq, and that it would keep him in Lebanon."[4] Out of such miscalculations came bloodshed.

This overall sense of confidence in Damascus, coupled with Bashar's doctrinaire views and desire to show toughness, culminated in the assassination of Rafiq Hariri, Lebanon's most important and popular politician. The affair began when Bashar sought to extend the term of puppet President Emile Lahoud for three years to ensure that Lebanon continued to follow Syrian orders. This was a trick Syria had used in the 1990s and once again, as he had done back then, Hariri said he would oppose it. To make matters worse, Hariri was expected to do well in the next elections, and Syria knew he was encouraging his friend, French President Jacques Chirac, to push through a UN resolution demanding Syrian withdrawal from Lebanon. Hariri was endangering Syria's all-important ownership of Lebanon, and Bashar was determined to put him in his place.

So on August 26, 2004, Bashar ordered Hariri to come to Damascus. Their meeting was very short and to the point: unless Hariri voted for the extension of Lahoud's term, thus abrogating Lebanese democracy for Syria's convenience, Bashar threatened he would break the Lebanese politician. According to Khaddam, paraphrasing Bashar, the Syrian president told Hariri, the neighboring country's prime minister, "You want to decide who the next Lebanese president will be? . . . I will not let you. I will crush anyone who tries to oppose our decision." Hariri was so upset that his nose began bleeding.[5] As he had done before, Hariri caved in, voted as Bashar ordered on September 3, and resigned as prime minister six days later. The Syrians tried to assassinate Druze member of parliament Marwan Hamade, who dared vote against the constitutional amendment, soon thereafter.

The victory in parliament should have satisfied Bashar. His father would have approved. The crisis had been handled neatly and Syria showed Hariri who was boss. Hafiz never hesitated to use violence when he felt it to be necessary, but his judgment was as cautious in practice as it was bloody-minded when required in execution. Hafiz, however, was no longer president of Syria, a country guided by Bashar's considerably less-experienced judgment.

The gathering of international forces behind Hariri was also a factor in Bashar's motive for murder. UN Security Council Resolution 1559, with U.S.

and French sponsorship along with Egyptian and Saudi support, was demanding Syrian withdrawal. Bashar had enjoyed a free ride in Lebanon because of his help back in 1991 during the Kuwait crisis. But that was 13 years ago. He had not made peace with Israel or done much for the West lately. On the contrary, Bashar had allied with Saddam and launched an insurgency in Iraq against America. On September 2, 2004, the resolution passed the UN Security Council unanimously.

Planning for a very special operation must have begun in Damascus not long after that. On February 14, 2005, Hariri's car drove over a large, one-ton bomb that had been dug into a paved downtown Beirut street; Hariri was instantly killed along with 22 others. No ordinary terrorist group acting alone could have pulled off an attack requiring so much pure control and immunity from the local security forces' suspicions. All Lebanon, at least outside of Hizballah, was shocked and horrified. There had been many acts of Syrian-backed terrorism against Lebanon before, but this one was not only the most brazen, it also killed the man who was the country's main hope for economic reconstruction and domestic tranquility.[6]

The decision to assassinate Hariri clearly came from Bashar himself. As Khaddam put it—and he was vice president of Syria at the time these events were taking place—"No security agency, or any other agency in Syria, could make such a decision on its own."[7] Only Syrian or pro-Syrian Lebanese security officials could have brought a ton or more of explosives into the center of Beirut and planted them in the middle of a major street, affirmed Khaddam. Neither "Ahmad Abu Adas [lentils] nor Ahmad Abu Humous [hummus]," could have done so, he asserted. In an interview with *Der Spiegel*, Bashar himself, while denying his country was responsible, explained, "If any Syrians are involved, it means I'm involved."[8]

After decades of quiescence to Syrian rule, Lebanon erupted into protests—at least from the Christian, Druze, Sunni Muslim majority—demanding a Syrian withdrawal. The Lebanese army refused to intervene. So great was the anger and pressure that pro-Syrian Prime Minister Umar al-Karami resigned on February 28. To counter this trend, Hizballah, Syria's ally, organized a pro-Syria rally on March 8 under the slogan—shocking to any Lebanese patriot—of "Fidelity to Syria."

This tactic backfired as it showed all too clearly that Hizballah placed loyalty to Syria over Lebanon. Bashar, who has a tendency to say things without any sense of their double meaning, highlighted the irony of this behavior. "Loyalty to one's country does not just mean [not] being a known agent of another country," he later explained. "Loyalty to one's country means rejecting foreign interference."[9] Now he would see the notion of resistance played out against Syria itself. On March 14, 2005, the largest demonstration in Middle East history took place in Beirut. Many Lebanese claimed that one million people participated, and even if this is exaggerated, the turnout was nonetheless remarkable.

Even Bashar felt the pressure. Perhaps he panicked. After almost 30 years of Syrian domination, he withdrew all of his troops from the country during the next six weeks, ending with the last uniformed Syrian soldier's departure on April 26. All was not lost, however, for Damascus. The intelligence apparatus and hundreds of thousands of Syrian workers remained behind. Hizballah and scores of Lebanese politicians on the payroll was still a Syrian fifth column for projecting its influence into the country. Pro-Syrian politicians, though beleaguered, were still in place.

It was ironic that an operation designed to preserve Syria's position in Lebanon ended by so badly damaging it. But problems stemming from Hariri's murder were just beginning. Syria might have escaped without any cost whatsoever, as had so often happened before, except for a minor detail that became extraordinarily important, the fact that President Chirac was a friend of Hariri and was angry at his murder. France had also always viewed Lebanon in sentimental terms as a sort of protégé. Thus, although Chirac was usually the Middle East dictators' best friend in Europe, this time he was out for revenge, even if it meant cooperating with the United States to do so.

With such a consensus, the UN Security Council created an international investigation under German judge Detlev Mehlis to discover who killed Hariri. Interim reports issued in October 2005 by Mehlis and Irish deputy police commissioner Peter FitzGerald blamed Syria. The Mehlis report concluded, "There is converging evidence pointing at both Lebanese and Syrian involvement in this terrorist act. . . . [G]iven the infiltration of Lebanese institutions and society by the Syrian and Lebanese intelligence services working in tandem, it would be difficult to envisage a scenario whereby such a complex assassination plot could have been carried out without their knowledge."[10] Syrian Interior Minister Ghazi Kanaan, after being questioned by Mehlis's investigators, was sent by Syria's rulers to sleep with the fishes on October 12—in effect, "suicided"—because, as head of Syria's intelligence operations in Lebanon from 1982 to 2003, he knew too much being alive and provided a good scapegoat if dead.

At any rate, Mehlis rejected this bait. Instead, while he did not accuse Bashar personally of murder, he did the next worse thing, pinning the hit on Mahir al-Assad, Bashar's brother, and General Asif Shawkat, his brother-in-law and the head of military intelligence. Next to Bashar himself, these were the two most powerful men in the regime. Also included as co-conspirators were the current chief of Syrian intelligence in Lebanon, Lieutenant General Rustum Ghazali; Syria's man in Lebanon, President Lahoud; and four pro-Syrian Lebanese intelligence officers. One of them, Ali Hajj, had been fired by Hariri as his chief bodyguard after he discovered Hajj was a Syrian spy. Another named co-conspirator was the Popular Front for the Liberation of Palestine–General Command (PFLP-GC), a Palestinian group that always followed the orders of Damascus. Syrian Foreign Minister Farouk al-Sharaa was also identified by the report as having lied to investigators. It is hard to remember any equivalent international indictment of a government's highest-level officials for direct involvement with terrorism.[11]

Nor was Hariri the only victim. Other prominent Lebanese critics of Syria were assassinated in 14 terror attacks during the remainder of 2005, both to eliminate them and to show the Lebanese there could be no peace or quiet without Syria being back in charge. On June 2, 2005, Samir Kassir, a columnist critical of Syria, was killed when his car exploded; George Hawi, the Communist party leader, was murdered a few days later. On July 12, it was the turn of Lebanese Defense Minister Elias al-Murr, who survived a bombing. He recounted that the attack came shortly after an argument with Ghazali. In September came the attempted murder of May Chidiac, a television anchorwoman for the Lebanese Broadcasting Company who had criticized Syria. The next month a car bomb nearly killed a judge, Nazim al-Khouri. In December, popular Lebanese politician Gibran Tuayni died at Syria's hands. Far from being intimidated by the Hariri case, Damascus simply repeated the formula whenever it pleased.

Faced with Syria's defiance, an October UN report, though written by Terje Roed-Larsen who had been a proven friend to Arab nationalists, blasted Syria for violating Resolution 1559 by its continued interference in Lebanon, including sending arms to militia groups there. So unhappy with Syrian sabotage of the investigation was the UN Security Council that it passed Resolution 1636 on October 31, demanding that Syria cooperate fully with the investigation or face "further action." The resolution was passed under the UN Charter's Chapter 7, which lets the Council impose further punishments up to and including the use of military force.[12] The December 12 Mehlis report raised additional criticisms of Syria. Even the European Council invoked restrictive measures on travel through Europe of those suspected of involvement in Hariri's murder.

Still, no one ever actually did anything about the continuing noncompliance. Once again, Syria seemed justified in banking on the international community's forgetfulness toward anything concerning its misdeeds. In the Mehlis report, the names of specific Syrian officials were edited out of the official text by UN Secretary-General Kofi Annan's office, though they had been included in the commission's draft. Instead the official report's text referred only to "senior Lebanese and Syrian officials."[13] Moreover, three members of the Security Council—Russia, China, and Algeria—stopped any threat of sanctions from being included in Resolution 1636. Here was the tip-off that even a final guilty verdict would bring no sentence, not even one of community service.

Syria, of course, had its own version of events, which, while laughable, was also a response largely accepted within the country and much of the Arab world. Its officials accused Hariri's own son of the murder,[14] along with the CIA and Mossad.[15] If the word did not seem so out of place, one might say that Bashar had been blessed with a surfeit of chutzpah. He assured the world that there would be no need for an international tribunal. If any Syrian had been involved in killing Hariri, he explained, it was an act of treason to his own country. The miscreant, he pledged, would be tried, and no doubt executed, very quickly to avoid the need for messy interrogations or probing investigations by anyone else.[16]

The full flow of Syrian invective—derived from Stalinism and typical of Arab nationalist discourse—was unleashed on anyone who might suggest that Syria was involved. Yet so violent is this rhetoric that it proves the exact opposite. And while its narrowness and cardboard phrases may seem amusing, they indicate the kind of thinking that really does dominate the views of those subjected to it.

Thus, in a special October 31, 2005, parliament session, one loyal son of Syria, Hassan Talib, proclaimed,

> The Syrian masses stress their loyalty to the homeland, and to the leader, Bashar al-Assad. They say, and I say on their behalf: "My soul I will sacrifice for you, Syria, and I will give everything for you." I have planted my heart and all I have in its soil. May Allah protect Assad, you are my sword. You are the mighty leader. You are my eyes. They chanted your name, Bashar, and I say: "I will sacrifice my eyes for you."

Here we have the sycophantic cult of personality at its ripest. And there is something to it, after all, since all gifts and privileges in Syria—and certainly Mr. Talib's lifestyle and honors of office—come from Bashar, who is indeed the great champion preserving the regime with his sword.

Taking up another theme, member of parliament Anwar Ubayd snapped at the ungrateful Lebanese who did not appreciate all that Syria had bestowed on them during its years of occupation, assassination, and theft. "We know the Lebanese leaders. Collaboration flows in their veins, and treachery thrives in their midst. Today they repay Syria's loyalty to them with treachery. They repay the attempts to help them with an effort to destroy Syria, and to put pressure on us."

For any Arab listener, the message was that these ingrates were collaborating with Israel and America, a crime punishable by death. Of course, this was a key reason for Hariri's murder, his work with America and France on the effort to force Syria out of Lebanon.

A third member of parliament also took up the theme of war:

> Syria in its entirety went [to battle] when some people wanted to attack it. The entire Syrian people, the young and the old, said: "We will dig their graves with our bare hands." . . . Today, too, we say: "With our hands, with our fingernails, with our children and our elderly, with our women and with our youth, we will dig their graves if they think of attacking [Damascus]."[17]

Finally, there was the need to counter their old comrade, Khaddam, who had blown the whistle on the murder of Hariri, one friend killed by Bashar, having defected after the killing of Kanaan, another friend murdered by Bashar. In a December parliamentary session, the traitor is cast into outer darkness in good 1930s vintage Soviet-style purge fashion. According to Abd al-Razzaq al-Yousuf, Khaddam "is mentally deranged. . . . His punishment . . . is known to all. He should be beaten with a shoe on his head until it breaks. My only fear is that the shoe would say: 'When a shoe hits Khaddam on the head, it cries out: what did I do to deserve this beating?'"[18]

Here, then, is the full Ba'thist political lexicon on view: glorifying the dictator; pinning all problems on foreigners; bullying other Arabs with the judo moves of Arab nationalism; proclaiming everyone who disagrees to be a traitor; discrediting dissidents and menacing them with death. It often seems as if no Syrian official can talk about anything without making threats. In the process of declaring themselves innocent of murder, they scream demands for murder in all directions. This is the political entity; this, the ideology; these, the leaders whom many in the West constantly believe can be engaged, appeased, and thus transformed into something else.

Although Khaddam had already been forced into retirement, his defection must have been a real blow to the regime. He was one of the very few members of the majority Sunni Muslim faith at the top of the government, and his decision to join the Muslim Brotherhood in an exile opposition front seemed to show a dangerous uniting of the majority group against the Alawite minority regime. Moreover, Khaddam was exceedingly well connected. One of his sons was married into the Atassi clan, a historic leader of the Sunni ruling elite, some of whose members were now active in the liberal opposition, while his wife was from a powerful Alawite clan. And the survivors of the murdered Ghazi Kanaan were from the same Alawite clan as the Assads. Indeed, Kanaan's son was wed to Bashar's cousin.

The murder or defection of key regime insiders, the withdrawal from Lebanon, U.S. anger at Syria's role in Lebanon, the criticism of Syrian reformers and Lebanese nationalists, plus the pressure over the Hariri case—along with the usual economic stagnation and corruption—made many observers in 2005 believe that Bashar was in serious trouble. This became a frequent topic in Western articles on Syria, but it also came from some Syrians. For example, Ali Sadr al-Din al-Biyanouni, exiled leader of the Syrian Muslim Brotherhood, predicted, "Khaddam's testimony will break up the power monopoly of the regime."[19]

At the time, it appeared as if the Hariri investigation would not go away. Within a year or so, it seemed quite possible that Bashar or at least his two key lieutenants—who also happened to be his brother and brother-in-law—would be indicted for murder. This was pretty heavy stuff. Former Jordanian Minister of Information Salih al-Qallab said that Bashar, "Does not care about southern Lebanon, the battle, or resistance, but about the assassination of Rafiq al-Hariri and the investigation into the assassination of Rafiq al-Hariri."[20]

The Americans, too, seemed to be pressing a bit on Syria at last. For example, in January 2006, Secretary of State Condoleezza Rice demanded Syria cooperate in the Hariri investigation, end support for terror groups, and permit Hizballah's being disarmed. Otherwise, she hinted, the United States might ask the UN Security Council for sanctions. "Syria's continuing provision of arms and other support to Hizballah and Palestinian terrorist groups serves to destabilize Lebanon, makes possible terrorist attacks within Lebanon, from Lebanese territory, and impedes the full implementation of Security Council resolutions," she said.[21]

Even the French were making uncharacteristic threats to Bashar. A high-ranking French official described the regime's behavior as "letting time pass and playing tricks" while "refusing to cooperate" in the Mehlis investigation. "Syria should realize it is digging its own grave," he said. He continued, Paris "had opposed regime change and advised the United States not to follow this route." But if Syria did not start cooperating fully with the UN investigation, France "w[ould] not be able to hold on to this position."[22] It is hard to think of any other time when France threatened to overthrow an Arab government in a half-century. Things were getting serious.

Consequently, Syria showed a little caution on the Iraq front. Cross-border infiltration did decline and Syria claimed to be closing its 375-mile-long frontier with Iraq. Much of the difference, however, was due to the coalition forces building a 15-foot-high border barrier protected by a much stronger Iraqi force. The cost for these improvements to the U.S. taxpayer was $300 million.[23] There were reports, too, that Syria had turned over some high-ranking Iraqi officials who had taken refuge there, including one of Saddam's half brothers.[24] But Syria's campaign of subversion continued. In December 2006, for example, Iraqi national security adviser Muwaffaq al-Rubaii accused Syria of hosting the leaders of those directing terrorism in Iraq and claimed that 90 percent of the terrorists bound for Iraq arrive at Damascus airport and then are allowed to cross the Syria-Iraq border.[25] And in January 2007, National Intelligence Director John Negroponte estimated that 40 to 70 foreign fighters—many or most of them seeking to be suicide bombers—enter Iraq through Syria every month.[26]

How was Bashar going to play Harry Houdini and escape from all these chains and manacles?

Option 1 was to respond to the pressures through concessions. He could cease backing Hizballah, leave Lebanon alone, stop running a covert war in Iraq, and cooperate with the Hariri murder investigation. Doing so, however, might well have brought his downfall.

Option 2 was to negotiate seriously, offering full peace with Israel in exchange for the whole Golan Heights and friendship with the West in exchange for help on economic development. He could even have conditioned more moderate behavior by demanding Lebanon be recognized as Syria's sphere of influence.

These alternatives, however, were not to his liking. Bashar wanted to have it all and pay nothing for getting everything. Besides, he and his colleagues thought they could succeed in this ambitious scheme, judging the apparent pressure on Syria to be largely illusory. If they ignored it, nothing would happen.

And so he responded with Option 3: militancy, demagoguery, and escalation—the oldest tricks in the Arab nationalist playbook. It would be the same issue about which Kilo had warned him—the conflict with Israel—that Bashar would turn into his way out of the dilemma. But a considerable dose of anti-American demagoguery and aggression toward fellow Arabs was also part of the mix. Indeed, Bashar would do nothing less than revitalize radical Arab nationalism, making a bold leap into the past, intended to make him leader of the Arab world.

While the regime did everything possible to prevent the reformers from advocating peace with Israel, they followed the same course regarding Lebanon. After all, despite endless professions of love toward that neighbor—for whom Syria claimed to have sacrificed so much—Damascus was waging an imperialist policy against it. The Syrian troops went home but the intelligence apparatus stayed behind. By threats, pay-offs, and terrorist attacks, Bashar was determined to show the Lebanese that they could not enjoy any peace unless they were under his thumb.

Despite their many assets in Lebanon, the Syrian leaders knew that it needed them only as long as two conditions applied: Lebanon was fighting Israel and no strong government could consolidate power there. The regime had to stoke Lebanon's external conflict and maintain its internal one. In a real sense, Hizballah was resisting a stable, independent Lebanon more than it was resisting Israel, a country having no interest in threatening that neighbor unless it was being used as a base for cross-border attacks.

As for Bashar, he was determined that his own people view Lebanon solely as an instrument of resistance and not as a country that had its own desires and interests. It was all very well for Syrians to shed tears over Lebanon as a victim of Israel, but he would make sure they did not embrace it as a true equal or as a victim of Syria. As a result, the biggest round-up of dissidents in Bashar's reign—including Kilo's arrest and imprisonment—took place in 2006 on the eve of the new Lebanon war.[27]

During the early summer of that year, Bashar seemed to be under attack from every direction simultaneously. A joint declaration of Lebanese and Syrian intellectuals to end Syrian domination of the smaller country, issued on May 12, was quickly followed on May 17 by UN Security Council Resolution 1680, demanding Syria establish full diplomatic relations with Lebanon and mutually define their borders. The new exiled opposition group, bringing together Khaddam, the Muslim Brotherhood, and Kurdish groups in a National Salvation Front, met in June in London.[28] And the investigation of the Hariri assassination was grinding toward a final report that would surely find Syria's top leaders to have been deeply involved. Things did not look good. And in the tradition of Arab regimes, Bashar knew this meant he must go on the offensive.

Ironically, one of the events promoting this decision was the reformers' own initiative to promote good Syrian-Lebanese relations, signed by several hundred people in both countries. To stress the equality being advocated between the two states, they called it "The Beirut-Damascus Declaration/Damascus-Beirut Declaration."[29] It was a mild and moderate, yet totally subversive, document.

Syrian-Lebanese relations, the manifesto pointed out, had worsened since two events—the extension of Lebanese President Emil Lahoud's term ("a violation of the spirit of the Lebanese constitution and contempt for the opinion of the Lebanese majority") and the killing of Hariri ("crimes of political assassination that have [also] led to the deaths or wounding of politicians, party members, media personnel, and citizens").[30] The declaration did not have to say so because everyone knew that the Syrian regime was directly responsible for both of these developments.

To solve this problem, the declaration called on Syria to recognize Lebanon's sovereignty and independence by establishing normal diplomatic relations and delineating the two countries' precise borders. In the kind of cute use of Arab nationalist ideology that was so clever but never actually availed them, the liberal authors urged Lebanon and Syria to "regain their occupied territories, by all possible means" but this could happen only, "after Syria officially declares that the Shabaa Farms are Lebanese," which Syria would never do.[31]

In short, they were calling Bashar's bluff: After all, it was just too obviously ridiculous that Syria demanded Israel return the Shabaa Farms to Lebanon and called Israel's refusal to do so a justification for armed struggle while at the very same time Syria still claimed that territory for itself! If Syria ever formally accepted that this little piece of worthless land (worthless except as a pretext for war on Israel) was part of Lebanon, Israel would probably hand it over to Lebanon just to spite Damascus.

But the reformers had highlighted such contradictions in Syria's position, a deed that always angered the regime and made it rush to arrest those daring to do so. Bashar would not let such insolence on the part of these intellectuals pass. This applied even more to hints that Syria's brotherly embrace of Lebanon was actually a stranglehold with one hand while the other picked Lebanon's pocket. The livelihood of the elite and the army would be at stake if Syria was forced to relinquish such profits.

There were also other messages in the declaration bound to give Bashar a headache. It urged Lebanon to take control of all its own territory, a reasonable demand but one which meant the central government would actually be governing the south and dispensing with the Syrian-backed Hizballah state within a state. It supported the international investigation of Hariri's assassination, a nice gesture at responsible international citizenry actually aimed at sending Syria's leaders to small rooms with bars on the window. And of course it called for democracy in both countries, a step which if actually implemented might lead, at best, to Syria's rulers being put on the country's long unemployment lines and at worst to enjoying a last cigarette and comfortable blindfold while a line of uniformed men raised their rifles in their direction and waited for the command to fire.

The regime responded as if it could not quite get that last image out of its collective head. The Syrian government's complaints had a strong element of unintentional humor as it strove to explain why demanding that Syria treat Lebanon fairly was such an outrageous notion. *Tishrin*'s response was a mélange between Jonathan Swift and Stalinist Russia. In an editorial entitled, "Syrian and Lebanese Intellectuals Join the Evil Attack on Syria," it was outraged to discover that these critics had forgotten, "All Syria's ... sacrifices for the sake of Lebanon, and have joined ... the evil and open attack led by Bush's American administration against Syria." [32] One can almost see the editor turning the pages of the Ba'th manual of insults, of which the longest chapter is about how all critics are just willing tools of Israel and America:

> How odd it is, too, that these Syrian and Lebanese intellectuals today issue a declaration in which they hint that Syria is threatening Lebanon—and forget Israel, its destructive role, and its unceasing aggression. Does exonerating Israel and the Bush administration of blame for everything that has happened and is happening, and [instead] blaming Syria, serve the interest of the two brother peoples? Why [did they issue this declaration] precisely at this time—while the American administration is applying its malicious pressure on the Security Council so that it will pass a resolution demanding that Syria establish diplomatic relations with Lebanon?[33]

This was a classic of Arab nationalist methodology, a work of art, which in the museum of that ideology should hold the place accorded in the Louvre of Paris to the Mona Lisa or the Winged Victory of Samothrace. The argument has everything: the nobility of the cause, the conspiracy against Syria, the Zionist and American plots, the equating of critics with enemy agents. And all of this vitriol was fired off in response to a declaration for merely demanding that Syria treat Lebanon as a sovereign country.

Naturally, arrests followed. Three days after the declaration was issued, Kilo was taken and 13 other signers followed him into the Adra prison, though three of them were soon released. The charges included a range of thought-crimes under Article 285: weakening national sentiment, arousing extremist ethnic or religious sentiment, publishing false or exaggerated news that might harm the state's honor or status, and insulting various branches of the government. Any of these misdeeds might be punished by death. But this was not Iraq but Syria, where a beating and prison term was more likely than a bullet in the head.[34]

Syrian reformers now put the world's fine words about democracy and human rights to the test by asking UN Secretary-General Kofi Annan and the international community to intervene in order to help release those imprisoned. Unfortunately, however, they all had previous engagements. Security men intimidating reformers could easily taunt them that no one outside Syria cared about their fate; nobody could protect them. And thus, surrendering to the regime was their best, indeed only, option.

Yet it was not enough for the government that the reformers be portrayed as traitors and shown as helpless and friendless. If possible, they also had to be made to embrace, however reluctantly, Big Brother himself. They had to be persuaded to support Bashar. How this was achieved in many cases is explained by an apparently twisted—yet compellingly logical—chain of circumstances along the following lines: Syria was a repressive dictatorship. Yet if that dictatorship fell, it might be replaced by an even worse radical Islamist dictatorship. The Ba'th regime just severely limited freedom; the Islamists would erase it altogether. At least with Bashar in power the urban middle class, the most likely recruits for the reform movement, could live a Western, modern lifestyle in terms of clothes, entertainment, women's rights, and so on. Bashar would not take that away, but the Islamists would.

Moreover, even if the Islamists did not actually gain power, a political vacuum could bring massive violence and social chaos. Syrian reformers merely needed to turn their eyes one way toward Iraq and the other way toward Lebanon to see what that was like. Syria itself had lived through such times between 1949 and 1971, an experience many of its citizens remembered vividly. The more Bashar refused to make reforms, the greater was the danger of a radical upheaval, and thus the need to support him by those who wanted reforms! Consequently, Bashar was to be preferred to the local equivalent of Hamas, Hizballah, and Iran.

This last point was the crowning irony of Syrian politics. A regime allied to radical Islamists and encouraging militant Islam at home must be supported lest it be replaced by . . . Islamists! Still, as absurd as this was, there was also a fair measure of logic in it.

Thus, the reformers might not truly love Big (Younger) Brother, but they still understood how they needed him. In the words of a visiting American reporter: "Syria has so thoroughly quashed organized opposition that even the most committed dissidents find themselves in a depressing bind: They're willing to risk prison by speaking out against the regime but are so convinced of their own weakness that they don't want the regime to fall, fearing that only chaos would follow."[35]

This paradox was embodied by Haytham al-Malih, an elderly human rights lawyer and influential opposition leader. He had been imprisoned by the regime for seven years in the 1980s. Despite the fact that he called the government of his country a "fascist dictatorship," Malih did not want to see it collapse because he saw nothing to replace it.[36] It is hard to think of a parallel situation anywhere else in the world.

Having such mastery at home and so easily crushing the liberals without foreign pressure, the regime understandably felt confident. Abroad, people spoke of Bashar's inexperience and the Syrian elite's alleged despair at being sad-dled with such a donkey. Yet the situation seemed to be the opposite: members of the elite were happy; the regime was united and ready to flex its muscles.

Reformers were quite aware of this mood. Ayman Abd al-Nour, a liberal-minded Ba'th party member, explained that the regime was no longer scared of America or anyone else. "They feel that the regime is about to escape the after-math of the Hariri assassination intact," he said.[37]

"The government is more comfortable than in the past," added Marwan Ka-balan, a political science professor at Damascus University. "They feel strong compared to six or seven months ago. They have survived the crisis before and they feel they can take the pressure. And now they feel the West is preoccupied with Iran and that they feel less concerned with Syria and the Syrian people. They have seen that the United States and Europe can't do much about arrests."[38]

It wasn't that the West was completely silent. Every time a leading figure was arrested, the United States issued a statement. For example, the White House voiced its "deep concern" at the November 10, 2005, detention of Kamal Labwani, who had already spent three years in prison, and called for his unconditional release. The fact that he was arrested on arrival at Damascus air-port, returning from a meeting at the White House, made this incident a direct slap in the face for the United States. "We stress," said the State Department spokesman, "that the United States stands with the Syrian people in their de-sire for freedom and democracy. . . . The Syrian government must cease its ha-rassment of Syrians peacefully seeking to bring democratic reform to their country."[39] But that kind of talk hardly made Bashar tremble.

Neither did the new U.S. sanctions in 2004 and in early 2006, nor the U.S. government's appropriation of a $5 million grant program to help non-governmental Syrian organizations function better. The European Union was also urging Syria to increase human rights as a condition in negotiations for Syria getting a better arrangement in trading with its members. All this didn't amount to very much, and Syria simply took the usual posture of indignant in-transigence. Arab dignity, Damascus proudly announced, was not for sale—a demagogic way of saying that its citizens were already fully owned by the regime.

Given the fact that Syria was then sponsoring terrorism at record levels and conducting a war on America in Iraq, to say that these efforts were pinpricks would be an exaggeration. If Bashar had been afraid of American efforts toward regime change, or felt heavy pressure after September 11, 2001, or when the United States overthrew Saddam in 2003, these concerns had dissipated. And when fear was dispelled, arrogance filled the vacuum. The dominant mood in

Damascus was that resistance and the occasional meaningless gesture had neutralized the United States. Syria could act as it pleased and fear no consequences.

After rejecting peace in 2000, Arafat had led the Palestinians into a new war on Israel, using anticivilian terrorism as its central strategy. Having no love for Arafat nor influence over him, Syria and Iran became cosponsors of Hamas and Islamic Jihad, whose energetic use of terrorism combined with their nationalist rival's incompetence to make them steadily more popular among Palestinians. Damascus was the main Hamas and Islamic Jihad headquarters; the Iranian-Syrian axis provided training and arms for both Islamist groups.

Meanwhile, Bashar was developing his comprehensive view of the situation, a stance he basically began formulating from the day he attained the presidency. By 2005, it was fully formed. One of the first presentations of this new world view and strategy was in his speech at the University of Damascus on November 11, 2005.[40] Syria would position itself as the leader of Arab resistance to the pernicious plots of America. It would counter democratization and regime change with a call to battle, a war carried out covertly through radical groups but trumpeted publicly as the only way to save Arabism and Islam from Western and Zionist designs. Basically, it was not different from the kind of ideas put forward by Nasser, Bashar's own father, Saddam, Khomeini, bin Ladin, and others. Yet it was refurbished and adapted for the early twenty-first century.

This strategy also fit the needs of Iran, facing its own potential threat of pressure on its nuclear arms program. On July 12, 2006, a few hours after Hizballah began a war by attacking Israel, the United States and other members asked the UN Security Council to force Iran to suspend its nuclear enrichment activities. "We called [Iran's] bluff today," a senior State Department official boasted.[41] However, in Hizballah Tehran had a secret weapon almost as potent as a nuclear one, and it was already completely ready.

The new situation also suited Hizballah, which was having its own problems. It could claim credit for Israel's earlier withdrawal as a great victory, but once Israel left, what need was there for Hizballah to be armed or to control southern Lebanon? Yes, it was nominally a part of the Lebanese government coalition, but its Syrian protector had left. Hizballah was in the minority, and it was being outmaneuvered by the anti-Syrian forces of the March 14 coalition. Of course, if Israel could be provoked to attack Lebanon, then Hizballah could again claim to be indispensable, while Syria would show that Lebanon could not be stable without its presence.

By late 2005 things were heating up on two tracks: Syria was escalating its militant rhetoric. "UN Reports Rising Flow of Arms from Syria into Lebanon," read a *New York Times* headline.[42] In November, Syria's deputy minister of waqf (religious foundations), Muhammad Abd al-Sattar, remarked on Syrian television, "Syria now represents the opposition to the Greater Middle East plan, . . . the last line of defense. All the forces of the Arab and Islamic nations everywhere must be mobilized to defend this last line of defense. The last line of defense is what guarantees that the values of this nation will endure."[43]

Sattar represented the regime's religious flank, focusing more on Islamist-style language. But other than the final Koranic invocation, he sounded very much like what Bashar would be saying. Indeed, the link between Islamism and Arab nationalism was the core of Bashar's argument. Only Syria stood between the Arabs and Muslims and the total destruction of everything they held dear or sacred. Therefore, it was the duty of every other country to defend Syria, every true Arab nationalist as well as each and every Islamist, too.

Of course, Syria was not so universally beloved even by its fellow Arabs. Lebanon had thrown out the Syrians; Egypt and Saudi Arabia had supported Lebanon's effort; Iraq was angry at Syria's covert war against itself. From now on, though, anyone who did not back Syria would be seen as a traitor. As Nasser in the 1950s, Syrian dictator Salah Jadid in the 1960s, and Saddam in the 1980s had done, Bashar was making a bid to be the Arab world's leader. Hafiz had never quite done this so boldly or blatantly, always acting as part of a coalition. It seems reasonable to suppose that Bashar did not really think he would become the leader of all the Arabs or Muslims—and he had to contend with his partner Iran's claim in the leadership department—but taking this stance was also a clever way to defend his regime at home. At first, this strategy seemed silly and futile, but the Lebanon-Israel war during the summer of 2006 would make it look brilliant.

Bashar had been raised on tales of great Arab warriors, acts of heroism, and the glory of revolution. His father had been in the political underground, an exile and conspirator, plotting coups, seizing power, overcoming foes, and building a powerful state apparatus almost from the ground up. Now, however, this young man was an administrator faced not only with dull problems but also with a lack of solutions to them. Where was the glory for him?

Aside from pure self-interest in supporting Hizballah as Syria's leading client in Lebanon, the romantic images of men in battle, defying the enemy and triumphing against tremendous odds—a virtual sea of testosterone—could not have failed to work their spell on Bashar. For his father, Hafiz, who had commanded armies, squadrons of airplanes, and fleets of tanks, some ragtag glorified militiamen on the payroll—Iran's, if not Syria's—were mere minions. Bashar saw matters differently. Yet, it was not just a young man's fancy. After all, Syria's army was not up to fighting Israel and had increasingly less value for controlling Lebanon in the new situation. Hizballah was more important for Syria precisely because Damascus was not going to be held as directly responsible for its antics. It was no mere semicovert terrorist group but rather the most powerful army in Lebanon. Syrian military planners were simply treating Hizballah as if it were an integral but deniable part of the Syrian armed forces.[44]

And so Bashar showed Hizballah more respect and gave it greater freedom of action. Hizballah was to make up for what the regular Syrian armed forces lacked in countering or even striking at Israel. His father never deigned to meet Hizballah's leader, whereas Bashar positively doted on Hassan Nasrallah, seeming, in Eyal Zisser's phrase, "to bask in Nasrallah's victorious glow," after Israel's withdrawal from south Lebanon. In return, Nasrallah patronized his own patron, "as if he would show the new boy the ropes." Such behavior would have driven Hafiz into a fury and Nasrallah would have soon been put in his place. Instead, Bashar did not try to restrain him from creating tensions on the Lebanon-Israel border from 2000 onward while delivering hundreds of rockets to Hizballah. Bashar was not only playing with fire, he was supplying it wholesale.[45]

Rockets and missiles played a central role in Syrian military strategy, perhaps more so than for any other country in the world. Realizing that they could not obtain military parity with Israel in conventional weapons during the 1980s, the regime's leaders sought an alternative. After all, their military technology was outdated; they lacked the needed money or credits from Moscow, and developing nuclear weapons was too difficult, expensive, and dangerous. Syrian generals had observed with great interest how Iran and Iraq had fired missiles against each other's cities during the Iran-Iraq war in the 1980s, as well as Saddam's use of missiles against Israel in 1991. For Damascus, rockets and missiles seemed a solution to their problem, what might be called the ideal poor man's nuclear weapon.

Ironically, the Syrians used a lot of the aid they had received with America's blessing for opposing Iraq in 1991 to buy missiles with which to fight Israel, mainly Scuds from North Korea and Iran. They also considered chemical and germ weaponry. Defense Minister Mustafa Tlas even published an article, "Biological (Germ) Warfare: A New and Effective Method in Modern Warfare," in an Iranian publication. But good old-fashioned high-explosive warheads seemed more reliable and less likely to provoke an uncontrollable escalation.[46]

By giving Hizballah thousands of rockets and some longer-range missiles, Syria and Iran had multiplied its power far beyond the machine-gun and assault-rifle level. It could literally hold Israel hostage by a large-scale targeting of that country's civilians. Iran took the lead in this process, seeing Hizballah's new offensive strength as an asset to ensure that its nuclear arms program was not attacked by Israel or the United States. But the policy was also what Damascus wanted.

Bashar predicted the course of the 2006 Lebanon crisis with impressive foresight five years earlier in an interview. "We know Israel has superiority over us in some military aspects," he explained, but the Arab side had in its favor two factors. One is "steadfastness," the willingness to take large numbers of casualties and a great deal of damage without seeking to end the conflict. The Arab side would only make peace on its own terms, no matter how long it took and how high the cost. "Even if we evaluate that the enemy would destroy a great deal of our infrastructure. In essence, we are poor and can tolerate more than expected, and rebuild what has been destroyed."

The other is the ability to attack Israel's civilian population through a combination of terrorism and rockets. "We know Israel has abandoned the idea of military invasion by [ground] forces, and it uses now a method of comprehensive destruction of its enemies' infrastructure using airplanes, or from a distance far enough to avoid the casualties of a direct confrontation," Bashar explained. But now the Arab side has "the ability to transfer the battle into the enemy's territories. . . . We can cause great damage to the enemy."[47]

Of course, if the war could be fought on Lebanon's soil, Syria would sustain no damage at all. If Syria could hit Israeli civilians, it would not have to defeat Israeli armies, ran the thinking. Another advantage would be gained with the old Arab nationalist principle that those who refuse to surrender and are indifferent to the costs are never defeated. A parallel concept, especially useful in the age of international media and political correctness, is that ostentatious suffering wins both Arab and Western support and cancels out any responsibility one might have for committing aggression. The blame goes not to the side that started the war or refuses to make peace but rather the one that has fewer casualties.

It is impossible to say the extent to which Tehran and Damascus coordinated Hizballah's aggressive policy in 2006. Clearly, though, whether or not they encouraged the specific attack that set off the war, these two sponsors did not object to its strategy of trying to seize hostages by raids into Israel. If Damascus and Tehran had not wanted such things to happen they would have stopped Hizballah in its tracks. The escalation by Hizballah also coincided with Bashar's new strategy into which it fit perfectly. Hizballah had been heating up the Lebanon-Israel border so blatantly in 2005 that even the UN Security Council concluded Hizballah was provoking a conflict. The council called on Lebanon's government to take control of the south and disarm Hizballah, as specified by the Taif Accord and previous UN resolutions. Beirut did nothing and neither did the UN.[48]

During this period, Hizballah organized several cross-border raids to kidnap Israeli soldiers.[49] On at least one occasion, Israel was able to intervene covertly and stop such an operation; on another, it reportedly got UN Secretary-General Annan to call up Bashar and convey a threat that worked: Syria must order Hizballah to cancel the attack or suffer direct consequences.[50] Israel was becoming impatient with the failure of the UN forces in southern Lebanon to do much to stop attacks and rocket firings, even when it passed them intelligence about impending Hizballah operations. In November, Israeli Chief of Staff Lieutenant General Dan Halutz said the army was expecting more attacks and kidnapping attempts in the near future because Hizballah wanted to fight, and Syria was pushing it to do so in order "to divert attention" from the Hariri investigation.[51]

Finally, on July 12, 2006, Hizbollah successfully attacked an Israeli border patrol, killing eight soldiers and kidnapping two more from a pair of vehicles. After having failed to retaliate against earlier attacks, Israel hit back hard. Israeli Prime Minister Ehud Olmert declared Hizballah's raid to be an act of war. And so it was. After all, Hizballah was part of the Lebanese government, authorized by the country's rulers to carry arms and run the south.

The fighting went on for a month. Israeli planes bombed Hizballah targets in south Lebanon and south Beirut. Hizballah fired four thousand rockets into Israel, of which 80 percent came from Syria.[52] A total of about one thousand people were killed including combatants. The United States was in no hurry to agree to a ceasefire; Hizballah and Syria wanted one only on their own terms. In much of Europe, Israel was portrayed as the villain.

Syria publicly distanced itself from direct involvement in the war while ensuring that the fighting continued. So eager was Damascus to avoid becoming engulfed in the battle that Syrian army headquarters renewed the order each morning not to fire on Israeli planes flying in range across the border in Lebanon. Even when Israel bombed trucks carrying weapons to Hizballah within a few yards of Syrian territory, Damascus kept quiet.[53]

Covertly, however, it was very active. On July 19, 2006, for example, U.S. intelligence satellites spotted Iranians loading eight Chinese-designed C802 antiship cruise missiles and three launchers onto a transport aircraft at the military section of Tehran's Mahrebad Airport for shipment to Hizballah via Syria. Such Iranian flights landed at three Syrian air bases: the military section of Mazza International Airport in Damascus; Nasiriyya, 36 miles from the

Lebanese border; and Qusayr, north of Damascus and 15 miles from the frontier. The markings on captured Hizballah arms, including Fagot and Kornet antitank missiles, showed they were Russian-made equipment and sold, respectively, to Iran and Syria. Some of the latter were stenciled, "Customer: Ministry of Defense of Syria. Supplier: KBP, Tula, Russia."[54] Indeed, when Syrian Chief of Staff Ali Habib visited Russia in January 2005, one of his main stops had been the plant where the Kornets, one of the world's best antitank missiles, were made.[55]

Lebanon was burning. Israel was burning. But Syria was glowing—and why not? A senior Western official arriving for a meeting with the Syrian leadership in Damascus was shocked. He explains, "I found [Bashar], his deputy Farouq al-Sharaa and Foreign Minister Walid al-Muallim, arrogant, in a good mood, buoyed and encouraged by the war in Lebanon."[56]

Why should he have been shocked? In terms of the straitjacket of Arab political and ideological structures, the Syrian strategy was unbeatable. It was totally unoriginal but, nevertheless, perfectly brilliant. Syria's first unbeatable maneuver was to define the goals of Israel and America—and sometimes of the West in general—as irredeemably aggressive and hostile. In the words of *Tishrin* editor Khalaf al-Jarrad, they would learn that their war and mass murder in Iraq, Palestine, and Lebanon would not force the Arab nation to be defeated or surrender. Syrian Minister of Expatriates Buthayna Shaban made the same point, "It is clear that the disarmament of the resistance [Hizballah], the destruction of Iraq, the tearing of the people of Iraq to pieces, and the threat to Syria—these are goals in the establishment of the New Middle East, in its Zionist-Western identity."[57]

Yet what were Israel and the United States really trying to do? Israel had no territorial claims on Lebanon and had withdrawn completely from its territory, demanding only that Lebanon not let people attack across the border. Regarding the Palestinians, it had agreed on a comprehensive peace with a Palestinian state, had withdrawn from the Gaza Strip, and was preparing to pull out of most of the West Bank. In Iraq, the United States was trying to support a government elected by the majority to achieve a stability that would ensure the country's permanent unity. Both Israel and the United States wanted to get out as fast as possible, both in terms of the way they defined their national interests and also for their leaders' political advantage. In the domestic politics of both countries, victory was defined not by a continuation of occupation but by the end of occupation.

In fact, it was the Arab "resistance" that was aggressive: keeping Lebanon damaged, divided, and weak; ensuring that the Palestinians would continue to suffer and not have a state; and murdering Iraqis in large numbers. Reality was being stood on its head, but this Syrian version was convincing to most Arabs and many in the West. After all, it coincided with a half-century-long Arab narrative, which continued to be promoted by virtually every school, government official, media outlet, and mosque in the Arab world.

At the end of the war, Israel and Lebanon had been damaged and bloodied whereas Syria had not sustained a single scratch. The Arab world was wildly enthusiastic for Hizballah's victory claim. Syria basked in the glow of being Hizballah's sponsor. At home, the Syrian regime was at the height of popularity. Forgotten were the lack of freedom, the economic mess, the repression of reformers, the Islamists' critique of the government, and the Sunni distaste for Alawite rulers. Lest anyone think that such things as higher living standards or more freedom were important, *Tishrin* explained, "Life, oh Arabs, is only [fighting] for one's honor" and martyrdom was the purest form of doing so.[58]

Perhaps the perfect expression of this prevailing attitude was a column by Yousuf al-Rashid in the Kuwaiti newspaper *al-Anba*. "The Lebanese people," he explains, "may have lost a lot of economic and human resources. . . . But away from figures and calculations, they have achieved a lot of gains." How can anyone be so crass, he seems to assert, as to worry about thousands of destroyed dwellings, billions in damage, and setting the economy back by decades, not to mention entrenching an extremist Islamist group as a second government? Killing some Israelis and damaging their country was supposedly far more important. Lebanon's "heroic resistance fighters," he writes, "have proven to the world that Lebanese borders are not open to Israeli tanks without a price. . . . Lebanon was victorious in the battle of dignity and honor."[59] Yet he could not even claim that Israeli forces could be kept out of Lebanon, only that they would suffer some losses in going where they pleased.

Even in the West, where French and American antagonism toward Syria remained, it seemed as if everyone was calling for diplomatic engagement with Damascus. Attacking Israel by proxy, turning Lebanon into a hostage, and creating a big mess, Syria had not made itself a pariah but a sought-after interlocutor. To be radical and anti-Western did not so much invite retaliation as it generated an urge to appease. The Hariri investigation disappeared from sight at the very moment it seemed potentially fatal for the regime. A pro-Syrian Lebanese politician gloated, "The wrecking of the formation of the international tribunal" on the case was the first benefit from the war.[60]

Bashar was vindicated.

But he was just getting started. Saddam had incurred tremendous damage to his country, international censure, and his own eventual overthrow by invading Iran and Kuwait. Bashar brought no damage to his country, hardly any foreign criticism, wild popularity at home, and offers of international concession by simply paying others to attack Iraq and Israel. As a special dividend, these actions also pushed Lebanon back toward Syrian hegemony.

At the same time, Bashar and his minions launched their campaign to exalt Syria and discredit every other Arab regime. Only Damascus was really fighting Israel, striking against America, and saving both Arabs and Muslims from imperialist enslavement. "Isn't it a disgrace," editorialized *al-Ba'th*, "that some [of the Arabs] speak as though they are on the side hostile to the Lebanese people, to its resistance, and to its national symbols?"[61] One must respect Syria's audacity. Here it was dragging Lebanon into an unwanted, unnecessary, destructive war and simultaneously claiming to be its victims' savior.

Responding to accusations that Damascus had embarked on a risky adventure, the newspaper insisted that "the Lebanese and Palestinian national and Islamic resistance"—no mention of Syria, as if it were an innocent bystander—"is not . . . 'adventurous.' They are defending the land, people, and honor of Lebanon and Palestine. . . . The 'adventurous' ones are those for whom honor and homeland have become contemptible [matters]."[62] Those who did not want to fight, who sought peace or complained about bloodshed, were cowards and traitors. Syrian leaders were free to posture as heroes of battle. Walid al-Muallim, on his first visit to Lebanon since Damascus withdrew, boasted that "as Syria's foreign minister I hope to be a soldier in the resistance."[63]

Within Syria, everyone played the vicarious victor. Everywhere there were posters of Nasrallah; ubiquitous were the group's yellow flags, its songs and slogans. Pictures of Bashar, Nasrallah, and Iranian President Mahmoud Ahmadinejad were plastered on minibuses and stores. When had there ever been so much celebration? A young television producer dressed in fashionable Western clothes—who would lose her job, freedom of dress, and perhaps even life (since she was an Alawite) if Islamists ever came to power in Damascus—was ecstatic, telling an American journalist, "If you think that the United States or anyone can offer the Syrian government a deal to abandon its support for [Hizballah and Hamas], you are crazy, because all Syrians support the resistance."[64]

The reformers were finished, mainly due to arrests, but also because how could calls for democracy compete with war cries? "The issue of Hizbollah and the war is no longer rational," one Syrian opposition figure said. "It is emotional." A young Syrian disagreeing with his friends, all engaged at the moment in showing their lack of Islamic piety by drinking beer, was accused of being an "American."[65] As the old Arab nationalist slogan put it, no voice should rise above the din of battle. Or in the words of Syrian filmmaker Umar Amiralay,

"The result reinforces the despotisms. Nobody is discussing reforms in a city where the merchants are flying the yellow flag of Hizballah."[66] A few days after saying this, he was arrested by the authorities.

Fighting Israel—or more often just talking about fighting Israel or praising others for doing it—was the highest of all virtues. Forgetting a half century of Arab defeat from such a value system, a television producer was convinced that victory was near. "The Roman empire did not last forever. There is no reason to believe that Israel will. It should have never existed to begin with, and all Arabs believe that it will be wiped out."[67] Nothing had been learned from two generations' worth of experience.

Syria's invincible argument was to insist that every Arab would have to choose sides with either Israel and the United States, or the resistance. "There are no other options," Jarrad said.[68] In effect, then, they would be held hostage by Syrian policy—and have to ignore their own interests—on the traditional principle that the most militant factor set the agenda. In Shaban's perfect phrase, "The Arabs need to understand today that 'everything that brings them together is right, and everything that sows dissension among them is wrong.'"[69] But of course the only acceptable unity was on Syrian terms under the leadership of Damascus.

Could Lebanon turn to the West to help it control its own national territory rather than have Hizballah, Syria, and Iran do so? No. Might Arabs negotiate peace with Israel for a compromise solution? No. Was it legitimate for Iraqis to seek American help to defeat terrorist insurgents who were murdering large numbers of Arab Muslims? No. Should the Arab states eschew endless conflict and focus instead on social and economic development along with more human rights? No. Only war, battle, and radicalism were permissible. There was only the Land of Resistance and the Land of Treason.

Yet what of Syrian-backed terrorism and disorder in Lebanon, did that sow dissension? No. How about the terrorist insurgency in Iraq, provoking bitterness between Sunni Arab Muslims and the Shia Arab Muslims, was that sowing dissension? No. And so on.

Only Syria was truly macho, upholding Arab nationalism and helping the gallant fighters while other Arab leaders were neutral ("drafting statements condemning the violence," complained *Tishrin*) or acting like Western lackeys ("wandering among the capitals of the superpowers begging for a ceasefire").[70]

The editor of *al-Thawra*, Abd al-Fattah al-Awad, mocked other Arab rulers as "rationalists and pragmatists and doves of peace" who drank toasts with the Americans in cups made from the skins of those killed in Lebanon. They did not understand that Israel had an "aggressive and barbaric nature . . . which it is impossible to change" except by defeating it.[71] Negotiations, then, were a waste of time. Yet might it be pointed out that if Syria and its clients had not promoted war, no one would have been killed? And if Syria advocated war as its strategy wouldn't that produce even more casualties forever? Who, then, was acting with an aggressive nature?

"All of those who were killed are our children," continued the editor. "Can the father forgive the murderer of his son?"[72] Yet, in this vein, hadn't Syria murdered the fathers of Lebanon's two leading political figures: Kemal, father of Walid Jumblatt, and Rafiq, father of Sa'd Hariri? Can the son forgive the murderer of his father? And precisely to add insult to injury, having inflicted this and other woes on Lebanon, Syrian leaders raged that Lebanon's leadership was ungrateful.

One reason why Syria was so ferocious in its threats, rhetoric, and punishments, however, was that its case—despite conforming so much to the accepted Arab worldview—was fragile. Only misrepresentation, stridency, and the exclusion of contradictory viewpoints could put it across. Fortunately for Syria's regime, though, that was easy to do at home and relatively simple to promote elsewhere in an Arab world whose media, intellectuals, clerics, and masses were eager for tales of revenge obtained and honor restored. Even in the West, the Syrian narrative drowned out its critics more often than might be expected.

The jingoism of the regime's mouthpieces knew no bounds in inciting people toward decades of unwinnable, costly warfare. "The time of our revival has now begun. . . . The era of war has not yet ended, and will never end as long as rights and land are plundered. . . . No one thinks that the [war] will be won today, tomorrow, or [even] next year—but it is the beginning of the end, and the road towards victory has begun." Thus spake *Tishrin.*[73]

And all this over a war in which Israel controlled the air and sea. Israeli losses were far smaller than in other conflicts (one-tenth of its casualties during the second Palestinian intifada), and it ended up in control of the battlefield. On one level, all this deliberately generated hysteria might seem insane, yet it was eminently functional. Syria was indeed the big winner, not so much over Israel but rather over its own people and other Arab states.

The rhetoric coming out of Damascus was indistinguishable from that of the 1950s and 1960s. "There can be no doubt," exulted *Tishrin,* "that the Middle East is indeed today in the throes of birth pangs. But the birth will be the birth of an Arab world which will be ruled by its noble sons who understand their own interests, are proud of their past, their present, and their future, and who sacrifice so that their children will have an honorable future in which the

Arabs will achieve this unification and cooperation, so that the Arab voice will prevail in the international arena."[74]

Bashar put himself at the head of the parade. In his message to the Syrian army on the anniversary of its founding, Bashar told his soldiers, "The time now is a time for popular and national resistance. This resistance succeeded in humiliating the occupiers, shattering their prestige in Iraq and Palestine, and so today in Lebanon, and it has proven to the world that the power of truth is stronger than all the hubris of the occupying power." The list of accusations against Israel applies much better—and it is startlingly apt—for Syria: perpetrating aggression, making whole nations hostile, holding thousands of prisoners, as well as "occupying our Arab lands in Palestine, the Golan Heights, and southern Lebanon."[75]

Yet by Syria's own maps, Israel didn't occupy any land in southern Lebanon, while Damascus opposed its giving back the other two areas in exchange for real peace.

The resistance fighters were fighting, cheered *al-Thawra,* to redeem their lands and defend their honor. And part of the battle is to expose "agents who have abandoned" fellow Arabs. Syria is "the strongest force and the force most determined to stand by our steadfast Arab people.... All the shouting of threats that the forces of hegemony, who support the aggression, are sounding will not deter us from continuing in the path of liberation, from supporting our brothers, and from providing aid to the resistance."[76] But of course as long as the threats meant nothing in practice, why should they?

The most important speech Bashar had ever made—and the fullest explanation of his worldview and strategy—was his talk to the Fourth General Conference of the Syrian Journalists Union on August 15, 2006. Many of these themes he had taken up before, and would do so again, but never was he so comprehensive. Much of it was a repetition of the ideas purveyed by Arab nationalists for the previous half century, yet Bashar's statement was, self-consciously, a reaffirmation on every point.[77] Muhammad Habash, a member of Syria's parliament, later praised Bashar by saying that this speech was a declaration of jihad,[78] and so it was, arguably against not only Israel, America, and the West but also most of the Arab world and the majority of people in Lebanon as well.

According to Bashar, what is the Arab world's problem: underdevelopment, dictatorship, the hold of the dead hand of tradition? No, instead it is the threat to mind and spirit, identity and heritage by a "systematic invasion." To make matters worse, many Arabs had betrayed their fellows through the "culture of defeat, submission, and blind drifting," which was in essence the retailing of the enemy's plan. For the Arabs, the sole choice, according to Bashar, was resistance or extinction. Clearly, he did not think resistance was a far more likely road toward extinction. At any rate, he argued that the 2006 war had proven him correct all along.

In reality, the new Middle East was a concept invented foolishly and naively, but also idealistically, by Israeli Foreign Minister Shimon Peres in the 1990s to describe a peaceful region in which everyone cooperated for their mutual benefit. In the U.S. government's view, it defined a region where democracy would reign and war would be banished.

To Bashar, however, all this was merely a cover for the "submission and humiliation and deprivation of peoples of their rights" so that they will be killed without mercy and enslaved without appeal.[79]

"They wanted Israel to be the dominating power in the Arab region and the Arabs would be laborers, slaves, and satellites revolving in the Israeli orbit." As an example, he gave Iraq, whose "destruction and ruination" had taken the country back to the Stone Age. Bashar did not mention that while the Americans had set off a crisis by overthrowing Saddam, it was his own regime that had ensured that the aftermath would be a seemingly endless nightmare of terrorism and sabotage.

The same point applies to the Arab-Israeli peace process of the 1990s. Israel did not want peace, Bashar said, quoting Israeli Prime Minister Yitzhak Shamir as saying in 1991, "We will make this process continue for 10 years." Bashar interpreted that to his audience as a rejection of a solution. Yet Shamir had been prophetic in a different way: almost exactly 10 years after he spoke Israel did offer Syria a serious solution and was turned down. It was Bashar's father who killed the process, not Shamir.

Bashar's diagnosis, however, was that the Arab mistake had been to adopt diplomacy and cancel "all the other options."[80] But if the Arab states abandoned war it was because they had been constantly defeated, and they expected that would happen again. If Bashar meant violence, this was not at all abandoned, since Syria continued to sponsor terrorism against Israel throughout the 1990s.

Regarding the moderate Arab bargaining position, Bashar characterized that as, in theory, "to offer everything to Israel," seek little for themselves, and end up getting nothing at all. This was completely bogus. After all, Egypt received all the territory it had lost in 1967 plus $2 billion in U.S. aid per year. Jordan gained a satisfactory solution for its state interests. The Palestinians obtained the return of tens of thousands of exiles, the receipt of billions of dollars in aid, and the establishment of a government, which could have become a state. It was Israel that got nothing, neither peace nor recognition, at least not from Syria, the Palestinians, or most Arab states.

The Arab mistake, according to Bashar, was not rejecting compromise but to have even considered it as an option. By trying "to appease Israel and the United States" they abandoned intimidation and ensured the indifference of the rest of the world. "They only take action when Israel suffers. Israel suffers only when we possess power. This means, in the final analysis, that the world will not be concerned with us and our interests, feelings, and rights unless we are powerful." Otherwise, instead of pressuring and criticizing Israel, the West demands things like better treatment for Syrian dissidents, or the UN passes resolutions protesting massacres in Sudan.

This is what happened when the Arabs wasted their time "discussing and negotiating with ourselves, convinced about a promised peace with an imaginary party that is [in fact] preparing itself for its next aggression against the Arabs."[81] But what if the Arabs could not truly be so powerful as he thought they were? Hadn't this happened before? Isn't this what befell Saddam?

And then Bashar coined a phrase, which may become known to history as his motto, words seemingly torn from the speeches of Nasser and of Bashar's father's predecessor and foe, Salah Jadid. "If wisdom, according to some Arabs, means defeat and humiliation, then by the same token, victory means adventure and recklessness."

Daring had pushed Israel out of southern Lebanon in 2000, Bashar continued, and he argued that the latest war had won a similar victory, not only against Israel and America but also over the treacherous Lebanese, who had supported Hariri and opposed Syrian occupation.[82] In the best Arab nationalist tradition, he redefined anyone who wanted Lebanon to be a sovereign, democratic state as a lackey of the Zionists and imperialists.

Hizballah had not only won, he claimed, but its actions had been wildly popular in the Arab world. The defeatists—Egypt, Jordan, Saudi Arabia, and Arab reformers—had been defeated. The real Arabs had reacted with pride, telling these odious seditionists, "We are Arabs and this is our resistance and whoever does not stand with us is not from us." And this all proved that Arab nationalist sentiment had not declined at all, was not a thing of the past to be replaced by liberalism, or Islamism, or even moderate nationalism. Rather, it "is at its peak."

What had now supposedly been proven—yet was consistently shown to be false by the previous half century of history, which Bashar had deleted—is that a self-confident resistance that represents its people "produces victory" no matter how well armed the enemy. If there is an unfavorable balance of power, righting it is only a matter of willpower, which will be overcome, "When we decide—and the decision is in our hands—to overcome this gap."[83]

For so ignoring material realities, Vladimir Lenin would have no hesitation about consigning Bashar to the category of infantile leftists. But Communism is dead and so Bashar can make the ultimate statement of philosophical idealism without any fear of shocking Moscow. He sums up the strategy of will power over material power in the following words: "We have decided to be weak but when we decide to be strong this balance will be changed." As for the global community, UN Security Council, or other countries' views, it was unnecessary to take their opinions into consideration. "National decisions take precedence over any international resolution, even if this leads to fighting or war."[84]

Now, the "political mercenaries" and "parasites" would be ignored, and "resistance as a way of thinking" would set the agenda. "After eight wars with Israel over almost 60 years, the Arab fighters' determination has increased."[85] This means there will be more wars, or at least threats of wars, until it is Israel that surrenders. Embarking on an unwinnable battle, ignoring so much experience about its costs, threatening not only Israel and the West but also most other Arab governments, walking on the edge of the abyss, is the policy Bashar advocates.

This political strategy could be suicidal, with miscalculation leading not only to massive bloodshed and destruction but also the downfall of regimes, including his own. The pattern he advocates is precisely the one of 1948 and 1967. Even at best, it is a formula for stagnation in the Arab world, postponing all the changes it needs.

Yet on another level Bashar's approach does make sense. It is the only strategy that will enable his regime and system to survive. Judge us not by our economic performance or delivery of services, he says in effect, but by our steadfastness and intransigence. The former are difficult prizes to deliver; the latter are just a matter of words and waging wars on other people's territory.

Moreover, experience has also shown him that the West is often eager to be fooled and usually willing to back down. Would the Europeans really stand up to a tough Syria, or would they rush to placate it? Why should Lebanese politicians defy Syria—and its ally Iran and client Hizballah—when they know the West will not really back them or put down Bashar? Thus, it is credible when Bashar says, if we are moderate they will make demands; if we are militant they will give concessions. He can well argue that the louder we yell and clash our weapons together, the more they will offer us in terms of money and territory. They will be galvanized into action in trying to prevent crisis, to understand why we are so aggrieved. The more we attack, threaten, and say no, the more they will tremble.

This kind of thinking is also the logic of his allies, Islamist Iran, Hamas, and Hizballah. It is also very much in line with historic Arab nationalist practice. And basically, it is the only strategy the Syrian regime can follow. For the sole useful alternative it is merely a time-out on the main militant approach. It is the one Hafiz used in the 1990s and Bashar manipulated briefly on taking power in 2000 as well as after the U.S. overthrow of Saddam in 2003: to pretend compliance and stall for time until Damascus could return to its posture of defiance and resistance.

During the speech to the journalists' organization, members of the audience who claimed to be Lebanese—no doubt planted there by Bashar's handlers since they permitted the interruptions—stood to thank Bashar loudly for all the things he had done for their country. With no sense of irony, one woman screamed, "Without the support of our sister country Syria, we would not be able to achieve what we have achieved." Given the country's wreckage, refugees, economic setbacks, ethnic strife, and the return of Syrian hegemony, it is hard to discern what any positive achievements might be.

The audience then broke into applause, shouting, "With our blood, with our soul, we redeem you, Oh Bashar!"[86] They need not worry. Bashar and his allies will make sure they continue to give him both.

CHAPTER TEN

THE ABYSS BECKONS

Khaddam, the former vice president who fled into exile and ought to know what he is talking about, said in January 2006 that the Syrian regime "cannot be reformed and there is nothing left but to bring it down."[1] Kilo, the most articulate internal critic, posited that same month, "The regime cannot surmount the present challenges, it has a choice of reconciliation with the outside and reform on the inside, meaning a different political system. There is no other choice."[2] Clearly, as Khaddam knew so well, the system cannot be reformed because change is so thoroughly against the rulers' interests. Its problems are structural, intrinsic to Syrian society's political, economic, and intellectual fabric. Its sense of mission—Arab leadership, Islamic-based antagonism to the West, imperial rule over its neighbors, and so on—is equally built-in.

Syria's difficult communal and geopolitical situation makes it fragile; the system was constructed to turn that weakness into a form of strength. The price, however, is extreme rigidity. That regime could no more survive a major structural change than the Soviet Union would have been capable of successfully transforming itself into a capitalist democracy. But this fact by no means proves the Syrian regime incapable of meeting the challenges it faces or that there is any force inside or outside the country able to bring it down.

Syrian strategy's more adventurous aspects at present may rest on Bashar's character, but this is a matter of degree and timing rather than substance. The problem is not that Bashar—or the leaders of Hizballah, Hamas, and Iran for that matter—are thoughtless fanatics. The trouble in fact, is the exact opposite: they act rationally in pursuing their interests as they define them in the world as they understand it. After all, the junior dictator did not invent the regime's ideology but merely dedicated himself to ensuring that the system survived by preserving its continuity. Syria's posture has always been radical even compared to all other Arab governments, going back as far as the 1930s. The estimation of a 1966 CIA report is quite accurate for today: "The question in regard to Syria's future then is not whether it will be moderate or radical, but what will be the kind and intensity of its radicalism."

As a result of the regime's nature, worldview, structure, and interests, it is not a government that can be reasoned into moderation or be partner in the negotiated settlement of some extremely difficult issues. Syria does not sponsor subversion and terrorism against Iraq, Israel, or Lebanon steadily, as well as Turkey or Jordan periodically, because of a misunderstanding. It did not assassinate Lebanon's leaders, wage war on Israel, or become a virtual state sponsor of al-Qaida in Iraq as a reaction to grievances that might be resolved.

The regime does not promote the most extreme and systematic anti-Americanism due to a desire to alter U.S. policies anywhere short of turning them into their opposite. Resolving the issues over which Syria fights cannot mollify that country, because Syria blocks any solution. And that regime does so because the process of continued struggle is so much more beneficial to it than the fruits of any compromise agreements or internal reforms would be.

On this and other matters, Syrian strategy, however, is aimed more at regime survival than at world conquest. Syria and its allies do want to defeat the West, destroy Israel, and take over the Middle East. But even if they know they will never even come close to succeeding with these goals—and some, though not all, are probably cynical on that point—the radicals still have very good reasons for acting as they do in order to keep their power and popular support.

Militancy is the glue that holds Syria together and keeps Bashar stuck to the throne. For other Arab countries, including Jordan, Saudi Arabia, and Egypt, a more limited, largely verbal militancy suffices because they already have a more coherent identity to hold together their societies. In contrast, Syria and Saddam-era Iraq had a greater need to incite foreign conflicts in order to hold together ethnically and religiously diverse countries that might not otherwise survive.

Syria's fragility in this respect was one more factor militating against democracy or economic reform. Alawites in the political-military elite enrich themselves through controlling the government, whereas Sunni Arabs would do best if the economy were more open. A liberal economy would tip both the economic and political equation by creating an independent entrepreneurial class inevitably demanding more changes and strengthening the

Sunni claim to govern. The fact that a Sunni—possibly Islamist—list would win any fair Syrian election gives the largely Alawite power structure and other non-Sunnis an additional incentive to reject democracy. The statistics of communal demography give the regime an antireform argument that is compelling for many, including the proportionately largest Christian community of any Arabic-speaking state. Fear of Sunni Islamists ties Christians and perhaps Druze to the regime even more tightly.

So, to return to Khaddam's argument, does this tough set of circumstances mean that the regime is going to be overthrown? This outcome is certainly possible, of course, yet one should not underestimate the system's strength and flexibility. Similar dictatorships in Germany, Italy, Japan, and Iraq fell only because they were overthrown by foreign countries in war. Communism was largely dismantled due to a reform movement from the top that went wrong.

By avoiding direct war, the Syrian regime seeks to escape the former fate, and by rejecting reform, it eludes the latter one. In this regard, Bashar's strategy has worked in discouraging foreign pressure, uniting the elite, and turning potential Islamists into Bashar-lovers. The wages of militancy have been praise, power, money, and glory. The Syrian government knows that it has mismanaged the country's economy, oppressed its people, and devastated its neighbors yet remains wildly popular at home and relatively influential abroad. Far from being on the verge of collapse, it has fooled or intimidated most of the world, freeing itself from the rules most other countries must obey while avoiding the external pressures other countries suffer. The regime has coopted the big potential opposition—Sunni Muslim Islamists—and crushed the far smaller actual opposition—liberal reformers. What possible incentive does it have to change its ways?

True, Syria's problems are very real in objective terms. There is a stagnant economy, rampant corruption, an ideology inhibiting freedom, and a system blocking progress. This is equally so for all the Arabic-speaking states in various ways, but it is worst in Syria. Given the power of nationalist and religious demagoguery to mobilize support, these material problems—as alien as this notion is to Western concepts of political pragmatism—can be overcome by satisfying psychological appetites instead.

The regime's greatest internal challenge would be an Islamist movement based on Syria's Sunni Muslim majority, whose energy it has so far successfully diverted to its own benefit. As Sunnis migrate from countryside to city, peasants grateful for the regime's past role in land reform may be transformed into people disoriented by their new environment, angry about problems they face, and eager to revive their idealized past through religion. This is what happened in Iran, where Shah-loving traditionalist villagers moved to cities and became Islamist revolutionaries.

Yet the regime has handled this issue very well by re-inventing itself as a proper Muslim one with Islamist political trimmings. As a result, the Syrian government was simultaneously repressing radical Islamist groups while building big mosques. In 2003, the Syrian government changed regulations to let soldiers pray while on army bases, a step that could increase Islamist influence in the military, and allow women students to wear head scarves in the schools, which was previously forbidden. Religious observance grows since people have no other outlet for their dreams and frustrations. But the resulting piety need not be political. And with Bashar accepted as defender of the faith, more religiosity enhances his control.[3]

The Syrian regime is no longer a secular government fighting Islamism but rather the main Arab state promoting it. The dictatorship shed its leftism in the 1970s and its secularism under Bashar. When Deputy Minister of Religious Endowments Muhammad Abd al-Sattar speaks he sounds just like Bashar—whom he quotes approvingly. Syria, Sattar explains, represents the "last line of defense" against the American-Zionist plan to take over the Middle East and to destroy both Arab society and Islam. These plots "aim to put on the throne of the Middle East the descendants of . . . those whom the Koran called the descendants of apes and pigs."[4]

Such rhetoric did not come from clerics alone. Islamist arguments and phrasing permeated the "secular" Ba'th media and came from regime supporters far removed from Islamic circles. In her *Tishrin* column, for example, Khadija Muhammad used a classical Islamist war cry and came close to proclaiming Nasrallah as messiah, all in the name of defending Arab nationalism.

> Declare before all your Arab identity and your Arab glory. . . . The Arab consciousness has spread to all, and the desire and yearning for martyrdom have grown strong. . . . Lo, the martyrs are rising towards the sun, on the jasmine roads of Damascus, with the fragrant [flowers] of Paradise, and they are waving the banner of victory, the banner of Hizballah. . . . Nasrallah, you are the leader who was foretold in prophecy, the one who will arrive on the steed of glory to write in the pages of history the first victories for the Arabs.[5]

This kind of talk is from the school of Khomeini and bin Ladin. Yet there was also something new here, a National Islamist mélange of Arab nationalism and Islamism. Aside from gaining support among the pious in particular, and Sunni Muslims in general, the regime's ploy had still another advantage for Syria's rulers. As Islamic forces seemed to become stronger—albeit under regime sponsorship—potential liberals were so afraid that the Assads might be replaced by an Islamist state that many of them preferred to support the status quo rather than seek reforms.

"The young in Syria, who have been exposed to the empty slogans of the Ba'th Party, feel lost and without a path, and this pushes them into the arms of fundamentalist Islam," explained Muhammad Aziz Shukri of the University of Damascus. "Elections would create a confrontation between the Ba'th Party and Islamic circles in Syria, and one must ask what the results would be and what would happen afterwards?" He points out how such a situation in Algeria led to a bloody civil war. An Islamist regime would mean a dim future for Syrian intellectuals, the sizable Christian minority, and more modern-oriented women, as well as an even more turbulent Middle East. Understandably, Shukri did not want to see such a disaster happen in Syria. He would choose Bashar over some Syrian version of bin Ladin or Khomeini.[6]

This strategy of promoting Islam at home and Islamism abroad is, then, a dangerous game that could backfire some day. The new young militant mullahs in Syria keep their rulers happy by never directly attacking the government, focusing instead on berating foreign, non-Muslim enemies. Yet they are also laying a foundation to subvert the regime, as when an influential prayer leader in Damascus first praised Bashar in his sermon, and then added that presidents should tremble because Islam is mightier than any power on earth and will triumph in the end.[7] If you wish, you can believe he is only talking about people like George Bush and Jacques Chirac, but any listener can think in such terms about a president closer to home.

An uprising in Syria could make Iraq's civil war look like a picnic. So far, though, there is no sign of the Islamist Frankenstein's monster turning on its creator. Islamist challenges to the regime have had only minimal results and little support.[8] A shadowy revolutionary Islamist group called Jund al-Sham has launched a few terrorist attacks within Syria. The group is either an imitator or a local franchise of al-Qaida, which is ironic since Syria helps that group's affiliate fight in Iraq.

In June 2006, a gun battle took place near the Defense Ministry in Damascus in which one policeman and four terrorists were killed. Two months later, another group tried to blow up the U.S. embassy there. By out-shooting the attackers, the Syrian regime brazenly claimed to have proven its antiterrorist credentials and earned U.S. gratitude. Whether or not this group is real—captured terrorists seem always to die conveniently before they can be questioned thoroughly—it does not pose much threat to the regime.

The Muslim Brotherhood exiles, led by Ali Sadr al-Din al-Bayanouni from his base in London, formed the National Salvation Front as a broad coalition with other opposition groups including some liberals, Communists, and Kurdish nationalists. Seeking international support against the regime, Bayanouni visited Washington, D.C., where he met secretly with U.S. officials. It is tempting for the United States to consider backing the Syrian Muslim Brotherhood, but this is also an extraordinarily dangerous gamble. After all, as his role model, Bayanouni cites Hamas, hardly an encouraging sign.[9] Of course, it also illustrates the amazing paradoxes of that country's situation that the biggest enemy of the Syrian government wants to imitate an extremist group, which is itself the client of that same regime.

The bottom line is that neither liberal reform nor Islamist revolt seriously threatens the Syrian regime. Even the West and Israel do not endanger it. Yet many observers still think they know better than Syria's rulers. Ignoring all the structural and ideological factors, they believe they can buy off or persuade Syria toward moderation, economic reform, cooperation with America, and making peace with Israel. Bashar encourages this misunderstanding because it benefits him. In interviews and meetings with Western visitors—but not in his Arabic language statements—he perpetually hints that if only treated nicely, he will behave.[10] In this regard, he persuades the unwise and unwary to serve him by urging negotiations and concessions to Syria. But the more they advocate such tactics, the more Bashar and his henchmen become confident that they will stand firm and the West will crumble. In short, the very policies intended to make him more flexible succeed in ensuring that he remains obdurate.

There are many examples of this phenomenon. Night-vision goggles are an awesome high-tech military tool enabling soldiers to fight in the dark as effectively as they do in sunlight. The U.S. government discovered that Syria gave night-vision goggles to Saddam's troops before the 2003 war and to Iraqi insurgents thereafter. Israel's military captured night-vision goggles that Syria supplied to Hizballah. After the 2006 Israel-Lebanon war European officials went to Syria and asked it to block arms smuggling to Hizballah, despite the fact that the regime itself was the main smuggler. We'd love to help, said Syrian officials, but we lack the proper equipment to be effective. Can you supply us with night-vision goggles? The Italian foreign minister seemed eager to fill this supposed gap in Syria's arsenal.[11]

It is quite conceivable that Syria may be given military equipment to be used in order to stop arms smuggling to Hizballah, which it then gives to Hizballah. In other words, Syria deflected criticism and pressure and won praise by promising to stop itself from helping Hizballah while daily announcing in Arabic that it would continue to arm Hizballah and facilitate more smuggling. As for English, Bashar later told the visiting U.S. Senator Arlen

Specter, who seemed to think him sincere, "If I know of one Syrian who is transferring arms to Hizballah I will make sure to stop it."[12]

The same period saw another case of this pattern. To stop smuggling, the Lebanese government asked the UN to put peacekeeping troops on the Lebanese-Syrian border. But Bashar refused to permit this, explaining that to do so "would mean creating hostility between Syria and Lebanon" and "violate Lebanon's sovereignty."[13] Bashar was claiming that he, not Lebanon's government, would determine what Lebanon's independence required. Rather than point out how Syria was subverting UN and international efforts, however, UN Secretary-General Annan praised Bashar for his nonexistent help and said the Syrian president had promised him that arms shipments to Hizballah would stop.[14] European states also accepted Syria's alleged cooperation at face value, though Syria was not only blocking close monitoring of the border but also hinting that UN forces might be attacked by terrorists if they did things Syria did not like. Syria and Iran rearmed Hizballah; the UN said and did nothing.

In contrast with its usual behavior, France opposed appeasement because of Chirac's anger over the murder of Hariri, but, as *Le Figaro* reported in August 2006, "France was isolated in its diplomatic boycott of Damascus." Spain led a majority of EU states that wanted a dialogue with Syria over Lebanon. This meant asking Damascus's help in stabilizing Lebanon, precisely the policy that had endorsed Syrian domination of that country for decades. Spanish Foreign Minister Miguel Angel Moratinos nonsensically claimed that Syria promised him it would make Hizballah act benign and support the Lebanese government of Prime Minister Fouad Siniora, which both Bashar and Nasrallah were busily trying to overthrow. Moratinos gushed that Bashar, "Conveyed to me a genuine wish and will to work in a constructive and positive manner." Syria, he asserted, is "part of the solution and not part of the problem."[15]

For his part, the German foreign minister said he would continue the dialogue with Syrian leaders until he got a constructive response from them, thus putting himself in the position of a supplicant ready to beg eternally.[16] Italian Prime Minister Romano Prodi boasted that Bashar had agreed to let European troops patrol the Lebanon-Syria border at the very moment he was publicly and repeatedly refusing to do so.[17] No European foreign or prime minister admitted that this uncooperative attitude showed that Syria was part of the problem and not part of the solution, even as the regime's mouthpieces were gloating at how they had fooled and divided the Europeans.[18]

Again and again, no harsh Syrian rhetoric, broken promises, or extremist action could kill off an expectation that Syria "must" want to cooperate, be eager to undertake domestic reforms, or be panting at the chance to make peace, because this idea seemed sensible to people whose worldview does not encompass what one must do to be Syria's dictator. At the same time, there were always Westerners advocating the idea that Syria had won and everyone should now surrender to it. "Syria thinks the United States used [its] withdrawal from Lebanon and the Hariri investigation to weaken it and nothing worked. So it now says it's time to remind the United States and Israel that they can't solve problems in the region without dealing with it," said Flynt Leverett, former CIA and National Security Council official who often talks in this way. According to Leverett, Bashar's real interest lies in realignment with the United States and in peace with Israel.[19]

In an article entitled "Illusion and Reality," and unintentionally embodying the "illusion" part, Leverett writes, "The United States should convey its interest in a broader strategic dialogue [with] Assad, with the aim of reestablishing U.S.-Syrian cooperation on important regional issues and with the promise of significant strategic benefits for Syria clearly on the table."[20] Such writings repeat all the past mistakes in dealing with Syria as if that history never happened. First, how can cooperation be "reestablished" when it never really existed between the United States and Syria at any point in history? Next, why should anyone accept the claim of Bashar's propagandists that the United States is in the position of weakness and must thus kowtow to Syrian interests? Last, why should the United States concede in advance the right to pressure Syria and give away "significant strategic benefits" before having received anything in return?

These are the kinds of ideas virtually no one would advance regarding negotiations with any other country in the world. Moreover, what was the United States going to give Syria that would suit its own interests: selling Lebanon back into slavery, dropping the Hariri murder investigation, ignoring Syria's role in terrorism and its human rights violations? How would taking such steps improve anything?

On top of all that, these ideas had all been tried before and failed repeatedly. It is not a matter of giving Syria a "second" chance since the number of such proffered and forfeited opportunities was already in the double digits. And finally, other than Bashar's flattering whispered sweet nothings to visitors, what possible reason was there to believe that Syria's interests and intentions lay in the direction of conciliation? Instead, Bashar was saying and showing daily that Syria had good reasons to prefer demagoguery about resistance and struggle. The regime was at the height of popularity at home, making a comeback in Lebanon, and basking in the light of its alliance with Iran. Who needs economic reform, higher living standards, or peace when war is paying off so well?

Hardly a day passed without Bashar and other Syrian leaders making it clear that they saw neither peace with Israel nor rapprochement with America as even possible, much less desirable. Such options are precluded by their assessments. For example, in his speech to the 2001 Arab Summit in Amman, Bashar explained that all Israeli leaders are the same and that Israel's nature makes peace impossible. He proclaimed, "In Israel, whoever murders a thousand Arabs belongs to the left, and whoever murders five thousand Arabs belongs to the right." The real problem was the average Israeli civilian who was bloodthirsty, completely set against peace, and determined to depose or even murder any leader who was not hard-line. "This is a racist society. More racist than the Nazis," Bashar explained.[21]

On another occasion he stated, "It is inconceivable that Israel will become a legitimate state even if the peace process is implemented, because its structure deviates from the region's norm, and maybe from the whole world. . . . As long as Israel exists, the threat exists. . . . Israel is based on treachery. . . . Since its very inception, Israel has been a threat. It is the Israeli nature, and for that Israel was established."[22] Nor was he well-disposed toward America. The U.S.-led conspiracy, said Bashar, was designed to reshape the Middle East and turn it over to Israel with all Arabs and Muslims as the victims. The only other way to interpret U.S. policy, he remarked sarcastically, would be to believe the Americans were acting out of charity, in which case, "We have to send them a cable of gratitude."[23]

Yet to say the regime was angry at the United States because it opposed American policies explains much less than it seems for several reasons. First, its perception of U.S. policy was distorted by Arab nationalist and Islamist propaganda into a caricature. Second, the regime needed to have that country as an enemy and thus willingly forfeited chances for a real rapprochement. Third, even if Bashar was convinced that what he said about America's imperialistic desire to enslave the Arabs and destroy Islam was false and believed it wanted an equitable solution to the Arab-Israeli conflict, he would be no better inclined toward the United States.

From Bashar's standpoint, it was bad enough if all America wanted was to deny him control over his neighbors and preferred a more democratic, moderate Syria. In that case, he would still be at odds with America and need to persuade his people that U.S. opposition to his regime was really a threat to all of them as well. Of course, it was in Bashar's interest to deflect what was really opposition to himself into being a threat to all Arabs and Muslims. Even a "pro-Arab" U.S. policy would inevitably be an anti-Bashar one. Syria's leader was quite right in believing that he was not on the same side as America.

Nor can his view of America and behavior toward it be attributed to resentment of the United States as an all-powerful bully since the regime's strategy was based on the assumption that it really was not. On the contrary, if he
truly feared or was awed by American power, Syria would act in a way much
less antagonistic to U.S. interests. A sense of this no-win-for-Washington situation in popular thinking is well conveyed by an ordinary Syrian's statement regarding the popular view of America in his country:

> As I was growing up in Syria, the consensus had always been that people like
> Saddam and the Assads are only in power because the Americans wanted them
> there. The conventional thinking has always been that they were agents of the
> West, handpicked to control their societies. Once the United States decided to
> remove a person like Saddam from power, such widespread predictions of a se-
> cret deal between America and Arab dictators were quickly forgotten. Tradi-
> tional conspiracy theories of such deals have given way to more conventional
> theories. The same people who criticized America for supporting people like
> Saddam and Assad quickly turned into thinking that rather than being agents
> supported by the West, these were great national heroes who are brave enough
> to stand up to the new crusaders dressed as American marines.[24]

Yet the regime had a somewhat different viewpoint. Bashar had concluded
that the risk of provoking the United States into doing something really damaging to Syria was low to nonexistent. He concluded that he could safely bait a
bull that was apparently blind, deaf, and had blunted horns.

This explains a seeming paradox in Syrian behavior. On one hand, the
regime insists that Syria has been continually attacked, menaced, and conspired against by powerful forces: America, the West, and Israel. Yet, on the
other hand, it does not hesitate to act in a belligerent manner. When the
regime trumpets its eagerness to fight to the last man and undergo any sacrifice
for the cause, one might see this as a sign of great courage. Actually, it is based
on the fact that Syria's leaders know they have little to fear, believing those they
portray as demons of steel are really tigers of paper. Syria is not frightened by
threats because it does not take them seriously.

This conclusion has been reached as the result of careful observation and
some experimentation. Things were not always so. At times during the 1990s
and between September 11, 2001, and around mid-2003, the United States did
scare Damascus into being relatively more cautious. British Foreign Secretary
Jack Straw explained, "What we also know from the history of dealing with
Syria . . . [is] that where the international community is firm and united, in the
end the Syrian government gets the message."[25] Similarly, as soon as there was
real international pressure to leave Lebanon, Bashar pulled out his army.

But when it became clear that the United States was too overextended in Iraq and divided internally to think of a real confrontation, much less attack, Syria knew a show of bravado brought many advantages and little risk. Similarly, Bashar understood that Israel, far from being so bloodthirsty and aggressive, wanted no war with Syria. Even when provoked into a conflict with Hizballah, it had no desire to widen the fighting by attacking Syria despite Bashar's role in supplying the rockets fired at its civilians.

Thus, Bashar could afford to ask, Why worry about what the West thinks or try to please it? Far better, he insisted, to follow the great majority of Arabs who wanted a militant policy of struggle. "When we make a courageous and clear resolution, 300 million [people] will support us morally and materially. If we don't, nobody, Arab or non-Arab, will stand by us and we will go from bad to worse." Willpower shall bring victory. "What is important is that if we act with determination we will get what we want."[26] In addition, rather than accept a Western view of reality, "We must make our own definitions and spread them." In other words, the West must be persuaded that Israel is aggressive, racist, and intransigent. This was obvious, Bashar explained, because the Arabs were exclusively victims. After all, he claimed with a rather creative sense of history, "Never have we attacked Israel."[27]

The regime never tried to hide, in its Arabic pronouncements at least, the fact that it did not believe in peace with Israel or feel it needed to compromise with the West, nor was it looking for reform or care about the domestic economic situation. Why then is there such a rush by the West to negotiate with Syria even when Damascus broadly hints that the West will get nothing in return? Even more curious, why do so many Western leaders, officials, and intellectuals believe that the problem is a lack of communication with Damascus, a failure on their part to understand what the regime wants?

The answer is a strange combination of factors. On one hand, Western diplomats and politicians genuinely want to avoid conflict and do believe that everyone in the region can and should work together for mutual benefit. On the other hand, they fear the trouble Syria can make for them. Democratic leaders have great difficulty in understanding dictatorships or the power of ideology for extremists. At the same time, they want to look as if they are doing something productive. When they see grievances, their impulse is to assuage them; when they perceive problems, they seek to solve them through pragmatic steps. This worldview builds into a powerful guide to action, the source of countless op-ed pieces and policy plans.

Some basic distortions in Western elite thinking make it far harder to understand a country like Syria or Iran, or movements like Hamas and Hizballah.

These misconceptions include the idea that all nations and people are generally alike in their priorities, that material benefits always trump ideology, and that no one can really be an extremist if the facts of life are only explained properly to them. Western guilt and greed also play a role in this process. Those involved in statecraft and diplomacy, as well as democratic politics, often evince such professional deformations as having a burning need to negotiate, to try and make a deal with someone no matter what the cost, and to prefer concession to confrontation.

Still another factor is misapplying the "realist" framework by which most policymakers operate. Realism views states as rational actors pursuing their national interests. But this theory can only work if one understands how another government actually defines its interests. Assuming Syria wants the same things as do Western democratic countries makes people expect that Bashar is eager for peace and reform because that is what they would do.

In this context, it is easy for them to believe that Syria is Iran's ally or Hizballah's patron only because it has not been offered a better alternative. They fail to comprehend that these are appropriate policies for the dictatorship and that extremism, demagoguery, and terrorism are rational responses to the situation of Syria's regime. Precisely because he is a rational actor, Bashar prefers conflict over peace, tyranny to reform, and demagoguery that pleases citizens rather than services that benefit them.

Actually, Bashar's biggest mistake may be not so much allying with Hizballah and Iran but giving up too much power to them over Syria's interests. This is especially true of Iran, for whom he has sacrificed his relations with Arab countries. Indeed, it seems likely that Bashar has gone so far that Syria will never again under the Assad regime be a part of the Arab political framework the way it was during the past half century.

Khaddam told an interesting story to illustrate this point. In the 1980s, during the Iran-Iraq war, he said, Saudi King Fahd asked Hafiz to intervene after Iran attacked a Saudi ship in the Gulf. Syria successfully mediated a solution. According to Khaddam, Hafiz sent a letter to the king saying, "We will never prefer our relations with any state to our relations with any of the Arab states, and the Iranians are aware of this."[28] But with Bashar in power, this kind of even-handedness had vanished. Many Arab leaders and writers expressed their feeling that his regime had crossed the line, was no longer part of their community. An Egyptian columnist, Hazim Abd al-Rahman, warned, "All Iran wants is to extend its hegemony over the eastern Arab countries."[29] Jumblatt claimed, "The New Middle East is the one that Iran [wants to impose] by means of the Syrian regime."[30]

It was through his alignment with Iran that Bashar hoped to secure his regime's survival and spread its influence. Tehran was indispensable as Syria's strategic guardian and financier. Moreover, Iran never required him to do anything he did not like—not reform or moderation, not the relinquishment of Lebanon or peace with Israel. Their interests meshed perfectly. And once Iran had nuclear weapons, it would provide Syria with even more protection, equal to that once granted by the Soviet Union. There is no way the West could pry apart these two countries. As the Lebanese journalist Michael Young explains, "Iran offers [Bashar] a way out of his regional isolation as well as a credible military deterrent against outside threats. Why surrender this?"[31]

The wild card, however, was whether Iran's embrace would some day turn into a stranglehold. When the Pope made a statement that many Muslims did not like, it was the Iranian leader's office in Damascus that organized the demonstrations in Syria. Iranian investment in Syria increased.[32] During 2006 alone, Iranian investments in Syria included two auto plants to assemble car kits from Iran, two big wheat silos, and a cement plant. Many other projects are under discussion, including the signing of a deal for Iran-Syria cooperation on nuclear research. As many as 500,000 Iranians make religious pilgrimages annually to Shia shrines in Syria.[33]

Hundreds of Syrians went to Iran for religious studies. Even Syria's prize client, Nasrallah, was more Iran's than Syria's man. After all, he was the official representative in Lebanon of Iranian spiritual guide Ayatollah Ali Khamenei. In Iraq, too, Iran, with its influence among the Shia majority, is more likely to become a dominant force than Syria, whose client is the much smaller Sunni majority. Ironically, the ultimate threat to Bashar's independence may prove to be neither America nor Israel but his own patron.

Still, with Saddam gone, the Iranians being Persian, and Egypt having given up on foreign adventures, Bashar was just about the only Arab ruler in contention. Does he really care very much whether people in Egypt or Saudi Arabia support him, or does he even expect that to happen? What is most important for Bashar is that Syrians see him as the universal Arab leader, so his prestige skyrockets among them. He wants the local folks to see him auditioning for the starring role that Nasser played in the 1950s and 1960s, and Saddam tried to fill in the 1980s and into the 1990s. Even if he doesn't get the part, just being in the running makes him the home-town favorite.

Here is how Bashar wanted to be seen, courtesy of the obliging editors of *Tishrin:*

Bashar al-Assad is the clearest and most explicit [Arab] voice today, articulat-
ing the goals of the Arab nation and its values and principles with vigor and
courage but also with logic, wisdom and discretion. He represents not only
Syria, which in itself constitutes an Arab and a regional force of importance,
but the aspirations of the [Arab] nation wherever it is, from the [Atlantic]
Ocean to the [Persian] Gulf, its hopes and its fears.[34]

Bashar himself explains well what he was trying to accomplish, "Many
have tried in the past to destroy the Arab national perception by attempting to
position it in confrontation with feelings of 'local patriotism' which ostensibly
are contaminated by separatism. Some tried to position Arabism in confrontation with Islam.... Others even tried to turn Arabism into the equivalent of
backwardness and isolationism.... But none of this, of course, is correct."[35]

Each of these points is significant. First, he insisted—in traditional Arab
nationalist fashion—that no country's local patriotism should prevail over the
welfare of the whole Arab nation. This means that the Egyptians, Saudis, Jordanians, or others could not legitimately put their own interests first. In theory,
this applies to Syria as well. Yet while any other Arab state defining its interests
apart from that of all Arabs is unacceptable, Syria is an exception, Bashar insisted. Since it represents the "aspirations"—in *Tishrin*'s phrase—of all Arabs,
Syria is entitled to set the course for everyone else. If Syria dominated
Lebanon, backed an insurgency in Iraq, or manipulated the Palestinians, this
was not an act of imperialism or "local patriotism" but the legitimate line all
Arabs must support.

Next, he rejected any idea that there might be a quarrel between Arabism
and Islamism. This was a tall order, seeming to defy every trend, since radical
Islamist movements had been trying to overthrow every Arab nationalist
regime. Yet Bashar was now maintaining that he, and not the Muslim Brotherhood, represented the interests of Islam. He was thus telling all Syrians that if
they were good Muslims and wanted Islam's triumph they should unite behind
his government. Sunni Arab Muslims were said to have no interests or identity
apart from his regime.

Finally, Bashar insisted that the Arabs' problem is not that they are bogged
down with an unworkable system, as liberals charge, and thus that keeping the
status quo does not inhibit progress. Foreign attack, and not dictatorship, is
what holds the Arabs back. The solution, then, is not reform but resistance,
not social change but struggle.

Clearly, Bashar does not lack confidence. Aside from Iran getting Syria
into a difficult situation, the other main threat to his regime is if Bashar believes his own propaganda enough to stumble into an armed confrontation

with the United States or Israel. He seems likely to avoid that trap but, as happened to Nasser in 1967 or Saddam in 1991 and 2003, other Arab dictators have made such big mistakes. Bashar's behavior is reminiscent of a story about when Muammar Qadhafi came to power in Libya in 1969. Egypt's president Nasser sent his confidante, the famous journalist Muhammad Haykal, to Libya to investigate. Haykal returned and told Nasser that the new dictator was "a catastrophe." "Why," asked Nasser, "is he against us?" "No, much worse," Haykal replied. "He is for us and actually believes the pan-Arab nationalist doctrine."[36] Haykal warned that Qadhafi's naiveté and adventurism might drag them all to disaster.

At times, the Syrian leadership seems to slide dangerously toward that precipice in its heated rhetoric and high levels of risk taking. During Foreign Minister Muallim's August 2006 visit to Lebanon, he got a bit carried away. "[We say] to regional war: 'Welcome.' We are prepared for it, and we do not hide [this fact]," adding that the military balance favored the Arabs over Israel.[37] Chided by other Arabs about its eagerness for the Lebanese to fight while it avoids shooting on the Golan Heights, Syrian officials began talking about liberating that territory at gunpoint. Bashar dropped many such hints. The establishment of a Popular Organization for the Liberation of the Golan was loudly announced in the media.[38] This might be mere hot air, but any attack by such a group across the Israel-Syria ceasefire lines could provoke war.

Less likely, but not out of the question, is some provocation to the United States that cannot be ignored. A hint in that direction came from an interview on Hizballah's al-Manar television by Muhammad Said Ramadhan al-Bouti. Bouti is very close to the Syrian government. In fact he is the most important Sunni cleric endorsing it politically and lending it religious legitimacy. Bouti stated that the United States was the real enemy and advocated blowing up its facilities and paralyzing that country in carefully planned attacks. It was alright, he said, to kill Americans "who are hostile to us" but not innocents.[39]

Syrian-sponsored and directed terrorists have attacked Americans before, notably in Lebanon during the 1980s, killing a total of about 300 Americans. One of those murdered was an American officer serving as a UN observer in south Lebanon who, according to his friend, former Deputy Secretary of State Richard Armitage, was "killed in the most heinous way, in a way I will not describe . . . because [you] will be horrified."[40]

What Hizballah and Syria could get away with in the 1980s without reprisal, however, might not sit so well in the post–September 11, 2001, policy environment. Again, though, only a major miscalculation by Bashar would bring confrontation. The United States, as the Syrian regime knows, though it often pretends otherwise, does not seek such a clash. On the contrary, it was American eagerness to conciliate with Syria that made it easier for the Assads to act as if they had the upper hand. Arriving in Damascus after Hafiz agreed to join the front against Saddam in 1991, Secretary of State James Baker gushed that the United States needed to "cooperate with a major Arab country [that] happens to share the same goals that we do."[41]

Of course, Syria's goals were quite different from those of the United States, something the Assads did not forget even if their interlocutors did. For a decade, Syria held off any U.S. steps against itself by dangling the hope that it would finally make peace, a maneuver that brought it billions of dollars in profits from having unchallenged hegemony over Lebanon. By 1998, Syria moved into an alliance with Iraq, without any U.S. steps to pressure or punish it as the biggest sanctions breaker. Sponsorship of terrorism never ceased. Yet in late 2006 Baker was still bragging—at the moment when Damascus's terrorism-sponsoring activities were at a record high—about how his frequent visits to Damascus supposedly weaned Syria away from supporting terrorism[42]

In explaining the 2006 Baker-Hamilton Iraq Study Group report, which advocated cooperation with Syria and bringing that country further into resolving the Iraq crisis, Baker explained,

> The reason I think we could get some help from Syria is because I ... believe Syria would rather ... get closer to the United States than [to] remain in her marriage of convenience with Iran. She would also improve her relations with her long-time allies, the other major Sunni Arab states. And I saw Syria when I was secretary of state ... change 25 years of policy because we worked with them. . . . I made [15 trips] to Damascus and she came and sat down face to face to negotiate peace with Israel, something she had resisted doing for 25 years, so I think there's a very good chance here.[43]

Yet in 2000 Syria had reneged on its claim to be seeking a negotiated solution with Israel, with no serious U.S. retaliation. Within a year, all was forgotten in the belief that Syria would prove helpful after September 11, 2001, an expectation that was again largely disappointed. Nevertheless, amnesia struck repeatedly thereafter. For example, Bashar lied to Secretary of State Powell about Syria's huge oil trade with Iraq during the American's 2001 trip to Damascus.

On May 2, 2003, aboard his plane once again on the way to Syria, Powell talked tough about how this time he was determined to see the Syrian government really do something about his demand that Bashar stop sponsoring terrorism. He pledged to remind his Syrian counterparts that he remembered how they had misled him two years earlier.[44] A few hours later, however, Bashar lied by telling him the terrorist groups' offices were closed. Powell was again taken in. When he found out about the deception, nothing was done. And the same cycle applied to Syria's sponsorship of terrorists to kill American soldiers in Iraq.

During the 2001–2005 period, five top-level U.S. government delegations visited Syria, along with numerous American congressional groups and notables, in an attempt to work things out with Bashar. They got nothing. These efforts were ended by the Bush administration not because it was so stubborn and doctrinaire—as its critics on this issue always seemed to suggest—but because the Syrian government blew up Hariri in February 2005. That is the type of deed that might get a regime branded permanently as a rogue pariah state, but that kind of thing does not happen to Syria.

So what exactly was U.S. policy toward Syria? Understandably, American policymakers saw Syria as an adversary, though this was not their preference. Yet considering what Syria had done, Washington's responses were still relatively mild. U.S. leaders seized every possible opportunity to claim that rapprochement was possible. Nobody in Washington was eager to engage Syria in a confrontation for which the United States lacked resources or allies. Periods of intense anger at Syria neither lasted very long nor resulted in systematic efforts beyond the largely symbolic gestures of sanctions.

An active effort to promote regime change in Syria was never very seriously considered but there was always a great temptation to fall back on appeasement. One of the few remaining options was to impose various sanctions, though the actions taken had only a very limited effect. For example, the 2003 Syria Accountability Act provided various minor pressures on Damascus that would not greatly inconvenience Syria.[45] The appeasement alternative was to reconcile Syria somehow, negotiating with it and offering it various inducements to be less extreme. Some in the academic and policy world went further, justifying Syrian claims and apologizing for the regime's actions. The top half-dozen American "experts" on Syria—people like Joshua Landis, Flyntt Leverett, and Bashar biographer David Lesch, as well as Hafiz court historian Patrick Seale—can be depended on for such responses.

Moreover, many who styled themselves as "realists" but knew very little about the real Syria were convinced that they could tame the lions of Damascus. The regime knew how to play these people like an angler reels in fish. An audience with Bashar and some Assad charm—including insistence that he really wanted to be moderate and make peace with everyone—went a long way. Success looked so easy to achieve, like crossing a nice smooth carpet of quicksand. What harm could it do, they asked, to give Assad a chance?

In December 2006 alone, for example, five U.S. senators visited Damascus. They included former presidential candidate John Kerry and his colleagues Bill Nelson, Christopher Dodd, and Arlen Specter. As a result, crowed Deputy Prime Minister Abdallah Dardari, "The former policy of political isolation of Syria has ended. . . . People are realizing in Western capitals that if you want to be influential in the Middle East, you have to come through Damascus."[46] While these visitors told the American media that they had made tough, as well as conciliatory, statements to Bashar, the Syrians spun the events in their own way. The Syrian media told its people and the Arab world that the senators had praised Syria's policy, reinforcing their belief that the radical policy was winning and restraint was unnecessary.

At times, the repertoire of Western response seemed reduced to the sole instrument of seeking dialogue, which was of course what Bashar wanted. While there is nothing wrong in theory about talking with the Syrian regime, in practice diplomatic engagement with Bashar is a disastrous strategy, historically shown to be a give-and-take that lets Syria do the taking and in the meantime insulates the regime from retribution for its continuing radical policies. Former Deputy Secretary of State Richard Armitage, who fancies himself a tough guy and had negotiated with the Syrians, glibly explained his support for more of the same by saying, "My personal belief is that diplomacy is the art of sitting down with someone and letting them have your way."[47] Yes, but that describes what the Syrians, not the Americans or Europeans, did.

There are at least eight basic reasons why negotiations with Syria or its allies—Hamas, Hizballah, and Iran, for that matter—will not solve the major crises and problems in which they are involved:

1. They have far-reaching goals. They want a Middle East without Israel; a world, or at least a region, without America; and to dominate the area for themselves. These people are not agrarian reformers; they are consistent totalitarians on a level with fascism and Communism.

2. They think they are winning, that the tide of history is running in their direction, especially since they reinterpret even their defeats as victories. How long it takes to achieve their goals or how much it costs themselves and others is of no consequence to them. Under these circumstances, it is better to be patient than make deals that are a form of treason, settling for far less than they could obtain through struggle.

3.	They believe their enemies to be weak and easily outfoxed. Syrian leaders must know that far from being victimized they have gotten away with behavior that would make neighbors and great powers crush a state anywhere else in the world. This conclusion was intensified by their interpreting the West's efforts to bridge disagreements with them—calls for concessions and negotiations—as proof of contemptible cowardice. Bashar even dared deliver a diatribe to UN Secretary-General Kofi Annan and his visiting delegation, who was trying to be conciliatory, depicting the Western powers as politically bankrupt and powerless.[48]

4.	They profit from militancy and benefit from conflict but would suffer from stability or moderation. One cannot make peace with a party that knows peace to be disastrous for its interests. Syria and Iran are anti-status quo powers that don't want diplomatic resolutions that freeze existing power balances. Hamas and Hizballah are revolutionary groups that seek total victory not compromise. Why then should they want negotiations to succeed if they expect to do better through violence? Why should they cooperate with the United States to end conflicts knowing that such successes would ensure an increase in U.S. influence in the region?

5.	The promises of the Syrian regime have repeatedly proved deceitful. Despite their "nice, sugar-coated words," says Walid Jumblatt, who has a lot of experience on this point, "We know the Syrian double-talk. They say one thing to international envoys and implement another thing on the ground."[49] After years of dialogue with Hafiz and Bashar, Chirac concluded that these talks led nowhere and that "the regime of Bashar seems incompatible with security and peace."[50] The many trips of Secretary of State Warren Christopher to beg Syria to make peace with Israel in exchange for the Golan Heights in the 1990s ended with Hafiz scuttling negotiations. Secretary of State Colin Powell believed Bashar's promises to stop illegal pipeline shipments of Saddam's oil and close terrorist offices only to find he had been told lies.

6.	The Syrians cynically milk the process itself for maximum value until it becomes counterproductive. Lebanese journalist Michael Young explained, "What Assad wants is a process that can protect him for a time from the United States, one that will pay him dividends, but which otherwise will never come to fruition."[51] This is how his father, Hafiz, handled things in the 1990s. By stalling, Syria gained immunity from pressure. By refusing to reduce its demands and threatening to walk out, Syria solicited Western concessions. The West had to stop criticism and pressure on Syria to avoid "discouraging" Damascus from continuing to talk. Either way, the Assads won. Negotiations in and of themselves were and are to Syria's advantage.

In contrast, the West gains nothing but is merely hooked by the lure, in Young's words, of "an empty process of dialogue with Syria, even offering concessions, without demanding that Syria make measurable concessions of its own beforehand."[52] In exchange Bashar wants the West to forget about the Hariri murder, the repression of Syrian liberals, the sponsorship of terrorism, and all the other things Syria does.

Its governments found it difficult to negotiate and be tough simultaneously, as if it were the diplomatic equivalent of trying to walk and chew gum at the same time. To get talks started and keep them going by proving Western good intentions to Damascus, the well-intentioned gave a series of concessions. It was made to seem so logical: How could Syria be expected to conduct negotiations, the regime argued, while under investigation for Hariri's murder? How could Syria be asked to stop instability in Lebanon unless it was given power there? Wasn't it a sign of hostility to accuse Syria of involvement with terrorism? If Syria sponsors terrorist attacks, subverts Lebanon, represses dissidents, or promotes violence in Iraq, nothing would be done to punish that country, hoping that the matter would be solved by the talking process. In the meantime, Syria would have a free hand to do what it pleases.

7. The negotiators cannot really offer Syria what it wants without further destabilizing the region. Should they force Lebanon once again to be a Syrian colony? Implant a government Syria likes in Iraq? Give the regime money so it can better pursue its ambitions? Hand it all the Golan Heights plus a slice of Israeli territory without Syria making full and permanent peace with Israel—an outcome that would strengthen Syria's position for attacking Israel in the future?

8. The objectives of Syria, along with those of other radical regimes and movements, are the opposite of the Western democratic states' goals. This fact is easy to demonstrate by the following list of key issues. Asked if they favor these propositions, Western states say "yes" while on every point the Syrian regime says "no."

- A peaceful situation in the region?
- An end to terrorism and punishment for state sponsors of covert violence against their neighbors?
- A calm Lebanon-Israel border with no attacks in either direction?
- A stable Lebanon with a strong, independent central government?
- A Palestinian-Israeli peace agreement that ends the conflict?
- A United States popular in the Arab world because it brokered successful peace agreements?
- A stop to Iran's nuclear program and a moderate democratic government in Tehran?
- An end to Iraq's bloody communal strife so that all groups there can live side by side in peace within a moderate democratic state?
- The achievement of real democracy in all Arabic-speaking states?
- A democratic Syria, which focuses on development rather than war and subversion?

If Syrian objectives are so divergent from those of the West in general and the United States in particular, then what is there to negotiate? Why should Syria's rulers be persuaded that their interests lie in another direction if they really do not? How can Syria be given at least part of what it wants if this moves the Middle East in an even more radical, violent, anti-Western direction? And should Syria be gifted money, territory, power, and immunity when it never really gives anything in return?

Consider, for example, how a fully frank dialogue with Syria over Iraq's future might go. If an American negotiator asked Bashar what kind of Iraq he would like, and he answered truthfully, the Syrian president would explain that he desired an anti-American Iraq that would support Hizballah and Hamas, be ready to fight the Arab-Israeli conflict forever, be a dictatorship dominated by a Sunni majority, suppress the Shia-Kurdish majority, be a close ally of Iran and possibly an Islamist state. Seen in this light, it's clear that nothing can be worked out. The United States and Syria do not have a common interest in Iraq, especially not one involving a peaceful, independent, democratic Iraq friendly to America.

This is amusing but not exaggerated. To read what Syrian leaders say, especially in Arabic, as well as examining their real interests should be enough to cure anyone of expectations that the dictatorship might change. The regime will not give up its enmity to an independent Lebanon or Israel under any circumstances, because it needs to control the former and fight the latter in order to win the struggle to retain popular support at home. The issues on which it has grievances cannot be resolved because its own actions and inflexibly maximalist demands are the very factors blocking a solution.

Thus, the problem of Syria cannot be fixed by solving the Arab-Israeli conflict because the regime wants a situation where it can complain while blocking progress that would jeopardize its own power. The regime cannot afford to lose so valuable an issue as a way to mobilize its own people to support it. As long as the regime and its network are in place, there will be no negotiated resolution of the conflict. At most, there will only be a long negotiating process leading nowhere and being exploited by Syria for unilateral gains. Aside from the question of Syrian goals and methods, there is the problem of serial memory lapses regarding past experiences in dealing with the regime. The 1990s showed how Syria continued its sponsorship of terrorism and anti-Western incitement even when given a free hand in Lebanon. It refused to make peace with Israel even when offered the entire Golan Heights.

A second important factor in devising an effective policy for dealing with Syria and other Arab states is an understanding of the structural reasons why those governments need such radical policies in order to preserve themselves. This list of requirements for survival includes the need to block real domestic reforms, a high priority on holding onto Lebanon (in Syria's case), as well as the benefits of sustaining both the Arab-Israeli conflict and a consistently high level of hysterical anti-Americanism.

Third, is seeing the way in which Syria created crises it then offered to solve for a very high price. Since regional problems cannot be solved without Syria's help, so went this argument, assistance must somehow be obtained on Syria's terms. "In all of the major challenges we have in the Middle East—Iraq, the Arab-Israeli conflict, the role of Hezbollah and Hamas, Iran—things are more complicated without Syria's cooperation," explained former U.S. ambassador to Syria Edward Djerejian.[53]

Syria has been brilliant at creating and maintaining such Catch-22 situations, where the only way to "solve" a problem is to buy Syrian "cooperation" with deals that would make things worse. Syria acted first as the arsonist who set the fire, then played the role of the fireman who would put it out only on the condition that the burning property be given to it. This was how Syria fomented terrorism in Lebanon against Western peacekeeping forces in the early 1980s, driving them out and then offering to stabilize Lebanon by controlling it completely. The same approach was applied to the Palestinians, post-Saddam Iraq, and to Lebanon again. Bashar, for example, disingenuously gave out the following I-told-you-so about Iraq: "Before the war, I told the Americans: There is no doubt that you will win this war, but then you will sink into a quagmire."[54] He did not say that the quagmire would happen largely because of his efforts.

Lebanon was indeed the masterpiece of this political genre. In the words of the Beirut *Daily Star,* "The Syrians realized that Hizballah's pariah status in the world community could work to their advantage, for who but Syria could ever hope to bring the violent party under control? To remain relevant in Lebanon and throughout the Middle East, the Syrians helped create a problem that only they could resolve."[55] The more problems Hizballah poses, the more Syria can demand power in Lebanon as the only one able to quiet down Hizballah. As the Lebanese journalist Michael Young wrote, "The Syrian president is likely to encourage Hizballah to periodically behave menacingly along Lebanon's southern border, so that Syria could be called in to 'moderate' its conduct."[56] Thus, Syrian Minister of Information Muhsin Bilal explained, "How can we be asked to disarm Hezbollah [since] we're out of Lebanon?"[57] But what if Syria was allowed to return to Lebanon in force, would it then clamp down on Hizballah? Well, on another occasion, Bilal was asked, "Will you be using your influence to persuade Hizballah to disarm, or not?" He responded, "Why on earth should we?"[58]

In fact, Syria has no intention of disarming Hizballah or pressing it to stop waging war on Israel. Quite the opposite, Hizballah is the main element in Syria's plan to recapture Lebanon entirely. As a Western ambassador put it, by asking that Syria disarm Hizballah, "You are asking them to connive in their own demise.... Persuading Hezbollah to commit hara-kiri doesn't make sense from Syria's point of view. It would mean the loss of their No. 1 card, not only in Lebanon, but with Israel."[59] If the West wants a stable Lebanon or to avoid more Lebanon-Israel wars it has to battle Syria, not make a deal with it.

By ignoring such Syrian statements, behavior, and interests, many rationales were constantly offered that played into the regime's game. For example, as happened in the 1990s—a peace process that spun out to be nine years long with no result whatsoever—Syria would not be asked for anything, since it would be expected to make concessions only at the end as part of a comprehensive negotiated settlement, an event that is never going to take place. Such Western gullibility has allowed Syria to tell lies and get away with it. The regime effectively split the West by taking advantage of Europe's eagerness to compete with the United States for diplomatic successes by proving that it was the nice one.

There are real costs and consequences to playing this game. For one thing, Syria becomes bolder and more intransigent rather than the opposite. With Americans flocking to Damascus after the U.S. invasion of Iraq, criticizing their own government's policy, and begging Bashar's help, Khaddam recalled, the leader became convinced "that the United States will come crawling to him to negotiate for Iraq and keep him in Lebanon. . . . This misreading led to later results."[60]

When the U.S. embassy in Damascus was attacked in September 2006 and Syrian guards killed the terrorists, White House press secretary Tony Snow thanked Syria by saying, "It illustrates the importance of the Syrians playing a constructive role in fighting terrorists." But the regime, which had done more than anyone to foment these problems, said the extremism and terrorism popping up in the region was America's fault. Syrian ambassador to the United States Imad Mustafa explained that the solution was for Washington, D.C., to stop trying to change Syrian policies and instead alter its own. "The ball," he concluded, "now is in the court of the American administration."[61] After having sponsored thousands of Hamas, Islamic Jihad, Hizballah, and Iraqi terrorist attacks, the regime argued on the basis of stopping one that it was the true force fighting terrorism and the United States should bargain with it rather than try to press it to behave differently.

Yet another point often forgotten is that Syria was targeting not only Israel but also Egypt, Iraq, Jordan, Saudi Arabia, and the majority in Lebanon for conquest. The Iran-Syria alliance was especially scary to Arabs in the Persian Gulf. If the United States tries to appease Syria it thus signals more moderate Arabs that they should give in as well. This danger was felt most immediately in Lebanon. Courting Syria, as Young put it, "would undermine what remains of U.S. credibility," with those rejecting an Iran-Syria-Hizballah takeover. "Reengagement would . . . practically invite a Syrian return to Lebanon."[62] Why should Lebanese risk their lives if they get no support from the West while their adversaries are treated like royalty?

Syria's first priority is to re-occupy Lebanon, if not by its own army then by its client Hizballah's militia. The Syrian media spared no insult in trying to incite violence and spread intimidation among the Lebanese majority. *Al-Thawra* called them devils; an *al-Ba'th* headline read, "Lebanese Politicians in the Service of the CIA and the Mossad."[63] Feisal Kalthoum, a member of Syria's parliament, called Sa'd Hariri—son of the man Bashar had murdered and now leader of the anti-Syrian forces—a mercenary agent protected by Israel who has "no future."[64] Muntaha al-Ramahi, host of an Arab satellite television show, pointed out the irony that Bashar had described at least 50 percent of the Lebanese people as "Israeli agents."[65]

Unintimidated, Hariri told a cheering audience gathered outside his home, "There is a neighboring president who is threatening to destroy the political regime in Lebanon because he could not [accept] the Lebanese people's decision to throw out his corruption and troops from Lebanon."[66] If Hariri and his colleagues are abandoned by the West and moderate Arabs, the radical forces in the region will take a big step forward, with terrorism and the chance for warfare increasing sharply.

While they are not capable of achieving much, throwing Syrian liberals to the wolves will also strengthen the regime and ensure even more unanimous domestic support for it. The respected cartoonist Ali Farazat was quite candid in expressing his belief that only Western action can help bring change in Syria: "Dictatorships of this type apparently cannot be toppled by anyone else. Since the Arab people cannot take any action or do anything, the only alternative is for the Americans or [others] to . . . remove those people who represent oppression."[67]

Humsi, a parliament member imprisoned for advocating political reforms, was equally outspoken. He explained, "The international community has been lenient with regimes that have had a free hand with their people, and that have made fortunes from exploiting their people without any accountability or deterrence." If the world let the Syrian regime win, "The danger of extremism and the insanity of rooted hatred" would continue to grow. The free peoples should "find new and peaceful ways to apply constant pressure in order to finally hold accountable those who have abused and continue to abuse the rights of the Syrian citizen, and so that this regime will know that Syria and its people are not the property of individuals, or a family."[68]

Worst of all, by acting as if Syria holds all the cards and bringing it in to settle the fates of Lebanon and Iraq, the West will show everyone in the region that Syria's methods work. Both Arab nationalists and Islamists will flock to the camp of "resistance" and jump on Iran's bandwagon. Not only will the United States and Europe be seen as kowtowing to Bashar, strange but true, they also will be perceived as endorsing him as the Arab world's leader.

To deal with Syria the United States needs a properly realistic assessment based on the facts about Bashar, the regime, and the country. Syria is a weak and fragile entity, dependent largely on oil income and European commerce. The regime has flourished to the degree it has from enjoying a free ride, lack of pressure except for American economic sanctions. There is a proper, traditional realpolitik way to handle such problems. It is not by propitiating aggressors and begging them to make a deal on their terms but rather by pressuring and deterring them. To do so requires credibility and patience, a demonstration that the West will not cave in or be worn down to surrender. In Syria's case, it must be denied assets, isolated, and its endeavors must be frustrated. This requires the use of everything in the foreign policy arsenal from trade to counteralliances, serious criticism, and covert operations.

The policy needed, therefore, is neither appeasement nor regime change, which will not work, but rather tough diplomacy backed up by strength and staying power. These are virtues unfortunately rarely visible in the history of Western dealings with Syria. The exceptions, though, prove the rule. When confronted by Turkish decisiveness in 1998 and international determination to force Syria out of Lebanon thereafter, Syria backed down. When worried about U.S. power in the 1990s and after September 11, 2001, the Assads were cautious until they no longer felt concerned about any such threat.

As the *Washington Post* put it in a December 2006 editorial, "As can be plainly seen in their public statements, Mr. Ahmadinejad and Mr. Assad are riding high: They believe they have the United States and its allies on the run across the Middle East. Perceiving no threat to their regimes, they see no reason for compromise. . . . The radicals are dangerously close to succeeding." The only solution was "decisive steps by the United States and its allies to counter the extremists and to force them to pay a price for their aggression. . . . 'Realism' in the Middle East means understanding that Syria and Iran won't stop waging war against the United States and its allies unless they are given reasons to fear they might lose."[69]

Part of such a campaign to contain Syria requires aiding those neighbors menaced by it and its allies: the Lebanese majority that opposes Syrian-Hizballah hegemony, Israel, and the majority in Iraq angered by Syria's role in murdering them. It also means working with Arab regimes like those in Egypt, Saudi Arabia, and Jordan that stand against the Iran-Syria-Hizballah-Hamas alliance due to their own interests. The United States and the West should show more regard for the interests of more moderate Arabs and Muslims rather than siding with the radicals against them. Likewise, Syrians must be shown that their leaders are failures and can offer neither lasting glory nor material gains. The regime must be contained until it crumbles or retreats. This can be a long process but it is ultimately a less costly one than the alternatives.

The starting point for an effective response is simply to understand the Syrian system on its own terms. The regime does not want to make peace, become moderate, or reform its economy. It wants to stay as it is and preferably to control Lebanon, continue the conflict with Israel forever, buy off the Islamists by supporting Hizballah and the Iraqi insurgency, and thus demagogically make its people cheer for Bashar as the great warrior of resistance.

What has the West taught the regime? Certainly not that aggression and human rights violations would make it a pariah or target for retribution. The regime did not suffer much for turning Lebanon into its own occupied territories for 30 years; killing Hariri, Jumblatt, Tueni, Gemayel, and many others; sponsoring terrorism; defying international sanctions on Iraq; failing economically; and repressing human rights at home. A Lebanese scholar complained, "Bashar has contempt for the West," but then added, "Given his experience, why shouldn't he?" If, however, Bashar has his way, he will help take the Arab world through another half century of disaster. It would be a Middle East in which a merger of radical Arab nationalism and Islamism preaches hatred and all-out war on the West; in which dictatorships continue to flourish; and in which war, terrorism, and social violence climb to steadily higher levels. Saddam and bin Ladin would be gone but their ideas would be triumphant.

The truth is that the Syrian regime has no interest in moderating Hizballah or breaking with Iran, making economic reform, allowing a stable, sovereign Lebanon, or getting the Golan Heights back by a peace treaty with Israel. Any alternative—a deal on the Golan, an EU economic association agreement—requires concessions Syria neither wants nor needs. Underlying the problem of Syria is not a whim of those in power there or hurt feelings at not being treated fairly. The root of the conflict is the regime's nature and interests. As Young explains, "The security edifice of Assad's regime requires a state of war with Israel and that edifice is essential to protecting Alawite rule in Syria."[70] The same thing applies to Bashar's sponsorship of radical Islamism in the region. It is a tool for maintaining the regime as well as a warning not to destabilize him lest the Islamists take over Syria.

Bashar, Young continues, not only wants but also needs to pursue regionally destabilizing policies that buttress his own regime. He asserts,

When Palestine goes up in smoke, when Lebanon collapses into war, when Iraq faces further violence, Assad sees events that allow him to keep his harsh security apparatus in place and silence and imprison domestic adversaries; that encourage timorous Arab states not to rock the Syrian boat; and, yes, that make American and European former and present officials advise that the road be taken to Damascus to "engage."[71]

Lebanon is the great financial and security prize for Damascus, much more valuable than the rocky Golan Heights. But to succeed he needs the support of a strong Hizballah, a group Bashar would like to make the local master of Lebanon. French Defense Minister Alain Richard put it best when he said, "One of Syria's main assets is its domination over Lebanon. Consequentially, any settlement that would call into question its domination over

Lebanon, even if it means regaining Syrian territory [from Israel], does not suit it."[72]

While others seek to "educate" the regime as to its "real" needs, the masters of Damascus understand such changes would in fact be disastrous for its interests. Given peace with Israel, Bashar has no answer as to why he must maintain a dictatorship with tight controls and no reform. Having good relations with America, how could he explain why elements of a system so successful there are so poisonous for Arabs and Muslims? With respect for Lebanon's sovereignty, he cannot produce the material rewards that Syrian domination brings. With no support for radical Islamists in Iraq, Lebanon, and among the Palestinians, he cannot explain away the fact that he is a non-Muslim ruling Syria and an enemy of the Islamists. The Islamification program at home would backfire and breed a massive opposition to the regime. Without sponsoring terrorism and radicalism, he cannot intimidate the West and demand that it appease him. Even more importantly, he cannot persuade his own people to cheer and obey him.

In many ways, the Syrian system is quite similar to that in the rest of the Arabic-speaking world and in Iran. Hatred is manipulated to keep a destructive system in power by persuading even those victimized by it to support the status quo. Two of the best illustrations of how this system works come from distant but parallel situations. The first is an old Communist cartoon from Latin America. A fat landlord lies content in a hammock held up at one end by a tree and on the other by a spindly peasant, trembling under the load. The plutocrat is telling him, "You know what those Communists want to do, Juan? They want to take away our tree." In the Middle East's case, one can substitute the words "Zionists and Crusaders" or "Israel and America" for the same effect. The great excuse, the external enemy, is used to justify a system that is ineffective except to fulfill an elite's greed and self-interest.

The other illustration is an explanation of how ruling groups maintained their hold on the segregationist American South even as they held back its progress and oppressed their own supporters. Bob Dylan vividly explained in his song "Only a Pawn in Their Game" how Southern politicians used the race card to keep poor whites in line by making them hate African Americans so much that they would support a status quo that hurt their interests in many ways. As a result, these leaders prospered while their people remained poor and powerless. In Dylan's words, while the elite benefited, the poor white man was used by them "like a tool." He was taught in school that he was superior and that the regime was on his side, protecting him from a terrible threat in order, "To keep up his hate/So he never thinks straight/'Bout the shape that he's in."

One can substitute American, Westerner, Jew, or Israeli for African Americans; Arab Muslim for poor white; and Islam or Arabism for what is being protected. Karl Marx called this phenomenon "false consciousness." In feudal and capitalist society, it developed largely without deliberate direction, but under Communism, fascism, and Ba'thism it was planned and institutionalized. Hatred is manipulated to keep a bad system in power. "All the better to fool you with," as the big bad wolf put it, or in William Shakespeare's words in "Hamlet": "One may smile, and smile, and be a villain."

In the strange case of Syria's radical dictatorship, seeing the regime clearly is the sole way to understand the truth about that country and the radical forces which pose the greatest threat to the peace and prosperity of the contemporary world.

NOTES

CHAPTER ONE

1. Syrian Arab Television, August 15, 2006. Translation in U.S. Department of Commerce, Foreign Broadcast Information Service (hereafter FBIS).
2. Fouad Ajami, "Arab Road," *Foreign Policy,* No. 47, Summer 1982, p. 16.
3. Christopher Andrew and Vasili Mitrokhin, *The World Was Going Our Way: The KGB and the Battle for the Third World* (New York, 2005), p. 212.
4. Syrian Arab Television, August 15, 2006. Translation in FBIS.
5. Ibid.
6. Many writers and scholars today routinely refer to Alawites as Shia Muslims, but there is almost no basis for this statement, aside from regime propaganda. Hafiz al-Assad persuaded the Lebanese Shia cleric Musa Sadr to accept this assertion, but Sadr was highly respected as a political leader, not as a theologian, and his opinion has not been formally endorsed by many others. Alawites in the past openly rejected the idea that they were Muslims, and their religious beliefs were very much at variance with those of Islam. It is appropriate to treat the idea that Alawites are Shia Muslims as a political myth even if Alawites (at least in public) and many other Muslims, though not all, accept this notion at present.
7. *Al-Gumhuriya,* October 7, 2001. Translation in Middle East Media Research Institute (hereafter MEMRI), No. 289, October 19, 2001, http://MEMRI.org/bin/articles.cgi?Page=archives&Area=sd&ID=SP28901#_edn1.
8. Quoted in the *New York Post,* September 3, 2006.
9. Tawfiq al-Hakim, *The Return of Consciousness* (New York, 1985), p. 50.
10. Ibid.
11. Text of United Press International interview in *British Foreign Office,* FO371 E8124/951/31, August 16, 1947.
12. *Tishrin,* August 14, 2006. Translation in MEMRI, No. 1250, August 16, 2006; *Al-Mustaqbal,* August 7, 2006. Translation in MEMRI, No. 1239, August 9, 2006. http://MEMRI.org/bin/articles.cgi?Page=archives&Area=sd&ID=SP123906
13. See, for example, Buthaynah Shaab, *Tishrin,* August 14, 2006. Translation in FBIS GMP20060814627003.
14. Al-Jazira TV, October 31, 2006. http://www.MEMRItv.org/search.asp?ACT=S9&P1=1309.
15. Syrian Arab Television, August 15, 2006.
16. *Tishrin,* August 3, 2006.
17. Speech of March 5, 1946. Text in http://www.fordham.edu/halsall/mod/churchill-iron.html.
18. IRINN TV, February 1, 2006. Translation in MEMRI, Clip No. 1019, <http://www.MEMRItv.org/Search.asp?ACT=S1>.
19. Sermon broadcast on Iranian Channel 1 television, September 1, 2006. Translation by MEMRI, http://www.MEMRItv.org/search.asp?ACT=S9&P1=1261.
20. Khalid al-Maaly, "Two Faces of Arab Intellectuals," *Berliner Zeitung,* September 14, 2006. Translation at <http://www.signandsight.com/features/993.html>.

21. Text in FBIS, November 8, 1979.

22. Al-Jazira television, October 7, 2001.

23. Interview on al-Jazira television, August 1, 2006. Translation in MEMRI, No. 1217, August 1, 2006; Al-Jazira television, August 29, 2006. Translation in MEMRI, Clip No. 129, http://www.MEMRItv.org/search.asp?ACT=S9&P1=1255.

24. *Associated Press* (hereafter *AP*), August 17, 2006.

25. "The Palestinian Problem in the Internal Political Report of the Extraordinary Regional Congress," March 10–27, 1966. Text in Abraham Ben Tzur, *The Syrian Baath Party and Israel* (Givat Haviva, 1968), p. 19.

26. *Al-Ahram,* August 14, 2006.

27. *Al-Ahram,* August 29, 2006.

28. "Yassir Arafat," *Third World Quarterly,* Vol. 8, No. 2 (April 1986), and also *South,* January 1986, p. 18; al-Anwar symposium of March 8, 1970, cited in Y. Harkabi, *The Palestinian Covenant and Its Meaning* (London, 1979), p. 12; Arafat statement, May 1969, *International Documents on Palestine* 1969 (hereafter *IDOP,* Beirut, 1970), op. cit., pp. 691–692.

29. Christopher Andrew and Vasili Mitrokhin, *The World Was Going Our Way* (New York, 2005), pp. 203–304.

30. Al-Manar television, July 29, 2006. Translation in MEMRI No. 1224, August 1, 2006, <http://MEMRI.org/bin/articles.cgi?Page=archives&Area=sd&ID=SP122406>.

31. Ibid.

32. Interview, January 22, 1968 in *IDOP,* 1968, p. 300.

33. *Filastin al-Thawra,* January 1970.

34. Raphael Israeli, *PLO in Lebanon: Selected Documents* (London, 1983), p. 31

35. The details are discussed in Barry Rubin, *The Arab States and the Palestine Question* (Syracuse, NY, 1982), pp. 187–188.

36. *Al-Safir,* July 28, 2006.

37. *Al-Madina,* August 31, 1982, FBIS, September 9, 1982.

38. Muhammad Anis, "An Interview with 'Isam Sartawi,'" *al-Musawwar,* March 25, 1983; Avner Yaniv, "Phoenix of Phantom? The PLO after Beirut," *Terrorism,* Vol. 7, No. 3, 1984.

39. Abu Kais, "Loving Life, Loving Death," in *From Beirut to the Beltway,* August 26, 2006, http://www.beirutbeltway.com/beirutbeltway/2006/08/loving_life_lov.html.

40. Ali Salem, "My Drive to Israel," *Middle East Quarterly,* Vol. 9, No. 1, Winter 2002. The full text is available at <http://www.meforum.org/article/130>.

41. *New York Times,* March 12, 2001.

42. *Al-Sharq Al-Awsat,* February 8, 2001. Translation in MEMRI, No. 49, February 16, 2001, <http://MEMRI.org/bin/articles.cgi?Page=archives&Area=ia&ID=IA4901#_edn1>.

43. *Al-Usbua,* August 14, 2006.

CHAPTER TWO

1. N. Yaish to Director Middle East, Het Tzadik 4219/12, Syr. 105.1, February 23, 1968, Israel State Archives.

2. Henry Laurence, *The Great Game: The Arab East and International Schemes* (Bengazi, Dar Al-Jamhiriyyah, 1993), p. 238. Cited in Yasin al-Haj Saleh, "The Political Culture Of Modern Syria: Its Formation, Structure and Interactions," <http://www.mafhoum.com/press7/225P9.pdf#search='quwatli%20%20prophets%20%20immensity%20of%20the%20task'>. Another version is given in Muhammad Hussanayn Heikal, "Heikal on Assad and the Syrian-Israeli peace talks," *Mideast Mirror,* February 7, 2000.

3. Sami al-Jundi, *al-Ba'th* (Beirut 1961), p. 27, cited in Bernard Lewis, *Semites and Anti-Semites* (London, 1986), pp. 147–148.

4. Matti Moosa, *Extremist Shiites: The Ghulat Sects* (Syracuse, NY, 1988), pp. 287–288.

5. This story is told in Barry Rubin, *The Great Powers in the Middle East 1941–1947: The Road to Cold War* (London, 1981).

6. U.S. Department of State Records, RG319 358722, February 27, 1948, p. 14; 291346, Mattison to Byrnes, July 17, 1946; Gorden Torrey, *Syrian Politics and the Military* (Columbus, OH, 1963),

pp. 103–106; CZA899/51 S25 9031, p. 63, June 16, 1946. On factionalism in the Syrian National Bloc, see RG319 345706, February 26, 1947; 346397, January 30, 1947; and 460590, April 20, 1948.

7.   RG59 867N.01/12–947, Pinkerton to Marshall, December 9, 1947. Central Intelligence Group Report 106729, September 3, 1947.

8.   For clippings of these articles from the Syrian press, see RG59 890D.00/12–1547, /12–1947 through /12–2347, /12–2647, /12–3147, /1–248, /1–1148, and /2–1248. FO371 E12263/3765/80 discusses Syrian objectives in Palestine.

9.   RG59 890E.00/2–1648, Pinkerton to Marshall, February 16, 1948; Torrey, *Syrian Politics and the Military,* p. 105.

10. Speech to Arab Writers' Union Conference, January 27, 2000.

11. For the regime's extremist behavior toward neighbors, see, for example, Joseph Mann, "The Syrian Neo-Ba'th Regime and the Kingdom of Saudi Arabia, 1966–1970," *Middle Eastern Studies,* Vol. 42, No. 5, September 2006.

12. Michel 'Aflaq, *Fi Sabil al'Ba'th* [In the Path of Ba'th] (Beirut, 1978, 20th Printing), p. 207; Hizb al-Ba'th al-Arabi, *Harakat Qawmiyya Sha'biyya Inqilabiyya Tunadhil fi Sabil al-Wahda al-Arabiya wal-Huriyya wal-Ishtirakiyya—Al-Dustur* [Arab Ba'th Party, Revolutionary Popular National Movement Struggling for the Arab Unity, Freedom and Socialism—The Constitution] (Damascus, 1947), both cited in Mordechai Kedar, "In Search of Legitimacy: Asad's [sic] Islamic Image in the Syrian Official Press," in Moshe Maoz et al., *Modern Syria: From Ottoman Rule to Pivotal Role in the Middle East* (Brighton, U.K., 1999).

13. *Jaysh al-Shaab,* April 25 and May 9, 1967. Cited in Eyal Zisser, "Syria, the Ba'th Regime and the Islamic Movement: Stepping on a New Path?" *Muslim World,* Vol. 95, Issue 1, January 2005.

14. Ibid.

15. Arab Socialist Ba'th Party, "Disagreement between the Two Ba'th Leaderships over War against Israel (Autumn 1965), Internal Circular (confidential) Concerning the Palestine Policy of the Party and the Summit Conference," No. 8/4, September 29, 1965. Text in Abraham Ben Tzur, *The Syrian Ba'th Party and Israel* (Givat Haviva), 1968.

16. See, for example, John Amos, *Palestinian Resistance: Organization of a Nationalist Movement* (New York, 1980), p. 56. It is interesting to note that at a time when Syria was sponsoring Fatah, the U.S. embassy in Damascus insisted there was no proof of any connection between them. RG59, Box 2606, Paganelli to Secretary of State, August 20, 1965.

17. Moshe Shemesh, *The Palestinian Entity: 1959–1974: Arab Politics and the PLO* (London, 1988), p. 113; see also Patrick Seale, *Assad of Syria* (London, 1988), p. 124.

18. Intelligence Memorandum No. 2205/66, December 2, 1966, in *U.S. Department of State, Foreign Relations of the United States, 1964–1968, Vol. 18, Arab-Israeli Dispute, 1964–1967* (Washington, DC, 2000), p. 699.

19. Amos, *Palestinian Resistance,* p. 56; RG59, Box 2606, Paganelli to Secretary of State, August 20, 1965.

20. British Foreign Office, E10711/7 G, November 20, 1965, recording a conversation with Syrian navy captain Adnan Abdallah, who told the British defense attaché on November 4, 1965, that Syria had no knowledge of Fatah.

21. Ghalib Kayyali, Syria's chargé d'affaires in Washington, told the State Department in October 1966 that Syria was no longer allowing Fatah operations from its territory and Syria had no connection with that group. RG59, Box 2406, Pol 23–9 Syr 32–1 Isr-Jordan, October 7, 1966.

22. Ibid.

23. British Foreign and Colonial Office 371, A.C. Goodison to D.J. Roberts, December 29, 1965. See also E10711/7 G, November 20, 1965, recording a conversation with Syrian navy captain Adnan Abdallah who told the British defense attaché on November 4, 1965, that Fatah was an Israeli front.

24. On the ineffectiveness of these attacks, see for example Stewart Steven, *The Spymasters of Israel* (New York, 1980), pp. 237–247.

25. Ehud Yaari, *Strike Terror* (New York, 1970), p. 61; *Foreign Relations of the United States.*

26. Alan Hart, *Arafat: A Political Biography* (Bloomington, IN, 1989), p. 177.

27. Andrew Gowers and Tony Walker, *Behind the Myth: Yasser Arafat and the Palestinian Revolution,* (London, 1990), p. 47.

28. Ibid., p. 48; Seale, *Assad of Syria,* p. 125; Amos, *Palestinian Resistance,* p. 50; Abu Iyad, *My Land: A Narrative of the Palestinian Struggle* (New York, 1981), p. 45; Hart, *Arafat: A Political Biography,* p. 201; Yaari, *Strike Terror,* pp. 86–89. This incident is said to have taken place in February or May by different sources. The U.S. State Department at the time gave the date as early June. RG59, Box 2606, Amman to Secretary of State, August 12, 1966.

29. Abu Iyad, *My Land,* p. 46.

30. May 21, June 1, and 14, 1967, *International Documents on Palestine 1967,* pp. 537, 605.

31. *Al-Ahram,* February 25, 1971.

32. U.S. State Department, From AmEm Amman to Department of State, "Joint Week," no. 26, December 28, 1965. From AmEm in Tel Aviv to Department of State, September 30, 1965.

33. *Washington Post,* August 24, 1993.

CHAPTER THREE

1. Patrick Seale, *Asad of Syria* (Berkeley, CA, 1988), p. 174.

2. *Boston Globe,* November 6, 2005.

3. *Al-Nahar,* June 16, 2000; *al-Hayat,* June 17, 2000.

4. The term "Regional" Committee is used for a very important symbolic Arab nationalist reason since the Ba'th claims to be the ruling party of the whole Arab world, of which Syria is merely one "region."

5. Raymond A. Hinnebusch, "State and Civil Society in Syria," *Middle East Journal,* Vol. 47, No. 2, Spring 1993, pp. 246–247, 257–258.

6. Cited in Zvi Bar'el, "Syria: Where Time Stood Still since 1963," *Ha'aretz,* September 25, 2003.

7. Al-Usbu, August 14, 2006. Translation in Middle East Media Research Institute (hereafter MEMRI), No. 1250, August 16, 2006.

8. *Tishrin,* August 14, 2006. Translation in ibid.

9. Syrian TV on August 22, 2006. View at Clip No. 1250, http://www.MEMRItv.org/search.asp? ACT=S9&P1=1250.

10. *Al-Hayat,* June 17, 2000; *al-Nahar,* June 16, 2000.

11. For an excellent discussion of these issues, see Daniel Pipes, "The Alawi Capture of Power in Syria," *Middle East Studies,* Vol. 25, No. 4, October 1989, pp. 429–50. Text at <http://www.danielpipes.org/article/>.

12. Eyal Zisser, *Decision Making in Asad's Syria* (Washington, 1998), pp. 17–27.

13. Eyal Zisser, "The Syrian Army on the Domestic and External Fronts," in Barry Rubin and Thomas Keaney, eds., *The Armed Forces in the Contemporary Middle East* (London, 2001), pp. 113–129.

14. *Al-Nahar,* June 16, 2000; *al-Hayat,* June 17, 2000; Andrew and Mitrokhin, p. 199.

15. For a discussion of U.S. military capabilities in the region, see Michael Eisenstadt, "U.S. Military Capabilities in the Post–Cold War Era: Implications for Middle East Allies," *MERIA Journal,* Vol. 2, No. 4 (December 1998), pp. 37–53. And Marvin Feuer, "U.S. Policy and Middle East Armed Forces," in Rubin and Keaney, eds., *Armed Forces in the Contemporary Middle East,* pp. 41–67.

16. Andrews and Mitrokhin, pp. 201, 207.

17. Eyal Zisser, *Asad's Legacy: Syria in Transition* (London, 2001), chapter 3.

18. *Der Spiegel,* June 22, 2006.

19. Ibid. *Asian Wall Street Journal,* January 27, 2005; *New York Times,* April 28. 2005.

20. Interview.

21. *Al-Quds al-Arabi,* January 11, 2002. Translation in MEMRI, No. 332, January 16, 2002. <http://MEMRI.org/bin/articles.cgi?Page=archives&Area=sd&ID=SP33202>.

22. Ibid.

23. Interview on Dubai television, August 23, 2006. Translation in MEMRI, No. 1265, August 23, 2006. http://www.MEMRI.org/bin/opener_latest.cgi?ID=SD126506.

24. *Al-Quds al-Arabi,* January 11, 2002.

25. Alan George, "In Syria, The Media is the System," *Middle East,* November 2000.

26. Middle East Watch, *Syria Unmasked* (New Haven, CT, 1991), p. 109.

27. On censorship, see ibid., chapter 9.

28. *Al-Quds al-Arabi*, April 24, 2006. Translation in MEMRI, No. 1172, May 25, 2006. http://www.MEMRI.org/bin/opener_latest.cgi?ID=SD117206.

29. Ibid.

30. The regime did create its own internet mouthpieces. See Tony Bedran, "Syrian-Saudi Media Wars," *Mideast Monitor,* Vol. 1, No. 3, September-October, 2006.

31. Najib Ghadbian, "Contesting the State Media Monopoly: Syria on al-Jazira Television," *MERIA Journal,* Vol. 5, No. 2 (June 2001).

32. George, "In Syria, The Media is the System."

33. *New York Times,* November 30, 2003; al-Rai, December 5, 2003; translation in MEMRI, No. 638, January 7, 2004. http://MEMRI.org/bin/articles.cgi?Page=archives&Area=sd&ID=SP63804.

34. *Al-Hayat,* January 20, 2001.

35. Eyal Zisser, "Syria, the Ba'th Regime and the Islamic Movement: Stepping on a New Path?" *Muslim World,* Vol. 95, Issue 1, January 2005; Martin Kramer, *Arab Awakening and Islamic Revival* (New Brunswick, NJ, 1996), pp. 195–201.

36. Ibid.

37. Zisser, "Syria, the Ba'th Regime and the Islamic Movement."

38. *New York Times,* October 20, 2003.

39. Ibid.

40. Syrian television, July 21, 2006. Translation in MEMRI, No. 1217, July 28, 2006. http://www.MEMRItv.org/search.asp?ACT=S9&P1=1206.

41. Ibid.

42. *Al-Safir,* September 13, 2004. Translation in MEMRI, No. 787, September 22, 2004. http://MEMRI.org/bin/articles.cgi?Page=archives&Area=sd&ID=SP78704.

43. *New York Times,* March 12, 2001.

44. *Al-Thawra,* February 16, 2006.

45. *Tishrin,* March 2, 2006. http://www.terrorism-info.org.il/malam_multimedia/English/eng_n/pdf/syria_as0506e.pdf

46. Al-Jazira TV, December 28, 2005. See MEMRI Clip No. 981, <http://www.MEMRItv.org/Transcript.asp?P1=984>.

47. Sami al-Jundi, quoted in Lewis, *Semites and Anti-Semites,* p. 147.

48. See, for example, *New York Times,* November 23, 1987, September 2, 1999, and October 26, 2005; *Agence France-Presse,* December 9, 2005; Rafael Dedoff, "Syria Sheltering War Criminals? Not the First Time," David S. Wyman Institute for Holocaust Studies newsletter, April 2003.

49. Syrian television, November 21 and 24, 2005. For the videos see MEMRI, Clip No. 941, http://www.MEMRItv.org/search.asp?ACT=S9&P1=941, and No. 938, http://www.MEMRItv.org/search.asp?ACT=S9&P1=938.

50. Speech, December 1980, cited in Daniel Pipes, "The Politics of Muslim Anti-Semitism," *Commentary,* Vol. 72, No. 3, August 1981, p. 39. See also Rushdi Abbas al-Amara, "The Historical and Religious Influences on Israel 's Behavior," *al-Siyasa al-Duwaliyya,* October 1982.

51. Interview.

52. *Al-Thawra,* August 11, 2006; *Tishrin,* August 8, 2006. Translation in MEMRI, No. 1244, August 11, 2006. http://MEMRI.org/bin/articles.cgi?Page=archives&Area=sd&ID=SP124406.

53. Syrian television, May 6, 2005. Translation in MEMRI, No. 1162, May 12, 2006. http://MEMRI.org/bin/articles.cgi?Page=archives&Area=sd&ID=SP116206#_ednref2.

54. Syrian television, May 6, 2005. Translation in MEMRI, No. 1162, May 12, 2006. http://www.MEMRI.org/bin/opener_latest.cgi?ID=SD116206.

55. Ibid.

56. Al-Arabiyya television, August 15, 2006. Translation in Foreign Broadcast Information Service GMP20060817602001.

CHAPTER FOUR

1. Fouad Ajami, "Arab Road," *Foreign Policy,* No. 47, Summer 1982, p. 16.

2. Radio Damascus, July 20, 2000. Cited in Eyal Zisser, "Who's Afraid of Syrian Nationalism? National and State Identity in Syria," *Middle Eastern Studies,* Vol. 42, No. 2, March 2006, p. 87.

3.   Martha Neff Kessler, *Syria: Fragile Mosaic of Power* (Washington DC, 1987), p. 114.

4.   *New York Times,* February 7 and March 12, 1991.

5.   "This Week with George Stephanopoulos," October 8, 2006.

6.   Al-Jazira TV, December 28, 2005. Middle East Media Research Institute (hereafter MEMRI), Clip No. 981, December 28, 2005. http://MEMRItv.org/Transcript.asp?P1=981.

7.   *Washington Post,* June 1, 1986.

8.   *Al-Hayat,* June 14, 1999. See Eyal Zisser, "Syria," in Ami Ayalon, *Middle East Contemporary Survey, Vol. 10, 1986–87* (Boulder, CO, 1989), pp. 606–607; Ami Ayalon, *Middle East Contemporary Survey, Vol. 11, 1987* (Boulder, CO, 1989), pp. 636–637; Ami Ayalon, *Middle East Contemporary Survey* (New York, 1994), p. 617; Andrew and Mitrokhin, op. cit., p. 198.

9.   Jim Hoagland, "A Clean Slate for Syria?" *Washington Post,* September 19, 1987.

10.   U.S. Treasury Department Press Release HP-60, August 15, 2006. http://www.whitehouse.gov/news/releases/2004/05/20040511–6.html.

11.   *Al-Usbu al-Adabi,* September 15, 2001. Translation in MEMRI, No. 275, September 25, 2001. http://www.MEMRI.org/bin/articles.cgi?Page=archives&Area=sd&ID=SP27501.

12.   It tells something about the state of Arab politics that even he admitted the regimes would do nothing more than issue statements of protest. *Kul al-Arab,* January 2, 2004. Translation in MEMRI, No. 646, January 19, 2004. http://www.MEMRI.org/bin/opener_latest.cgi?ID=SD64604.

13.   Radio Damascus, October 27, 2005. Cited in Intelligence and Terrorism Information Center at the Center for Special Studies (hereafter CSS), "Syrian Media Glorify the Terrorist Suicide Bombing in Hadera," October 30, 2005. <http://www.terrorism-info.org.il/malam_multimedia/English/eng_n/pdf/syrian_gl.pdf>.

14.   Radio Damascus, December 5, 2005, cited in CSS, "The Palestinian Islamic Jihad Carries Out Another Suicide Bombing Attack," December 6, 2005. <http://www.terrorism-info.org.il/malam_multimedia/English/eng_n/pdf/pij_e1205.pdf>.

15.   Reuven Erlich, "Terrorism as a Preferred Instrument of Syrian Policy," October 10, 2001. <http://www.ict.org.il/articles/articledet.cfm?articleid=400>.

16.   Ibid. See also CSS report, April 4, 2005. <http://www.terrorism-info.org.il/malam_multimedia//ENGLISH/COUNTERTERRORISM-DATA/PDF/APR13_05.PDFBulletin>.

17.   Kamal Junbalat, *I Speak for Lebanon* (London, 1982), p. 28.

18.   Seale, *Assad of Syria* op. cit., p. 348; *Tishrin,* July 9, 1983.

19.   Mohammed Heikal, *The Road to Ramadan* (New York, 1975), pp. 63–64.

20.   Moshe Shemesh, *The Palestinian Entity: 1959–1974: Arab Politics and the PLO* (Totowa, NJ, 1988), pp. 116–117.

21.   Baruch Kimmerling and Joel Migdal, *Palestinians: The Making of a People* (New York, 1993), p. 229; Shemesh, *Palestinian Entity,* p. 144; Lester Sobel, ed., *Palestinian Impasse* (New York, 1997), p. 82.

22.   PREM 15/202 <http://www.pro.gov.uk/releases/nyo2001/hijack3.htm>, Telex Amman-London, September 13, 1970; Cab 128/47, "Conclusions of a Meeting of the Cabinet," September 21, 1970 at 10 Downing 10:30 am.

23.   Andrew Gowers and Tony Walker, *Behind the Myth: Yasser Arafat and the Palestinian Revolution* (London, 1990), p. 85; Abu Iyad, op. cit., p. 80.

24.   James Lunt, *Hussein of Jordan: A Political Biography* (London, 1989), p. 144; Gowers and Walker, *Behind the Myth,* p. 87; Anthony Nutting, *Nasser* (New York, 1972), p. 475; Abu Iyad, op. cit., p. 90.

25.   Muhammad Heikal, *Road to Ramadan* (New York, 1975), p. 121.

26.   Gowers and Walker, *Behind the Myth,* p. 84.

27.   Ibid., p. 63; Sobel, *Palestinian Impasse,* p. 14.

28.   Ibid.

29.   *Al-Majalla,* December 4, 1982, Damascus television, December 15, 1982 (BBC, *Survey of World Broadcasts,* December 17, 1982); Abu Musa, NIN (Belgrade), October 30, 1983, translation in U.S. Department of Commerce, Joint Publications Research Service, November 22, 1983.

30.   Eric Rouleau, "The Future of the PLO," *Foreign Affairs,* Vol. 62, No. 1, Fall 1983, p. 145.

31. The rebels' political leaders included PNC chairman Khalid al-Fahoum and Nimr Salah (Abu Salah), a Marxist founder of Fatah who had been the PLO's liaison and arms supplier to the Lebanese left.

32. *Al-Watan,* May 26, 1983; al-Anba, October 3, 1987.

33. See the text of the statement in Foreign Broadcast Information Service (hereafter FBIS), May 17, 1983, p. A4.

34. Yezid Sayigh, "Fatah: The First Twenty Years," *Journal of Palestine Studies,* Vol. 13, No. 4, Summer 1984, p. 115; al-Anba, October 3, 1987. See also Fouad Moughrabi, "The Palestinians After Lebanon," *Arab Studies Quarterly,* Vol. 5, No. 3, Summer 1983, p. 211.

35. Adam Garfinkle, "Sources of the al-Fatah Mutiny," *Orbis,* Vol. 27, Fall 1983, p. 637.

36. In addition to their long-standing hatred of Arafat and clash of interests in Lebanon, the Syrians may have also wanted revenge for Arafat's help to Islamist revolutionaries within Syria, another possible example of his meddling in the politics of Arab states. *Tishrin,* June 25, 1983; *al-Thawra,* June 30, 1983.

37. Garfinkle, "Sources of the al-Fatah Mutiny"; Rouleau, "The Future of the PLO," pp. 142–143; Robert Baer, *See No Evil: The True Story of a Ground Soldier in the CIA's War on Terrorism* (New York, 2002), p. 124; *Washington Post,* June 14, 1983.

38. Bassam Abu Sharif and Uzi Mahnaimi, *Tried by Fire* (London, 1995), p. 205.

39. Thomas Friedman, *From Beirut to Jerusalem* (New York, 1989), p. 174.

40. Ibid.

41. William Harris, *Faces of Lebanon: Sects, Wars and Global Extensions* (Princeton NJ, 1997), p. 184.

42. Text, *Journal of Palestine Studies,* Vol. 14, No. 3, Spring 1985, p. 201.

43. Text of testimony of Phil Wilcox, State Department Coordinator for Counter-Terrorism, House International Relations Committee, July 25, 1996. On King Hussein's charges against Syria, see *Palestine Report,* August 16, 1996.

44. Agence France-Presse, August 24, 1993, in FBIS, August 24, 1993; *New York Times,* August 25, 1993.

45. Tlas as quoted in *al-Safir* and *Daily Star,* August 3, 1999. The Syrian media only covered Tlas's denial of making such comments.

46. *Al-Hayat,* August 20, 1995; in FBIS, August 25, 1995.

47. Adeed Dawisha, "Comprehensive Peace in the Middle East and the Comprehension of Arab Politics," *Middle East Journal,* Vol. 37, 1983, pp. 147–148.

48. Damascus radio, July 16, 1985, in FBIS, July 16, 1985.

49. Al-Mustaqbal TV, August 27, 2006. Translation in FBIS GMP20060828622001.

50. Interview.

51. Inaugural speech, July 17, 2000, Syrian News Agency. Translation in MEMRI, No. 116, July 21, 2000.

52. *Tishrin,* January 11, 1981.

53. Andrew and Mitrokhin, op. cit., pp. 211–212.

54. Curtis R. Ryan, "The Odd Couple: Ending the Jordanian-Syrian Cold War," *Middle East Journal,* Vol. 60, No. 1, Winter 2006, pp. 33–56.

CHAPTER FIVE

1. *Washington Post,* March 9, 1998.

2. Eyal Zisser, "Syria," in *Middle East Contemporary Survey,* Volume 14, 1990 (New York, 1991), p 653. Raymond A. Hinnebusch, "State and Civil Society in Syria," *Middle East Journal,* Vol. 47, No. 2, Spring 1993, p. 242.

3. *Al-Sharq al-Awsat,* February 18, 2001.

4. Speech of October 1, 1981. For the full text, see Barry Rubin and Judith Colp Rubin, *Anti-American Terrorism and the Middle East* (New York, 2002), p. 113.

5. *New York Times,* April 28, 1992.

6. The clearest presentation of Saddam's position was in his speech to the Arab Cooperation Council, February 24, 1990. See Rubin and Rubin, *Anti-American Terrorism,* pp. 119–126.

7. Al-Mustaqbal TV, August 27, 2006. Translation in Foreign Broadcast Information Service (hereafter FBIS) GMP20060828622001.

8. Inaugural speech, July 17, 2000, Syrian News Agency. Translation in Middle East Media Research Institute (hereafter MEMRI), No. 116, July 21, 2000.

9. Sharaa speech of January 27, 2000, to the Arab Writers Union Conference in Damascus. The text is from *al-Usbu al-Adabi,* February 12, 2000. See <http://www.awu-dam.com>. The question-and-answer session is from "Al-Sharaa Answers Questions on Peace," *al-Safir,* February 12, 2000. Translations are from FBIS-NES-2000–0216, February 12, 2000.

10. Ibid.

11. SIPRI, *Yearbook 2006: Armaments, Disarmament and International Security* (New York, 2006), pp. 342, 348–349.

12. Sharaa speech.

13. Roula Khalaf, *Financial Times,* October 13, 1999.

14. Majid Muawwad in *al-Thawra,* July 9, 1999. Translation by FBIS.

15. *Christian Science Monitor,* July 12, 2000.

16. Ibid.

17. Sharaa speech.

18. The Palestinian equivalent of this ploy was to demand all "occupied" territory, leaving it ambiguous as to whether this meant that captured by Israel in 1967—that is, the Gaza Strip and West Bank—or the territory on which Israel had been created in 1948, that is, the elimination of Israel altogether.

19. Sharaa speech.

20. Ibid.

21. Ibid.

22. Yossi Ben-Aharon, "Negotiating with Syria: A First-Hand Account," *MERIA Journal,* Vol. 4, No. 2, June 2000, pp. 1–13. http://meria.idc.ac.il/journal/2000/issue2/Ben-Aharon.pdf.

23. Sharaa speech.

24. Ibid.

25. Ibid.

26. Ben-Aharon, "Negotiating with Syria."

27. Ibid.

28. Ibid.

29. Ibid.

30. Itamar Rabinovitch, *The Brink of Peace: The Israeli-Syrian Negotiations* (Princeton, NJ, 1998), p. 96.

31. Ibid., p. 168.

32. Ibid., p. 104.

33. Ibid., p. 106.

34. Ibid., pp. 208–228.

35. *International Herald Tribune,* October 25, 1994; *New York Times,* October 28, 1994.

36. *Arab Times,* May 19, 2005.

37. Sharaa speech.

38. Ibid.

39. Al-Thawra, July 13, 1999.

40. "The Palestine Problem in the Political Report and the Resolutions of the Eight All-Arab Baath Congress (Spring 1965), Aggressive Strategy against Israel's Existence," in Ben-Tzur, op. cit.

41. Quoted in George Gruen, "Turkey's Potential Contribution to Arab-Israeli Peace," *Turkish Review of Middle East Studies,* Vol.10, 1998–1999, pp. 200–201.

42. Aysegul Sever, "Turkey and the Syrian-Israeli Peace Talks in the 1990s," *MERIA Journal,* Vol. 5, No. 3, September 2001.

43. Cited in ibid.

44. See, for example, Mustafa Aydin et al., "Political Conditionality of Economic Relations Between Paternalist States," *Arab Studies Quarterly,* Vol. 27, No. 2, Winter/Spring2005; Bulent Aras et al, "Turkish-Syrian Relations Revisited," *Arab Studies Quarterly,* Vol. 24, Issue 4, Fall 2002; Mahmut Bali Aykan, "The Turkish-Syrian crisis of October 1998: A Turkish View," *Middle East Policy,* Vol. 6, Issue 4, June 1999. pp. 174–191.

45. Cited in Etienne Sakr, "The Politics and Liberation of Lebanon," *MERIA Journal,* Vol. 9, No. 4, December 2005, p. 90. http://meria.idc.ac.il/journal/2005/issue4/Abu%20Arz%20pdf.pdf.

46. Human Rights Watch, "An Alliance Beyond the Law: Enforced Disappearances in Lebanon," May 1997.

47. Gary C. Gambill and Elie Abou Aoun, "Special Report: How Syria Orchestrates Lebanon 's Elections," *Mideast Monitor,* August 14, 2000.

48. Cited in Khalaf, *Financial Times,* October 13, 1999.

CHAPTER SIX

1. *New York Times,* January 22, 1994.

2. The following draws on Eyal Zisser, "Appearance and Reality: Syria's Decisionmaking Structure," *MERIA Journal,* Vol. 2, No. 2, May 1998.

3. Henry Kissinger, *Years of Upheaval* (Boston, 1982), pp. 780–781, 1083.

4. Ibid., p. 448.

5. Ibid., p. 457.

6. Ilham Abu-Salih, "Qiraati," Second Section for First Grade, Damascus, p. 56; Ahmad al-Qadiri, Anwar Karimi, and Salim al-Zaim, "Uktub wa-Uhsub," First Section, Damascus, p. 33, exercise no. 5. Cited in Ben-Aharon, pp. 5–6.

7. James A. Baker III, *The Politics of Diplomacy* (New York, 1995), p. 456.

8. Kissinger, *Years of Upheaval,* pp. 1087, 1068.

9. *Washington Post,* February 9, 1998.

10. "Dossier: Rifat Assad," *Middle East Intelligence Bulletin,* Vol. 2, No. 5, June 2000, <http://www.meib.org/articles/0006_sd.htm>.

11. Patrick Seale, *Assad: The Struggle for the Middle East* (Berkeley, CA, 1988), p. 433. This story might be a public relations' concoction, of course.

12. *Al-Nahar,* October 21, 1999.

13. *Yediot Ahronot,* June 5, 1999; Eyal Zisser, "Heir Apparent," *New Republic,* October 11, 1999.

14. *Al-Sharq al-Awsat,* February 18, 2000

15. *Al-Majalla,* June 6, 1999. Translation by Foreign Broadcast Information Service (hereafter FBIS), FTS19990611000312, June 11, 1999.

16. For information on the society, see http://www.scs-syria.com/SCS.

17. In Hasan Khadir, "And Now, A Dynastic Republic," *al-Ayyam,* June 13, 2000. See also Fuad Abu Hijla, al-Hayat al-Jadida, June 13, 2000. *Al-Ayyam,* June 14, 2000. All translations are from Middle East Media Research Institute (hereafter MEMRI), No. 102, June 16, 2000. http://MEMRI.org/bin/articles.cgi?Page=archives&Area=sd&ID=SP10200.

18. *Washington Post,* July 17, 1998; *New York Times,* July 18, 1998.

19. *New York Times* and *Washington Post,* June 11, 2000.

20. *The Australian, Daily Telegraph, The Times, New York Times, Philadelphia Inquirer,* June 14, 2000.

21. *New York Times,* June 12, 19, 21, 28, and July 12, 2000.

22. *Al-Sharq al-Awsat,* February 12, 1999.

23. Al-Jazira television, June 26, 2000. Cited in Ghadbian, op. cit.

24. Inaugural speech, July 17, 2000, Syrian News Agency. Translation in MEMRI, No. 116, July 21, 2000.

25. Ibid.

26. Cited in Gary C. Gambill, "The Myth of Syria's Old Guard," *Middle East Intelligence Bulletin,* Vol. 6, No. 2–3, February-March 2004.

27. *New York Times,* May 16, 2000; *Middle East Economic Digest,* June 2, 2000; *Financial Times,* May 22, 2000.

28. Full text at http://yalibnan.com/site/archives/2005/11/full_arabic_eng.php or http://www.eyeon-theun.org/assets/attachments/documents/assad_speech_11-11-05.doc.

29. *Al-Safir,* July 16, 2001. Translation in MEMRI, No. 244, July 20, 2001. http://MEMRI.org/bin/articles.cgi?Page=archives&Area=sd&ID=SP24401.

30. Dennis Ross, "U.S. Policy toward a Weak Assad," *Washington Quarterly,* Summer 2005.

31. http://www.elaph.com/ElaphWeb/Politics/2006/6/153652.htm.

32.   Al-Mustaqbal television, August 27, 2006. Translation in FBIS GMP20060828622001.
33.   Ibid.
34.   Speech to conference of Syrian Expatriates, *al-Ba'th,* October 9, 2004. Translation in MEMRI, No. 799, October 14, 2004. http://MEMRI.org/bin/articles.cgi?Page=archives&Area=sd&ID=SP79904.
35.   *Al-Safir,* July 16, 2001. Translation in MEMRI, No. 244, July 20, 2001. http://MEMRI.org/bin/articles.cgi?Page=archives&Area=sd&ID=SP24401.
36.   Ibid.
37.   *New York Times,* November 30, 2003.
38.   Ibid.
39.   *Al-Hayat,* June 26, 2006. Translation in FBIS FEA20060627024631.
40.   Ibid.
41.   Interview, July 27, 2006. <http://www.cfr.org/publication/11169/>.
42.   Interview in *al-Safir,* July 16, 2001.

CHAPTER SEVEN

1.   Alan George, "Syria at the Crossroads," *The Middle East,* February 2000. See also Nimrod Raphaeli, "The Syrian Economy Under Bashar al-Assad," MEMRI, No. 259, January 13, 2005. <http://MEMRI.org/bin/latestnews.cgi?ID=IA25906>. See also Peter Kiernan, "Syria's Economic Dilemma," *The Middle East,* Issue 228, March 1999, pp. 35–37.
2.   Cited in Zvi Bar'el, "Syria: Where Time Stood Still Since 1963," *Haaretz,* September 25, 2003.
3.   Reuters, April 12, 1999; *al-Nahar,* October 4, 1999; Zisser, "Syria: The Renewed Struggle for Power,"op. cit; *Al-Hayat,* July 26, 1999; *al-Safir,* August 29, 1999
4.   CIA, *The World Fact Book,* October 5, 2006. https://www.cia.gov/cia/publications/factbook/index.html.
5.   *New York Times,* January 17, 2000.
6.   Interview with the BBC, October 9, 2006. Text at Syrian Arab News Agency, <http://www.sana.org/eng/21/2006/10/09/74408.htm>.
7.   Bassam Haddad, "Left to Its Domestic Devices: How the Syrian Regime Boxed Itself In," *Royal Institute of International and Strategic Studies,* No. 43, Madrid, Spain, 2005.
8.   Begun originally in the Superman comics, Bizarro world posited a place where all rules, behavior, and values are the reverse of those on earth. For the best literary representation of the Bizarro world concept as a source of evil, see William Shakespeare, *King Richard the Third,* Act One, Scene One.
9.   *Al-Ahram Weekly,* November 10–16, 2005.
10.   Speech to conference of Syrian Expatriates, October 8, 2004, *al-Ba'th,* October 9, 2004. Translation in MEMRI, No. 799, October 14, 2004. http://MEMRI.org/bin/articles.cgi?Page=archives&Area=sd&ID=SP79904.
11.   See, for example, Gary Gambill, "Lebanese Farmers and the Syrian Occupation," *Middle East Intelligence Bulletin,* Vol. 5, Issue 10, October 2003; Eric V. Thompson, "Will Syria Have to Withdraw from Lebanon?" *Middle East Journal,* Vol. 56, No.1, Winter 2002, pp. 72–93; Habib Malik, *Between Damascus and Jerusalem: Lebanon and Middle East Peace* (Washington, DC, 2000).
12.   Al-Mustaqbal TV, August 27, 2006. Translation in FBIS GMP20060828622001.
13.   The following draws heavily on George and Raphaeli, op. cit.
14.   *Al-Sharq al-Awsat,* December 26, 2005.
15.   International Monetary Fund report, cited in Raphaeli, op. cit
16.   International Monetary Fund, "Syrian Arab Republic," *Staff Report for the 2005, Article IV Consultation.* Washington, DC, p. 4. Syrian Arab News Agency, January 12, 2007.
17.   Independent Inquiry Committee into the United Nations Oil-for-Food Program, *Management of the Oil-for-Food Program,* September 7, 2005, Vol. II, Chapter 4, pp. 240–242.
18.   *New York Times,* October 19, 1990; *Financial Times,* October 23 and November 2, 1990.
19.   World Bank, *World Development Indicators,* 2001, op. cit., pp. 94–96.
20.   Ibid., pp. 306–308.
21.   *New York Times,* January 27, 2000. See also Roula Khalaf, "Syria's Golden Opportunity," *Financial Times,* October 13, 1999.

22. Najib Ghadbian, "Contesting the State Media Monopoly: Syria on al-Jazira Television," *MERIA Journal*, Vol. 5, No. 2, June 2001, pp. 75–87. http://meria.idc.ac.il/journal/2001/issue2/ghadbian.pdf.

23. Ibid.

24. Arabic News, <http://www.arabicnews.com/ansub/Daily/Day/000526/2000052611.html>.

25. See, for example, "An Open Letter to Dr. Bashar al-Assad," *al-Nahar*, March 23, 2000. Excerpts are translated in "We Are Not a Syrian Province," *Middle East Quarterly*, Vol. 7, No. 2 (June 2000).

26. Hazim Saghiyya, "The Speech That Bashar al-Assad Will Never Make," *al-Hayat*, June 25, 2000. Translation in MEMRI, No. 112, July 6, 2000. <http://MEMRI.org/bin/articles.cgi?Page=archives&Area=sd&ID=SP11200>.

27. *Al-Quds al-Arabi*, February 20, 2001.

28. *Al-Quds al-Arabi*, February 19, 2001.

29. Syrian Press Agency, July 17, 2000.

30. *Al-Sharq al-Awsat*, February 8, 2001.

31. *Al-Hayat*, January 15, 2001; al-Sharq al-Awsat, February 8, 2001.

32. *Al-Hayat*, January 15, 2001.

33. Reuters, February 27, 2001.

34. *Guardian*, July 27, 2002.

35. *Al-Nahar* and *al-Safir*, September 26, 2000.

36. *Al-Hayat*, January 16, 2001.

37. *Al-Quds Al-Arabi*, February 2, 2001. See also *al-Safir*, January 24, 2001.

38. *Al-Hayat*, January 13, 2001. Translation in MEMRI, No. 47, February 9, 2001. http://MEMRI.org/bin/articles.cgi?Page=archives&Area=ia&ID=IA4701.

39. Hinnebusch, op. cit., p. 253.

40. *Guardian*, July 27, 2002.

41. Ibid.

42. *Al-Sharq al-Awsat*, February 17, 2001.

43. *Al-Sharq al-Awsat*, February 18, 2001.

44. Ibid.; *Al-Nahar*, February 19, 2001. Translation in MEMRI, No. 51, February 28, 2001, http://MEMRI.org/bin/articles.cgi?Page=archives&Area=ia&ID=IA5101. *al-Sharq al-Awsat*. February 8, 2001. Translation in MEMRI, No. 49, February 16, 2001. http://MEMRI.org/bin/articles.cgi?Page=archives&Area=ia&ID=IA4901

45. Abd al-Raouf Haddad, *Akhbar al-Sharq*, June 20, 2002.

46. Mahmoud Al-Mahamid, *Akhbar al Sharq*, June 20, 2002.

47. *Al-Nahar*, October 11, 2003. Translated in MEMRI, No. 599, October 30, 2003. See also http://www.MEMRI.org/bin/opener_latest.cgi?ID=SD59903.

48. *New York Times*, March 12, 2001.

49. See, for example, Khaddam's statement quoted in *al-Sharq al-Awsat*, February 18, 2001.

50. *Al-Sharq al-Awsat*, February 18, 2001.

51. *Al-Hayat*, January 21, 2001.

52. Gary C. Gambill, "Syria and the Saudi Peace Initiative," *Middle East Intelligence Bulletin*, Vol. 4, No. 3, March-April 2002.

53. *Al-Hayat*, February 9, March 2, and March 21, 2000. Translation in MEMRI, No. 84 April 6, 2000. http://MEMRI.org/bin/articles.cgi?Page=archives&Area=sd&ID=SP8400.

54. *Al-Hayat*, February 9, 2000. Translation in MEMRI, No. 84, April 6, 2000. http://MEMRI.org/bin/articles.cgi?Page=archives&Area=sd&ID=SP8400.

55. *Al-Hayat*, February 9, March 2, and March 21, 2000. Translation in MEMRI, No. 84, April 6, 2000. http://MEMRI.org/bin/articles.cgi?Page=archives&Area=sd&ID=SP400

56. *Times*, September 17, 2002.

57. *Al-Nahar*, October 11, 2003. Translation in MEMRI, No. 599, October 30, 2003, No. 599. See also http://www.MEMRI.org/bin/opener_latest.cgi?ID=SD59903.

58. *Al-Sharq al-Awsat*, February 8, 2001. Translation in MEMRI, No. 49, February 16, 2001. http://MEMRI.org/bin/articles.cgi?Page=archives&Area=ia&ID=IA4901.

59. *Al-Usbu al-Adabi*, December 16, 2000.

60.   Gary Gambill, "Dark Days Ahead for Syria's Liberal Reformers," *Middle East Intelligence Bulletin,* Vol. 3, No. 2, February 2001.

61.   *Al-Quds,* October 11, 2000. Translation in MEMRI, No. 48, February 12, 2001. *Al-Hayat,* February 1, 2001. <http://MEMRI.org/bin/articles.cgi?Page=archives&Area=ia&ID=IA4801>.

62.   *Al-Sharq al-Awsat,* February 8, 2001.

63.   *Al-Ba'th,* February 1, 2001.

64.   *Al-Safir,* July 16, 2001. Translation in MEMRI, No. 244, July 20, 2001. <http://MEMRI.org/bin/articles.cgi?Page=archives&Area=sd&ID=SP24401>.

65.   *New York Times,* December 2, 2003.

66.   *Tishrin,* March 28, 2001. Translation in MEMRI, No. 202, April 2001. <http://MEMRI.org/bin/articles.cgi?Page=archives&Area=sd&ID=SP20201>.

67.   *Al-Mustaqbal,* May 3, 2001; *al-Hayat,* May 4, 2001, and *al-Sharq al-Awsat,* May 6, 2001. Translation in MEMRI, No. 56, May 24, 2001. <http://MEMRI.org/bin/articles.cgi?Page=archives&Area=ia&ID=IA5601>.

68.   *Al-Sharq al-Awsat,* February 8, 2001. Translation in MEMRI, No. 49, February 16, 2001. http://MEMRI.org/bin/articles.cgi?Page=archives&Area=ia&ID=IA4901

CHAPTER EIGHT

1.   Volker Perthes, *International Herald Tribune,* October 5, 2005.

2.   *Guardian,* October 6, 2003.

3.   Associated Press, September 19, 2006.

4.   Interview by Foreign Secretary Jack Straw and U.S. Secretary of State Condoleezza Rice on BBC Television, October 23, 2005. Website of UK Mission to the UN. <http://www.ukun.org/search/Search_show.asp?Aid=1060&T=1>.

5.   Future TV on February 14, 2006. Clip No. 1038, http://www.MEMRItv.org/search.asp?ACT=S9&P1=1038.

6.   *Al-Hayat,* June 29, 2006.

7.   Robert Rabil, *Daily Star,* June 9, 2003.

8.   *Akhbar al-Sharq,* June 1, 2003. See also http://www.reformsyria.com/documents/Intellectuals%20appeal%20for%20Syria%20reforms.pdf.

9.   Tarek Heggy, "We . . .and the Reality Around Us," *al-Ahram,* May 11, 2003.

10.   *Syrian Monitor,* June 29, 2006. http://syriamonitor.typepad.com/news/2006/06/mamoun_homsi_in.html.

11.   Rabil, *Daily Star,* June 9, 2003. On repression in Syria, see Syrian Human Rights Committee, *Annual Report 2003* (London, 2003).

12.   BBC, March 20, 2002.

13.   *Democracy Digest,* Vol. 1, No. 13, July 29, 2004.

14.   The group's leader, Aktham Naisse, a lawyer from Latakia, had spent seven years in jail for founding a human rights group in 1991. Associated Press, March 8 and 10, 2004; text of petition, *al-Nahar,* February 10, 2004. For a good analysis of the reform movement, see Tony Badran, "Divided They Stand: The Syrian Opposition," *Mideast Monitor,* Vol. 1, No. 3, September-October 2006.

15.   Middle East Transparent, http://www.metransparent.com/texts/riad_seif_beaten_by_security_agents.htm, September 5, 2006. Translation in MEMRI, No. 1292, September 19, 2006. <http://www.MEMRI.org/bin/opener_latest.cgi?ID=SD129206>.

16.   Ibid.

17.   Ibid.

18.   *Syrian Monitor,* June 29, 2006. http://syriamonitor.typepad.com/news/2006/06/mamoun_homsi_in.html.

19.   *New York Times,* July 2, 2005.

20.   *Elaph,* http://www.elaph.com/ElaphWeb/Politics/2006/10/184639.htm.

21.   *Al-Ba'th,* January 8, 2002; *al-Hayat,* January 9, 2002. Translation in MEMRI, No. 332, January 16, 2002. http://MEMRI.org/bin/articles.cgi?Page=archives&Area=sd&ID=SP33202.

22. *Al-Quds Al-Arabi,* January 11, 2002, MEMRI, No. 332, January 16, 2002. http://MEMRI.org/bin/articles.cgi?Page=archives&Area=sd&ID=SP33202.

23. *New York Times,* January 14, 2002.

24. *Washington Post,* July 25, 2002.

25. *New York Times,* January 14, 2002.

26. *Washington Post,* July 25, 2002.

27. Ibid.

28. Eyal Zisser, "Syria and the United States: Bad Habits Die Hard," *Middle East Quarterly,* Vol. 10, No. 3 (Summer 2003). <http://www.meforum.org/article/555>.

29. On the wanted Hizballah men, see http://www.fbi.gov/wanted/terrorists/teratwa.htm, http://www.fbi.gov/wanted/terrorists/terizzaldin.htm, and http://www.fbi.gov/wanted/terrorists/termugniyah.htm.

30. Reuters, October 11, 2001.

31. Ibid.

32. Robert Baer, *See No Evil: The True Story of a Ground Soldier in the CIA's War on Terrorism* (New York, 2002), pp. 129–130. "FBI Most Wanted List," October 10, 2001, in Barry Rubin and Judith Colp Rubin, *Anti-American Terrorism and the Middle East* (New York, 2002), pp. 189–204; *Newsweek,* November 15, 1999.

33. Ibid.

34. Ibid.

35. *New York Times,* December 20, 1998; *Tishrin,* February 9, 1999; MECS 1998, p. 576; *al-Hayat,* February 25, 1999; Reuters, February 15, 1999.

36. *Al-Siyasa and al-Hayat,* April 15, 2003.

37. *Al-Safir,* March 27, 2003.

38. *Al-Hayat,* March 13, 2000. The following section benefits greatly from Eyal Zisser, "Syria and the War in Iraq," op. cit.

39. United Press International, January 23, 2001.

40. *Christian Science Monitor,* May 16, 2002.

41. *New York Times,* April 26, 1999.

42. Economist Intelligence Unit (hereafter EIU), *Syrian Country Profile,* 2002 (London, 2002), pp. 2–5; Reuters, October 29, 2002; *al-Quds al-Arabi,* October 10, 2000; *Times,* December 16, 2002.

43. *Times,* December 16, 2002; EIU, *Syrian Country Profile;* Reuters, October 29, 2002; *International Oil Daily,* February 26, March 31, and April 8, 2003; *Washington Post,* January 24, 2001; *Wall Street Journal,* January 24, 2001; *Los Angeles Times,* January 23, 2001.

44. *Los Angeles Times,* December 30, 2003.

45. *Al-Hayat,* October 26, 2001, December 13, 2002; *al-Safir,* November 23, 2000; Reuters, March 31, 2001, January 4, 2002; *al-Sharq al-Awsat,* August 30, 2001; Knight Ridder/Tribune News Service, March 3, 2001.

46. Interviews with former U.S. government officials having direct knowledge of this incident.

47. *Al-Safir,* March 27, 2003; see also Bashar speech at the Sharm al-Shaykh Arab summit, March 1, 2003, Syrian TV, translated by Foreign Broadcast Information Service (hereafter FBIS); Radio Damascus, March 10, 2003, translated by FBIS; see also *al-Hayat,* March 10, 2003.

48. *Al-Safir,* March 27, 2003. Translation in MEMRI, No. 488, March 30, 2003. http://MEMRI.org/bin/articles.cgi?Page=archives&Area=sd&ID=SP48803.

49. Radio Damascus, March 9, 2003, translated by FBIS; see also *al-Safir,* March 10, 2003.

50. Radio Damascus, March 27, 29, 2003, translated by FBIS. Associated Press, March 28, and April 13, 2003; Reuters, April 9, 2003; Fox News, April 14, 2003.

51. Press conference with French Foreign Minister Dominique de Villepin. *Al-Rai al-Am,* April 13, 2003; see also Reuters, April 12, 2003, and Syrian Arab News Agency, March 30, 2003.

52. CNN, April 13, 2003. See *al-Hayat,* April 21, 2003; see also Reuters, April 21, 2003.

53. *Tishrin,* April 6, 9, 13, 2003

54. *Washington Post,* May 3, 2003

55. *New York Times,* May 5, 2003.

56. *Al-Sharq al-Awsat,* January 19, 2004.

57. AFP and United Press International, March 27, 2003.

58. *Wall Street Journal,* March 26, 2003.

59. United Press International, September 17, 2003; Reuters, September 26, 2003; *International Herald Tribune,* April 17, 2003.

60. For U.S. complaints about Syria's role, see for example, *Washington Post,* December 6, 2004; *Christian Science Monitor,* December 16 and 23, 2004; Bremer, p. 104.

61. *New York Times,* October 21, 2003, and October 22, 2004; *Washington Post,* September 20, 2004.

62. Associated Press, September 29, 2003.

63. United Press International, June 30, 2003.

64. Paul Bremer, *My Year in Iraq: The Struggle to Build a Future of Hope* (New York, 2006), p. 198.

65. *New Republic,* May 26, 2003. See also Associated Press, October 7, 2003, BBC, April 1, 2003.

66. *Al-Hayat,* October 7, 2003.

67. U. S. Department of State, *Patterns of Global Terrorism—2001,* May 21, 2002, p. 68.

68. U.S. Department of State, *Patterns of Global Terrorism—2002,* April 30, 2003, p. 81.

69. U.S. Department of State, daily press briefing, October 8, 2003; United Press International, September 22, 2003; *Washington Post,* October 6, 2003.

70. Syrian Arab Republic Radio, October 16, 2003. Translation by BBC Survey of World Broadcasts.

71. Gary Gambill, "Implications of the Israeli Reprisal in Syria," *Middle East Intelligence Bulletin,* Vol. 5, Issue 10, October 2003.

72. UN Security Council minutes, October 5, 2003, <http://domino.un.org/unispal.nsf/22f431edb91c6f548525678a0051be1d/57b65178624842ee85256db8005213c9!OpenDocument>.

73. Ibid.

74. *New York Times* and *Washington Post,* May 12, 2004. For a good overview of U.S. sanctions, see Albert B. Prados, "Syria: U.S. Relations and Bilateral Issues," *Congressional Research Service Report,* August 18, 2006. Texts of laws and executive orders at http://www.fas.org/sgp/crs/mideast/RL33487.pdf and http://www.whitehouse.gov/news/releases/2004/05/20040511-8.html.

75. Neil Ford, *The Middle East,* Issue 347, July 2004, pp. 16–17.

76. Ibid.; *Financial Times,* December 11, 2003.

77. Syrian Television, November 24, 2005. View at <http://www.MEMRItv.org/Search.asp?ACT=S9&P1=940>. Translation by MEMRI, Clip No. 940, November 24, 2005. http://www.MEMRItv.org/Transcript.asp?P1=940.

78. *Wall Street Journal,* November 21, 2003.

79. *Arab Times (Kuwait),* December 16, 2003.

80. *Arab Times (Saudi Arabia),* December 15, 2003.

81. Ibid.

CHAPTER NINE

1. *Al-Nahar,* October 11, 2003. Translation in MEMRI, no. 599, October 30, 2003, available at http://MEMRI.org/bin/articles.cgi?Page=archives&Area=sd&ID=SP59903.

2. For a detailed discussion of these issues, see Rubin and Rubin, *Yasir Arafat,* op. cit.

3. Sermon, June 4, 2004, available at http://www.qaradawi.net/site/topics/article.asp?cu_no=2&item_no=3321&version=1&template_id=104&parent_id=15#%20__%20__%20__%20__%20__%20__.; al-Qatar television, December 2, 2005. Translation in MEMRI, no. 1045, December 9, 2005, available at http://MEMRI.org/bin/articles.cgi?Page=archives&Area=sd&ID=SP104505.

4. Al-Arabiyya television, December 31, 2005, available at http://www.MEMRItv.org/Transcript.asp?P1=985. For transcript see MEMRI, January 5, 2006, available at http://www.MEMRItv.org/search.asp?ACT=S9&P1=984.

5. Ibid.

6. Ibid.

7. Ibid.

8. Ibid. See also *New York Times,* January 6, 2006.

9. Interview on Dubai television, August 23, 2006. Translation in MEMRI, no. 1244, August 23, 2006, available at http://www.MEMRItv.org/search.asp?ACT=S9&P1=1244.

10. For the FitzGerald report text, see http://www.al-bab.com/Arab/docs/lebanon/unhariri.htm. For the October 2005 Mehlis report, see "Report of the International Independent Investigation Commission Established Pursuant to Security Council Resolution 1595 (2005)," United Nations (October 2005), available at http://www.un.org/News/dh/docs/mehlisreport/.

11. The text of the report as released is at http://www.mideastweb.org/mehlis_report2.htm. The original version names in paragraph 96: Mahir Assad, Asif Shawkat, Hassan Khalil, Bahjat Sulayman, and Jamil al-Sayyid. For the unedited version, see http://www.metransparent.com/texts/mehlis_1_report.htm.

12. *New York Times,* November 1, 2005.

13. Compare http://www.mideastweb.org/mehlis_report2.htm to the unedited version, see http://www.metransparent.com/texts/mehlis_1_report.htm.

14. Al-Thawra, October 14 and 16, 2005. Translation in MEMRI, no. 1023, November 11, 2005, available at http://www.MEMRI.org/bin/opener_latest.cgi?ID=SD102305.

15. Minister of Information Muhsin Bilal, interview with *La Republica,* August 17, 2006. Translation in FBIS, EUP20060817058012. See also *Al-Thawra,* July 27, 2006. Translation in MEMRI, no. 1249, August 15, 2006, available at http://www.MEMRI.org/bin/opener_latest.cgi?ID=SD124906.

16. Interview with the BBC, September 8, 2006, available at http://www.sana.org/eng/21/2006/10/09/74408.htm.

17. Syrian television, October 31, 2005, available at http://MEMRItv.org/search.asp?ACT=S9&P1=910.

18. Al-Arabiyya television, December 31, 2005, available at http://www.MEMRItv.org/search.asp?ACT=S9&P1=986.

19. Cited in Robert Rabil, "Khaddam's Revelations: Is the Asad Regime Unraveling?" *Washington Institute Policy Watch,* no. 1068, January 6, 2006.

20. Al-Arabiyya, August 15, 2006. Translation in FBIS GMP20060817602001.

21. See http://abcnews.go.com/Politics/wireStory?id=1517820.

22. *Al-Sharq al-Awsat,* November 23, 2005.

23. Gary Gambill, "How Significant is Syria's Role in Iraq?" *Terrorism Monitor 2,* no. 19 (October 7, 2004), 3–6; *Chicago Tribune,* April 19, 2005; AP, December 27, 2004; *Daily Telegraph,* January 11, 2006; *Wall Street Journal,* December 10, 2004.

24. *New York Times,* February 28, 2005. al-Jazira, August 25, 2006, available at http://english.al-jazeera.net/NR/exeres/225CBBA9–9AB7–46ED-BBE0-DE20FE29ABFA.htm.

25. *Al-Sharq al-Awsat,* December 7, 2006.

26. *Los Angeles Times,* January 12, 2007.

27. On the Kilo arrest, see Reporters sans Frontieres, October 23, 2006, available at http://www.rsf.org/article.php3?id_article=19408.

28. *New York Times,* May 24, 2006.

29. For the text of the declaration, see http://www.thisissyria.net/2006/05/12/releases/05.html. The quotations below are taken from this text.

30. Ibid.

31. Ibid

32. *Tishrin,* May 17, 2006.

33. Ibid.

34. Those arrested included Anwar al-Bunni, an attorney and Hurriyat [Freedom] Center spokesman; Mahmoud Meri, secretary of the Arab Organization for Human Rights in Syria; Nidal Darwish, a leader of the Committees for the Defense of Democratic Liberties and Human Rights in Syria; Khalil Hussein, of the Kurdish Al-Mustaqbal movement; Mahmoud Issa, Communist Labor Party; and human rights activists, Akram Al-Bunni, Khaled Khalifa, Sulayman Al-Shammar, Kamal Shaykho, Abbas Abbas, Ghaleb Amr, Safwan Tayfour, and Muhammad Mahfouz. Khalifa, Abbas and Shaykho were quickly released. Al-Mustaqbal, May 19, 2006; *al-Safir,* May 18, 2006; *al-Sharq al-Awsat,* May 18, 2006; *al-Quds al-Arabi,* May 18, 2006.

35. *Boston Globe,* November 6, 2005.

36. Ibid.
37. Reuters, February 27, 2006.
38. *Christian Science Monitor,* May 25, 2006.
39. State Department Press Release, "United States Calls for Release of Syrian Dissident," Nov. 10, 2005.
40. Retrieved from http://www.eyeontheun.org/assets/attachments/documents/assad_speech_11–11–05.doc and the Syrian Arab News Agency but is no longer available.
41. *Los Angeles Times,* July 12, 2006.
42. *New York Times,* October 27, 2005.
43. Syrian TV, November 8, 2005, available at http://www.MEMRItv.org/search.asp?ACT=S9&P1=914.
44. See Zisser, "In the Name of the Father," op. cit., pp. 231–32, 271–77.
45. Ibid.
46. Mustafa Talas [sic], "Biological Warfare, a New and Effective Method in Modern Warfare," *Tehran SAFF,* FBIS, April 20, 2000, 38-42; see also Anthony H. Cordesman, "Syria and Weapons of Mass Destruction" (Washington DC, 2000), 22–8.
47. *Al-Safir,* July 16, 2001. Translation in MEMRI, no. 244, July 20, 2001.
48. UPI, November 24, 2005.
49. In October 2000, Hizballah had kidnapped three Israeli soldiers and exchanged them for many of its own prisoners in Israeli hands.
50. Interviews.
51. *Maariv* and *Jerusalem Post,* November 23, 2005.
52. Yaakov Amidor, "Misreading the Second Lebanon War," *Jerusalem Issue Brief,* Vol. 16, No. 16, January 16, 2007.
53. Interviews.
54. *Janes' Defense Weekly,* September 7, 2006; *Daily Telegraph,* August 15, 2006.
55. *Asian Wall Street Journal,* January 27, 2005; *Beirut Daily Star,* January 26, 2005; *Die Welt,* February 6, 2007.
56. *Ma'ariv,* August 1, 2006.
57. *Tishrin,* July 31, 2006; *al-Sharq al-Awsat,* July 31, 2006.
58. *Tishrin,* August 3, 2006.
59. AP, August 17, 2006.
60. *Al-Nahar,* July 18, 2006.
61. *Al-Ba'th,* July 17, 2006.
62. Ibid.
63. AP, August 6, 2006.
64. Interview with Lee Smith.
65. *Washington Post,* August 13, 2006.
66. *Actualité,* August 19, 2006, available at http://www.lefigaro.fr/actualite.
67. Interview with Lee Smith.
68. *Tishrin,* July 31, 2006.
69. Ibid.; *al-Sharq al-Awsat,* July 31, 2006.
70. *Tishrin,* August 3, 2006. Translation in MEMRI, no. 1232, August 4, 2006, available at http://www.MEMRI.org/bin/opener_latest.cgi?ID=SD123206.
71. *Al-Thawra,* August 1, 2006.
72. Ibid.
73. *Tishrin,* August 3, 2006. Translation in MEMRI, no. 1232, August 4, 2006, available at http://www.MEMRI.org/bin/opener_latest.cgi?ID=SD123206.
74. *Tishrin,* July 31, 2006.
75. *Al-Thawra,* August 1, 2006.
76. Ibid.
77. All quotes from the speech are taken from Syrian TV1, August 15, 2006. Translation in FBIS GMP20060815607001.
78. Habash, al-Arabiyya television, August 15, 2006. Translation in FBIS GMP20060817602001.
79. Syrian TV1, August 15, 2006. Translation in FBIS GMP20060815607001.

80. Ibid.
81. Ibid.
82. Ibid.
83. Ibid.
84. Ibid.
85. Ibid.
86. Ibid.

CHAPTER TEN

1. *Al-Sharq al-Awsat,* January 6, 2006. Translation in MEMRI, no. 259, January 13, 2006, available at http://MEMRI.org/bin/latestnews.cgi?ID=IA25906.
2. *Arabian Business,* January 8, 2006.
3. See for example, Paul L. Heck, "Religious Renewal in Syria: The Case of Muhammad al-Habash," *Islam and Christian-Muslim Relations* 15, no. 2 (April 2004): 185–207.
4. Syrian television, November 8, 2006. Translation in MEMRI, no. 914, November 8, 2005, available at http://www.MEMRItv.org/search.asp?ACT=S9&P1=914.
5. *Tishrin,* August 6, 2006. Translation in MEMRI, no. 1239, August 9, 2006, available at http://MEMRI.org/bin/articles.cgi?Page=countries&Area=iran&ID=SP123906.
6. *Financial Times,* May 15, 2001.
7. *Washington Post,* January 23, 2006.
8. Chris Kutschera, "Syrie: L'Eclipse des Frères Musulmans," *Cahiers de L'Orient* 7, no. 3, 1987, available at http://www.chris-kutschera.com/syrie_eclipse_fm.htm.
9. Reuters, March 20, 2006.
10. *New York Times,* December 1, 2003.
11. UPI, June 30, 2003; *Washington Times,* August 16, 2004; AP, March 28, April 13, 2003, and July 5, 2005; Reuters, April 9, 2003; *Financial Times,* September 14, 2006.
12. Specter interview, *Ha'aretz,* December 29, 2006.
13. Interview, Dubai television, August 25, 2006. Translation in MEMRI, no. 1265, available at http://www.MEMRI.org/bin/opener_latest.cgi?ID=SD126506 and http://www.MEMRItv.org/search.asp?ACT=S9&P1=1244.
14. *Washington Post,* September 1, 2006; Reuters, August 8, 2006.
15. Interview with *Ha'aretz,* October 18, 2006.
16. Ibid.
17. AFP and Reuters, September 10, 2006. On Bashar's rejection of this idea, see Reuters, September 22, 2006.
18. Ibrahim Hamidi, *al-Hayat,* September 23, 2006.
19. *Financial Times,* October 23, 2006.
20. Flynt Leverett, "Illusion and Reality," *The American Prospect,* September 12, 2006.
21. *Tishrin,* March 28, 2001. Translation in MEMRI, no. 202, April 4, 2001, available at http://MEMRI.org/bin/articles.cgi?Page=archives&Area=sd&ID=SP20201.
22. *Al Safir,* March 27, 2003. Translation in MEMRI, no. 488, March 30, 2003, available at http://MEMRI.org/bin/articles.cgi?Page=archives&Area=sd&ID=SP48803.
23. Speech to Arab lawyers meeting, January 21, 2006, *Tishrin,* January 22, 2006.
24. A Syrian citizen writing, available at http://joshualandis.com/blog/?p=58#comment–299.
25. Transcript, Interview, BBC Television, October 23, 2005.
26. Speech to Arab summit meeting, *Tishrin,* March 28, 2001. Translation in MEMRI, no. 202, April 4, 2001, available at http://MEMRI.org/bin/articles.cgi?Page=archives&Area=sd&ID=SP20201.
27. Ibid.
28. Future TV, August 27, 2006. Translation in FBIS GMP20060828622001.
29. *Al-Ahram,* August 6, 2006. Translation in MEMRI, no. 1249, August 15, 2006, available at http://www.MEMRI.org/bin/opener_latest.cgi?ID=SD124906.
30. *Al-Nahar,* August 7, 2006.
31. Michael Young, *Beirut Daily Star,* September 7, 2006.

32. See for example, http://www.adnki.com/index_2Level_Arab.php?cat=Business&loid=8.0.34941 4524&par=0 and Iran-Syria-Samand http://www.irna.ir/en/news/view/menu–234/06101754441 93819.htm.

33. *New York Times,* December 28, 2006; Syrian Arab News Agency, December 27, 2006.

34. *Tishrin,* December 16, 2002, cited in Zisser, "What Does the Future Hold for Syria," op. cit.

35. Radio Damascus, November 28, 2002, cited in Zisser, "What Does the Future Hold for Syria," op. cit.

36. Interview.

37. *Al-Mustaqbal,* August 7, 2006. Translation in MEMRI, no. 1239, August 9, 2006, available at http://www.MEMRI.org/bin/opener_latest.cgi?ID=SD123906.

38. *Al-Usbu,* August 14, 2006; *al-Rai al-Am,* August 25, 2006. Translation in MEMRI, no. 1270 and 1267, August 29, 2006, available at http://www.MEMRI.org/bin/opener_latest.cgi?ID=SD127006.

39. *Al-Manar,* August 11, 2006. Translation in MEMRI, no. 1245, accessed from http://www.MEM-RItv.org/Transcript.asp?P1=1230. Available at http://www.MEMRI.org/bin/opener_latest.cgi?ID=SD124506.

40. Interview, al-Jazeera television, August 25, 2006, available at http://english.aljazeera.net/NR/exeres/225CBBA9–9AB7–46ED-BBE0-DE20FE29ABFA.htm.

41. Cited in Eric V. Thompson, "Will Syria Have to Withdraw from Lebanon?" *Middle East Journal* 56, no. 1 (Winter 2002): 88.

42. "This Week with George Stephanopoulos," ABC Television, October 8, 2006.

43. Interview on PBS, December 6, 2006, available at http://www.pbs.org/newshour/bb/middle_east/july-dec06/bakerhamilton__12–06.html.

44. Text from http://www.state.gov/secretary/former/powell/remarks/2003/20156.htm.

45. Albert B. Prados, "Syria: U.S. Relations and Bilateral Issues," *Congressional Research Service Report,* August 18, 2006, available at http://www.fas.org/sgp/crs/mideast/RL33487.pdf.

46. *Financial Times,* December 22, 2006. For a detailed look at the Specter case, see *Philadelphia Inquirer,* December 28, 2006.

47. Interview with al-Jazira, August 25, 2006, available at http://english.aljazeera.net/NR/exeres/225CBBA9–9AB7–46ED-BBE0-DE20FE29ABFA.htm.

48. *New York Times,* September 11, 2006.

49. *Globe and Mail,* September 1, 2006.

50. *Le Monde,* July 26, 2006.

51. Michael Young, *Beirut Daily Star,* September 7, 2006.

52. Ibid.

53. Corine Hegland, "Syria Gets the Silent Treatment," *National Journal* 38, no. 40 (October 7, 2006): 55.

54. Interview, *Der Spiegel,* September 24, 2006.

55. *Beirut Daily Star,* August 4, 2006.

56. Michael Young, *Beirut Daily Star,* September 7, 2006.

57. Cited from http://free-syria.com/loadarticle.php?articleid=9538.

58. *La Repubblica,* August 17, 2006. Translation in FBIS 06EUP20060817058012.

59. *New York Times,* July 26, 2006.

60. Interview, al-Arabiyya television, December 31, 2005, available at http://www.alarabiya.net/Articles/2005/12/31/19936.htm.

61. Available at http://news.bbc.co.uk/2/hi/middle_east/5339834.stm; http://us.cnn.com/2006/WORLD/meast/09/12/syria.embassy/index.html.

62. Michael Young, *Beirut Daily Star,* September 7, 2006.

63. *Al-Thawra* and *al-Ba'th,* August 7, 2006.

64. Al-Jazira television, August 17, 2006. Translation in FBIS GMP20060817642002.

65. Panorama show, al-Arabiyya television, August 15, 2006. Translation in FBIS GMP20060817602001.

66. Al-Jazira television, August 6, 2006. Translation in FBIS GMP20060817607001.

67. Al-Jazira television, April 30, 2006, available at http://www.MEMRItv.org/search.asp?ACT=S9&P1=1128 *Clip # 1128.

68. Middle East Transparent, June 29, 2006. Translated in *Syria Monitor,* June 2006, available at http://syriamonitor.typepad.com/news/2006/06/mamoun_homsi_in.html.

69. *Washington Post,* December 16, 2006.

70. Young, op. cit.

71. Ibid.

72. *L'Orient-Le Jour,* April 19, 2000.

INDEX